For the Prosecution

For the Prosecution

How to Prosecute
Criminal Cases

C. J. Williams

ROWMAN & LITTLEFIELD
Lanham • Boulder • New York • London

Published by Rowman & Littlefield
An imprint of The Rowman & Littlefield Publishing Group, Inc.
4501 Forbes Boulevard, Suite 200, Lanham, Maryland 20706
www.rowman.com

6 Tinworth Street, London SE11 5AL, United Kingdom

British Library Cataloguing in Publication Information Available

Library of Congress Cataloging-in-Publication Data Available

ISBN 978-1-5381-3847-2 (pbk.: alk. paper)
ISBN 978-1-5381-3848-9 (electronic)

∞™ The paper used in this publication meets the minimum requirements of
American National Standard for Information Sciences—Permanence of Paper
for Printed Library Materials, ANSI/NISO Z39.48-1992.

This book is dedicated to all of the prosecutors and law enforcement officers who, with their guidance, by their example, and through their patience, helped me become a better prosecutor and person

Contents

Acknowledgments   ix

Introduction   1

1   Thinking Like a Prosecutor   5

2   Working with Law Enforcement Officers   11

3   Working with Prosecution Team Members   27

4   Working with Defense Attorneys   35

5   Relationship with the Court   45

6   Managing a Caseload and Other Duties   49

7   Strategies for Prosecuting Criminals   71

8   Working with Cooperators   91

9   Developing Evidence   105

10   Working with Grand Juries   115

11   Charging Strategies and Tactics   131

12   Discovery   161

13   Handling Pretrial Motions   173

14   Plea Negotiations and Plea Hearings   185

15   Preparing for the Case-in-Chief   195

16   Preparing for the Defense Case   227

17   Expert Witnesses   239

18   Working with Crime Victims   253

19   Preparing for Jury Selection   261

20   Preparing Openings and Closings   319

21   Handling Sentencing Hearings   323

22   Appeals   337

Notes   343

Bibliography   347

Index of Cases   355

Index   361

About the Author   367

Acknowledgments

Serving as a prosecutor was an honor and a privilege. I found great satisfaction in performing my duties, knowing that each day I did something to make the world just a little bit better. After I became a judge, I realized how quickly I was forgetting all that I knew about how to prosecute cases. As a judge, all I saw was what prosecutors did in the courtroom. Yet, I knew that the real job of a prosecutor, and what made prosecutors successful, was everything a prosecutor did outside of the courtroom. I resolved, then, to write down what I knew of the job I used to hold and love before I forgot all that I learned. It is my hope that this book will help those who, like me, strive to become effective prosecutors.

I am grateful to the US Department of Justice and the US Attorney's Office for the Northern District of Iowa for providing me the opportunity to serve my country as a federal prosecutor. In particular, I am thankful to Steven Rapp, former US Attorney for the Northern District of Iowa, and Richard Murphy, an Assistant US Attorney and then Criminal Chief in the Northern District of Iowa, for hiring me in 1997. Rich is a prosecutor's prosecutor and I learned much from him. I am also grateful to all of my former colleagues at the US Attorney's Office, and at the Department of Justice and in the other US Attorney's Offices with whom, during my prosecution career, I had the privilege of working; I became a better prosecutor by their example.

I extend a special thanks for those who read all or parts of the manuscript and provided me with thoughtful and insightful feedback. Sean Berry, my former colleague at the US Attorney's Office, my fellow adjunct professor at the University of Iowa College of Law, and my friend, read the entire manuscript and provided me with invaluable comments and suggestions. Sean possesses judgment, insight, and wisdom seldom found in such depth in any person or prosecutor, and without his counsel over the years we worked together I would not have become the prosecutor I was nor the judge I am. I thank, too, Sali VanWeelden, currently my Judicial Assistant, formerly a paralegal in the US Attorney's Office, and throughout my friend, who read and provided suggestions on portions of the manuscript. Similarly, two former law enforcement agents, Bill Basler (Iowa Division of Criminal Investigation, Special Agent [ret.]) and John Graham (Iowa Division of Narcotics Enforcement, Special Agent [ret.]), read portions of the manuscript dealing with law enforcement officers. Bill and John are the gold standard for outstanding law enforcement officers and dear friends to take time out of their retirement to, once again, provide valuable feedback to their former prosecutor.

Finally, I want to thank my editors, Ashleigh Cooke, Kathryn Knigge, Charlotte Gosnell, Kate Hertzog, and the entire production team at Rowman & Littlefield, without whom this book would not have been possible.

Introduction

For more than two decades, I announced in court that I was appearing for the prosecution; I prosecuted federal criminal cases. I was a trial attorney with the Criminal Division of the Department of Justice in Washington, D.C., and later served as an Assistant US Attorney for almost twenty years before I became a federal judge. For a few years and in a few cases early in my career, between times when I served as a prosecutor, I also represented criminal defendants in federal court. I came to realize over time that 90 percent of the work prosecutors perform occurs outside the courtroom. Most of the work involves prosecutors interfacing with law enforcement officers, witnesses, and victims; developing an investigation; deciding who to charge and how to prosecute cases; identifying what charges to bring and how to draft the charges; negotiating plea agreements; marshaling and organizing evidence for hearings and trial; and preparing for grand jury presentations, motions hearings, trials, sentencing hearings, and appeals. Much more of a prosecutor's real life is spent in the field, at jails, in conference rooms, on the phone, and behind a desk than it is standing in a courtroom before a jury. And whether a prosecutor prevails in jury trials depends entirely on the work performed long before opening statements.

Law schools teach students some criminal law and criminal procedure, and some trial advocacy skills, but they do not teach the practicalities of practice as a prosecutor. I learned how to think like a prosecutor and develop criminal cases for prosecution over the course of time by watching others, through experimentation, and from learning after making my own mistakes. The Department of Justice, with all of its resources and otherwise excellent formal training programs at the National Advocacy Center, had not generated a treatise or book on how to think like a prosecutor and prepare a case for prosecution. My hope is that this book will fill the gap and impart to others the knowledge I gained through my service with the Department of Justice.

This book strives to provide prosecutors and those who want to become prosecutors with guidance on how to successfully investigate and prosecute criminal cases. The focus of this book is on the strategies and tactics involved in the job of being a prosecutor and the soft skills required to manage cases and manage people. This book examines how to think about criminal cases and guide investigations with an eye toward successful prosecution. It provides suggestions for breaking down complex issues into manageable pieces and how to organize all the pieces of a complex case in a persuasive manner. Similarly, the book outlines ways for prosecutors to organize and prioritize their caseloads and other demands on their limited time. The book describes successful strategies for taking down criminal organizations and tactics for turning criminals into cooperators. The book advises prosecutors about working with the wide variety of personalities involved in criminal cases, from federal agents and local law enforcement officers to crime victims and judges.

This book addresses these issues as they relate to prosecution at either the federal or state level. There are many strategies and tactics, and personal skills, that apply with equal force in state and local criminal prosecutions. There are, however, significant differences between the prosecution of federal versus state and local cases, as will be pointed out from time to time in the text, not the least of which is the critical role of the grand jury and the impact it has in federal cases. Although there are a lot of books in print regarding prosecution of state cases, few address federal prosecution, and none have federal prosecution as its focus. As will be discussed in greater detail later, federal prosecutors tend to be much more involved with criminal investigations than state prosecutors. So federal prosecutors have a greater ability to shape the scope and alter the direction of criminal investigations and affect the nature and quality of the evidence generated through the course of the investigation. This book will address in detail the role of federal prosecutors during the investigation stage of criminal cases.

This book may also be of value to defense attorneys who work with and against prosecutors. It is always an advantage to know more about one's opponent. During my five years in private practice I represented a few defendants in criminal cases and had one federal criminal trial. My prior experience as a prosecutor was invaluable to me in defending my client. This book can provide insight to defense counsel who do not have any prosecution experience to understand how prosecutors work and why they do the things they do. This, in turn, can aid defense counsel in helping their clients navigate a criminal prosecution.

I want to make it clear that this book is not a book on trial advocacy. This book does not provide detailed instruction on how to formulate effective opening statements or produce persuasive closing arguments. It does not provide tips for conducting direct examination or advice for cunning cross-examinations. Indeed, this book does not discuss the skills involved in courtroom performance at all. There are several reasons why I have chosen to bypass that portion of a prosecutor's job. First, there are already many excellent books on the topic of trial advocacy. Indeed, those few books already in print about criminal prosecution focus primarily on trial advocacy skills. Second, very few criminal cases result in trials; the vast majority of cases end in guilty pleas, while others are dismissed for various reasons by the government or courts. Thus, although trial advocacy skills are important to learn, this book deals with all of the work involved outside the courtroom that is critical in successfully investigating and prosecuting criminal cases. A prosecutor's courtroom performance is of little import if the prosecutor has not carefully and fully investigated the case and prepared the case for prosecution. A prosecutor's courtroom performance is at its best, on the other hand, when the prosecutor has thoroughly supervised the investigation and prepared the case for trial. In the end, the raw material the prosecutor has to work with in the courtroom—the evidence—is a product of all of the work the prosecutor performed outside the courtroom. Thus, although there will be repeated references to how to use evidence and information to advantage in the courtroom, this book will not dwell on what a prosecutor does in the courtroom.

I am sure that prosecutors who read this book will identify issues I missed and will take issue with some of the suggestions and observations I make. That is fair because prosecuting a criminal case is more of an art than a science. In this book I have attempted to record and relate the lessons I learned and the advice I would give to new prosecutors based on my personal experiences. The reader should understand that this book does not purport to provide the definitive way for prosecutors to prepare a case for prosecution. On the other hand, the reader will benefit by learning from my experience and my mistakes, giving them the advantage of my experience without suffering my setbacks. It is my hope that the reader comes away from this book with a better understanding of the process of prosecution and gains practical guidance on how to successfully prosecute criminal cases.

Chapter One

Thinking Like a Prosecutor

When I left my judicial clerkship to become a federal prosecutor, my friend and fellow law clerk gave me a going-away card in which he copied the well-known description of a federal prosecutor written by US Supreme Court Justice Sutherland:

> The United States Attorney is the representative not of an ordinary party to a controversy, but of a sovereignty whose obligation to govern impartially is as compelling as its obligation to govern at all; and whose interest, therefore, in a criminal prosecution is not that it shall win a case, but that justice shall be done. As such, he is in a peculiar and very definite sense the servant of the law, the twofold aim of which is that guilt shall not escape or innocence suffer. He may prosecute with earnestness and vigor—indeed, he should do so. But, while he may strike hard blows, he is not at liberty to strike foul ones. It is as much his duty to refrain from improper methods calculated to produce a wrongful conviction as it is to use every legitimate means to bring about a just one.

Berger v. United States, 295 US 78, 88 (1935). My friend,[1] who later became a federal public defender, hoped that as a prosecutor I would approach my job with this description in mind. I tried to do so to the best of my ability. Prosecutors possess a tremendous amount of power and discretion. This is particularly true for federal prosecutors. Speaking of federal prosecutors, then Attorney General Robert H. Jackson described the scope of power and discretion federal prosecutors hold.

> The prosecutor has more control over life, liberty, and reputation than any other person in America. His discretion is tremendous.

Robert H. Jackson, *The Federal Prosecutor*, 24 J. Am. Jud. Soc. 18, 18 (1940).

Unlike their state and local counterparts, federal prosecutors can choose their cases. Generally, federal charges are brought against defendants only with the assistance of and approval by an Assistant US Attorney, either through the filing of a criminal complaint or by seeking a grand jury indictment. State and county prosecutors, on the other hand, are usually handed cases they must deal with where local law enforcement officers have arrested defendants without input from or involvement by the state or county prosecutor. Both state and federal prosecutors possess wide discretion to determine what charges to bring, which often dictates the extent of punishment to which a defendant may be subject. Prosecutors have discretion plea bargaining, choosing whether and what charges to drop or change or concessions to make regarding sentences. Finally, prosecutors have significant discretion in sentencing advocacy. This is particularly true for federal prosecutors who decide which guideline enhancements to seek at sentencing, and whether to move for or oppose departures or variances from the advisory US Sentencing Guidelines sentence.

With great power comes great responsibility. It is difficult to better articulate the essence of what it is to be a responsible prosecutor than Justice Sutherland did in his 1935 *Berger* decision. What I can offer here, however, is an elaboration of how federal prosecutors can incorporate this proper mindset, described by Justice Sutherland, in their approach to criminal cases. I can also describe why and how this mindset leads to success as a prosecutor. In doing so, I should start by defining success for a federal prosecutor.

Justice defines success for a federal prosecutor. A prosecutor's success is not measured by the number of defendants convicted or the length of sentences imposed. A prosecutor's success is not defined by statistics or quotas, the number of indictments brought, trials won, or cases closed. Certainly, wining at trial, when cases proceed to trial, is important to success. Nevertheless, the vast majority of criminal cases do not result in trials. Thus, whether a prosecutor has been successful is best determined by an examination of whether justice was done in each of the cases handled.

In determining how to use their tremendous power to achieve justice, prosecutors should approach each decision by asking themselves not what can they do, but what should they do. Prosecutors can (and sometimes should) take a hard line, bring the most serious charges, present evidence to the fullest extent possible under the most expansive reading of the rules of evidence, and demand the harshest sentence possible under the law. Prosecutors should, however, ponder whether they should do so in every case.

It is important that prosecutors understand that justice may be achieved in some cases by not prosecuting a person, or not prosecuting them to the fullest extent of the law. This may mean choosing to not prosecute the person at all, or by having the defendant charged in state court, instead of federal court, because the state charge would carry a more lenient sentence. It may mean not bringing the most serious charges possible against the defendant. Or it may mean striking a generous plea bargain, or advocating for a sentence that is less than the maximum sentence permitted by statute. Good prosecutors recognize they have this discretion and realize that sometimes exercising that discretion in a manner that gives defendants breaks is appropriate and in the interest of justice. Unfortunately, most of the general population and some judges are not aware that prosecutors sometimes decline prosecution in the interest of fairness, or give other breaks to defendants in the form of charges, plea bargaining, or sentencing decision. Thus, prosecutors should understand that their generous exercise of discretion may often go unnoticed and unappreciated.

Doing justice also means fully complying with the rules. Ours is a nation of laws. Courts are rule-bound and compliance is expected, particularly in federal court. Deadlines are firm, discovery obligations are mandatory, and rules of evidence apply. But enforcement of the rules relies upon the awareness that they have been breached by a person with the ability to bring it to the court's attention and a court's willingness to demand compliance. In practice, rules are not always followed, and their breach not always known or raised, or enforced when they are raised. Nevertheless, prosecutors should not take advantage of the lackadaisical application or enforcement of court rules. Rather, prosecutors should toe the line of all rules at all times. Like the saying that a person's character is judged by what he or she does when no one is looking, a prosecutor's character is judged by whether he or she follows the rules regardless of whether the opposing party would catch him or her breaching or ignoring the rules. When prosecutors faithfully adhere to the rules, they earn the trust and respect of defense counsel and judges. This trust and respect in turn places prosecutors in a better position to negotiate with defense counsel and leads judges to place greater reliance on prosecutors' representations.

Similarly, prosecutors should err on the side of disclosure of information and evidence to defense counsel. Both state and federal courts have discovery rules dictating the information that prosecutors must disclose to defense counsel. In most states, the scope of discovery is far more liberal than in federal courts. In state prosecutions, for instance, defense attorneys can take depositions of government witnesses, whereas that tool is not available to defense attorneys in federal criminal cases. Federal Rule of Criminal Procedure 16 and the Jencks Act are really the only provisions that govern federal prosecutors' obligation to provide discovery to defense counsel. The Supreme Court's decisions in *Brady v. Maryland*, 373 US 83 (1963), and *Giglio v. United States*, 405 US 150 (1972), also require prosecutors to provide a criminal defendant with materially exculpatory evidence and information that could be used to impeach a government witness. Prosecutors can apply a narrow reading to the scope of the rules and provide the bare minimum of evidence to the accused. Prosecutors can also take risks with *Brady* and *Giglio* information, seeking refuge behind the materiality requirement or making late disclosure of the information to make it more difficult for opposing counsel to use it. That is not, however, how it should be. Good prosecutors recognize that justice means giving defense counsel the fairest chance possible to defend the accused. Good prosecutors appreciate that their goal is not conviction, but justice. If disclosure of information to the defense weakens the government's case, then it deserves to be weakened. Of course, sometimes the safety of witnesses or other security issues compete with the need to disclose information to the defense. Those instances occur infrequently, however, and prosecutors should not use the screen of "security concerns" to unnecessarily delay disclosure of information to the defense. As will be noted in more detail in a later chapter, full disclosure of the government's evidence carries many advantages for prosecutors, not the least of which is avoiding reversible error for failing to properly disclose evidence to defendants.

Prosecutors who have internalized the goal of seeking justice in every case take on the responsibility to ensure defendants are fully aware of their rights and are adequately represented. Generally speaking, criminal defense attorneys are good and competent. Nevertheless, some are new and not all are good, even after years of experience. Prosecutors should hesitate to take advantage of a defense attorney's ignorance of the law or facts. In some cases, it may be more appropriate for the prosecutor to inform and aid a defense attorney if it is apparent that the attorney would otherwise be rendering ineffective assistance of counsel. Prosecutors should be as concerned that defendants are effectively represented as they are about obtaining a conviction. Indeed, prosecutors must often defend a conviction in post-conviction litigation against allegations of ineffective assistance of counsel. Wise prosecutors, then, try to ensure effective assistance of counsel whenever possible so as to minimize the possibility of having the conviction reversed later.

When prosecutors internalize the proper mental state of what it means to represent the government in criminal prosecutions, when they strive to ensure that justice is done, they will be successful. The benefits that arise from approaching the job of being a prosecutor with this mentality are many. The greatest benefit, of course, is that it makes it much more likely that the guilty shall not escape justice or the innocent suffer wrongful conviction. Another benefit, however, is that rightful convictions are more likely to be affirmed on appeal and successfully defended in post-conviction litigation. Finally, when prosecutors approach criminal cases with the goal of seeking justice, it decreases the likelihood that the prosecutors will be found to have violated rules or obligations.

Other benefits of maintaining a proper mental attitude as a prosecutor are more indirect, but no less important. When defense counsel, defendants, and judges perceive that the prosecutor is seeking justice and not notches on his or her belt, it increases the level of trust each of them has in the prosecutor. As will be discussed at greater length in a later chapter, developing a trusting relationship with defense counsel, defendants who may become cooperators, and judges is important to developing a successful working relationship with these other actors in the criminal justice system. There is also a real benefit when law enforcement officers, paralegals, and other members of the prosecutor's team understand that the prosecutor's goal is justice and not winning. The proper mental attitude can be contagious. Other team members are less likely to fudge on the truth, hide evidence, or bend rules if they come to appreciate that the prosecutor's goal in every case is to see that justice is done, regardless of the outcome of the case.

Finally, to the extent the public becomes aware, directly or indirectly, of the government's attitude toward prosecution, it enhances the confidence the public has in the criminal justice system. That confidence in turn may further assist the government in the prosecution of criminal cases. A public that has confidence in the criminal justice system is more likely to report crime, cooperate in criminal investigations, and be willing to testify than a public that has lost confidence in the system. A public that has confidence in the criminal justice system will also produce better jurors, and citizens more willing to serve as jurors, than a public that lacks such confidence.

Adopting the correct prosecution attitude, and maintaining that attitude, is not easy. It requires mental discipline. No one likes to lose. When a prosecutor is working on a case, it can sometimes become personal. It may become personal when a defense attorney alleges the prosecutor acted unfairly or unethically, or accuses a law enforcement agent with whom the prosecutor works of unlawful or unconstitutional conduct. When cases involve victims of violent crime or child victims, it is often difficult for prosecutors and everyone else involved to remain objective. In the end, however, it is critically important that prosecutors do not let cases become personal. Prosecutors cannot allow the outcome of the case to define success.

John F. Kennedy once said that "[w]e choose to go to the moon in this decade and do the other things, not because they are easy, but because they are hard" (Rice Stadium, September 12, 1962). Lawyers choose to become prosecutors not because it is an easy job, but because it is hard. Prosecution presents difficult challenges at every step. The first challenge is adopting the proper mental attitude. But when prosecutors internalize the attitude that their goal is justice and not winning, the other challenges of the job become easier to overcome.

Chapter Two

Working with Law Enforcement Officers

A federal prosecutor is the face of the federal case, the leader, the front person. But it is the law enforcement officers—federal agents, state investigators, local police officers—that comprise the front line of the case. Law enforcement officers are the ones who face the dangers, kick in the doors, and arrest people. Law enforcement officers conduct the witness interviews and gather and process the evidence. And, ultimately, law enforcement officers are the ones who take the stand, testify, and present the evidence upon which the prosecutor's case rests. Federal prosecutors, in particular, work hand in hand with law enforcement officers both during the investigation of a case and in its presentation at trial. It is critical, then, that prosecutors develop an appropriate, respectful, and healthy working relationship with law enforcement officers.

Developing a successful working relationship with law enforcement officers requires attention to several factors. First, prosecutors need to recognize and learn to work with the power dynamics surrounding their interaction with law enforcement officers. Second, prosecutors need to develop leadership skills that will help them persuade and motivate law enforcement officers to perform the way prosecutors desire. Third, prosecutors should identify and attempt to fulfill the law enforcement officers' needs. Fourth, it is important that prosecutors make sure that they and law enforcement officers stay within their own lanes. Finally, good prosecutors learn to maintain an appropriate professional relationship with law enforcement officers. I will discuss each of these factors in turn. I will then conclude this chapter by noting some nuances that exist for federal prosecutors in developing good working relationships with state and local law enforcement officers that may not be present in their relationships with federal agents.

POWER DYNAMICS

Prosecutors work with a variety of law enforcement officers, from local police officers, to agents for state law enforcement agencies, to federal law enforcement agents. The one thing in common with them all is that none of them work directly for prosecutors. To form a good working relationship with law enforcement officers, prosecutors need to understand and fully appreciate the truism that officers do not answer directly to prosecutors. They are not in the same chain of command. Prosecutors do not hire or fire law enforcement officers. Prosecutors do not decide whether law enforcement officers get raises or year-end bonuses. Prosecutors, thus, cannot demand or command that law enforcement officers do anything. Rather, they can only ask and persuade. I once took a college class on presidential power in which the professor emphasized that the only real power a president of the United States has is the power of persuasion. The same can be said of prosecutors, in my estimation, regarding their relationship with law enforcement officers.

Although this seems obvious, it was my observation that not all federal prosecutors fully understood this power dynamic or appreciated what it meant for how they should perform their jobs in working with law enforcement officers. During my career as a federal prosecutor, I sometimes observed federal prosecutors attempt to dictate to law enforcement officers what to do, both orally and in writing. I know from observation as well that this kind of treatment of officers by federal prosecutors does not go over well with law enforcement officers. Nor did the law enforcement officers always do as asked, sometimes simply out of defiance.

Successful prosecutors recognize that they must form a partnership with law enforcement officers when they work together to achieve the same goals. Prosecutors cannot succeed in the prosecution unless the law enforcement officers cooperate and help develop the case in the manner the prosecutor believes is necessary to win at trial. To do this, prosecutors must persuade law enforcement officers to work with them, not try to order them to do so. Of course, law enforcement officers must also understand that they need to cooperate and assist prosecutors, or else their cases will not be prosecuted, or may not be successfully prosecuted.

Persuasion begins with the prosecutor evincing the proper respect for the law enforcement officer and making sure the officer recognizes that the prosecutor appreciates that the officer does not work for the prosecutor. Law enforcement officers need to see that the prosecutor sees them as part of a partnership and not an inferior partner. Prosecutors should ensure that the law enforcement officers understand that the prosecutor recognizes the difficulty of their jobs and the skills and contributions that the law enforcement officers bring to the case. Prosecutors can reflect this mindset in a manner apparent to the law enforcement officer through thoughtful communication. Prosecutors should request and ask officers to perform a task, not command or tell them to do so. Prosecutors should use the words "please" and "thank you." When speaking of the plan for or goals of the investigation and prosecution of a case, prosecutors should use terms that reflect a partnership, such as "we" and "us" and "our." One sure way for prosecutors to offend law enforcement officers is to use possessive language in referring to officers or cases, such as referring to "my officer," "my agent," or "my case." Like all lawyers, pros-ecutors can be arrogant and self-important and view themselves as the center of the case. It is far more conducive to a good working relationship with law enforcement officers, however, when prosecutors see themselves as only part of a partnership, no more and no less important than their law enforcement partners.

One way for a prosecutor to build a healthy relationship with law enforce-ment officers is to make an effort to go to them instead of always insisting that officers come to the prosecutor's office. There will be times when it is necessary for the officers to come to the prosecutor's office, of course, but there will be many other occasions when meetings could take place at the officer's location. Prosecutors should make a point of going to the officer's office as often as possible.

It is also important in persuading law enforcement officers to work in a cooperative manner with prosecutors that prosecutors take time to explain to the officers why the prosecutor desires that the officers perform a particular task in furtherance of the investigation and prosecution. Rather than simply telling an agent, for example, that the prosecutor wants an officer to interview a particular witness, it is far better to have a discussion with the officer about why the prosecutor believes a particular witness should be interviewed and discuss the benefits that could arise from such an interview. Indeed, when a prosecutor engages in a discussion about an investigation or prosecution task with a law enforcement officer, it often generates new and sometimes better approaches and ideas. Discussing tasks and tactics together and arriving at an agreed-upon plan also results in buy-in by the officer into the tasks that are ultimately, jointly, recognized as appropriate. That requires prosecutors to take the time to talk to law enforcement officers, to keep them informed, and to have face time with them. For example, grand jury testimony is a critical step in a criminal investigation, as I will discuss in a later chapter, but the rules do not permit law enforcement officers to be present in the grand jury room to hear the testimony. It is important, then, for prosecutors to take the time after each grand jury session to fill in the law enforcement officers about what occurred in the grand jury room, discuss the impact the testimony may have on the direction of the investigation and development of leads, and map out together with the law enforcement officers plans for the next steps in the investigation, including identifying future grand jury witnesses.

Sometimes to persuade law enforcement officers to perform tasks the prosecutor believes are in the best interest of the case it requires the prosecutor to take time to provide a lengthy explanation to the officers. The law may, for example, require more work from the officer than the officer realizes. For example, an officer may not fully appreciate the legal nuances of establishing probable cause to search files within a computer seized during a search or understand that a second warrant may be necessary based on what an officer saw in plain view while making an arrest. Rather than being impatient with the officer, the prosecutor should see this as a teaching opportunity, recognizing that explaining the law will not only help the officer understand why the requested task is necessary, but also help improve the officer's performance in the future.

On occasion, officers may push back or flatly refuse to perform tasks that the prosecutor believes are either necessary or beneficial for the case. When this occurs, a prosecutor should first re-examine the matter and re-evaluate the necessity or urgency of the task. Perhaps the prosecutor did not appreciate the cost in law enforcement resources involved in performing the task, or perhaps the officer suggested an alternative means to achieve the same goal. A prosecutor must be willing to change positions based on feedback from the agents. If the prosecutor nevertheless concludes that the task must or should be done and feels strongly about it, the prosecutor may need to exert pressure on the officer to persuade the officer to perform the task. Prosecutors have a lot of power over the cases officers bring to them for prosecution, even if the prosecutor does not have direct supervisory authority over the officer. The prosecutor can refuse to take the case, or chose to dismiss or reduce charges, or strike a generous plea agreement, or forgo a sentencing enhancement, if those actions are called for in light of an officer's refusal to take a necessary step in the investigation. To maintain a good working relationship with law enforcement officers, prosecutors should use this power sparingly, and when they do exercise that power, they should explain to the officer why that decision was, or would be, necessary because of the officer's refusal to undertake the necessary task. When exercising this pressure, prosecutors should not use an imperious or threatening tone with officers, but, rather, adopt a calm attitude and use a tone that reflects reason and not emotion.

Finally, it is important for prosecutors to empathize with law enforcement officers. By the time law enforcement officers bring cases to prosecutors for consideration, they have likely already expended a lot of hours and effort investigating the cases. They may have already risked their lives in undercover operations or while executing warrants or may have been exposed to gruesome crime scenes or disturbing evidence. They are professionally and sometimes emotionally wrapped up in their investigations. Success in the law enforcement officers' careers may also be tied to the successful prosecution of the cases they investigate. Prosecutors should consider the officers' position when setting the tone and tenor of the relationship they form with officers.

LEADING LAW ENFORCEMENT OFFICERS

Prosecutors serve as leaders of a prosecution team, of which law enforcement officers are key members. Federal prosecutors occupy this leadership role because it is the prosecutor who ultimately makes the critical decisions regarding the prosecution. Prosecutors decide whether to charge defendants, what charges to bring, what evidence to present to the grand jury to obtain the indictment, whether to agree to a plea bargain or go to trial, what evidence to present at trial, what sentence to seek, and what evidence to present at the sentencing hearing.

Law enforcement officers serve a supporting role, investigating the case and securing evidence. Without leadership, however, law enforcement officers' efforts may not advance the prosecution in the way the prosecutor desires or believes is factually or legally necessary. It is thus incumbent upon prosecutors to provide leadership to law enforcement officers so that they work in partnership to achieve the same goal.

Leadership involves having a vision and providing a plan for the investigation and prosecution of the case and coordinating the efforts of all of the law enforcement officers involved. Prosecutors are responsible for formulating a plan for completing the investigation and prosecuting the case. This is particularly true in federal prosecutions when prosecutors are often deeply involved with the investigation of cases. A prosecutor's role frequently involves coordinating the efforts of multiple law enforcement officers or agencies, paralegals, victim advocates, and others. In federal cases, a law enforcement officer will serve as the "case agent," meaning that one particular law enforcement officer, usually but not always a federal agent, will be the lead agent. Prosecutors should work with and through the case agent to identify tasks that need completed and identify the law enforcement officers who will be assigned those tasks. The case agent should then be responsible for coordinating the efforts, collecting the evidence, and providing it to the prosecutor. In more complex cases, it may be necessary for prosecutors to have meetings with all of the law enforcement officers to help coordinate all of the tasks. As will be discussed in a later chapter, law enforcement officers are members of an often much larger prosecution team including multiple law enforcement officers and agencies, paralegals, support staff, and prosecutors. It is the prosecutor's responsibility to lead this group to all pull oars in the same direction.

A critical component to effective leadership of law enforcement officers is communication. Law enforcement officers not only desire but also deserve to be kept informed about the case into which they have invested so much time and effort and emotion. Prosecutors should regularly communicate with law enforcement officers about the investigation and prosecution of the case. Good prosecutors regularly communicate with the law enforcement agents about their cases. Good prosecutors discuss investigation and prosecution strategies with the law enforcement officers. They keep the officers advised of scheduled events, such as time before the grand jury, and hearing and trial and sentencing dates. To the extent possible, prosecutors should be sensitive to scheduling conflicts and discuss timing issues with agents in advance. Some schedules are, of course, not within the prosecutor's control, such as hearing and trial dates. Others, such as grand jury presentations, are constrained by others' schedules but somewhat within the prosecutor's control. Still other dates, such as setting up prosecution team meetings or preparing witnesses for trial, are largely within the prosecutor's control. Prosecutors should consult with officers about other scheduling conflicts the officers may have whenever prosecutors have any control over scheduling matters.

The key is to communicate regularly with the law enforcement agents. For good reason, law enforcement agents become agitated, frustrated, and sometimes angry when they are not kept informed. I have heard agents voice strong complaints about prosecutors who did not advise them of when a guilty plea or sentencing hearing was to occur. There is no excuse for prosecutors who fail to keep the officers advised of such important stages in the progress of the case. Further, prosecutors should regularly keep law enforcement officers advised of delays in the progress of cases. Law enforcement officers may be unaware of other time constraints or demands on the prosecutor's limited time and become frustrated at what they perceive to be an unwarranted delay in the prosecution of their case. Prosecutors can mitigate this frustration by keeping the officers informed about the other deadlines the prosecutor is facing and the plan for fitting the officers' cases into the prosecutor's overall schedule. Finally, prosecutors should be responsive to law enforcement agents. That means returning their calls and answering their questions. Again, there is no excuse for prosecutors to fail to return phone calls or, perhaps worse, fail to clear their voice mailbox so that officers are unable to even leave new messages.

Although a prosecutor's client is the government, and hence the people, in a limited sense law enforcement officers occupy a quasi-client role. They represent the people to the extent that they have brought a criminal investigation to the prosecutor on behalf of the people. In any form of legal practice, attorney-client communication is very important. In private practice, one of the leading causes of complaints about, and disciplinary actions against, attorneys is an attorney's failure to keep the client informed. Thus, just as it is important in private practice to keep clients informed and be responsive to them, so too is it important for prosecutors to keep the law enforcement officers informed and be responsive to them.

Effective leadership also involves active listening. Prosecutors should listen to the law enforcement officers' needs and ideas. Timing of such things as search and arrest warrants, for example, often must depend on the availability of law enforcement officers. Significant operational planning is involved by law enforcement officers when they engage with criminals, and prosecutors need to be aware of and respect those arrangements for officer and public safety. It is also important that prosecutors listen to law enforcement officers' suggestions and ideas. Although a prosecutor should lead by having a vision of and a plan for the investigation and prosecution of the case, the prosecutor must also be prepared for change in light of suggestions by law enforcement officers.

To be an effective leader, prosecutors must also be there when needed to give direction. Law enforcement officers will often work before 9:00 a.m. and after 5:00 p.m., particularly when they are conducting law enforcement operations such as undercover buys or executing search warrants. Sometimes the officers' plans go off script when something changes in the heat of battle. It is imperative that prosecutors are available on those occasions to respond immediately to the officers' inquiries about strategy, tactics, and legal issues that arise because of unanticipated changes in circumstances to maintain the investigation's integrity. In short, prosecutors must be available to law enforcement officers twenty-four hours a day, seven days a week.

Sometimes serving as a leader of law enforcement officers requires prosecutors to deal with conflicts between individual officers or between law enforcement agencies. Occasionally, disputes arise among law enforcement officers. When they do, they are often a form of turf warfare; that is, an officer believes that another officer or law enforcement agency has infringed on the officer's work or scope of responsibility. The officer may be worried about losing control of the direction of the investigation or his or her share of the credit for success. Whatever the source of dispute or motive of the officers, prosecutors should help resolve the dispute to advance the best interest of the case. In wading into the internecine dispute, prosecutors should recall that none of the officers works for the prosecutor, and the prosecutor cannot order anyone to do anything. Rather, the prosecutor should work to decrease the tensions, hear the officers out (separately or together, depending on the circumstances), and try to find a resolution to the problem. It helps to remind the officers of the end goal and to emphasize that the dispute may impair the prosecution team from achieving those goals. It is important that prosecutors not appear to play favorites among officers. In the end, however, prosecutors must do what is best for the case.

Leadership also involves motivating others by recognizing and rewarding them for their efforts. Although prosecutors are not law enforcement officers' supervisors and cannot promote them or give them raises for work well done, that does not mean that prosecutors cannot recognize and reward such efforts. It is important to acknowledge good work and find ways to reward it, both as a show of appreciation to that individual but also to incentivize other officers. Prosecutors should look for opportunities, then, to publicly recognize outstanding efforts by law enforcement officers. There are many ways for prosecutors to do this. Prosecutors can send letters to the officers' supervisors praising good work. This takes little effort by prosecutors but is deeply appreciated by officers and may help them in being considered for promotions or raises. Prosecutors can also have their offices generate award certificates or acquire plaques referencing particularly good work. Prosecutors can also nominate officers for various awards for particularly outstanding law enforcement work. For example, the Department of Justice confers some awards on law enforcement officers (such as a Director's Award), as do other various law enforcement organizations (such as the Organized Crime Drug Enforcement Task Force Award).

Prosecutors should think carefully about when and how to recognize good work by law enforcement officers. Recognizing officers for their work in every case waters down the importance of the recognition; it's like every child on a losing team getting a "participation" award. On the other hand, failing to recognize truly outstanding work by officers may lead the officers to infer that the prosecutor does not fully appreciate the effort expended, which will make it less likely that officer and others will expend that level of effort in the future. Also, there are different levels of awards or recognition, with letters to officers' supervisors perhaps at the bottom and a Department of Justice Director's Award near the top. Prosecutors should afford the level of recognition that is commensurate with the significance of the case and the quality of the work the officer performed. But the need to recognize law enforcement officers' hard work in some way cannot be overemphasized. In writing this book, one former law enforcement officer I worked with informed me that the most appreciated recognition he received were simply emails I sent to him praising his work, emails that he has kept to this day.

In deciding when officers deserve recognition, prosecutors should also be thoughtful about what effort deserves recognition and how to articulate the recognition. Awards should not be based on things like how many defendants were convicted or how long their sentences were. Rather, awards should emphasize the officer's conduct (e.g., facing danger, working long hours, dealing with difficult or disturbing evidence, unraveling a complex crime) or the impact the officer's conduct had on the community (e.g., shut down a drug ring, removed violent criminals from the street, stopped a fraudster from duping more victims). In articulating (either in a letter or on a certificate or award) what the officers did that deserves recognition, prosecutors should imagine those words appearing on the front page of the local newspaper and make sure that they properly convey recognition for efforts toward justice.

Finally, effective leaders lead by example. Prosecutors should work as long or longer than the officers, as hard or harder than the officers. Prosecutors' conduct and words should reflect a focus on a just outcome and teamwork and not on racking up statistics or seeking advantage over other prosecutors or offices. Prosecutors should never denigrate judges or defense counsel, coworkers, or even defendants. Regarding criminal defendants, prosecutors should act and speak in a way that shows law enforcement officers that the defendant's conduct is the focus of the investigation, not the defendant's character. By showing respect for everyone in the criminal justice system, prosecutors convey a message to law enforcement officers about the values that should drive their efforts.

UNDERSTANDING LAW ENFORCEMENT OFFICERS' NEEDS

In working with law enforcement officers, it is important that prosecutors understand the officers' needs, the demands on their time, and the constraints on their actions. As mentioned, it is important that prosecutors empathize with law enforcement officers. This means in part that prosecutors should learn what officers do and how they do it, what steps they must take to perform a task, the approval process they are required to go through to perform certain tasks, and the ramifications for them personally and for their agencies when performing tasks.

For example, a prosecutor may determine that surveillance of a subject is an appropriate step that should be taken in an investigation. Before a prosecutor requests that an officer conduct surveillance, the prosecutor should have some appreciation of what that involves. It may mean long, mind-numbing, boring hours sitting in a car drinking bad coffee. It may require the officer to obtain permission for overtime pay or require other officers to take on some of the officer's other duties. Hours of surveillance on the prosecutor's case may deprive the officer of time that could be spent on other tasks or other cases or time with family. Surveillance in a bad area could place the officer in danger.

As another example, prosecutors may need to understand law enforcement officers' need for and relationship with confidential sources. Good investigators develop relationships with people who are on the periphery of, or slightly in, the criminal world. This may be the result of catching, but releasing, a person with a user amount of drugs in order to develop that person as a confidential source of information. These relationships depend on the confidential source trusting the law enforcement officer and often include an express or tacit understanding that the law enforcement officer will not reveal the source's identity. Prosecutors approach cases from the mindset of proving the case at hand and, to a prosecutor, a confidential source may appear to be a wonderful witness for the case. The short-term benefit of having the source testify in the case, however, could destroy years of work by the agent in developing the witness as a confidential source. It may also jeopardize the officer's ability to develop other confidential sources when the word gets out, as it will, that the officer is unable to keep the source's identity confidential. So good prosecutors learn things like this and learn to find ways to work around without jeopardizing the officer's work and relationship with confidential sources.

To make informed decisions about working with law enforcement officers, it is incumbent upon prosecutors to learn about law enforcement officers, their agencies, and their duties. Prosecutors should ask questions and invite input from officers about steps in the investigation and prosecution. Prosecutors may want to visit the officer's agency or obtain briefings about various law enforcement activities. Prosecutors should also learn about the officer's job generally. A lot of this education about law enforcement officers' needs and demands will come to an attentive prosecutor over time through the process of working with officers. Early on in their careers or when working with a new agency, however, prosecutors should endeavor to learn as much as possible and not simply wait for the knowledge to accumulate over time.

STAYING WITHIN THE LANES

Just as law enforcement officers do not work for prosecutors, prosecutors do not work for law enforcement officers. Some law enforcement officers fail to recognize this, just as some prosecutors fail to recognize it. Particularly early in a prosecutor's career, law enforcement officers may be much older and have many more years' experience than the prosecutor. Some officers approach cases with an agenda, wanting "their case" prosecuted ahead of others, and in the way they think is appropriate, and may try to cajole or pressure the inexperienced prosecutor to do what the officer wants, regardless of whether it is what's best for the case or justice. Some law enforcement officers are known for never having seen a bad case; in other words, they fail to see any problems with their cases, any holes in their investigations, and any doubt that the defendants are guilty, and will not listen to anyone who thinks otherwise. Sometimes agents also have underlying agendas behind their demands or suggestions. For example, some agencies may require agents to engage in certain investigative techniques (like a wiretap) before officers can be considered for raises or promotions. Finally, some law enforcement officers will attempt to influence a prosecutor's decision about who should be charged with what crimes, what evidence should be presented, what witnesses called, and what sentence to be sought based on factors the prosecutor may deem inappropriate.

It is important for prosecutors to listen to input from law enforcement officers but not let law enforcement officers improperly influence how the prosecutor performs the prosecutor's duties. Prosecutors cannot allow themselves to be bullied into doing what they believe is not in the best interest of the case or justice. Law enforcement officers, particularly experienced ones, often have great insight and judgment, and their advice and suggestions on the investigation and prosecution can be invaluable. Indeed, among those officers may be some who also have law degrees and may have practiced law. Prosecutors should welcome their input and counsel. Nevertheless, it is the prosecutor's duty to make the fundamental decisions about how a case is charged and prosecuted, and to some degree what judicial resources should be used in an investigation. A prosecutor should, for example, agree to seek judicial approval for a wiretap only if the investigation truly calls for a wiretap and a wiretap can be justified under the statutory standard, and not simply seek a wiretap to allow the officer to check a box on a work review form. It is incumbent upon prosecutors to maintain an objective and critical view of the case, not allow it to become personal, and assess the evidence so as to only pursue prosecution when the prosecutor is convinced beyond a reasonable doubt of the target's guilt, regardless of how confident the officer may be that the officer just "knows" the target is guilty.

In dealing with heavy-handed law enforcement officers, prosecutors may need to explicitly draw a line defining the roles of the prosecutor and the officer. While indicating that the prosecutor is interested in the officer's input, the prosecutor should make it clear which decisions belong to the prosecutor to make. If the prosecutor intends to make a decision contrary to the advice or demands of an officer (say, for example, by turning down a request to seek a wiretap), a new prosecutor may want to first seek input from a supervisor and then indicate to the officer that the decision was made with the supervisor's input to foreclose the officer trying to go over the prosecutor's head or concluding that the prosecutor's judgment is poor because of lack of experience. In the end, it is imperative that prosecutors establish a relationship of mutual respect with law enforcement officers while making it clear that they expect the officers to stay within their lanes.

To ensure that law enforcement officers stay within their lanes, it is important that prosecutors not allow officers to pass around the prosecutor (or as law enforcement officers call it, "prosecutor shopping"). When a prosecutor denies a law enforcement officer's request or demand, that officer may attempt to go around the prosecutor to another prosecutor or go over the prosecutor's head to a supervisor. Prosecutors must guard against this manipulation. Prosecutors should not denigrate another prosecutor or allow an officer to bypass another prosecutor solely because the officer is dissatisfied with that prosecutor's answer. If a prosecutor truly believes another prosecutor has erred, that should be addressed internally, through the proper chain of command. Similarly, supervisors should be hesitant to reverse a line prosecutor's decision simply because an officer is dissatisfied with the decision. Only if the decision is truly erroneous should the supervisor reverse it, and when doing so the supervisor should communicate directly with the line prosecutor and have that prosecutor reverse the decision and convey that information to the law enforcement officers, not do so directly.

At the same time, it is important that prosecutors learn to remain in their own lanes. When working with law enforcement officers on an investigation, the prosecutor's role is to direct and guide the prosecution with the goal of obtaining evidence that will support the charges and ensure a conviction of the target of the investigation. There is a real temptation, however, for prosecutors to veer into the lane occupied by law enforcement officers. Prosecutors are not investigators and should not assume that role. Law enforcement officers are trained to perform their tasks, and prosecutors should let them perform their tasks. For example, it is not a prosecutor's place to weigh in on operational decisions, such as how to execute a search warrant or effect an arrest warrant. Law enforcement officers may have legal questions regarding these matters (e.g., can they search vehicles located within the curtilage of the property, or under what circumstances can they enter a target's house to effectuate an arrest). It is dangerous, however, for prosecutors to influence how law enforcement officers actually execute operational tasks. Similarly, federal prosecutors often participate in debriefing cooperating defendants in so-called proffer sessions. It is primarily the law enforcement officer's role to question the cooperator; officers are trained and often very experienced in conducting such interviews. There are sometimes tactics involved in questioning people, such as determining how to approach difficult areas for the cooperator to talk about or deciding what topics to address and in what order. Prosecutors should refrain from interfering with the officer's interview unless the prosecutor has greater knowledge or experience (for example, in a complex white-collar fraud case) or the prosecutor believes the law enforcement officer has made a mistake. Prosecutors may also need to weigh in from time to time if, for example, the cooperator is perceived to be lying or recalcitrant, or to clarify an answer or elicit more detail on a matter that the prosecutor knows may have legal ramifications (such as drug quantity for purposes of sentencing). Nevertheless, prosecutors should generally let law enforcement officers conduct such interviews in the manner that the officer desires, with minimal interference.

MAINTAINING A PROFESSIONAL RELATIONSHIP

Prosecutors work closely with law enforcement officers and may develop friendships with them. This is particularly true when prosecutors work with officers in a long-term investigation and prosecution, on particularly emotionally draining cases, or in small districts where prosecutors and officers work together repeatedly over a course of years. There is nothing inappropriate about prosecutors becoming friends with law enforcement officers. Indeed, to this day I count several law enforcement officers among my good friends.

Nevertheless, prosecutors must remain objective. They cannot allow their friendships with law enforcement officers to cloud their judgment. Prosecutors need to ensure that officers tell the truth and not cut corners or engage in improper conduct, regardless of how close the prosecutor may be to the officer. Prosecutors should make decisions based on what is best for the case and justice, and not based on what may be best for an officer or the officer's career or agency. Just as prosecutors cannot allow themselves to be bullied into making decisions, nor can they allow themselves to be influenced in making decisions based on friendship. Prosecutors cannot overlook violations of the law, or dishonesty, by law enforcement officers out of a sense of friendship. In the end, prosecutors must remember that their highest duty is to the rule of law, and their decisions must be based on what will result in justice.

It is also important that prosecutors have a frank discussion with law enforcement officers to stress the importance that they, too, set friendship aside when working on the case. Law enforcement officers cannot make decisions about an investigation based on what they think would please or help a prosecutor who has also become a friend. Maintaining a professional relationship is particularly important for law enforcement officers to make good, credible witnesses. Testifying is stressful and difficult for even the most experienced law enforcement officers. When officers take the stand, to be effective they must be able to shut out the outside world, set aside any personal views or feelings they have, forget their personal worries and issues, and testify frankly and candidly about the facts of the case. In this role, law enforcement officers cannot be thinking about how their answers to questions may affect their friendship with the prosecutor.

STATE AND LOCAL LAW ENFORCEMENT OFFICERS

A final note is appropriate to address the unique relationship that arises when federal prosecutors work with state and local law enforcement officers. In some US Attorneys' Offices, there is a practice or policy that cases will not be prosecuted without the involvement of or sponsorship by a federal agent or agency. Other US Attorneys' Offices will take cases referred directly by local law enforcement officers without requiring involvement of a federal agency. This is particularly true in smaller and more rural districts. In either case, state and local law enforcement officers are working in sometimes unfamiliar territory when their cases are prosecuted in federal court. In working with state and local law enforcement officers, then, there are certain things that federal prosecutors should keep in mind.

First, it has been my experience that many state and local law enforcement officers are highly trained and perform outstanding work. Indeed, some of the best law enforcement officers I ever worked with as a federal prosecutor were state agents. On the other hand, prosecutors should recognize that the quality of work by state and local officers may vary significantly. Thus, prosecutors should not treat state and local officers differently or with less respect than their federal counterparts, but nevertheless should be alert to indications that their work may not be of the necessary quality. This may require the prosecutor to ensure that additional work is performed to shore up any weaknesses in the investigation. This may require, for example, follow-up or piggyback search warrants if necessary to overcome the effects of prior errors.

Further, state and local officers do not necessarily always work in a manner that meets federal standards. For example, for a no-knock or nighttime federal search warrant to be valid, the affidavit supporting the warrant must establish facts justifying a no-knock entry or nighttime search. Some state laws may not require such a showing in the affidavit. By the time the case reaches the prosecutor's desk, it may be too late to change or affect the investigation that had thus far been conducted. But federal prosecutors may want to educate the state officers about nuances of federal law and procedure with which they are unfamiliar to the extent it may affect future work on the case at hand or other cases.

State and local officers may also be unfamiliar with various practices in federal court. For example, state and local officers may be completely unfamiliar with the need to be advised of and disclose to a defendant information that may affect an officer's credibility (a requirement under *Giglio* that will be discussed in a later chapter). Similarly, state and local officers may be unfamiliar with the creation of "taint teams" or the walling off of information from the investigative team to avoid exposure to information to prevent fruit-of-the-poisonous-tree results. In other words, federal prosecutors have developed a practice of creating taint teams to handle parts of investigations that may develop evidence subject to suppression, such as seizure of possible attorney-client communication or evidence that may have been obtained in violation of a defendant's constitutional rights. Taint teams filter the evidence and provide to the investigation team only that evidence that is not subject to suppression so that the greater investigation is not tainted by exposure to the suppressible evidence. What may be common practice in the federal system, however, may be completely foreign to state and local law enforcement officers. Prosecutors must be alert to these issues and take the time to explain the procedures, and reasons for the procedures, to officers who are unfamiliar with them.

Similarly, the atmosphere of federal court is very different than in most state courts. Many state and local officers have never testified in federal court or observed proceedings in federal court. Grand juries are seldom used in many states, so the state and local law enforcement agents may be completely in the dark about the workings of a federal grand jury or what it is like to testify before one. Prosecutors should devote additional time in preparing state and local officers for testifying before a grand jury, in hearings before a federal judge, and at a jury trial.

Finally, prosecutors may want to make a special effort to ensure that state and local law enforcement officers are not made to feel inferior. Federal court is not better than state court, it is just different. There are many federal agents who are inferior to many state and local law enforcement officers. State and local officers will be better members of the prosecution team, and perform better, when they are treated as equals to federal agents.

Chapter Three

Working with Prosecution Team Members

Every criminal case requires a team of people to prosecute it. That team may consist of only a prosecutor and a law enforcement officer. In larger and more significant cases, however, the prosecution team may consist of multiple people, sometimes scores of people, particularly in federal criminal cases. Depending on the nature, size, and complexity of a criminal case, the prosecution may involve a team of professionals along with the prosecutor and law enforcement officers. Team members may consist of other prosecutors, multiple law enforcement officers, paralegals, legal assistants, victim and witness coordinators, and IT specialists. Working effectively with a prosecution team requires skills not typically taught in law school.

There are many issues that arise in working with a large prosecution team. First, prosecutors need to determine the size and membership of the prosecution team. Second, prosecutors must determine the positions needed on the team, identify the people who will fulfill those roles, and assign tasks to the various members. Third, prosecutors should monitor progress and coordinate the team members' efforts. Fourth, prosecutors may be tasked with the burden of resolving disputes or conflicts among team members. Finally, prosecutors need to provide effective leadership to the team. I will discuss each of these issues below.

SIZE AND MEMBERSHIP OF A PROSECUTION TEAM

A lead prosecutor should thoughtfully determine the size and makeup of the prosecution team and not allow it to be a result of haphazard events or decisions by other team members. There are forces, however, that tend to make teams begin or become too large. Agency heads and supervisors may have agendas, such as developing officers, prosecutors, or others for promotion, that compel them to try to influence team membership. Although the goals behind the agenda may be completely legitimate, the lead prosecutor needs to weigh the benefits of achieving these goals against the costs of decreasing the effectiveness of the team. Members of the team themselves may also cause the team to grow by delegating work or inviting others to join the team. Other members of the team, including other prosecutors, may pressure the lead prosecutor to add others they like to work with, while on other occasions a prosecution team grows like a snowball, gathering more and more members as it rolls toward trial. The lead prosecutor must be in control of both the size and membership of the prosecution team. It is the lead prosecutor's responsibility (typically with supervisory approval) to determine the size of the prosecution team and identify its members.

As for the size of a team, the best advice I can give is to make it as small as possible. The larger any group is, the more difficult it is to manage and direct. In large teams, effective communication can become complicated and difficult, tasks are harder to coordinate, and consensus is more difficult to achieve. Generally speaking, it is best to keep the number of core team decision-makers limited to about three to six, but never more than a dozen, people.

It may be necessary, in truly large and significant cases, to create an executive council, of sorts, or develop a lead team with subsidiary teams dedicated to specific roles. For example, if an investigation and prosecution involves multiple, but connected, targets, it may be appropriate to have teams for each target or closely associated groups of targets, with an executive team in charge of coordinating the subsidiary teams. Conversely, if an investigation and prosecution involves different types of criminal conduct by the same person or group of people, or the investigation of multiple criminal events, then it may make the most sense to form teams based on the type of criminal conduct or the criminal events. For example, when I was a prosecutor I was involved in a case involving both complex financial crimes and complex immigration violations. We formed one team to focus on the financial crimes and another team to focus on the immigration violations. In another case, I had a series of drug-related deaths tied to multiple sources of heroin suppliers; we formed teams based on each death, and when it was determined the deaths were tied to a particular supplier, those sub-teams formed new teams focused on the common supplier.

In determining the membership of a prosecution team, a lead prosecutor must carefully assess the anticipated needs of the prosecution team and the skills of various people who could join the team. This requires some deliberate thought about and prediction of the course of the investigation and prosecution. A team is only as strong as its weakest member. Thus, deciding the membership of a prosecution team is critical.

The lead prosecutor must try to identify all of the skills that will be needed and assess the volume of the labor that will be involved in the case. In doing this, it may be helpful for the lead prosecutor to sketch out what the prosecution may look like in terms of who might be charged with which crimes, how many indictments may be brought, and how many trials in what order may result. Through this process, the lead prosecutor should determine how many people with what skills should occupy which positions to successfully prosecute the resulting cases. In identifying the members of the team, the lead prosecutor should consider a person's skills and experience, workload and other demands on their time, and the person's ability to work well with others. Lead prosecutors are not always able to determine whom other agencies, such as law enforcement agencies, choose to include in a given case. The lead prosecutor can, however, determine who that prosecutor will include as a member of the decision-making prosecution team. Other law enforcement officers may be involved in performing tasks in furtherance of the case, but their participation in the case does not dictate that they have a place at the table when key decisions have to be made about the course and scope of the investigation and prosecution.

Finally, a lead prosecutor must continuously monitor, assess, and, when necessary, adjust the size of the prosecution team. Through inertia, some prosecution teams remain too small for the task, while through accretion some prosecution teams grow beyond their need. Large investigations and prosecutions also evolve and are dynamic. The lead prosecutor must account for all these factors in determining whether the prosecution team needs to grow, shrink, or change. If the team appears to be growing by accretion, that is through members involving and inviting others into the case, it may be necessary for the lead prosecutor to address that matter and cut the additional personnel from the case. On the other hand, if it becomes apparent that team members are unable to complete their tasks in a timely manner, the lead prosecutor may need to shift tasks among the team members or consider increasing the size of the team. Likewise, the lead prosecutor may need to reorganize the team, perhaps creating sub-teams, as an investigation evolves into finite targets or areas of investigation. The bottom line is that the lead prosecutor must put careful thought into not only the initial formation of the team but also its size and constitution throughout the existence of the prosecution team.

IDENTIFYING THE ROLES AND ASSIGNING TASKS

In consultation with other team members, a lead prosecutor must organize the team's efforts. This requires an analysis of the targets of the investigation and the potential charges, an identification of the tasks involved in developing the case against the targets and the order in which those tasks should be undertaken, and an assessment of the personnel on the prosecution team regarding their skill sets and ability to successfully complete the identified tasks. It is often best to identify roles and assign tasks by first sketching out the targets of the prosecution and developing an outline of the tasks that are deemed necessary to pursue those targets. Once that is accomplished, then the lead prosecutor can assign finite tasks to team members. For example, imagine a case involving multiple drug dealers believed to be obtaining drugs from the same source of supply. The lead prosecutor should decide how to attempt to take down the organization with a goal of getting to the source of supply. This may involve attempting to make controlled buys from some of the dealers, executing search warrants, and developing cooperators and informants. Once the targets are identified and the tasks enumerated, then the lead prosecutor can begin to assign tasks to team members.

Some of the roles and tasks are easier to identify and assign than others. For example, if the case involves victims, then the victim coordinator is obviously going to assume the lead role in working with the victims. Even this assignment, however, may require thought as to whether a law enforcement officer should work in partnership with the victim coordinator, perhaps because of a pre-existing relationship between the officer and victims formed during the investigation. Other roles and tasks are more difficult to identify. It may be difficult, especially at the beginning of the investigation, to identify all of the targets or discern ways of developing evidence against those targets.

With that in mind, and recalling the need for the lead prosecutor to continuously assess the constitution and size of the prosecution team, it is the responsibility of the lead prosecutor to similarly continuously reassess the identities and roles of team members and the tasks for them to accomplish. Developments in the investigation may require reassignment of tasks and a shifting in the roles of team members. It may become apparent that certain tasks are harder to accomplish than anticipated, or that certain investigation plans have not been successful, requiring a reassessment and reassignment. Likewise, through monitoring progress of the investigation, the lead prosecutor may learn of weaknesses or shortcomings in team members or discover unrealized skills or proficiency in other team members that call for a reassessment of roles or reassignment of tasks.

In particularly large cases involving multiple prosecutors, law enforcement officers, and other professionals, it is often advisable to form sub-teams or other units of the team. As mentioned, depending on the nature of the investigation, smaller teams may be formed to focus on particular targets or victims or crimes. The heads of these sub-teams would be responsible for running their own sub-team and reporting to the executive prosecution team. It may also be helpful to assign certain support staff to take on a lead role for similar positions. For example, in a case involving multiple prosecutors it may be advisable to have one legal assistant assigned the role of lead legal assistant for the case to better delegate responsibility and coordinate efforts among other legal assistants.

MONITORING PROGRESS AND COORDINATING EFFORTS

Regular communication with the prosecution team is necessary for the lead prosecutor to monitor the progress of the case, coordinate efforts among team members, and assess the need for expanding or contracting the size of the prosecution team or realignment of roles among team members. This is usually best accomplished by having regularly scheduled meetings with the prosecution team and, sometimes, specially scheduled meetings when necessary to react to a development in the case. For the regular meetings to be productive, the lead prosecutor should establish agendas, maintain notes of the assigned tasks, and set dates for when team members are expected to accomplish the tasks.

During the meeting, the lead prosecutor should go through the topics on the agenda, discuss the various tasks that were previously identified, obtain feedback from team members regarding progress in accomplishing those tasks, and take careful notes reflecting the status of the work. It is best when the lead prosecutor maintains control of the meeting and ensures an orderly discussion of issues but at the same time encourages a full discussion of matters and elicits feedback from team members. It has been my experience that these meetings often serve as productive brainstorming sessions.

If the case involves sub-teams or groups of team members involved in accomplishing finite tasks, the lead person in charge of those sub-teams or groups must similarly have regular communication with the personnel in those groups and monitor progress by the group. The lead prosecutor may want to be present at those meetings or, depending on the personalities and leadership skills of the lead members of those groups, stay out of it and let that lead person report to the lead prosecutor. It may also be necessary to have one or more of the sub-teams or groups meet together to coordinate efforts. I recall using multiple sub-teams on a case, each devoted to the investigation of the deaths of specific victims. It became necessary in that case to have the groups meet periodically to share information to identify overlap among witnesses and targets as more and more information became available through the investigation.

RESOLVING CONFLICTS

Prosecution teams are made up of people with different agendas, interests, and personalities, which sometimes leads to conflicts. These conflicts may be personal in nature, when one team member rubs another the wrong way, or may arise over feelings that a particular team member is not carrying a fair share of the weight. Conflicts may also arise among agencies whose members constitute the prosecution team. Even when the agents themselves work cooperatively at a personal level, law enforcement agencies may come into conflict over sharing resources or perceived crossing of lines of demarcation between the roles or turf of law enforcement agencies. Sometimes these conflicts come to the lead prosecutor's attention when they flare up during regular meetings. More often, these conflicts remain below the surface, bubbling up from time to time, but nevertheless corrode the success of the team.

The lead prosecutor must be vigilant and maintain an awareness for these conflicts. When they arise, it is the lead prosecutor's responsibility to deal with the conflict in an effective way. This may require intervention to ensure that team members are working hard enough or not encroaching into others' territory or areas of responsibility. It may require the lead prosecutor to refocus the group as a whole on the goals of the prosecution and the need to put petty differences aside for the greater good. When conflicts seriously impair the progress of the case, however, it may be necessary for the lead prosecutor to make reassignments of roles on the prosecution team, or in extreme cases to remove people from the prosecution team. In deciding how to resolve a conflict, it is important that the lead prosecutor do so from a perspective of what is best for the case, regardless of whether it may have adverse consequences on individuals.

LEADING A PROSECUTION TEAM

Effectively leading a prosecution team, like leading law enforcement officers, is not always easy. It requires the lead prosecutor to be organized yet dynamic, diplomatic yet decisive. It requires the lead prosecutor to be willing to listen to and consult with team members, and yet make sure that the lead prosecutor's decisions and directions are followed. All of the leadership skills involved in working with law enforcement officers apply to leading a prosecution team. The lead prosecutor should have a clear vision of the goals of the investigation and a clear plan on how the team will achieve those goals. The lead prosecutor should encourage and compliment and when the time comes reward team members for their efforts. Lead prosecutors need to maintain open lines of communication with the team members, not only encouraging information to flow from team members to the lead prosecutor, but also ensuring that the lead prosecutor adequately and timely provides information to the team members about developments in the case, decisions affecting the outcome of the case, and important events in the investigation and prosecution. Finally, the lead prosecutor should lead by example, by working harder than everyone else and by reflecting the highest principles in seeking a just outcome.

Chapter Four

Working with Defense Attorneys

Criminal cases involve a host of people occupying various roles. Of all of these people, next, perhaps, to law enforcement officers, prosecutors have the greatest contact with defense attorneys. From the time a case is charged, and sometimes well before that, prosecutors interact with defense attorneys inside and outside the courtroom. Prosecutors negotiate plea agreements, litigate motions, work on compromises regarding evidentiary issues, and present closing arguments in opposition to defense counsel. A key part of being a successful prosecutor, then, is learning how to work with defense attorneys. I will discuss here a general philosophical approach prosecutors should take in working with defense counsel, address practical practices for handling disputes with defense counsel when they arise in the course of a criminal case, and then examine constitutional implications when prosecutors make personal attacks on defense counsel.

GENERAL PHILOSOPHY

The title of this chapter, "Working with Defense Attorneys," reflects my general philosophy for the proper relationship prosecutors should have with defense attorneys. I did not title this chapter "Working against Defense Attorneys." Although the criminal justice system is an adversarial one, that does not mean that prosecutors and defense attorneys should always be adversaries. Calling the system adversarial reflects a belief that when two parties are able to present competing positions, justice will win out. It does not mean that the attorneys representing the parties must or should become enemies in the process of presenting opposing positions in court.

Prosecutors should have the utmost respect for the critical role defense attorneys have in the criminal justice system. Defense attorneys are charged with the awesome responsibility of zealously representing their clients, whose liberty, and sometimes lives, are at stake. The criminal justice system thrives when defense attorneys fulfill this duty. Prosecutors, whose goal is that justice is done, should respect attorneys willing to take on the sometimes unpopular and always difficult role of criminal defense attorney.

Fortunately, it has been my observation that prosecutors generally exhibit proper respect for defense attorneys and treat them professionally. I observed this as both a prosecutor and during my limited experience as a criminal defense attorney. While prosecuting cases, I became friends with several defense attorneys. I continue to count several of them as my friends to this day. Defense attorneys were often invited to my fellow prosecutors' weddings, baby showers, and parties, and defense attorneys were among mourners at the funerals of prosecutors' family members, and vice versa. In the courtroom prosecutors and defense attorneys fought hard against each other, but they would often share beers after hours.

As a federal judge, I have gained a perspective I did not have as a lawyer. As a judge I have been able to observe how civil attorneys interact compared to how criminal attorneys interact, and there is a definite difference. Although the best civil practitioners display professional behavior and get along well with opposing counsel, more often attorneys in civil practice make vicious personal attacks against each other, use derogatory, pejorative, and downright nasty and rude terms for each other (particularly in emails), and engage in at best sharp practices and at worst underhanded and unethical conduct. Indeed, I have been surprised and sometimes shocked at the lack of respect and professionalism exhibited by civil practitioners.

I have a theory for why the attorneys who practice criminal law treat each other with so much more respect, and interact so much more professionally, than do their counterparts in private practice. First, the criminal bar in many courts is relatively small. The same prosecutors will see and face the same defense attorneys over and over again. What comes around, goes around, so prosecutors and defense attorneys realize that if they treat the opposing counsel poorly, make personal attacks, or engage in sharp practices, it will come around to bite them because they are very likely going to be dealing with the same attorney in the future. In civil practice, in contrast, the bar is much larger and often more geographically disbursed. Although civil attorneys will sometimes find themselves across the aisle from the same opposing counsel from time to time, especially in specialized areas of practice or small geographic areas, it is much less common. Civil practitioners can get away with more hostile tactics because they are much less likely to ever face the opposing counsel again.

Second, prosecutors and defense attorneys have no financial stake in the outcome of a case. Prosecutors are salaried, as are public defenders. Appointed counsel gets paid a set hourly rate, and it is unethical for privately retained counsel to be paid based on the outcome of a criminal case. Civil practitioners, on the other hand, solicit and strive to retain well-paying clients. Civil attorneys' long-term compensation depends upon keeping these lucrative clients happy at all costs. Civil attorneys' compensation in many cases may also hinge on the verdicts, with the attorney getting a share of jury awards or settlements, or with attorney fee awards depending upon success in the outcome of the cases. When attorneys have a personal stake in the outcome of a case, the case can become personal. When, however, neither prosecutors nor defense attorneys have a direct financial stake in the outcome of individual cases, they are free to do what they think is right, not what may make them more money. To be sure, an indirect financial motive can be present for privately retained criminal defense counsel. The more cases they win, the more clients they attract, and the more money they make. This does, sometimes, render privately retained criminal defense attorneys more difficult to work with.

Finally, the unique role of prosecutors in the criminal justice system creates more of a partnership with criminal defense attorneys. Prosecutors seek justice. In some instances, just decisions comport with the best interests of criminal defendants. Both the prosecutor and criminal defense attorney may agree that a fair outcome in a case would be a plea to a lesser-included offense or a reduced sentence. It is also in the prosecutor's best interest in some instances to assist criminal defendants. For example, prosecutors want and need criminal defendants to cooperate in many investigations in order to advance the case and work up the chain of command in a criminal organization. Criminal defendants who cooperate can receive a reduced sentence. Thus, in those cases both the prosecutor and criminal defense attorney are working together to get the most out of the defendant's cooperation. It is also the case that prosecutors benefit from helping criminal defense attorneys do their job well. Good prosecutors look out for criminal defense attorneys, helping them fulfil their responsibilities to their clients because when criminal defense attorneys fail to do so it can result in a reversal of a conviction either on direct appeal or during post-conviction litigation.

To be sure, criminal defense attorneys do not fully share prosecutors' goal. Justice to a criminal defense attorney is whatever is best for the client in that particular case. A criminal defense attorney's duty is only to the defendant and no one else. A criminal defense attorney cannot and does not care if the government's investigation against others succeeds unless it assists the client in some way. Criminal defense attorneys also do not have the same obligation to divulge information to prosecutors. Although prosecutors must disclose exculpatory information to defendants, criminal defense attorneys have no obligation to disclose inculpatory information to prosecutors; indeed, to do so would violate the criminal defense attorney's duty to the defendant. So prosecutors and criminal defense attorneys work in partnership only when their mutual interests align.

Prosecutors should adopt an attitude of treating defense attorneys with the highest degree of professionalism. Prosecutors should be scrupulously honest with defense attorneys. Prosecutors should invariably be polite and respectful. Although there will inevitably be exceptions, defense attorneys will reciprocate when they are treated in this way. And even when prosecutors encounter defense attorneys who engage in unprofessional practices, prosecutors cannot lower themselves to that level. Prosecutors need to remember they are the representative not of an ordinary party to a controversy, but of the people. More is expected of prosecutors as a result, and prosecutors have a responsibility to live up to that expectation.

PRACTICAL PRACTICES

It is one thing to understand the prosecutor's obligation to treat defense attorneys professionally, but it is altogether another thing to put it into practice. There is some practical advice that will help prosecutors live up to the standard expected of their positions.

Referring to Defense Attorneys

Prosecutors should rarely refer to defense counsel before a judge or jury, and prosecutors should never personally attack them. Prosecutors need to remember that it is the defendant who is the party in the case. The defense attorney is a representative of the defendant. What a defense attorney says and does, then, is really the words and actions of the defendant. By always referring to the defendant instead of the defense attorney, prosecutors remove the defense attorney from the equation. It is no longer a personal thing between the prosecutor and the defense attorney. It is, rather, a matter between the government and the defendant. By removing the personal reference to the defense attorney and concentrating on the merits of the defendant's argument, a prosecutor is less likely to make an improper reference to the intent or motive the prosecutor believes the defense attorney may have. When prosecutors get into the habit of simply never referring to defense attorneys, they remove the possibility of making a personal attack against defense attorneys.

So when a prosecutor might be tempted to respond to a defense argument at a hearing over a discovery dispute that the defense attorney is being disingenuous (a not so veiled allegation that the defense attorney is lying), the prosecutor should instead state that the defendant's position is inaccurate and then correct the record. Instead of a prosecutor arguing in closing that "the defense attorney is using a red herring and trying to mislead you," the prosecutor should instead argue that "the defendant's position is really a red herring and could mislead you." The prosecutor's attack in the first instance in each example is on the defense attorney and focuses on the defense attorney's state of mind. The prosecutor's attack in the second instance in each example is on the merits of the argument and the focus is on the effect it may have on the judge's or jurors' states of mind. The first statements are improper attacks on defense attorneys; courts would find the second statements proper comments about the evidence.

Although it is most important that prosecutors not personally attack a defense attorney in the presence of a jury because it can lead to constitutional error, prosecutors should similarly refrain from doing so in front of a judge. Judges rightfully take umbrage at attorneys attacking other attorneys. When an attorney attacks another attorney, it erodes the attacking attorney's credibility with the judge and causes the judge to question the attacking attorney's integrity and judgment. This is especially true when the attacking attorney is a prosecutor. Judges justifiably hold prosecutors to a higher standard.

Referring to Strategy or Tactics

Prosecutors should also refrain from making references to defense strategies or tactics. A strategy or tactic is the result of mental analysis. The mind behind a defense strategy or tactic belongs to the defense attorney. So a comment about a strategy or tactic is a comment about the defense attorney's state of mind. Derogatory comments about a strategy or tactic, then, become derogatory comments about a defense attorney's intent or motive.

Derogatory attacks on defense strategy or tactic usually take the form of popular metaphors or analogies. Prosecutors will sometimes use phrases like "pulling the wool over your eyes," "trying to mislead you," "using a red herring," or "using smoke and mirrors." It does not solve the problem by substituting the word "defendant" for "defense attorney" because the defendant is not the one actually speaking to the judge during a hearing or the jury in a closing argument. Rather than use words to characterize the strategy, prosecutors should use words to describe the possible effect a defendant's argument may have on the listener. So a prosecutor may characterize a defense position a red herring that could distract the listener from the important facts,[1] without referencing what anyone intended it to be. Similarly, a prosecutor may argue that the effect of the defense position is that it could mislead the jury to render a verdict on an erroneous basis, regardless of whether anyone intended to mislead the jury.

Responding to Personal Attacks

There may be times when defense attorneys make a personal attack against prosecutors. This can arise before a court, with an accusation that the prosecutor lied to defense counsel or intentionally hid evidence or misrepresented some matter. On other occasions, it can occur during a trial, when a defense attorney impugns the prosecutor's integrity by attacking the prosecutor's honesty or accuses the prosecutor of misconduct or misleading the jury. There are several things prosecutors should keep in mind regarding personal attacks by criminal defense attorneys.

Prosecutors should document their interactions with criminal defense attorneys. Oral discussions and phone calls should be later memorialized in emails to defense counsel or reduced to writing in a letter or agreement. If the oral conversation takes place outside court but connected to a hearing or trial (say, for example, right before the hearing before the judge has taken the bench or during a break in the midst of a jury trial), the prosecutor should make it part of the record of the proceeding by summarizing the statements or agreement once the hearing or trial has resumed. Production of discovery to a criminal defense attorney should be fully documented with date, time, and a description of what the prosecutor produced (ideally including Bates numbers). By documenting every interaction with a criminal defense attorney, a prosecutor will be able to respond to a personal attack with facts, not emotion.

Prosecutors also need to develop a thick skin. They cannot allow a criminal case to become a personal dispute with defense counsel. Prosecutors must, of course, defend themselves vigorously against unwarranted and untrue attacks on their integrity. When the attacks occur outside the presence of the judge or jury, prosecutors should respond by dispassionately setting the record straight, bringing the matter to the court's attention when necessary and asking for a court finding that the accusation was unwarranted. When attacks are made in emails, letters, or pleadings, prosecutors should respond with a factual retort, stripped of emotion and venom, to set the record straight. Prosecutors should not retaliate or engage in a round of name-calling with defense counsel.

When a defense attorney attacks a prosecutor's integrity in the presence of a jury, such as during closing argument, the prosecutor must respond, but be cautious in doing so. When possible and a judge is willing, prosecutors should raise the matter with the judge outside the jury's presence before responding. For example, if a defense attorney suggests through cross-examination questions that the prosecutor improperly coached a witness or had something to do with the destruction or alteration of evidence, the prosecutor should ask for a sidebar or bring the matter to the judge's attention during a break. The prosecutor should set the record straight before the judge. Whenever speaking about such a matter, prosecutors should address all comments to the judge and not to defense counsel. Prosecutors should not get into a childish arguing match with a criminal defense attorney, even if the defense attorney directs statements or questions directly to the prosecutor.

When arguing the matter to the judge, the prosecutor should also stress the effect of the defense attorney's statements or conduct. Prosecutors should not be defensive and express offense at the comments. Nor should prosecutors accuse the defense attorney of an evil motive or intent. What matters is the impression the jury may derive from the comments or conduct, not whether the prosecutor has been offended or what the defense attorney intended. The prosecutor should then ask the judge for an appropriate remedy. The remedy could take the form of a curative instruction, informing the jury that the prosecutor did nothing wrong and that the jurors should disregard the defense attorney's question or statement. If the attack is part of a pattern of such conduct, the prosecutor may also ask the court to direct counsel from repeating the conduct. If the defense attorney then persists the court can, in the appropriate case, sanction the attorney for violating the court's order.

If a judge is unwilling to take up the issue, a prosecutor should attempt to correct the record with facts and evidence. In doing this, prosecutors must remain careful not to impugn defense counsel or attribute to them a sinister motive, even if the prosecutor believes there was one. Rather, through redirect examination or another witness, prosecutors should merely reference the prior improper question or comment without characterizing it as such, then elicit the facts necessary to correct the record.

When a defense attorney's improper attack comes during a closing argument, a careful prosecutor should again try to speak to the judge outside the presence of the jury before responding. Prosecutors have the right to respond in kind, to some degree, to an improper attack. *See, e.g., United States v. Young*, 470 US 1, 12–13 (1985) (attorneys may "right the scale" by responding to improper comments during their respective closing arguments); *United States v. Collins*, 642 F.3d 654, 658 (8th Cir. 2011) ("An advocate is permitted considerable latitude in responding to his opponent's arguments"). Under the "invited response" doctrine, a "defense argument may, in a proper case, 'open the door' to otherwise inadmissible prosecution rebuttal," because prosecutors must be allowed to offer "legitimate responses" to defense attorneys' arguments. *United States v. Rivera*, 971 F.2d 876, 883 (2d Cir. 1992).

When possible, however, the best course is to discuss the matter with the judge before responding. The trial judge may not share the prosecutor's opinion that the defense attorney's comment was improper or agree that the prosecutor's intended response is proportional. By clearing it with the judge in advance and obtaining a judicial imprimatur on the prosecutor's response, the prosecutor can substantially decrease the chance that a reviewing court would later find that the prosecutor engaged in misconduct.

Preparing for Rebuttal Closing Arguments

Finally, prosecutors should prepare rebuttal closing arguments in advance to the degree possible. Prosecutors will likely know from the nature and tone of the defense attorney's opening statement, cross-examination, and affirmative case (if there was one) the nature of the defense argument. A prosecutor is likely to have concluded long before closing argument that, in the prosecutor's opinion, the defense counsel is using or will use smoke and mirrors or the like to mislead the jury. When a prosecutor prepares a response in advance, it is far more likely the prosecutor will be able to carefully craft cautious wording that constitutes an attack on the merits of the argument instead of an improper attack on the integrity of the arguer. A significant number of reported cases addressing alleged prosecutorial misconduct involve personal attacks on defense counsel that arise in prosecutors' rebuttal closing arguments. All too often when prosecutors get up to present a rebuttal closing argument they have not properly prepared and they argue extemporaneously. When prosecutors do that, they tend to take more risks and make more mistakes than when they think carefully in advance about what they intend to say.

CONSTITUTIONAL IMPLICATIONS

If professionalism and a sense of fair play are not sufficient to motivate prosecutors to treat defense attorneys with respect and professionalism, then the possibility that failing to do so could violate a defendant's constitutional rights should. When made in the presence of jurors, a personal attack on a defense attorney can jeopardizes a defendant's right to a fair trial. *Viereck v. United States*, 318 US 236, 247–48 (1943). "A personal attack on defense counsel's integrity [can] constitute misconduct." *United States v. Santiago*, 46 F.3d 885, 892 (9th Cir. 1995); *see also United States v. Tomsha-Miguel*, 766 F.3d 1041, 1047 (9th Cir. 2014) (A "prosecutor may not 'distort' the trial process by leading the jury to believe that defense counsel is dishonest" [citation omitted]). A personal attack on a defense attorney can suggest that a jury should consider the integrity of the defense attorney in arriving at the verdict. A statement or an argument that impugns the integrity of the defense attorney can also have the effect, intended or not, of besmirching the defendant's character through the defendant's association with his attorney. A personal attack on a defense attorney, and by extension on the defendant, then, is a form of jury nullification, turning the factual and legal dispute into a personality contest.

When prosecutors impugn the integrity and honesty of defense attorneys, it can lead to reversal of convictions. Prosecutors' personal attacks usually occur during closing arguments, most often rebuttal closing arguments, and they usually take some form of suggesting that the defense attorney is being untruthful. *See, e.g., United States v. Milk*, 447 F.3d 593, 601-02 (8th Cir. 2006) (finding it improper when prosecutor suggested in closing that defense attorney was trying to "mislead" the jury with "red herring" evidence and accused defense attorney "distract you[,] to take you off the path" and implored jury not to let defense attorney "twist those facts" or "con you"); *United States v. Holmes*, 413 F.3d 770, 775 (8th Cir. 2005) (reversing a conviction when in closing argument prosecutor focused "on the conduct and role of [the defendant's] attorney rather than on the evidence of [the defendant's] guilt" by suggesting defense attorney was distracting jury with red herrings, and insinuating that defense attorney and defendant had conspired to fabricate a defense); *Bruno v. Rushen*, 721 F.2d 1193, 1195 (9th Cir. 1983) (finding prosecutor's comments equating defendant's hiring of counsel with guilt and attacking integrity of defense counsel without evidence improper and error of constitutional dimension).

As noted above, prosecutors should exercise restraint, keep their emotions in check, and calmly rebut a defense case by focusing on the evidence and not the defense attorney or the defense attorney's motives. By adopting the practice of not making any reference to a criminal defense attorney, particularly when arguing to a jury, prosecutors can avoid turning the matter into a personality contest. By refraining from describing what the prosecutor believes to be the defense attorney's motive, intents, strategy, or tactic, the prosecutor can shift the focus to the impact the defense argument might have on the jury and in the jurors' minds. Then, by alerting the jurors of the danger of going down the wrong path or focusing on a red herring, the prosecutor can refocus the jury's attention back on the evidence and the truth.

Chapter Five

Relationship with the Court

Prosecutors' relationship with the court, with judges, is fundamentally and materially different from that of any other lawyers. First, as noted in the first chapter of this book, prosecutors occupy a unique position as representatives of the government to fulfill a duty to the people to do justice, not just advocate for a client. Second, prosecutors have regular ex parte and in camera contact with judges in carrying out the duties of their office. This unique relationship prosecutors have with judges carries great responsibility and risks.

Although in a sense every lawyer is an officer of the court, a prosecutor is one in a very real and true sense. Like judges, prosecutors are public servants. Just as judges do, prosecutors take an oath to protect and defend the Constitution against all enemies, foreign and domestic. Judges share prosecutors' goal to see that justice is done. Although public defenders are also public employees, they owe a duty to zealously represent their clients. Thus, no other attorney appearing in court is so closely aligned with judges as prosecutors.

Prosecutors also tend to have much more contact with judges than any other category of lawyer. Prosecutors appear before judges more often as a group than any other group of attorneys simply as a result of the large number of criminal cases and proceedings and the relatively small number of prosecutors. In many civil cases the lawyers may never appear before a judge before settling the case. Judges decide most civil motions on the pleadings, and less than 1 percent of all civil cases proceed to trial. Criminal proceedings require the defendant, and thus the prosecutor, to appear before a judge often, such as for arraignment, detention hearings, change of plea hearings, trials, and sentencing hearings. Approximately 5 to 10 percent of criminal cases proceed to trial. Thus, judges come to know prosecutors far more than they do any other lawyers, creating a relationship with them that is different from the relationship with any other group of attorneys.

The criminal justice system also requires prosecutors to regularly have contact with judges outside the courtroom. Prosecutors and officers meet in chambers (and sometimes at judges' houses) to swear out material witness warrants, search warrants, criminal complaints, and wiretap applications. Prosecutors seek judicial approval for trap and trace authorizations and to obtain tax information about suspects. When grand jury witnesses refuse to testify, prosecutors go to judges to obtain compulsion orders and, when that fails, to initiate contempt proceedings. Prosecutors participate in and advise the court in the empaneling of new grand juries. Prosecutors may also permissively meet with judges ex parte during the course of a trial when there is reason to believe that the defendant is engaging in witness or jury tampering or some other form of obstruction. No other lawyer has this type of regular, ex parte contact with judges.

Finally, prosecutors and judges must engage in more cooperation and coordination on logistical and scheduling matters than judges do with any other group of attorneys. Prosecutors control the timing of the return of indictments from the grand jury and must coordinate with chambers to have the indictments returned in open court. Prosecutors control the timing of arrests and must be in communication with chambers to coordinate initial appearances. In some instances when the government intends to arrest a large number of defendants on a single occasion, special coordination may be required to ensure the court can prepare for the large number of defendants entering the criminal justice system. In short, because prosecutors control the entry into the criminal justice system pipeline, it requires them to have frequent communication and coordinate with the court.

The frequent contact prosecutors have with judges and the greater familiarity they have with judges has some benefits. When prosecutors are good and reliable and fair, judges come to trust the prosecutors. Judges rely on prosecutors to be forthright and candid, and they will have confidence that prosecutors' briefs accurately reflect the facts and the law when prosecutors prove themselves to be trustworthy. A judge who trusts a prosecutor may be more likely to heed a prosecutor's request for a sidebar discussion, assuming the prosecutor is exercising sound judgment in interrupting the trial, than the judge might heed another lawyer's judgment of whether a sidebar is really necessary. A judge who trusts a prosecutor may also be more skeptical of allegations of prosecutorial misconduct and more willing to keep an open mind when evaluating such claims.

The familiarity between judges and prosecutors can, however, lead to an improper development of a "team spirit" between judges and prosecutors.[1] The frequent ex parte contact between judges and prosecutors, and the judge's necessary insight into investigations, can sometimes lead prosecutors to disclose more than they should, particularly during ex parte, in camera contacts. Some judges may contribute to this by expressing a natural curiosity about the government's case and strategies. Prosecutors may feel an equally natural desire to satisfy a judge's curiosity. Judges are not part of any prosecution team, however, and prosecutors must maintain a separation. The line between proper and improper interaction between judges and prosecutors is often the result of "laxity, inattention, or simple ignorance of the law."[2] It is the prosecutor's responsibility to ensure this does not happen.

Crossing the line may be more than an ethical issue. For example, Rule 6(e) of the Federal Rules of Criminal Procedure requires grand jury proceedings to be kept confidential, even to a judge, unless judicial intervention is necessary (to compel a witness's testimony, for example). Further, the *Leon* good faith exception to the exclusionary rule[3] is premised, in part, on a finding that the judicial officer approving a search warrant did so as an independent judicial officer. Likewise, judges and prosecutors need to maintain a wall of separation so that defendants cannot successfully move for recusal on the ground that the judge was too aligned with the prosecution. Just as prosecutors and law enforcement officers must stay in their own lanes, so too must prosecutors and judges. Although prosecutors should maintain friendly and cordial relations with judges, the relationship must remain at a professional level and at arm's length. It is important not only that justice is done, but that there is an appearance of justice in order for the public to maintain confidence in the criminal justice system.[4]

Prosecutors and judges also do not always share the same vision of justice. Prosecutors represent the executive branch of the government, and judges occupy the third branch. These branches are separate to ensure a balance of power. Thus, although each may seek the same goal of justice in principle, they may not share the same vision of that goal or agree on the means of achieving that goal. Prosecutors should be cautious, then, to maintain their independence from the judiciary. Judges may attempt to exert influence over prosecutorial decisions and pressure prosecutors to do what the judges believe is right, but prosecutors must do what they believe is right even if it is at odds with the judiciary's view.

Another risk for prosecutors is living up to judges' expectations. Judges may trust prosecutors, as I said, until they do not. Once a judge finds that a prosecutor has failed to be fully candid, or believes a prosecutor misled the judge on the law (intentionally or not), the judge is likely to feel betrayed and offended more than they would have if another attorney had done the same thing. Once a prosecutor has lost a judge's trust, it is very difficult to earn it back again. Judges simply hold prosecutors to a higher standard. Prosecutors should strive to live up to that higher standard.

Chapter Six

Managing a Caseload and Other Duties

One of a prosecutor's greatest challenges is managing a caseload and other duties and demands on the prosecutor's limited time. Depending on whether prosecutors work for the state or federal government, and the type of cases prosecutors handle, prosecutors sometimes have scores of cases pending at any given time. Even when the cases are relatively few in number, such as with a federal prosecutor handling white-collar cases, the time demands on those few cases may be as great as a larger number of less complex cases. Each case on a prosecutor's docket will have numerous deadlines that must be met, hearings the prosecutor must attend, and myriad tasks the prosecutor must perform to keep the cases successfully moving toward resolution. Unlike in civil litigation, in criminal cases these deadlines are often short and firm as the courts protect defendants' speedy trial and due process rights.

In addition to handling all of the demands of their cases, prosecutors often have collateral duties as a member of the office. Some prosecutors are also supervisors and are responsible not only for their own caseloads, but also overseeing those of other prosecutors. Other prosecutors may have duties such as training, hiring, ethics compliance, or any number of other program or office initiatives. Finally, prosecutors also have a life outside work with all of the duties and responsibilities attendant to everyday existence, and the need for time for relaxation, socialization, and enjoyment of life.

All of these demands on a prosecutor's time can be daunting and, at times, overwhelming. Keeping every case moving forward and meeting every deadline while fulfilling every other obligation is like trying to keep a dozen or more plates spinning on poles at the same time or juggling a dozen balls. To do it successfully requires concentration, attention, and effort.

Law schools do not teach law students how to handle this practical part of the practice of law. Nor is it common for prosecutors' offices to devote time and resources in training new prosecutors how to juggle all of these demands, manage their caseloads, or deal with crises that arise when everything goes awry. Generally, new prosecutors learn how to deal with all of these demands through trial and error, learning from mistakes, some more successfully than others. The goal of this chapter is to describe the nature of the problems with managing a caseload and other duties, provide some insight into factors that affect timing of events in the prosecution of criminal cases, and provide suggestions to prosecutors for successfully handling the myriad demands for their limited time.

THE LIFE OF A CRIMINAL CASE

To solve the problem of managing a criminal caseload, it is first necessary to understand the nature of a criminal case and appreciate the time demands connected to the various stages of a criminal case. For purposes of this illustration, this discussion will focus on the various stages of the life of federal criminal cases. Many of the same time demands are present in the prosecution of state and local criminal cases as well, while others, such as grand jury presentations, may not be.

Investigation

A federal criminal case starts with the investigation. Some cases are so-called reactive cases, and others can be labeled proactive cases. The demands on a prosecutor's time are often different depending on whether the case is reactive or proactive.

Reactive cases are ones where law enforcement officers have reacted to a crime that has already been committed. Typically, the defendant has already been apprehended. The defendant may be in custody temporarily on state charges or under a probable case arrest on federal charge, or officers may need federal charging documents immediately. The interdiction of drugs on the highway or at an airport, a bank robbery, child exploitation, human trafficking, and violent crimes like murder are all examples of reactive cases. Reactive cases are ones that catch law enforcement by surprise, resulting from sudden events or discoveries by law enforcement officers or reports of crimes by the public or victims.

In reactive cases, much of the evidence that will exist in the case is generated from the immediate investigation of the crime before law enforcement officers bring the case to the prosecutor for prosecution. Reactive cases often have a significant front-end, short-term demand on the prosecutor's time during the investigation stage. Because law enforcement officers have reacted to a crime, time is often of the essence during the investigation stage to secure evidence before it disappears or dissipates. Officers may have an immediate need for search warrants or grand jury subpoenas to obtain records or "freeze" letters to internet or social media providers to require preservation of electronic data before it is automatically erased.

How often these reactive cases affect a given prosecutor depends on the type of cases the prosecutor handles. Drug prosecutors or general crimes prosecutors will likely have to deal with reactive cases far more often than a white-collar crime prosecutor, for example. It is important to understand, however, that reactive cases can arise even in white-collar investigations. No prosecutor is immune from having to deal with reactive cases, at least from time to time.

When prosecutors are assigned to reactive cases, it often means that they must drop everything else they are working on at the time and respond to the immediate needs of the investigation. Sometimes this occurs during regular working hours, but as often as not prosecutors are called in at night or on weekends to help officers react to the case. Because reactive cases are, by their nature, surprises to law enforcement officers, prosecutors cannot mark off time on their calendars in advance to deal with the demands on their time during the investigative stage of reactive cases. The best a prosecutor can do is anticipate reactive cases will arise and build in enough lead time in complying with other deadlines and demands on their time to absorb the time demands of reactive cases when they arise.

Some prosecutors' offices help manage the time demands of reactive cases by various means. Some offices, for example, have so-called duty attorneys. That is, the office requires attorneys to assume the responsibility of handling any reactive case that arises during a given time frame (say, for example, a week). While serving as a duty attorney, the prosecutor is responsible for handling any reactive cases that arise during his or her assigned time period. Law enforcement officers are directed to take their reactive cases to the duty attorney. The duty attorney will assist law enforcement officers with whatever they need during the investigation stage, such as search warrants or arrest warrants, but responsibility for the prosecution of the case will ultimately be assigned to another prosecutor once the immediate emergency has passed. Some prosecution offices also assign attorneys to prosecution units responsible for handling reactive cases, such as drug interdiction cases, so that the unpredictable time demands of reactive cases do not fall on other prosecutors.

It is important for prosecutors to understand that the investigation does not end, even in reactive cases, when charges are brought against the subject. Although most of the evidence that will exist in the case may be obtained in the course of a few hours or days immediately following the commission of the crime, good prosecutors handling reactive cases will continue to evaluate the need for further investigation. For example, a prosecutor handling a reactive drug interdiction case may investigate further ties to drug suppliers or organizations by conducting forensic examinations of cell phones seized from the drug mules, or by tracing the courier's route and trying to obtain records from hotels along the route. Thus, in handling reactive cases and anticipating the time demands of those cases, prosecutors should account for the need to devote additional hours in a further follow-up investigation from the leads generated by the initial seizure of evidence.

Proactive cases are ones where law enforcement officers initiate an investigation into past or ongoing criminal activity. These investigations are typically not rushed or an emergency in nature. Rather, proactive cases seek to investigate criminal activity methodically and thoroughly, and typically without the target becoming aware of the investigation as long as possible. Proactive investigations often involve a significant use of the grand jury, including the issuance of subpoenas for documents and questioning of witnesses before the grand jury. Proactive cases sometimes take months or even years to complete, particularly in white-collar criminal investigations.

Proactive cases impose a less immediate, but more long-term demand on a prosecutor's time. Prosecutors typically have a greater ability to anticipate the time demands during the investigative stage of a proactive case and work them into their schedule. Proactive cases, however, also demand more of a prosecutor's limited time. Typically, proactive cases generate a greater volume of evidence, more documents, and more witnesses than reactive cases. Organizing and managing the volume of the evidence, analyzing it, and planning further investigative steps takes time.

Proactive cases require prosecutors to regularly revisit the cases with law enforcement officers to monitor the progress of the investigations and keep the cases moving toward proper dispositions. When prosecutors also have a number of reactive cases they must deal with on a daily basis, it is easy for them to push proactive cases to the back burner and neglect them. The same is true for the law enforcement officers working on proactive cases. If prosecutors fail to keep proactive cases current and maintain steady progress on them, it actually increases the time demands generated from the case. When prosecutors ignore proactive cases for prolonged periods, it requires more time for them to get back up to speed on the case than it does when the prosecutors keep the case fresh in their minds by regularly and methodically working on the case.

It is also important to recognize that reactive cases and proactive cases sometimes evolve and shift from one category to the other. The investigation of a reactive case may, for example, lead to the development of a proactive investigation arising from information and evidence obtained through the investigation of the reactive case. Likewise, while conducting a proactive investigation, an event may occur that requires an immediate reaction by law enforcement officers, generating a reactive case as part of the otherwise proactive investigation. For example, the DEA may be working with the prosecutor on a proactive investigation of a drug organization, methodically conducting controlled buys, surveillance, and phone analysis when a state trooper happens to make a traffic stop of a drug mule working for the organization and discovers pounds of controlled substances during a roadside search. In managing their caseloads, then, prosecutors need to anticipate the possibility of their cases evolving in different directions with different time demands and build in enough flexibility in their schedule to deal with these changes.

Whether a case is a reactive case or a proactive case, a prosecutor needs to anticipate and budget for the amount of the prosecutor's time the investigation will take. This is very difficult to do because each case will be different in time demands. With experience, prosecutors develop a sense of how much of the prosecutor's time a typical bank robbery case will require, for example, or how much time a proactive bank fraud case will demand, during the investigation stage. Until prosecutors gain that knowledge from experience, it is best for them to work closely with a mentor, supervisor, or other experienced prosecutor.

Grand Jury Presentation

In the federal system, prosecutors are generally required to use the grand jury to charge a defendant with a felony offense. The Fifth Amendment to the US Constitution provides, in pertinent part: "No person shall be held to answer for a capital, or otherwise infamous crime, unless on a presentment or indictment of a Grand Jury" US CONST., AMEND. V. Thus, unless waived (for example, as part of a plea deal), the Fifth Amendment requires prosecutors to present evidence to a grand jury establishing probable cause to believe the defendant committed the crime alleged in the indictment. But a federal grand jury more than simply decides whether to formally charge defendants.

A federal grand jury serves two basic functions. First, it is an investigatory body with the power to call witnesses and subpoena documents and other things in an effort to investigate the underlying criminal activity. Second, it must decide, in conjunction with the federal prosecutor, whether there is probable cause to believe that the target of the investigation committed the federal offense under investigation. Thus, federal prosecutors work with grand juries, using the grand jury subpoena power as a tool to investigate criminal activity. Federal prosecutors also work with grand juries to determine whether and against whom to bring criminal charges.

In some larger federal districts, grand juries are designated to hear either reactive cases or proactive cases. In other words, so-called accusatory grand juries hear testimony, review evidence, and vote on indictments only on reactive cases. The presentation of evidence to these grand juries is typically very short and often involves testimony only from the case agent. As a result, an accusatory grand jury may review evidence and vote on indictments on a dozen or more cases in a single day.

The Federal Rules of Evidence do not apply in proceedings before a federal grand jury. Thus, hearsay evidence is admissible before a grand jury. *See United States v. Calandra*, 414 US 338 (1974). A fundamental reason that the evidence rules do not apply is because a grand jury proceeding takes place at the investigatory stage of the case. A grand jury is investigating leads to evidence that would prove a criminal case, just like a police officer may rely on hearsay statements to pursue leads that result in the discovery of admissible evidence. Because the evidence rules do not apply in grand jury proceedings, there is no requirement that the government present any or all the witnesses with firsthand or personal knowledge of a case before a grand jury. Thus, it is common in reactive cases to present all of the evidence to an accusatory grand jury through a single case agent.

For example, imagine a case where a drug trafficker is pulled over in a traffic stop and the officer finds a hidden stash of thirty pounds of methamphetamine. Perhaps the trafficker makes incriminating statements, or other incriminating evidence is found in the car, but there is nothing else really known about the target or his criminal conduct. In such a case, the prosecutor may simply have the case agent, like the DEA agent who submitted the case to the office for prosecution, testify before the grand jury by summarizing the evidence from the traffic stop. The agent can do this even when the agent was not present at the traffic stop and has no personal knowledge of the events.

Another type of grand jury is a so-called investigatory grand jury. These grand juries review evidence and vote on indictments regarding proactive cases. These long-term investigations may involve presenting evidence to a grand jury over the course of several months or even years. These grand jury presentations typically involve the prosecutor calling many witnesses before the grand jury and using the grand jury power to subpoena multiple entities or individuals to obtains documents pertinent to the investigation. As a result, investigatory grand juries may be convened and be in session for just as many hours and days as an accusatory grand jury but vote on a small fraction of indictments that an accusatory grand jury would during the same time period.

Other federal districts do not distinguish between accusatory and investigatory grand juries. Rather, these grand juries consider evidence and vote on both reactive and proactive cases. In these districts the grand juries will hear testimony on whatever types of cases the prosecutors bring before them. Some cases will be reactive cases where only a case agent testifies and the grand jury is asked to deliberate on an indictment immediately after the agent's testimony. Other cases will be proactive ones where the grand jury hears testimony from one or more witnesses during each grand jury session, over the course of months or years, before being asked to deliberate on an indictment.

In a later chapter I will discuss the work that prosecutors must perform in preparing for a grand jury presentation in both types of investigations. For purposes of this chapter, however, the point is that both types of grand jury presentations take a significant amount of preparation to be done well. That means prosecutors need to budget time to prepare for and present cases to the grand jury. The time demands on a federal prosecutor presenting evidence to a grand jury on reactive cases is much less than for proactive cases. Reactive cases require less preparation for and consume less time in presentation to grand juries than proactive cases. Because each case is different, it is difficult to provide significant guidance as to how much time a prosecutor should budget for grand jury presentations. That said, I found that typically a reactive case required several hours to prepare for and present the case to the grand jury (not counting the time necessary to draft and obtain approval of the indictment). I can offer no general rule for proactive cases because the amount of time varies so significantly based on the facts of those cases.

Charging

Prosecutors need to account for the amount of time necessary to draft charging documents and have them approved by supervisors. In federal court, a prosecutor can bring charges against a defendant by way of a criminal complaint, a criminal information, or a grand jury indictment. Each form of charging document takes time to prepare.

The requirements for filing a criminal complaint are contained in Rule 3 of the Federal Rules of Criminal Procedure, and they are simple. A criminal complaint "is a written statement of the essential facts constituting the offense charged." FED. R. CRIM. P. 3. The government must submit a sworn affidavit in support of a criminal complaint. An agent signs the affidavit, swearing that the information contained in the affidavit is true and correct to the best of the agent's knowledge and belief. The affidavit submitted to the judicial officer must establish probable cause to believe the defendant has committed criminal offense. If the judge agrees that probable cause exists to believe the defendant has committed a criminal offense, then the judge will issue a warrant for the defendant's arrest, unless the prosecutor asks for another means, such as a summons, to require the defendant to appear in court to answer to the charges. Fed. R. Crim. P. 4.

The government almost always utilizes criminal complaints as a temporary charging document. Criminal complaints are issued in situations where there is an immediate need to charge a person with a crime because the person poses a danger to the community or constitutes a flight risk. It follows, then, that criminal complaints are most often used in reactive cases.

A criminal information is another form of charging document. The United States may charge a defendant with a misdemeanor offense by criminal information without leave of the court and without any presentation of evidence to or review by a grand jury. Fed. R. Crim. P. 7(a). A misdemeanor crime is an offense punishable by one year or less in prison. Federal prosecutors are not barred from using the grand jury to investigate a misdemeanor offense, however, even if an indictment is never presented to the grand jury for deliberation. A prosecutor may also file a criminal information against a defendant to charge a felony offense, but may try, or accept a guilty plea from, a criminal defendant only if the defendant waives his right to have the felony charge considered and returned by a grand jury in the form of an indictment. Fed. R. Crim. P. 7(a). Unlike indictments, which must be returned by a grand jury, a federal prosecutor charges a crime by filing a criminal information on his or her own authority. In form, a criminal information generally appears the same as an indictment, only the caption says "Information" and it is signed only by the prosecutor. The form of an indictment is addressed below.

As mentioned, indictments are charging documents returned by grand juries after a finding of probable cause. After the grand jury returns an indictment, called a true bill, the prosecutor and the grand jury present the indictment to a judicial officer. Upon ensuring that the indictment and the grand jury voting ballot are complete and valid on their face, the judge will order the indictment filed with the district court.

Whatever the form of charging document used, they take time to draft. Prosecutors must determine the appropriate charge, review the applicable statutes, draft the document, and have the document reviewed and approved by a supervisor. The amount of time consumed by this step of the process will vary depending on the type of charging document and the facts of the case. In federal cases, the prosecutor is typically integrally involved in drafting the affidavit in support of a criminal complaint. Often law enforcement officers will present the prosecutor with a draft affidavit, which the prosecutor then must review to ensure that it establishes probable cause to support each element of the offense charged. It is common that the affidavit requires revisions, sometimes significant ones. Once the affidavit is prepared, the prosecutor must draft the other supporting paperwork for the criminal complaint, including the application for the complaint, the complaint itself, an arrest warrant, and other clerk of court forms. Typically, the prosecutor's legal assistant performs this task with instruction from the prosecutor, but the prosecutor must review the charging documents to ensure their accuracy.

The drafting of informations and indictments are the sole responsibility of the prosecutor. Depending on the number and types of charges, the drafting of these charging documents can be very time-consuming, while others take much less time. The Department of Justice provides forms for charging most types of federal offenses. Some, like for drug or immigration offenses, are simple and short and are quick to draft. The forms for other types of offenses, such as for fraud offenses, are more like shells that require the prosecutor to insert a significant amount of facts and other language. Some informations and indictments charging white-collar crimes can end up being quite lengthy, depending on the number of charges and the nature of the crime committed. Drafting an indictment on a white-collar case can sometimes take days, involving multiple rewrites and revisions.

Whatever the form of charging document, a supervisor must review the document. This sometimes leads to revisions. Prosecutors may have to discuss the charges with the supervisor or wait in the supervisor's office while the charging document is reviewed. This review process takes time. Further, criminal complaints must be presented to a judicial officer for review, which also requires a devotion of time by the prosecutor.

Initial Hearings

After a defendant is charged, there follows initial hearings that the prosecutor must attend. These include initial appearances, arraignments, preliminary hearings, and detention hearings. Each takes time.

Rule 5 of the Federal Rules of Criminal Procedure requires that, upon arrest, the government must bring the defendant before a judicial officer without unnecessary delay. When the defendant appears before the judge for the first time, it is called, appropriately enough, the "initial appearance." Typically, this hearing occurs before a federal magistrate judge. The judge appoints an attorney to represent the defendant at the hearing, if the defendant does not already have one. During the brief hearing, the judge will apprise the defendant of the nature of the charges against him or her and explain to the defendant his or her rights under the Constitution. The judge will also determine if the government is seeking detention of the defendant pending trial. These hearings typically take less than fifteen minutes.

When a defendant has been charged by a criminal complaint, and the matter has not yet been submitted to the grand jury, the defendant is entitled to a preliminary hearing. FED. R. CRIM. P. 5.1. A defendant may waive a preliminary hearing. *Id.* Otherwise, the court must hold a "preliminary hearing" or "probable cause hearing" within fourteen days of arraignment if the defendant is in custody, or within twenty days of arraignment if the defendant has been released pending trial. FED. R. CRIM. P. 5.1(c). During a preliminary hearing, the government must present evidence to establish probable cause to believe the defendant committed the crime in question. FED. R. CRIM. P. 5.1(e). The government may satisfy the requirement for showing probable cause through hearsay evidence such as by a case agent. *Id.* Preliminary hearings are typically relatively short, taking only half an hour or an hour. In many cases preliminary hearings become unnecessary. If a defendant is indicted between the time of an initial appearance and the preliminary hearing, then the grand jury's probable cause finding negates the need for a preliminary hearing.

One of the decisions a prosecutor must make when arresting a defendant is whether to seek detention of the defendant in jail pending the trial in the matter. Whether a defendant is eligible for release pending trial is governed by Title 18, US Code, Sections 3142 and 3144. *See* FED. R. CRIM. P. 46(a). The prosecutor must move for detention at the time of the defendant's initial appearance or it is waived. If the prosecutor moves for detention, the court must conduct a detention hearing to determine whether detention is appropriate. The detention hearing must be held at the time of the defendant's initial appearance unless either party seeks an extension of time. 18 U.S.C. § 3142(f). The law provides, though, that "except for good cause," such an extension cannot exceed five days (if the defendant sought the extension) or three days (if the government sought the extension), not counting weekends and holidays. *Id.* During any such continuance, the defendant must be detained. *Id.* At the detention hearing, the rules of evidence do not apply. *Id.* Thus, the government's presentation is again typically short, involving the testimony of only a case agent. Prosecutors may also proffer evidence in lieu of presenting live testimony. If the defendant does not contest the proffer, the court can base its decision on the proffered evidence. It is also sometimes the case that the basis for detention is the defendant's history and characteristics, as reflected in the pretrial services report (sometimes called a bond report). Again, the prosecutor can proffer the information contained in the pretrial services report and, unless contested, the court can rely on that information to determine whether to detain the defendant. Sometimes judges combine detention hearings with preliminary hearings because the evidence the government presents often overlaps.

In deciding which witnesses to call at preliminary or detention hearings, prosecutors should remember that the Federal Rules of Evidence do not apply, and they should consider the effect of generating prior sworn testimony by key witnesses. In other words, it is often best to call the case agent at these hearings to summarize the testimony of witnesses with personal knowledge instead of calling those witnesses. Although the case agent's testimony may be based largely on hearsay, the presentation of the evidence is more efficient and it avoids having witnesses present testimony that can later be used against them for impeachment purposes. Even the most honest witness may make mistakes or make statements that expose him or her to later cross-examination for perceived inconsistencies. Presenting testimony through the case agent also prevents defense counsel from using preliminary and detention hearings to conduct discovery. At the same time, however, prosecutors should consider the effect of presenting hearsay statements on the judge. Although hearsay is admissible in these proceedings, the judge need not afford it as much weight as testimony by witnesses with personal knowledge of the events. Thus, prosecutors must balance the need for persuasive evidence against the costs of presenting testimony by witnesses with personal knowledge.

Once a grand jury has indicted a defendant (or the defendant has been charged by way of a criminal information), and the defendant has been arrested, the defendant must be arraigned before a federal judicial officer, which again often takes place before a federal magistrate judge. FED. R. CRIM. P. 10. During an arraignment, the judge advises the defendant of charges pending against him or her. Unless waived, the judge must read verbatim the indictment pending against the defendant. At the time of arraignment, the defendant enters a plea. FED. R. CRIM. P. 10(a)(3). When a defendant's first appearance in court is after being charged by an information or indictment, the arraignment coincides with his or her initial appearance. Again, these are typically very short hearings, lasting ten to fifteen minutes.

Discovery

In the federal system, discovery is limited. There are no depositions. Most US Attorneys' Offices have adopted policies whereby they provide defense counsel with copies of or access to essentially all of the government evidence, which significantly diminishes the amount of time a prosecutor must spend dealing or litigating discovery disputes. Nevertheless, prosecutors need to budget some time to work with office staff to ensure that discovery is provided to defense counsel and to deal with any problems arising from that discovery. Thankfully, in most cases prosecutors do not have to spend a lot of time dealing with these issues.

Motions Practice

It is common for defense counsel to file motions of various sorts in every criminal case. They may file discovery motions, motions for bills of particular, motions to strike portions of or to dismiss the indictment, motions to suppress evidence, motions for change of venue, or any number of other types of pretrial motions. Prosecutors must respond to these motions, drafting written responses and, when necessary, presenting evidence at hearings on the motions.

The demand on a prosecutor's time dealing with motions differs significantly from case to case. The more complex the case, the higher the stakes (because of the prominence of the defendant or the length of the possible sentence, for example), the greater the number of motions filed. Some defense attorneys file more motions than other defense attorneys. Retained counsel hired by defendants with significant resources are more likely to file motions than other defense attorneys. Some motions (such as motions to suppress) almost always require evidentiary hearings, while other motions (such as motions to dismiss) do not. Some judges entertain oral arguments on all motions, but other judges never hold argument hearings on pretrial motions.

Prosecutors may be able to predict the amount of time that will be required to deal with pretrial motions in some cases and budget for the time accordingly. Prosecutors should have a feel, for example, whether a case will likely draw a motion to suppress based on the nature of the law enforcement officers' conduct and the facts of the case. Similarly, knowing the defense attorney and judge may clue in the prosecutor as to the likelihood of there being a large number of motions or lengthy hearings.

The amount of time necessary to research and draft written responses to motions will, of course, vary significantly depending on the type of motion, the issues raised, and the facts of the case. When evidentiary hearings are involved, prosecutors must figure that there will be time needed to review the evidence, identify witnesses and exhibits, prepare witnesses to testify, and for the actual hearing itself. For every hour of testimony, a federal prosecutor typically spends two to three hours in preparation. So pretrial motions, and in particular motions to suppress, can constitute a significant drain on a prosecutor's limited time.

Plea Negotiations

Every criminal case will involve plea negotiations. Between about 90 and 95 percent of all criminal cases, both state and federal, are resolved by way of guilty pleas. Even in those criminal cases that do not end in guilty pleas, there are inevitably plea negotiations. And plea negotiations constitute another demand on a prosecutor's time.

Plea negotiations require communication with defense counsel. Discussing plea deals can sometimes be relatively quick, and other times be quite lengthy. Plea negotiations may involve multiple exchanges of letters or emails. Sometimes plea negotiations require the prosecutor to sit down with a criminal defendant and the defendant's attorney to review the evidence and explain the plea deal. When a plea deal involves a defendant agreeing to be a cooperator, it typically requires the prosecutor to participate in a debrief of the defendant during which the defendant proffers the information he or she has that will be of assistance in the government's investigation. The prosecutor's presence is important during proffer sessions because it is necessary for the prosecutor to determine whether the defendant is being truthful and thus whether to enter into a cooperation plea agreement with the defendant. Again, depending on the nature of the case and the length of time and extent to which the defendant was involved in the criminal activity, proffer sessions can consume an hour or may take days.

Every plea agreement should be written, and in the federal system the Department of Justice requires them to be. Most of the language in plea agreements are stock, and generating most of a plea agreement can be accomplished in fifteen minutes by selecting from an electronic form the boilerplate language that is appropriate for the particular case depending on the facts and charges and tweaking the language and filling in blanks to make the stock language fit the case at hand. Other parts of a plea agreement, however, may take much more time to draft. Good plea agreements will contain stipulations of fact which reflect, at the very least, all of the facts necessary to satisfy each element of each offense to which the defendant is pleading guilty. Many plea agreements in the federal system also attempt to reflect an agreement by the parties regarding how they believe the US Sentencing Guidelines should apply to the case. This requires the prosecutor to analyze the guidelines and their application notes and sometimes conduct research regarding the legal application of the guidelines.

Finally, every plea agreement is reviewed and approved by a supervisor. This, again, takes time. It may be necessary for the prosecutor to explain the reasoning behind or justify the plea deal being offered. The supervisor may require the prosecutor to revise or correct errors in the plea agreement as well. Each time changes are thereafter made to a written plea agreement as a result of the back and forth of plea discussions with defense counsel, the prosecutor must repeat the process of obtaining supervisory approval of the plea agreement.

Plea Hearings

When a defendant decides to plead guilty, a change of plea hearing must take place before a federal judge, under the requirements set forth in Rule 11 of the Federal Rules of Criminal Procedure. The amount of work involved in preparing for a change of plea hearing may differ from court to court. Most courts require the government to provide basic information to the judge in advance of the hearing so that the judge can properly prepare for the hearing. This may take the form of a so-called "Rule 11 letter," in which the prosecutor informs the court of the charge or charges to which the defendant is pleading guilty, the elements of those offenses, the factual basis for defendant's guilty plea to each charge, and a description of any collateral consequences that may arise from the guilty plea (such as restitution, registration as a sex offender, or deportation). Typically, the court will also require the prosecutor to provide the court with a copy of any written plea agreement. The amount of time required to draft and produce the documents the court requires in advance of a change of plea hearing will vary from case to case depending on the number and nature of the charges to which the defendant is pleading guilty. Typically, this task takes no more than an hour or two.

The actual change of plea hearing is typically short. The typical change of plea hearing takes less than half an hour. When, however, an interpreter is needed, or the defendant is pleading guilty to a large number of counts, or the factual basis for the plea is unusually complex, change of plea hearings can last longer.

Trial Preparation

As will be discussed in later chapters, preparing for a trial can require a significant amount of work. Prosecutors must select and sometimes develop evidence and exhibits, organize them, identify witnesses and prepare each witness for testifying, generate outlines for direct examination and cross-examination for each witness, review information about prospective jurors and draft questions for voir dire, and write opening statements and closing arguments, just to name a few of the tasks involved in preparing for trial. Depending on the nature of the case, trial preparation can take only a few days, or it may take months.

In relation to managing a caseload, trials constitute the single greatest challenge for prosecutors in managing their time. This is for two reasons. First, although a prosecutor may know that less than 10 percent of all of the cases charged will result in trials, the prosecutor does not know for sure which cases will comprise the 10 percent. Second, trial preparation constitutes the single largest demand on a prosecutor's time. For every day of trial, a prosecutor typically spends two to three days in preparation, if not more. Every trial, even a one-day trial, requires a significant amount of preparation. When a prosecutor is preparing for trial, every other demand on the prosecutor's time must take a back seat. Yet, prosecutors cannot drop the balls in the other cases.

Prosecutors may have some limited ability to anticipate which cases may result in a trial and prepare accordingly. A prosecutor may know, for example, that an indictment that charges crimes that result in significant mandatory minimum sentences are more likely to go to trial. Or a prosecutor may know enough about the defendant's personality or history in the criminal justice system to anticipate that the defendant is more or less likely to plead guilty. A prosecutor can anticipate that the stronger the evidence, the more likely the defendant is to plead guilty. Finally, certain defense attorneys are more likely to be willing to go to trial while others are known for always pleading their cases out. Regardless, however, prosecutors will inevitably be surprised when cases they were certain would go to trial result in guilty pleas and cases they just knew would end in a guilty plea result in a trial. Just to make their lives more difficult than they already are, it is also not uncommon for defendants to enter last-minute guilty pleas, after the prosecutor has already put in most if not all of the time preparing for trial. It is typical that prosecutors will prepare for trial two to three times the number of cases that actually result in trials. In the end, prudent prosecutors anticipate that any case they charge may result in a trial and budget accordingly in determining the number of cases they charge and other responsibilities they assume.

Trial

Trials constitute the second greatest demand on a prosecutor's time per case, second only to preparing for trials. As noted, the length of trials varies significantly depending on the nature and number of the charges and defendants and the facts of the case. When budgeting their time and deciding how much work they can handle, it is important for prosecutors to consider the likelihood of any given case going to trial and the likely length of the resulting trial.

Post-Trial Motions

After every trial that results in a conviction, the defense will file post-trial motions seeking a new trial or judgment of acquittal, despite the jury's guilty verdict. Defendant must file these motions within fourteen days of the verdict. *See* FED. R. CRIM. P. 29(c) (judgment of acquittal) and 33(b)(2) (new trial). The government then has a very short time to file responsive pleadings.

Sometimes, although seldom, courts will hold hearings on these motions. The demand on the prosecutor's time in dealing with these post-trial motions will vary, of course, on the nature of the grounds raised, the length and complexity of the trial, and the evidence presented. Prosecutors should, however, assume that every trial will require time afterwards to respond to post-trial motions.

Pre-Sentencing Preparation

Every convicted defendant will be sentenced, and every sentencing requires preparation by the prosecutor. Prosecutors should prepare offense conduct statements, review and object to presentence investigation reports, draft sentencing briefs, and sometimes prepare evidence and witnesses for the sentencing hearing. Each of these tasks constitutes another draw on the prosecutor's limited supply of time.

The sentencing process begins with the US Probation Office drafting a presentence investigation report (PSR) for the court. Shortly after a conviction, federal prosecutors typically prepare an offense conduct statement that they provide to the probation officer to aid the officer in preparation of the PSR. In the offense conduct statement, the prosecutor usually provides a factual description of the crime committed. Again, depending on the case, the factual description of the criminal conduct in an offense conduct statement can be quite lengthy and take a lot of time to write. An offense conduct statement also typically includes a description of the defendant's criminal history, with citations to case and docket numbers to aid the probation office in researching the defendant's criminal history. Finally, an offense conduct statement will include the prosecutor's view of how the US Sentencing Guidelines would apply to the defendant's case. If the defendant has pleaded guilty under a written plea agreement that included a stipulation by the parties as to how the guidelines should apply, then this portion of the offense conduct statement has already been completed and is a simple function of cutting and pasting the stipulation from the plea agreement. When, however, the parties were unable to stipulate to the application of the guidelines or a jury found the defendant guilty after a trial, then the prosecutor must analyze the guidelines, apply them to the facts of the case, and calculate the defendant's base offense level, adjustments, criminal history score, and guideline range. As noted, this can sometimes be complicated and take a significant amount of time.

When the probation officer has completed a draft of the presentence investigation report, the officer provides the parties with copies of the report. The parties then have fourteen days to file objections to the probation officer's draft report. So, the prosecutor must read the draft report, look for errors, and draft a responsive pleading either voicing objections or the absence of objections to the draft report. Sometimes there are no errors, sometimes minor errors that take little effort to point out, and still other times the prosecutors may believe the probation office significantly erred, such as in the recitation of the facts or in the application of the guidelines. Drafting the objection letter may take a matter of minutes or may take hours, depending on the nature of the perceived error. After the probation officer makes all of the corrections the officer believes are appropriate to the draft PSR, the officer will issue a final PSR. The probation officer will provide the parties again with a copy of the final report and the sentencing judge will receive a copy as well. The final report will indicate whether there are contested issues that the court will have to resolve at the time of the sentencing hearing.

In preparation for all but the most routine sentencing hearings (such as in immigration illegal re-entry cases), federal prosecutors typically draft and file sentencing memoranda. In a sentencing memorandum, a prosecutor identifies the contested issues that the judge will have to resolve at the sentencing hearing, summarizes the law regarding those issues, and applies the law to the facts of the case, articulating the government's position on the issue and the ruling the government seeks from the court. The length and amount of work, and thus the drain on the prosecutor's time, depends again on the nature of the case and legal and factual issues in dispute. Prosecutors should plan, however, on spending time, sometimes hours, in drafting a sentencing memorandum. Prosecutors must also determine if there are victims who desire to address the court. Victims have the right to do so, regardless of whether there are contested issues at the sentencing hearing.

When sentencing issues turn on resolving factual disputes, the government may have to present evidence at the sentencing hearing. When this occurs, the prosecutor must identify the necessary evidence and witnesses. Exhibits must be marked, and witnesses prepared for the hearing.

Whether there are contested issues or not, a prosecutor must prepare for the sentencing hearing. The prosecutor must decide what sentence to seek, whether to seek a departure or variance from the advisory guideline range, and draft notes for the argument the prosecutor intends to make in support of whatever position the prosecutor takes. Typically, supervisory approval is required for the prosecutor to seek a sentence outside the advisory guideline range. Getting this approval takes time.

Sentencing Hearing

Sentencing hearings in federal court can require a significant commitment of a prosecutor's time. The vast majority of sentencing hearings involve few or no contested issues and take less than an hour. Other contested sentencing hearings, however, can last hours and sometimes days. They can be as time-consuming as, and sometimes more time-consuming than, a trial on the merits of the case. They can resemble mini–bench trials in many ways. Preparing for direct examination and cross-examination of witnesses at a sentencing hearing takes almost just as much time and preparation as preparing for the direct examination and cross-examination of witnesses at a trial.

Appellate Briefing

Line prosecutors are often required to handle their own appellate work, while some larger offices have appellate units that assume that responsibility. When line prosecutors are responsible for their own appellate work, they have to budget time for it. Prosecutors can assume that every case that proceeds to trial will result in an appeal. On the other hand, the vast majority of cases resolved by way of guilty pleas do not result in appeals unless they are conditional pleas (the defendant pleads guilty but reserves the right to appeal an adverse ruling on a motion to suppress or dismiss) or there are contested sentencing issues.

In managing a caseload, prosecutors should consider the appellate possibilities. In some instances, prosecutors can require a defendant to waive appellate rights as part of a quid-pro-quo in plea negotiations. Prosecutors may also want to consider whether to strike a plea bargain that is more favorable for the defendant to avoid an appeal, particularly if the prosecutor believes an appeal may be risky. Finally, prosecutors should consider agreeing to conditional guilty pleas. A conditional plea is when a defendant agrees to plead guilty with the condition that the defendant reserves the right to appeal an adverse district court ruling, such as an order denying a defendant's motion to suppress evidence. Absent agreeing to a conditional plea, the defendant will go to trial and if found guilty will appeal. Thus, absent a not-guilty verdict at trial, either way the prosecutor will be dealing with appeal.

Appeals require prosecutors to draft appellate briefs and sometimes argue the case before a court of appeals. Appellate briefs can be very time-consuming, particularly if the appeal comes after a trial. Defendants frequently raise insufficiency of the evidence as one of the grounds for the appeal, requiring the government to take great pains to summarize all of the material trial evidence and explain how the evidence proved all of the elements of all of the offenses beyond a reasonable doubt. Appellate briefing schedules are generally generous, giving the prosecutor several weeks to draft a responsive brief. Nevertheless, with all of the prosecutor's other responsibilities, that time can disappear quickly.

Appellate Argument

Courts of appeal vary in how often they grant oral argument, but generally speaking they do so about two-thirds of the time. Appellate arguments can also be time-consuming. Often they take place in cities other than where the prosecutor resides, requiring travel time. Prosecutors must prepare for the oral argument, and this can be a lot of work. Keeping in mind that the prosecutor will typically be arguing before three very intelligent appellate judges who may barrage the prosecutor with probing questions, it is a foolish prosecutor indeed who does not devote hours in preparation for an appellate argument. Then, of course, there is the time spent in the argument itself. Appellate courts usually allow only ten to twenty minutes of argument time per side, so a single argument will usually consume half an hour to an hour. Appellate courts will hear multiple arguments in any given session, and typically the prosecutor will have to wait while the court hears other arguments before the prosecutor's case is called. Thus, prosecutors should generally assume that half of a day will be consumed waiting for and presenting an appellate argument.

Post-Conviction Litigation

In both state and federal prosecutions, criminal defendants have the right to make collateral challenges to their convictions after exhausting all appellate options. This post-conviction relief litigation, although technically a civil action, challenges the constitutionality of the underlying criminal conviction. Title 28, US Code, Section 2255 is the federal statute authorizing such collateral challenges. Generally, defendants have a year after exhausting all appellate avenues to file a petition for post-conviction relief.

Post-conviction litigation can again constitute a significant drain on a prosecutor's time, and most line prosecutors are responsible for handling post-conviction litigation on the cases they prosecuted. Although there are hurdles for defendants to obtain evidentiary hearings on post-conviction petitions, they are sometimes granted. When that happens, the litigation can again resemble a mini–bench trial. In some cases, these hearings can be very significant. Although an extreme case, I litigated a post-conviction hearing on a death penalty case that involved weeks of testimony and generated more transcript pages than the underlying trial.

Thankfully from the prosecutor's point of view, most post-conviction cases do not involve evidentiary hearings. They do require, however, significant briefing and sometimes additional evidence in the form of affidavits. To bring some claims in a post-conviction petition, the defendant must show an excuse for failing to raise the issue before the district court or on appeal. The most common basis for asserting an excuse is to claim ineffective assistance of counsel, meaning that the defendant blames the defense attorney for failing to raise issues below. The focus in the post-conviction litigation then evolves into a question of whether the defense attorney was ineffective in that the performance was so deficient that it deprived the defendant of the Sixth Amendment right of counsel and, if so, whether the defendant was prejudiced by the poor performance. Whether the defense attorney was ineffective requires sometimes finding out what the defense attorney knew, what the defense attorney communicated to the defendant, and why the defense attorney acted or failed to act as a matter of strategy or as a matter of ignorance or mistake.

Another complicating factor in handling post-conviction litigation is that usually a significant amount of time has passed since the defendant's guilty plea or trial and the case is no longer fresh in the prosecutor's mind. It is not unusual for a year to pass between the disposition of a criminal case at the district court level and the resolution of the case on appeal. A defendant then has a year to file a post-conviction petition. The district court then conducts an initial review of the petition to determine whether it is defective or insufficient in some way, or whether it should be litigated by briefing or evidentiary hearings. The defendant is typically then appointed counsel and that attorney is usually given a generous amount of time to draft the defendant's brief. Thus, it may be as much as three or more years since the trial of the case that the prosecutor first receives a post-conviction petition challenging the conviction. Drafting a brief on a case that is fresh in the prosecutor's mind is much easier than trying to do so when it is stale and the prosecutor no longer remembers all of the facts or where to find the necessary documents or pleadings.

CONTROLLING THE FLOW IN THE PIPELINE

Considering all of the time demands during the life of a typical criminal case outlined in the prior section, and multiplying those time demands by the ten, twenty, thirty, or more cases on a prosecutor's docket, the reader gets a sense of the incredible burden facing a prosecutor in managing such a caseload. Any given case on the prosecutor's docket may be at any given stage of the criminal case. Each case will have its own deadlines, demands, and problems. Then, as if this is not already enough, prosecutors almost always have other collateral duties to perform as part of their job.

Considered as a whole, a prosecutor's responsibility for handling a large caseload may appear overwhelming and unmanageable. The first thing prosecutors should remember is not to panic. When starting out as a new prosecutor it may appear that there is simply no way for the prosecutor to successfully complete all of the many required tasks in the available time. I found, however, that things have a way of working out, so long as the prosecutor stays organized and works diligently. When it may seem that there is simply too much work to handle, something almost inevitably happens to alleviate the pressure; a defendant who appeared headed to trial pleads and frees up time, or a defendant is granted a continuance of a trial or briefing deadline, or an issue that appeared would take a tremendous amount of time to brief ends up being much easier and quicker to address than anticipated.

Organization and planning are key to managing a large caseload. One way to do this is to look at time management at both a micro and macro level. In other words, prosecutors should examine the time demands of each case but consider the time demands on the prosecutor's time as a whole. The time demands on each prosecutor may vary based on the type of cases prosecuted and other collateral demands on the prosecutor's time. For example, when I prosecuted drug, gun, and violent crime cases and had the collateral duty as training officer, I could divide up my time by percentages based on all of the demands on my time. I estimated that in any given year I spent 15 percent of my time working with law enforcement officers during the investigation stages of my cases (including grand jury presentations), 5 percent in drafting charging documents, 5 percent in motions practice, 10 percent in plea negotiations and plea hearings, 20 percent in trial preparation, 10 percent in trial, 5 percent handling post-trial motions, 15 percent in sentencing, 5 percent on appellate work, and 5 percent on post-conviction litigation. The final 5 percent of my time was consumed by collateral duties, such as my training responsibilities. Having a sense, then, of how much of my time I could generally devote to any given demand, I could make a more informed decision about whether to take on a new case or when to bring charges.

Another key to caseload management is to pay attention to timing. Prosecutors, particularly federal prosecutors, have a lot of control of the timing of when to bring charges. Although there will be some reactive cases, generally prosecutors have some flexibility in the timing of charging decisions. Prosecutors should plot out the timing of cases, anticipating the usual length of cases from charge to disposition, consider the number of cases currently charged and where in the pipeline those cases are, and bring new charges at times when they will fit in the pipeline well and not lead to clogging up.

It is also important that prosecutors learn to ask for help. Prosecutors tend to have strong Type A personalities. They do not often willingly admit weaknesses or want it to appear that they are unable to handle their own caseloads. No matter how good a prosecutor is, however, there will be occasions when the prosecutor is overwhelmed, when the timing did not work out as planned, when the prosecutor bit off more than he or she could chew. Wise prosecutors remain humble enough to recognize when they need help and asks for it from a colleague or a supervisor.

Good prosecutors also must learn to say no. The better the prosecutor, the more work that will flow to the prosecutor. Law enforcement officers will want their cases handled by the best prosecutors, and management will want the best prosecutors to handle the most difficult cases. A prosecutor's ego can get in the way of remaining a good prosecutor. Prosecutors have to learn when it is necessary to say no and turn down cases or assignments.

Finally, to be a really good prosecutor, it is critically important that the prosecutor maintain a healthy work/life balance. Prosecution is difficult work, and it can be exhausting physically, mentally, and emotionally. Prosecutors who fail to maintain a life outside work can burn out, and a burned-out prosecutor makes mistakes that can lead to a downward spiral. Most prosecutors chose the profession because they wanted to right wrongs, to make a difference in the world, and it is often hard for them to accept that they cannot right every wrong and solve every case. Over time, however, experienced prosecutors accept the truth; crime will always exist. No matter how hard the prosecutor works or how many cases the prosecutor prosecutes, criminals will still commit crimes and people will still be hurt. Prosecutors have to come to terms with that truth, enjoy the life they have, and be content with knowing that they are helping right wrongs, even if they are unable to right them all.

Chapter Seven

Strategies for Prosecuting Criminals

If they serve for any significant period of time, prosecutors will encounter a wide variety of criminal cases. Crimes can run the gamut from sudden random acts of violence to long-term, carefully thought-out orchestrated frauds. A single individual may be responsible for a crime, or the crime may be the result of joint, coordinated action by two or more people or by highly structured criminal organizations. There are general strategies that prosecutors can employ to successfully prosecute crimes of any nature. There are other strategies, however, that are more effectively tailored to particular types of criminal activity. In this chapter, I will describe the types of criminal cases prosecutors encounter, discuss general strategies for prosecuting criminals, and then review strategies for prosecuting various types of criminal activity.

REACTIVE VERSUS PROACTIVE CASES

Before discussing prosecution strategies, it is first important to remind the reader that prosecutors will encounter two types of criminal cases: reactive and proactive. As noted, a reactive case is one where the crime has already occurred, police have arrested the suspect or suspects, and there is no ongoing criminal activity. A proactive case is where the crime may or may not be complete, police have not identified and arrested a suspect or suspects, or if a suspect has been arrested, there remains ongoing criminal activity. The scope of options available to a prosecutor for developing the case for prosecution will differ significantly depending on whether the case is a reactive case or a proactive case. To appreciate this, it is helpful to give some examples of both types of cases.

One example of a reactive case would be a bank robbery where shortly after the robbery officers stop the suspect's car and find evidence of the robbery inside. Another example of a reactive case would be a drug interdiction stop where an officer stops a car for speeding, develops probable cause to believe the car is carrying drugs, and a search of the car reveals a large quantity of controlled substances. A final example of a reactive case might be a murder where the suspect is caught shortly after the act. In each of these cases, the immediate crime is complete.

The nature of a reactive case is that the prosecutor is in a position of having to react quickly to a completed crime and a charged criminal. In reactive cases, prosecutors have generally not had the ability to work with law enforcement officers to develop the investigation, identify suspects, or pursue lines of investigation. In reactive cases, prosecutors immediately face deadlines created by the arrest of the suspect, including those posed by speedy trial statutes. With reactive cases, prosecutors have limited strategies available to further develop the case, uncover additional evidence, or make charging decisions. On the other hand, because the immediate crime is complete, the prosecutor is not faced with an ongoing concern to prevent additional criminal conduct or harm to other victims.

Proactive cases, on the other hand, may encompass a wide variety of criminal cases. The primary factor that distinguishes a reactive case from a proactive case is the absence of ongoing criminal conduct. A bank robbery could be a proactive case if, for example, no suspect was apprehended, particularly if it is believed that the robbery was part of a series of bank robberies. A drug interdiction stop may be a reactive case as it relates to the driver of the car, but is a proactive case insofar as it involves trying to identify and prosecute the drug supplier or intended recipients of the shipment. Other examples of other proactive cases may be much more complex. A bank may discover through an audit, for example, that the accounts receivables pledged by a company for a multimillion-dollar loan have been inflated based on false invoices. The prosecutor faced with this case does not know who in the company was involved, how the fraud was committed, or the full scope of the fraudulent conduct.

Law enforcement officers present proactive cases to prosecutors at a stage of the investigation when more steps can and should be taken. Because of the timing of their involvement in these cases, prosecutors have many more options to employ strategies to further develop the case, identify suspects, and shape the course of the prosecution. With proactive cases, prosecutors are not faced with immediate court-imposed deadlines that restrict their options. On the other hand, depending on the nature of the case, a prosecutor may be presented with time limitations posed by the existence of ongoing criminal conduct, especially when innocent people may become victims of the criminal conduct. The need to stop the criminal conduct before more and possibly irreparable harm occurs may restrict a prosecutor's options.

GENERAL PROSECUTION STRATEGIES

With an understanding of how reactive and proactive cases impact a prosecutor's investigative options, there are some general strategies that apply to both types of cases. The most basic strategy is to exhaust all covert investigation techniques first before engaging in techniques that are overt or known to the suspect. Second, when the criminal activity involves more than one person, prosecutors should identify the people involved and work first on the weak links. Finally, when the criminal activity involves more than one person in some type of hierarchical relationship, prosecutors should work up the chain of the organization. I will discuss each of these general strategies in turn.

Exhaust Covert Techniques First

There are a wide variety of investigatory tools available to prosecutors, some or all of which may be available to a prosecutor. Generally, these tools can be placed in categories as either covert or overt. A covert investigatory tool is one that can be employed unbeknownst to the target of the investigation. An overt investigatory tool is one which, if employed, will be known to the target of the investigation. The primary strategy for prosecutors in any case is to exhaust covert investigation techniques before engaging in overt ones. There are multiple reasons why prosecutors would desire to exhaust covert methods before turning to overt ones. When targets become aware they are under criminal investigation, it can motivate them to destroy or tamper with evidence; influence, threaten, or kill witnesses; or flee the jurisdiction. Targets can also sometimes hamper the government's ability to investigate them by changing telephones, by changing methods and manner of communicating and traveling, and by temporarily ceasing criminal activity. Finally, targets with assets potentially subject to seizure in the future can liquidate, transfer ownership, or remove such assets from the jurisdiction.

Covert investigation techniques would include undercover operations. The nature of undercover operations can vary significantly. In drug cases, an undercover operation may involve using a confidential informant to make a controlled buy of narcotics from a suspect, or it may involve an officer posing as a drug dealer. In a fraud case, an undercover operation may involve having a victim place a recorded call to the suspect to discuss the victim's investment, or an officer posing as an investor. The common thread among undercover operations is an attempt to engage with the suspect regarding the criminal conduct in an effort to develop evidence of the crime.

Monitoring of communications is also an example of a covert investigation technique. Law enforcement officers may monitor communication through a wiretap, when a court has authorized the interception of communication between the suspect and others over the suspect's phone or computer. Wiretaps clearly invade privacy, so the government must obtain a court order after demonstrating probable cause to believe that the phone, location, or device which it seeks to monitor is being used to conduct, or will produce evidence of, criminal conduct. The specific federal requirements for obtaining permission to wiretap are numerous and strict (*see* Title 18, US Code, Section 2510 *et seq.*) because wiretaps are, by their very nature, so invasive of privacy. Although the regulations and requirements are set up so that wiretaps are not used as a routine method of investigation, it also does not mean that the government must exhaust every other method available before resorting to a wiretap. *See United States v. Macklin*, 902 F.2d 1320, 1326 (8th Cir. 1990).

Wiretaps are extremely labor intensive, especially for law enforcement agents, requiring many, many hours of tedious monitoring of phone calls or other communication. The government must minimize the invasion of privacy by attempting to determine, as the communication is occurring, whether it is nonprivileged communication and whether it references criminal activity. If it does, the government may listen and record. If it does not, the agents must stop monitoring the communication for a few minutes, check again, determine if they can monitor, and if not, stop monitoring for a few minutes, and repeat. This is called "minimization." Wiretaps often also involve interception of communication in foreign languages or in the form of coded communication of varying sophistication. This, obviously, requires interpretation and decoding, a further tax on limited government resources. While a wiretap is in place, the government must make frequent disclosures to the court in camera (meaning to the court only and not publicly filed) and ex parte (meaning no disclosure is made to an opposing party) so that the court can ensure that the wiretap is still appropriate and supported by probable cause, and that the agents are engaging in proper minimization. Despite all these hurdles, in the appropriate case wiretap evidence may be necessary and can be extremely valuable. Prosecutors help determine when a wiretap is appropriate and are responsible to ensure that it complies with federal law.

Law enforcement officers may also monitor communication through other means, such as accessing the suspect's publicly available social media. Surprisingly, many criminals will publicly post messages to others on social media, such as Facebook or Twitter, that contain incriminating statements and often incriminating photographs. So long as the officer is accessing only the information that the suspect has made public, no court order or subpoena is required to access this evidence.

Officers may gain some limited information about the people with whom a suspect is communicating by monitoring telephone traffic through pen registers or trap and trace devices. These investigation techniques will not reveal the underlying conversations or messages, but will reveal the phone numbers with whom the suspect has contact. Court approval is necessary to obtain a pen register or trap and trace information, requiring a showing that it is being requested by a law enforcement officer or agent and that the information likely to be obtained is relevant to an ongoing criminal investigation. Title 18, US Code, Section 3122. Because the information recorded is otherwise exposed to the public, in the sense that the telephone company must necessarily know the numbers called, the use of pen registers or trap and trace devices does not constitute a search under the Fourth Amendment. *Smith v. Maryland*, 442 US 735, 743–44 (1979).

Officers may also monitor a limited amount of information about a suspect's communication through a mail cover. In a mail cover, a prosecutor may request that the post office report to the investigator information about the suspect's mail that is available without opening the mail, such as the date, cancellation stamp, sender and recipient, and characteristics about the mail, such as its weight, size, and appearance. The recording of such information does not violate a person's constitutional rights or constitute a search under the Fourth Amendment to the Constitution. Nevertheless, a prosecutor must obtain authorization of the Chief Postal Inspector to conduct a mail cover. *See, e.g., United States v. Hinton*, 222 F.3d 664, 674 (9th Cir. 2000); *United States v. Krauth*, 769 F.2d 473, 475 (8th Cir. 1985). Mail covers are especially useful in cases when law enforcement officers are attempting to determine the identity of other members of a criminal organization, the location of assets or accounts, or the scope and nature of a fraudulent scheme that uses the mail.

Surveillance is another form of covert investigation. Surveillance can encompass a wide variety of techniques, such as officers sitting in a car outside the suspect's house, to long-range surveillance by officers with high-powered telescopes and cameras, to pole cameras (cameras mounted, for example, on a telephone pole near the suspect's house), to aerial surveillance. It is well settled that visual observation alone does not constitute an invasion of privacy, necessitating a search warrant, even if the object of the surveillance, such as a house, is itself protected by the Fourth Amendment. *Dow Chemical Co. v. United States*, 476 US 227, 234–25 (1986). For aerial surveillance, the law is generally that there is no Fourth Amendment violation so long as the surveillance is conducted from airspace normally open to aircraft. *See, e.g., Florida v. Riley*, 488 US 445, 457 (1989); *California v.*

Ciraolo, 476 US 207, 213 (1986). Some forms of surveillance require court approval. For example, thermal imaging of a residence requires a search warrant. *See Kyllo v. United States*, 533 US 27, 40 (2001). So, too, does the placing of a tracking device on a suspect's vehicle. *See United States v. Jones*, 565 US 400, 411–12 (2012).

Officers may also conduct some forms of evidence collection in a covert manner. For example, officers may collect a suspect's trash placed on the curb for pickup (called a trash rip or a trash pull) because the person has abandoned any privacy interest in the property. *California v. Greenwood*, 486 US 35, 41 (1988). Trash rips can sometimes reveal a significant amount of evidence or can provide evidence (drug use paraphernalia, for example) that could allow for the use of other investigation techniques, such as a search warrant. Officers may seize other items discarded by a suspect that may carry the suspect's DNA, such as a cigarette butt or a paper cup. Law enforcement officers have increasingly used this type of evidence collection in cold murder cases when they have used DNA analysis from a crime scene to focus on a particular suspect. Finally, officers can, with court approval, execute search warrants without immediately disclosing the search of the property to the suspect. These delayed-notification searches can include searches of a suspect's computers or internet activity, or even a suspect's home. *See* 18 U.S.C. § 3103a(b) (authorizing delayed notification of search warrants generally); 18 U.S.C. § 2705(a)(A) (authorizing delayed notification of a search warrant for electronic communication "if the court determines that there is reason to believe that notification of the existence of the court order may have an adverse result," such as destruction of evidence or flight). FED. R. CRIM. P. 41(f)(3) ("Upon the government's request, a magistrate judge—or if authorized by Rule 41(b), a judge of a state court of record—may delay any notice required by this rule if the delay is authorized by statute").

Researching public record data about the suspect can almost always be conducted without the suspect's knowledge. A suspect would likely have no way of knowing, for example, that a law enforcement officer went to the recorder's office to find out information about the defendant's residence, accessed the Department of Transportation records to find out about a suspect's vehicles, or accessed the suspect's criminal history records. Officers can access most of this information online without interaction with any individual. Even when, however, an officer must interact with a person to get the information, that person is a government employee and is unlikely to reveal the inquiry to anyone. It should be noted, again, that accessing some information about a suspect from public records requires court approval. For example, a court must authorize a law enforcement officer to access a suspect's tax records.

Researching nonpublic records about a suspect can oftentimes be conducted without the suspect's knowledge. A prosecutor can use a grand jury subpoena to obtain information about the suspect from a third party. For example, the government could issue a grand jury subpoena to a cellular service to obtain subscriber information about a phone number, or an internet carrier to get information about an IP address, or a financial institution to get information about a suspect's financial transactions. In many instances, federal statutes proscribe third parties from at least immediately disclosing to suspects the government's access of this information. In other instances, however, there are no statutory prohibitions. For example, a car dealer would be free to alert a suspect that the government used a grand jury subpoena to get details about the suspect's purchase of a vehicle. So prosecutors should proceed with caution in obtaining information from third parties about a suspect because it may not always be covert or remain covert for long.

Finally, interviewing of witnesses, or questioning them before a grand jury may be covert, depending on the individual. Some witnesses are unlikely to knowingly disclose to a suspect that they have spoken to law enforcement officers or testified before a grand jury. For example, government employees, such as a coroner, will generally maintain the confidentiality of a criminal investigation, even if not necessarily legally required to do so. Crime victims usually have little motivation to reveal their cooperation to a suspect. Similarly, bystanders or other third parties with no connection or loyalty to a suspect would be unlikely to reveal their cooperation to a suspect. Other people, such as the suspect's family, friends, and associates, are very likely to reveal to the suspect that law enforcement officers questioned them or that they were subpoenaed to testify before a grand jury. And prosecutors should be aware that a witness is free to tell anyone that he or she was subpoenaed to a grand jury and disclose what questions he or she was asked and what answers he or she gave. Although some witnesses also may not be likely to directly reveal contact with law enforcement officers to a suspect, they may do so inadvertently or unintentionally by telling another person, who in turn tells others. In deciding whether to question a potential witness as part of a covert investigation, then, prosecutors must carefully weigh the possibility or probability of disclosure by the interviewee.

Grand jury proceedings are conducted in secret. Under Rule 6(e) of the Federal Rules of Criminal Procedure, generally only the prosecutor, the court reporter, the witness, the grand jurors, and, when necessary, interpreters are permitted to be in the grand jury room while testimony is obtained. Further, documents produced under the grand jury subpoena are similarly held in confidence by the grand jury and the government. Except for certain types of documents in certain types of criminal investigations, however, a person or entity can reveal to others the fact of the subpoena and disclose what was produced to the grand jury. So, for example, federal law prohibits a financial institution from disclosing anything about a grand jury subpoena if the investigation involves potential money-laundering charges. *See* 18 U.S.C. § 1510(b). The financial institution could, however, reveal the existence of the grand jury subpoena for the same documents if the investigation involved a different crime, like kidnapping.

Overt investigation techniques, or techniques of which the suspect would be aware, include questioning witnesses close to the suspect, some document and record searches when the third party may disclose the inquiry to the suspect, search warrants (other than delayed-notification warrants), and questioning the suspect directly. These are not, by any means, all of the methods available to federal law enforcement officers.

A criminal investigation should almost always exploit and use all covert methods of investigation first before going overt. This ensures that the evidence can be collected without the target of the investigation knowing about the investigation and doing anything to destroy or alter evidence. Sometimes other factors require the use of overt investigation techniques, however, before exhausting all covert options. Prosecutors should work with agents to weigh the benefits of covert investigation techniques against other considerations, such as whether the defendant may pose a danger to the public, or whether evidence may be lost if an overt method is not used. For example, the government may judge it necessary to execute a search warrant at the defendant's house to seize a shipment of cocaine to prevent the loss of the evidence or the danger to the public posed by the controlled substance, even though by doing so there will be no more chance of conducting a covert investigation.

Work on Weak Links

When the criminal conduct under investigation involves more than one suspect, it is important for prosecutors to develop a strategy for the prosecution of the multiple defendants. A sound prosecution strategy involves trying to identify and focus on the weak links in the group. A weak link are criminals who, for various reasons, may be the easiest member of a group to prosecute and the most likely to fold and cooperate with the government's investigation. Attacking weak links first allows a prosecutor to begin to unravel the criminal organization while at the same time gaining knowledge about the organization before the prosecutor tries to take down the leadership of the organization.

A suspect may be deemed weak because of the characteristics or life circumstances of the individual. For example, a suspect may be a weak link because the person has significantly more to lose personally or professionally from the prosecution than others. Perhaps the person is a professional with a license or has dependents who may suffer from the person's prosecution. That person may have a greater motivation to plead guilty and cooperate against others because of those weaknesses than someone without those circumstances. Other people may be weak links because they simply do not have strong personalities. Some people are emotionally and psychologically crushed by criminal charges and fold easily and quickly, while others are hardened, perhaps because of prior run-ins with the law, and are tougher characters all around.

A suspect may also be deemed a weak link because of the nature of the relationship the suspect has with others. A person with only loose ties to the other criminal suspects may be more likely to plead guilty and cooperate than someone with close ties and a sense of loyalty. For example, a short-term girlfriend of a drug dealer may be more likely to cooperate than the drug dealer's loyal lieutenant of many years. On the other hand, a long-term girlfriend may be less likely to cooperate than a suspect who had only one or two drug transactions with the drug dealer. Similarly, a suspect may be a weak link because of a dislike for others. Perhaps, for example, an accounts payable clerk dislikes the boss who got her involved in forging invoices or blames that boss for getting her in trouble.

A suspect may be a weak link based on the nature of the evidence. If the evidence is particularly overwhelming against a suspect, that person is more likely to plead guilty and cooperate than those against whom the evidence is not as strong. Similarly, a suspect who was in a key position and is able to inform on many other suspects is a weaker link to the entire group than a person who occupied a position that would have provided only limited access to information.

Finally, the sentencing ramifications may make a suspect a weak link. A suspect who is facing a severe mandatory minimum sentence, for example, would have a great motivation to plead guilty and cooperate if by doing so the person could avoid the mandatory minimum sentence. Conversely, a suspect who had no criminal history may be motivated to plead guilty and cooperate if by doing so it may make him or her eligible for probation or even the dismissal of charges.

To break up the group and gain access to inside information through cooperation, prosecutors should thus focus their initial efforts on the weak links. This may mean charging those individuals before the others. Or it may mean entering into early plea negotiations with the weak links. In some cases, prosecutors may want to offer the most favorable plea deals to the weak links to get them to plead early and cooperate. Even in cases when a weak link refuses to cooperate, there is still a benefit to taking out the weak links first.

Other suspects may not know whether the weak link is cooperating or will cooperate. Further, sometimes when one defendant pleads guilty it starts a chain reaction of others doing the same, like a row of dominoes falling down.

Work Up the Chain of Command

When, again, more than one suspect is under investigation or has been charged already in a reactive case, prosecutors should strive to determine if there is any hierarchical relationship between them. If there is one, the sound prosecution strategy is to work up the chain rather than down the chain. In other words, prosecutors should try to work out plea deals with people lower in the organization first, giving them the best deals, rather than give the biggest breaks to those higher in the organization. The primary reason for this is that people higher in the criminal organization have a greater criminal culpability and generally should receive commensurately greater punishment.

Further, working up a chain of an organization helps the prosecutor more fully understand the scope of the criminal conduct before negotiating plea deals with the most criminally culpable members. A prosecutor may not fully comprehend the scope of the criminal conduct like a low-level member of the criminal organization might. If the prosecutor works out a plea deal with a person high in the organization before fully understanding the scope of the conduct, the person high in the organization may not be held fully accountable. Although that same danger exists in working out a deal with a low-level person, the consequences are not as great if the low-level person generally has lower criminal culpability in the first place.

TAILORED PROSECUTION STRATEGIES

In addition to the general strategies of performing all covert operations before engaging in overt investigation techniques, taking out weak links first, and working up the chain of an organization, there are additional strategy considerations for prosecutors. Other strategy decisions may depend on the nature of the criminal conduct itself. There are strategies that may work well against a group of suspects that would be of little use against an individual, or strategies for investigation of a series of crimes that would not apply to the investigation of a single criminal act. Likewise, attacking a crime organization engaged in a series of criminal acts may require a different strategy than attacking a series of criminal acts committed by a group of unorganized individuals.

Lone Criminals

In many cases prosecutors will encounter crimes committed by single individuals, committed without the knowing aid of accomplices and unconnected to any other criminal actors. Many times these will be crimes of violence (like bank robberies) or possession-based charges (like felon in possession of a firearm) or white-collar cases (such as bank fraud). Many of the general strategies outlined above presuppose multiple criminal actors, and those strategies will not assist a prosecutor attempting to develop and prosecute a case against a lone criminal actor.

The first thing for prosecutors to recognize in attacking cases involving lone criminal actors is that no criminal is ever truly alone. Even if others were not knowingly involved in the criminal conduct, that does not necessarily mean that those around the suspect do not have valuable information that could advance the investigation and prosecution. A suspect's friends, family, coworkers, and associates may have evidence that could help establish an opportunity and motive, reveal the suspect's state of mind, establish the suspect's whereabouts at important times, or identify locations where evidence of the crime may be found. These associates may also eliminate possible defenses, such as an alibi defense.

It is important, then, that prosecutors direct the investigation toward exploring the people who are within the suspect's orbit of association. A productive way to approach this part of the investigation is to take the knowledge the prosecutor now has and work backward. For example, if a prosecutor knows a person robbed a bank with a handgun on a particular date and time, the prosecutor should then investigate the suspect's life and try to determine who among his associates might be able to shed light on the case. A drinking buddy may have heard the suspect talk about being broke. A best friend may have seen the suspect with a handgun in the past, indeed, may have even gone out to a shooting range with the suspect. Coworkers may be able to indicate when the suspect worked or failed to show up to work. Monitoring the suspect's social media, subpoenaing the suspect's work records, and canvassing the suspect's neighborhood are all ways of trying to identify the people associated with the suspect. The important point is to make sure that law enforcement officers pursue these connections and ask questions of a suspect's associates, even when law enforcement officers are convinced the suspect acted alone in committing the crime.

Another strategy to use when trying to develop a lone-actor case for prosecution is to work backward from the crime to piece together the suspect's movements and then follow leads to develop additional evidence. A bank robber got to the bank somehow. Identifying the car he or she drove to the bank, whether the car was stolen, his or her own car, or a friend's car could lead to evidence tying him or her to the crime. The drug courier came from somewhere before law enforcement officers stopped him or her on the highway. The route the courier took, the places he or she stopped along the way could reveal evidence showing his or her knowledge that drugs were hidden in the car. Prosecutors should guide investigators to keep working backward from the crime scene as far as possible, gathering receipts and records, identifying witnesses, and seizing evidence. That evidence may lead to discovery of coworkers, family, associates, or other witnesses.

Finally, a thorough research of the lone actor's background is important. This seems obvious, but there is a tendency in lone-actor cases for law enforcement officers and prosecutors to focus solely on the crime under investigation. This is particularly so when it appears that the lone actor committed a single criminal act, like a bank robbery. The reality is that criminals seldom get caught the very first time they commit a crime. Although the suspect's criminal history may provide some valuable evidence and is clearly relevant for sentencing purposes, it is likely that the suspect committed other crimes that were never detected. Prosecutors should approach lone-actor cases with an assumption that the suspect has committed similar crimes in the past, even if it does not show up on the suspect's criminal history. With this in mind, the prosecutor should look further into the suspect's background. For example, in a bank robbery case the prosecutor should find out if there are other unsolved bank robberies in the area, and particularly find out if they were committed in a manner similar to the robbery under investigation. If so, then the prosecutor should investigate whether it is possible the suspect committed other robberies. In a fraud case involving embezzlement, the prosecutor should have law enforcement officers question the suspect's prior employers to determine if the suspect may have embezzled from them. The prior employer may not have even been aware of it.

Unorganized Crime

Prosecutors are sometimes faced with a rash of criminal conduct that is a product of multiple actors with no connection or only a loose association. For example, when I was a prosecutor our community suffered from a dramatic increase in shootings and murders by and of young men and innocent bystanders in a particular neighborhood. It was not the product of gang disputes or a drug war, and the shooters and victims were not all connected in a cohesive group. Similarly, the opioid epidemic struck our district a little earlier than it hit many other districts in the country, resulting in a sudden rise in heroin overdose deaths over a short period of time. The heroin was seeping into the community from multiple sources and not as a result of a single drug organization. It can be difficult for law enforcement officers to have an impact on this type of unorganized criminal conduct when investigating each crime one at a time. So they will sometimes approach prosecutors to help them develop a strategy for attacking the problem more holistically or comprehensively. Prosecutors can provide valuable guidance and leadership in coordinating the response to these seemingly disparate criminal acts.

In addressing this type of unorganized crime, one of the first tasks is to define the problem. Defining the problem involves identifying the nature of the crime or crimes under investigation and a description of the targets of the prosecution and establishing the geographic and time parameters that will be the focus of the investigation and prosecution. Defining the problem will place parameters on the scope of the task ahead.

For example, when faced with the sudden rise in heroin overdose deaths, we determined that we would investigate the overdose deaths both for potential charges related to the deaths for those who distributed the heroin that caused the deaths, and also for potential drug trafficking charges. Under both state and federal law, a person who intentionally distributes a controlled substance to a person who then dies from that substance can be held criminally responsible for the death under certain circumstances. Further, we decided that to make the task manageable, we would look backward three years at any heroin-related overdose deaths, and that the geographic scope of our efforts would be limited to a five-county area surrounding our city.

Having defined the problem and established the scope of the investigation, the next step is to identify the cause of the problem. In other words, the trick is to try to figure out what has given rise to this particular type of unorganized criminal conduct. With lone actors, the causation turns on the individual's motives, be they greed, addiction, vengeance, or the like. With organized crime, the causation is almost always greed, with the organization's ultimate goal being the accumulation of criminal proceeds. In contrast, there is often a number of factors that cause a group of unassociated or loosely associated people to engage in a similar course of criminal conduct. The problem is often acute, but it can be chronic in nature. If a prosecutor can identify the factor or factors giving rise to the rash of criminal activity, the prosecutor will be more successful in resolving the real problem. It is a little like an illness. A doctor is more successful in curing the problem if the source of the illness can be identified; otherwise, the doctor is left with treating symptoms.

It is important for prosecutors to recognize that the factors leading to the unorganized criminal activity may not be ones that can be directly addressed by criminal prosecution. For example, the rash of heroin overdose deaths may be the consequence of an opioid epidemic in which patients first became addicted to opioids prescribed to them for pain, which led to heroin use when opioids were unavailable, or heroin was cheaper. The heroin epidemic itself may be the result of over-prescription of opioids. A prosecutor may not be able to directly address the underlying source of the problem through prosecution, but identifying the causes can help guide the prosecution as a component of the solution. For example, knowing that many of the heroin overdose victims are former opioid users may help the prosecutor identify how these people, who were otherwise not involved in criminal activity, got connected to a criminal heroin distribution network. That may, in turn, provide an idea for how an undercover law enforcement agent may pose as a former patient and get plugged into the network to make contact with the heroin sources and make controlled buys.

It may also be appropriate for prosecutors to work with others outside the criminal justice system to develop a more holistic approach to addressing the problem. With a heroin overdose problem, for example, the prosecutor may work to team up with treatment providers and counselors to help identify, educate, and treat the addicts. Working as part of a team to approach problems like this can ultimately aid the prosecution because it can result in law enforcement officers making contact and developing relationships with addicts in a positive environment, which in turn may lead to more addicts being willing to work with law enforcement officers in identifying their sources of supply. Working with youth counselors to build relationships with young men associated with others involved in a rash of violent shootings could similarly help prosecutors develop leads and possible cooperators.

Sometimes it is necessary for prosecutors to take the lead in developing an ad hoc task force to address a crisis. The benefit of a task force approach is that it concentrates resources, for a limited period of time, to address a specific problem. Task forces can also result in the integration of different specialties or skill sets that can be brought to bear on a problem with a coordinated effort. For example, when our community was hit by that wave of heroin overdose deaths, I formed a task force consisting of both state and federal law enforcement officers from the area. The agencies committed their agents to the task force for a six-month period. I also formed the task force with both narcotics agents and homicide detectives. The narcotics agents focused on identifying the sources of supply for the heroin using traditional drug investigation techniques. Meanwhile, the homicide detectives worked on investigating each heroin death as if it were a homicide. They poured over and analyzed the evidence from the scene of the death and interviewed witnesses in an effort to identify the persons who supplied the heroin that killed the victims. As a result, the task force successfully prosecuted more than a score of heroin dealers, holding nearly half of them responsible for causing the deaths of specific victims.

Organized Crime

Organized crime refers to criminal activities coordinated and carried out by structured and usually hierarchical groups of criminals, on a large scale, often over extended periods of time. This can include drug trafficking organizations, human trafficking organizations, white-collar criminals, and crime families or the mafia. As a caveat to this section, I will note that in my career I never handled the prosecution of mafia members.[1] I do not hold myself out as having any expertise in prosecuting the mafia; there are federal prosecutors who do, and I suspect there are aspects of investigation and prosecution of the mafia that are particularly unique. So in my discussion of organized crime, I will not attempt to address that particular type of organized crime.

The most important step in taking down a crime organization is to determine how it is structured. Organized crime varies in the degree of organization, but by definition there is some structure to the group. Although some may resemble an oligarchy, with more than one leader, they are more often autocracies, with one person occupying the top position. Some organizations have very structured layers below the top, with defined roles or geographic areas of control, while others may be more loosely structured below the top two or three layers. It is important for prosecutors to recognize that not all crime organizations have the same type of structure. It is also important for prosecutors to recognize that the structure of the organization often changes over time. How the organization was structured at the start of the criminal activity under investigation may not resemble how it was structured during the most recent criminal activity.

Developing organizational charts is a critical first step in identifying how to attack the problem. An organizational chart allows investigators and prosecutors to visually comprehend the nature of the organization and the relationship among the various members. This, in turn, aids in identifying weak links in the organization that can be exploited. The danger with organizational charts, however, is that there is a temptation to become wedded to the first iteration of the chart. Once investigators and prosecutors identify who they believe is the top of the organization, it is often difficult to reach a different conclusion despite evidence showing otherwise. Known as confirmation bias, the phenomenon involves the tendency to interpret new evidence as confirmation of one's existing beliefs or theories. Confirmation bias is a danger that exists in all aspects of a criminal investigation, but it has been my experience that it is particularly strong when making organizational charts. Thus, prosecutors should be very careful in evaluating evidence regarding the perceived structure of a crime organization and be prepared to alter the organizational chart to fit the evidence, not the other way around.

Discerning the structure of a crime organization can be very difficult. Investigators and prosecutors are on the outside of the organization trying to look in, and, of course, the criminals take pains to conceal their organizations. Some circumstantial evidence can aid in discerning a structure of a crime organization. For example, in making a controlled buy from a street dealer, the dealer may reference his or her source by name, or may indicate the geographic limits of his or her territory. The appearance of drugs or the way drugs are packaged may lead prosecutors to tie them to a particular organization. A pattern of movement among suspects, or connections between suspects engaged in financial transactions or other activities, may also provide clues as to the structure of the organization.

The key to learning how a crime organization is structured, however, is to get inside the organization. There are several ways to do this. One way is to infiltrate the organization with an undercover officer. This is very difficult to do, however, because crime organizations do not welcome newcomers and the more organized they are, the less likely a cop will be able to get inside. Another way is to pick off a member of the organization and flip that person. In some cases, this cooperator may be placed back into the organization to perform undercover work for the government. In all instances, the benefit of the cooperator is to tell the government how the crime organization is structured. A danger with this method is that the cooperator may lie or may turn and reveal to the crime organization that it is under investigation. Finally, covert interception of communication between the members of the crime organization such as through a wiretap, for example, is another way to get inside a criminal organization. A difficulty with relying on wiretaps, however, is that criminals will often talk in code, and they seldom directly make statements that clearly define the structure of the organization.

Another key to taking down a crime organization is to learn how it commits the criminal conduct. In other words, it is critical to fully understand how the organization operates, how it carries out its criminal activities. If a prosecutor can fully comprehend how the organization operates, it can facilitate looking for weaknesses in the organization, or identify sources of evidence that the government can exploit. For example, knowing the details of how drug proceeds are laundered by a drug trafficking organization may allow the prosecutor to issue subpoenas for financial documents that reveal the source and origin, as well as destination, of the drug proceeds and the identity of the people conducting the financial transactions. As outsiders, it may not be readily apparent to law enforcement officers and prosecutors the details of how the targets are committing the criminal conduct. Sometimes documents and records can provide some insight into the operations of a criminal organization, but more often it requires flipping one or more members of the criminal organization to gain the insight into the operations.

Figuring out the structure of the criminal organization is only the beginning of the prosecutor's task. To dismantle a criminal organization, prosecutors must carefully develop a plan. As the investigation develops evidence against members of the organization, prosecutors need to determine how to dismantle the organization. Ideally, a prosecutor is in a position to charge all members of the organization in one indictment. Depending on the number of members, however, charging all suspects at the same time may prove unwieldy from a purely logistical standpoint. If a prosecutor started picking off weak links, it may give a highly structured criminal organization time to adjust and take counteractions by harming cooperators, destroying evidence, or going underground. Thus, prosecutors should strive to find a way to immediately hobble the criminal organization. One way to do this is to take out key players in the organization in the first round of indictments, depriving the organization of leadership. Another way to hobble organized crime is financially. Remembering that organized crime is almost always a profit-driven enterprise, prosecutors can use criminal and civil forfeiture tools to freeze and seize bank accounts and other assets that the organization relies upon to operate.

Complex and Difficult Cases

The mine-run criminal case demands a lot of work and attention from prosecutors, but prosecutors will encounter complex cases that pose even greater difficulties. On occasion, a law enforcement officer will come to a prosecutor with evidence that someone committed a crime but is stymied regarding who and how the person committed the crime. On other occasions, a law enforcement officer will come to a prosecutor with evidence that a person committed some crime but it is apparent that the known evidence is just the tip of an iceberg of other unknown criminal conduct. In some instances it may appear that the target committed other crimes, in other instances that the target had other unknown cohorts, and in still other instances it may appear that there are both additional crimes and targets at issue.

There are some common strategies that prosecutors may use to attack complex cases to identify the crimes and criminals, and then how to take them down. To begin with, it is important that prosecutors be slow to fix on a particular target or targets and avoid locking into a particular theory of what occurred or why or how a crime was committed. This requires mental discipline to resist the predisposition to reach premature conclusions. Keeping an open mind exposes a prosecutor to a wider variety of possibilities and decreases the likelihood of a prosecutor missing something or going down the wrong road.

A good strategy is to create a timeline of the events then known to the prosecutor, and then add to the timeline as progress is made in the investigation. Placing the evidence in chronological order often provides visual insight into patterns or relationships that can provide enlightenment. Similar to this is the task of creating organization tables by target and/or subject matter. This may involve, for example, listing several targets on a chart and then listing overt acts or events associated with that target irrespective of the time line of the acts or events. The same thing can be used for possible crimes, listing the people involved and events without respect to the timing of the events.

Sometimes the best way to unravel a complex crime is to work backward from what is known to arrive at what is not known. In any case brought to a prosecutor by law enforcement officers, there will be a body of information that is known. These are facts of past conduct or events. Each act or event was necessarily the result of acts or events that came before and led to the event under investigation. Working backward from the known facts in search of the causation can generate leads and expose a web of connections of other acts and actors. For example, if a bank discovers a false invoice during an audit of the books of a company to whom the bank has loaned money, then the focus should be on determining who in the company could have been involved in handling that invoice. The invoice would have reached the file through some internal process and it is possible to identify the various people involved in the process who could have touched the false invoice. Discovering who handled the one false invoice can lead to identifying other false invoices. If multiple false invoices are discovered, analyzing who could have been connected to all of the of false documents can narrow down the possible suspects. In other words, a half-dozen people may have had contact with a single false invoice, but only one or two could have touched all of the false invoices. Tracing the document backward through the process can also reveal how and when in the process the invoice was falsified.

Brainstorming the case with other prosecutors can also be very helpful. Sometimes it is difficult to see the forest for the trees. When prosecutors are close to a case it may be difficult for them to see leads or explanations that may be more apparent to someone new to the case. In some complex cases, I recruited fellow prosecutors multiple times to discuss the same case at various stages of the life of the investigation. It is important that prosecutors should evaluate and re-evaluate the evidence over and over again.

Some cases are complex simply because of the large volume of the evidence. Some white-collar, financial, or money-laundering cases may implicate scores of legal entities, bank accounts, and financial transactions. A broadly drafted grand jury subpoena may result in the production of thousands of documents, only some of which may provide anything of evidentiary value. In other cases, during a search law enforcement officers may seize boxes and boxes of files and documents because there might be evidence of a crime within them. Especially in this digital world, a criminal investigation may involve terabits of data that may contain evidence of the possible criminal activity. Organizing that evidence and developing a strategy for searching it for valuable information is the key to discerning meaning and finding value in the evidence. Separating the wheat from the chaff in these cases is critical.

There are several strategies to wade through a large volume of material to find evidence of value. One strategy is to take samples. In other words, instead of reviewing every single document that could possibly have evidentiary value, only sample documents are viewed at first. The goal is to use sampling to identify a better way to search the whole population of documents and to look for patterns that reveal the type of information that will lead to valuable evidence.

For example, in a fraud case a prosecutor could issue a grand jury subpoena to a bank requiring the bank to produce documents for all of a target's financial transactions for the past year. This broad subpoena, however, would likely generate a tremendous amount of data of little or no value, and the documents of real evidentiary value would be hard to find. Instead, a prosecutor may tailor a more narrowly drafted subpoena, seeking copies of any documents reflecting financial transactions over a certain dollar limit (say $1,000), and only for January, April, July, and October. Then looking through this smaller volume of documents, investigators may discern a pattern of financial documents that look suspicious, or may find documents that involve financial transactions with particular parties that are pertinent to the investigation. Armed with this insight, the prosecutor can then draft further subpoenas more narrowly tailored to obtain records related to certain types of transactions or particular persons. This same type of sampling strategy can be used whether it involves subpoenaing documents, searching through seized physical documents, or viewing digitally stored data.

With regard to digitally stored data in particular, there are numerous software programs that provide robust search capabilities. Some programs allow a person to reorganize the data by various criteria that may make it easier to search only those documents most likely to have value. Some programs also allow word searches with various degrees of sophistication. Some are similar to Westlaw or Nexis and allow a person to search for particular words or word patterns within various parameters, while others are more limited and permit only searching by key words. This software can be very valuable, when the person searching is properly trained in using it, to quickly search through very large volumes of data to find documents of real evidentiary value.

One of the difficulties with cases involving a large volume of evidence is less the physical challenge than it is the personnel challenge. By this I mean that sometimes finding the people and the hours to search through large volumes of evidence can be tough. Prosecutors seldom have time to personally conduct these searches. Persuading law enforcement officers to spend hours and hours looking for and reading through documents can be difficult. In some cases prosecutors may need to put an effort into finding the human resources necessary to get the job done. This may mean utilizing paralegal resources in the prosecutor's office. In other cases, it may be working with the law enforcement agency to free up some resources if even for a short period. Several times in my career I worked with agencies to devote other agents for a finite period or with specific, limited documents to assist my case agent in searching through a large volume of evidence. In other instances, the prosecutor may need to recruit other law enforcement agencies to assist on the case. The Internal Revenue Service Criminal Investigation Division, for example, has agents trained in the examination of financial documents. When, on occasion, I had a case that unexpectedly evolved into a large-volume financial document case, I would persuade an IRS agent to join forces with the other agencies on the case. Finally, in some cases the prosecutor may need to seek additional resources outside the government. In a couple instances I hired contractors to help search and organize large volumes of documentary evidence. This last solution, however, obviously raises issues because, for example, contractors would not be allowed to see documents deemed covered by the grand jury secrecy requirements of Federal Rule of Criminal Procedure 6(e).

Chapter Eight

Working with Cooperators

Part of every prosecutor's job involves working with cooperators. A cooperator is someone connected with criminal activity who is providing assistance to the government in the investigation and prosecution of others. A cooperator may be someone who has been apprehended in an unrelated case but has information helpful to the government on another case or who is in a position to engage in undercover work, perhaps making a controlled buy of narcotics, for example. A cooperator may be a co-defendant in a case the prosecutor is handling who chooses to plead guilty and cooperate with the government against co-defendants. Cooperators, or informants, may also include people who are connected to people in the criminal world and are willing to cooperate with law enforcement officers against criminals in exchange for money.

Cooperation can take many forms. Cooperation can consist of the cooperator simply providing information to the government. Sometimes cooperation simply starts with a proffer of information and is followed by other activities. Defendants usually provide information (or proffer information) to the government in anticipation of entering into a cooperation plea agreement on impending or pending charges. During proffer sessions cooperators debrief and tell all they know about their own criminal activity and the criminal activity of others. The information is often proffered on the condition that it cannot be used against the defendant. In other words, the defendant talks under a grant of so-called "use immunity," meaning that the government cannot use against the defendant what he or she says during a proffer. It is not, however, transactional immunity. In other words, a proffer agreement does not prevent the government from prosecuting the defendant based on other evidence.

Cooperation may go far beyond simply a defendant telling the government what the defendant knows during a protected proffer session. Cooperation may involve proactive work, such as making controlled buys of drugs or guns, controlled deliveries of cash, or recorded phone calls or meetings. Cooperation often also involves cooperators testifying before grand juries, at hearings, or in trial.

Whatever the form the cooperation takes, cooperators are working with the government for selfish reasons. Cooperators stand to benefit in some way through their cooperation, or they would not be cooperating. Many times, they cooperate to avoid being charged, in exchange for reduced charges, or in the hope of receiving a more lenient sentence. Other cooperators or informants help the government in exchange for money. They are literally paid informants, compensated either at a flat rate to provide information to law enforcement officers or paid by the task, such as for making a controlled buy of narcotics.

Prosecutors become involved in working with cooperators in a number of different ways. Prosecutors often decide in the first instance whether to provide defendants the opportunity to cooperate and, if so, under what terms. Sometimes prosecutors endeavor to convince criminal targets or defendants to become cooperators, that is, to "flip" the defendant. Prosecutors are responsible to ensure that the cooperator's conduct in working with law enforcement officers is lawful and constitutional. Prosecutors must work with many cooperators as witnesses, either in grand jury, hearings, or trial. Prosecutors are responsible to ensure that cooperators are being truthful and for dealing harshly with cooperators who lie. Finally, prosecutors are often involved in deciding or influencing the reward a cooperator receives for cooperating.

A prosecutor's responsibility in working with a cooperator is a significant and serious one. As one court aptly described that responsibility:

> A prosecutor who does not appreciate the perils of using rewarded criminals as witnesses risks compromising the truth-seeking mission of our criminal justice system. Because the government decides whether and when to use such witnesses, and what, if anything, to give them for their service, the government stands uniquely positioned to guard against untruthfulness. By its action the government can either contribute to or eliminate the problem. Accordingly, we expect prosecutors and investigators to take all reasonable measures to safeguard the system against treachery.

United States v. Bernal-Obeso, 989 F.2d 331, 333-34 (9th Cir. 1993)

Despite all of the dangers inherent in working with cooperators, there are significant benefits for prosecutors to use cooperators. Using cooperators can enable the prosecutor to work up the chain of command. By getting people lower in the criminal organization to cooperate, the prosecutor can use them to prosecute the next person higher in the organization, hopefully flip that person too, and then keep going up the chain. In determining who to use as cooperators in this a way, it is important to make sure the prosecutor is working up the chain of command and not the other way around. Prosecutors want to use drug dealers to catch drug suppliers, accountants to catch chief executive officers, and soldiers to catch mob bosses. Sometimes using cooperators is the only way to take down criminal organizations because they are so disciplined and insular that it is not possible to infiltrate them using undercover law enforcement officers.

Also, sometimes using a cooperator is the only way that a prosecutor can learn the scope of the criminal activity or organization, or how the targets committed or are committing the criminal conduct. There is only so much information law enforcement officers can learn about criminal operations through other traditional law enforcement techniques. Controlled buys from dealers will not often provide law enforcement officers insight into the dealer's source of supply. Reviewing financial documents in the aftermath of a massive fraud scheme may not disclose who was involved in committing the fraud or how it was committed. Cooperators have the ability to turn on the light of the otherwise dark room of criminals and criminal conduct.

There are a number of issues involved with prosecutors performing this critical role of working with cooperators. Prosecutors should strive to understand and address the problems posed by cooperators' mental states and motivations. Prosecutors have to develop ways to persuade cooperators to cooperate and to do so honestly. Prosecutors should adopt practices that serve as a check on the cooperator's conduct and make rewards dependent on complete honesty. Prosecutors should also learn how to develop cases around cooperators, using them for all the benefits they provide while minimizing dependence upon them. Finally, prosecutors are required to find methods to present cooperators as believable witnesses.

THE MENTALITY OF COOPERATORS

The first trick in working with cooperators is to fully understand their mental states, why they are cooperating, what makes them tick. Anyone cooperating with the government has an ulterior motive. Concerned citizens cooperate out of a sense of duty, or to make their own neighborhood safer for them and their children, or because they want to right a wrong. Cooperators, in the sense of the term used in this chapter, on the other hand, have no such altruistic or noble thoughts motivating them. The cooperators I am talking about in this chapter are motivated, rather, by selfish considerations. They are seeking money or, what is even more valuable, freedom.

Because cooperators are operating under selfish motives, they do not necessarily have a strong adherence to honesty. They are motivated to tell prosecutors what they think prosecutors want to hear. They may have little adherence to the truth if they believe that a lie will get them a better deal. Cooperators are also reluctant to divulge information that may be harmful to them or decrease the chance of getting a favorable deal. Some cooperators may also be motivated by vengeance, particularly if they are cooperating against other cooperators, competitors, or others they believe have done them wrong. Conversely, some cooperators may also be motivated to lie to protect others from prosecution, either out of friendship or fear.

Prosecutors must also consider that cooperators are, or have been, criminals. They are crooks, dope dealers, con artists, liars, and cheats. They have shown by their own prior conduct that they have little regard for the strictures of society, law and order, or honesty.

Further, cooperators do not want to appear to be cooperating for any selfish reasons or be seen as the criminals they are. Cooperators are known in the criminal world by derogatory labels, such as snitch, weasel, and rat. To avoid these labels, if even in their own mind, cooperators will often proclaim more honorable motives animated their decisions to cooperate. They may claim to have found God, or had an epiphany, or claim they want to help eradicate crime. They may have even convinced themselves of these fallacious explanations for their decision to cooperate.

Finally, most cooperators are frightened, often for good reason. They know full well how cooperators are viewed by their fellow criminals. They are aware that by cooperating they are likely placing themselves and their loved ones in danger. They recognize the power of the criminal elements against whom they are cooperating and have to weigh that power in their minds against the power the government has over their futures. In many cases, defendants are far more afraid of what other criminals might do to them and their loved ones than of what prosecutors are capable of doing to them and their futures.

To develop an effective working relationship with cooperators, prosecutors should start by recognizing the motivations and fears cooperators have. Prosecutors should not trust cooperators. Prosecutors should be skeptical of anything that comes out of a cooperator's mouth. Prosecutors should endeavor to corroborate and test everything a cooperator says. At the same time, it is important for prosecutors to empathize with cooperators, to imagine what it is like to be in their positions, what may be motivating them to shade the truth and in what way they are likely to do so. Recognizing cooperators for who they are, and what factors may influence their decision to cooperate and the truthfulness of their cooperation, prosecutors can then tailor their communications and dealings with cooperators to be responsive to cooperators' motivations and mindsets.

PERSUADING PEOPLE TO COOPERATE

In most instances, by the time the prosecutor deals with cooperators, the cooperators have already made the decisions to cooperate. Perhaps law enforcement officers have already developed an informant and have a co-operation agreement with the person paying them for their cooperation. On other occasions, defendants agree to cooperate with officers immediately upon their arrests. In most instances when cooperators have been charged with criminal offenses, they make the decision to cooperate after consultation with their defense attorney. In some instances, however, prosecutors find themselves in the position of needing to persuade a person to cooperate. This may involve persuading a person who may not be exposed to criminal charges to cooperate, such as a child, parent, spouse, girlfriend, boyfriend, or associate. It also may involve persuading a target or a criminal defendant to cooperate against others.

Persuading non-criminal actors to cooperate in a criminal investigation requires prosecutors to practice empathy, get an understanding of why the person may be reluctant to testify, and then attempt to directly address the person's concerns. The people who fall into this category of cooperators can include anyone from an innocent bystander or eyewitness to a crime, to a member of the target's family, to associates of the target who, frankly, are probably involved in criminal conduct but against whom the prosecutor has insufficient evidence to charge them. People in this category may be reluctant to testify out of fear, loyalty, or apprehension of exposing themselves to criminal charges. It is important to get these people to articulate why they are reluctant to testify. Prosecutors should be understanding and listen attentively, assuring the person that they care and do want to hear about the person's concerns. Once the person has explained the reason why he or she is reluctant to testify, the prosecutor can address those concerns. In some cases the prosecutor may be able to assure the person that concerns are not realistic or will be mitigated as a result of the prosecution, but prosecutors should be very cautious against saying anything that amounts to a promise. In most cases, however, the prosecutor may attempt to address the concern by working with law enforcement officers to implement security measures, or by the prosecutor entering into a proffer agreement with persons worried about incriminating themselves. Prosecutors may also want to talk to the potential cooperating individual about the importance of his or her cooperation. The bottom line is that with these people, prosecutors have little power to compel cooperation. The degree of cooperation the prosecutor receives may be wholly dependent on the prosecutor's ability to build rapport with the person and gain the person's trust.

It is sometimes the case with criminal defendants that they do not fully understand the need to cooperate and benefits they may receive for cooperating because it has not been effectively communicated to them by their defense attorneys. Sometimes this is because the defense attorneys themselves do not adequately understand it or are incapable of articulating the factors to a defendant in a way that should convince a defendant to cooperate. More often, criminal defendants are simply unreceptive and unwilling to believe their defense attorneys. Defense attorneys are occasionally hesitant to put the matter to their clients in terms too stark and startling for fear that their clients will lose faith in the attorney and the attorney's wiliness to defend his or her client at trial, if necessary.

Whenever a prosecutor believes a defendant's cooperation would help the case, and that it is truly in a defendant's interest to cooperate, it is sometimes effective for the prosecutor to approach the defense attorney and ask for an opportunity to "talk at" the defendant. When I did this I would tell the defense attorney that I truly believed it was in the defendant's best interest to cooperate and asked for permission to explain things to the defendant without asking the defendant any questions. I would tell the defense attorney that during the meeting I would fully summarize the strength of the government's case against the defendant and why I believed that if he or she went to trial a jury would convict him or her. I would also explain the possible benefits to the defendant if the defendant plead guilty and cooperated. I told defense attorneys that I can be the person delivering the bad news to the defendant and be the one explaining why cooperation was a good thing so that the defendant did not lose faith in the defense attorney. I would assure the defense attorney that I would not require an answer from the defendant on the spot and would give the defendant a few days to talk about it. I would also point out that there was really nothing for the defendant or defense counsel to lose from agreeing to the session because at the very least I would be providing the defendant with an advanced version of my opening statement and closing argument. When defense attorneys let me have these meetings with defendants, I was almost always able to persuade the defendant to cooperate.

Keeping in mind what is likely going through the person's mind, there are some key things to remember in effectively persuading a person to cooperate with the government. First, prosecutors must be completely honest with the person. It is critical that prosecutors are completely accurate in describing the evidence and not exaggerate or overstate the case. The defendant likely knows exactly what happened and any misstatements or exaggerations will destroy the prosecutor's credibility and decrease the chances the defendant will cooperate. Prosecutors should also not minimize the dangers of cooperating or exaggerate the rewards or likelihood of being rewarded for cooperation.

Second, prosecutors should attempt to respond to what is likely to motivate the person to cooperate. In some cases if the person has been victimized by another, a prosecutor can help the person realize that cooperating may be an opportunity to break out of the abusive relationship. It is important in these instances that the prosecutor not denigrate the alleged offender for a number of reasons. The potential cooperator may still be protective of the victimizer and attacking him or her may backfire. The person also may not be correct or accurate in the description of how he or she has been wronged. It is also critical that prosecutors address this motivation by emphasizing the benefit to the cooperator as opposed to the punishment to the alleged offender. Prosecutors do not want to motivate people to cooperate out of a sense of vengeance.

If a person is apprehensive about the charges or sentence the person faces, the prosecutor can explain the process by which those matters are decided and how the person's cooperation can influence the outcome of these decisions. It is important in these cases that the prosecutor carefully explain the cooperation process and the factors that determine whether the person gets a benefit and the extent of the benefit from cooperating, emphasizing the compelling need for truthfulness. It is also important that the prosecutor make sure the person understands that there are no promises that the cooperator will receive a benefit, even if the person does everything asked, because others, including the judge, will ultimately be making the decisions. Although prosecutors can explain and hold out the options that may give the person hope for receiving benefits from cooperating, prosecutors cannot mislead the person into believing that it will ever be anything more than a hope.

If the person is reluctant to cooperate because of fear of repercussions for them or their loved ones, the prosecutor can ask questions to get a true sense of the threat and then identify things the government can do to address those concerns. The government can often offer a number of options along a continuum from extra police patrols at the person's house to the Witness Protection Program. It is important when talking with cooperators about their fears that prosecutors not belittle or be dismissive of the person's fears or treat them as illegitimate. Even if the prosecutor believes the fears are unwarranted or exaggerated, it is important that the prosecutor ensures the person knows the prosecutor respects the person's fears, acknowledges that the person truly has those fears, and attempts to address ways of mitigating the things that are making the person fearful of cooperating.

CHECKS AND BALANCES ON COOPERATORS

Because of the motives compelling cooperators to prevaricate, prosecutors need to develop checks and balances in working with cooperators to counteract and overcome those motives with equally compelling reasons for cooperators to be honest, and with methods designed to make sure they are. There is a saying in the diplomatic corps: Trust but verify. In working with cooperators, a more apt saying would be: Distrust and verify. Wise prosecutors approach working with cooperators with the assumption that cooperators are lying to them. So instead of trusting that what a cooperator says is true, prosecutors should assume it is not true and view the information skeptically, looking for inconsistencies and inaccuracies. Prosecutors should turn a cooperator's story upside down and inside out, testing it for holes and gaps, mixed-up timelines, and improbable or unlikely explanations or developments. If a story sounds too good to be true, it probably is.

To effectively check on a cooperator's story, prosecutors should search for ways to corroborate or disprove the story. The best way to do this is to solicit as much detail as possible from the cooperator. If a cooperator claims to have made a drug run with a target of the investigation to Texas, for example, the prosecutor should demand details about the trip: dates, times, locations, roads traveled, stops made, texts sent or received, money spent. If the cooperator provides these details, the prosecutor can have officers try to corroborate it by getting receipts, running phone tolls, checking road routes and times, and eliminating the possibility the cooperator was somewhere else, like in jail or work. If a cooperator is unable to provide details or equivocates in providing answers or responds to questions with questions, the prosecutor should assume the cooperator is lying.

Another key check in working with cooperators is to ensure that the government does not reveal information to the cooperator. Rather, the government should draw information from the cooperator. In other words, the prosecutor and law enforcement officers must be vigilant in not revealing information about the investigation to the cooperator. The government should not let the cooperator know the targets of the investigation or the scope or details of the information law enforcement officers already know. In all likelihood, the defense attorney will have already, and quite properly, provided the cooperator with a lot of this information in the process of disclosing to the cooperator the contents of the government's discovery. Nevertheless, there may still be some things that have not yet made it into discovery, or the focus of the investigation or identity of the targets not readily apparent from a review of the discovery. Prosecutors should approach working with cooperators with the assumption that the cooperator will tell the prosecutor what he or she thinks the prosecutor wants to know, and the more the cooperator knows of the government's case, the easier that will be.

One of the most significant checks on a defendant's cooperation is in the form of the written agreements the government reaches with cooperators. These include so-called proffer agreements and plea agreements. Prosecutors have control over the written terms of such agreements and do not have to enter into agreements unless they contain language that induces truthfulness.

A proffer agreement is a contract setting out the terms of a debriefing session with a potential cooperator. A proffer agreement does not address what the government will or will not do for the cooperator in terms of charges or sentences; rather, it is confined to what the government agrees to do or not do with the information proffered by the cooperator during a debriefing session. A typical proffer agreement provides that the defendant will provide information and the government will not use the defendant's statements against him or her. Importantly, however, this promise by the government should be contingent upon the cooperator's complete truthfulness and, by its terms the agreement becomes null and void if the defendant is found to have lied. It is advisable to enter into proffer agreements and obtain a proffer from a defendant before entering into a plea agreement that contains cooperation provisions. Prosecutors should not enter into cooperation plea agreements with defendants they do not believe are being fully honest in the proffer session.

Plea agreements address the concessions the government is willing to make on charges or sentencing issues in exchange for truthful cooperation. The best plea agreements for ensuring truthful cooperation include several provisions. First, to the extent possible prosecutors should not reduce charges or sentencing options in exchange for cooperation. When these concessions are made, the cooperator has already obtained a large part of the benefit of cooperating perhaps before the cooperation is complete or has been put to the test by the crucible of cross-examination at trial. Rather, the better plea agreement is one that provides the benefit to the cooperator on the back end, at the time of sentencing, after all cooperation is complete and has withstood the adversarial process. The federal sentencing system provides a vehicle for federal prosecutors to make motions at the time of sentencing, or even after a defendant has been sentenced, to reward the defendant for cooperation. Even these plea agreements, however, should not set forth the amount of reduction in the sentence the government intends to provide in exchange for cooperation. It is far more inducive of encouraging truthful cooperation for a plea agreement to provide that the determination of how much the government will recommend the court reduce the defendant's sentence will only be made at the time of sentencing, after all cooperation is complete. Further, as with the proffer agreement, the best cooperation plea agreement provides that the government's obligation to consider a motion for a reduced sentence is forfeited if the defendant is found to be lying. Finally, the plea agreement should not only contain a carrot (in the form of a potential reduction in sentence) but also a stick. In other words, the plea agreement should contain a provision that makes it clear that if the defendant is found to have lied in the process of providing cooperation, not only does he or she not receive a benefit of a reduced sentence, but he or she will also be prosecuted for perjury or obstruction of justice. Prosecutors should carry through with the threat of prosecution when appropriate not only to punish the wrongdoer but also to deter other cooperators from lying.

DEVELOPING CASES WITH
AND AROUND COOPERATORS

Although cooperators are useful and sometimes necessary for prosecutors to use in criminal cases, they pose significant problems if the strength of the government's case depends too much on cooperators. Cooperators typically make poor witnesses and are often easily impeached because they have criminal histories or have lied in the past (or possibly even in the process of cooperating). Also, for all the reasons outlined above, cooperators have motives to be dishonest that are readily apparent to most jurors and will be amply pointed out by defense counsel to any jurors who have not already figured it out. Thus, prosecutors should strive to minimize dependence on cooperators.

To begin with, prosecutors should consider having cooperators testify before the grand jury. This has several benefits. First, it requires the cooperator to testify under oath, which may serve to further motivate the cooperator to tell the truth and, if not, make prosecution for perjury an option. Second, grand jurors sometimes ask questions that reveal flaws in the cooperator's story that got by the prosecutor. Third, when cooperators are truthful in grand jury, it provides the target of the government's investigation with a clear indication of the extent and strength of the government's case against the target. This makes it more likely that the target will him- or herself plead guilty than if the same statements from the cooperator appear in an officer's interview report.

In a way, the best cooperator is the one that the prosecutor never has to call as a witness at trial. Prosecutors should work with law enforcement officers to use the information the cooperator provided to develop evidence to prove the case independent of the cooperator's testimony. This is seldom completely possible, but it is surprisingly frequent that parts of the cooperator's story can be corroborated and proven without the cooperator's testimony. Also, every piece of corroborating evidence that can be developed helps shore up the believability of the cooperator on the portions of his or her story that are not capable of independent corroboration. It is also often the case that the government calls multiple cooperators to testify in the same trial. The cooperators' testimony should corroborate one another.

One last way to use cooperators other than having them testify is to use them as a source of information for questioning other witnesses at trial. This is particularly true when cross-examining defense witnesses who might have been involved in the criminal activity. The cooperator may have firsthand knowledge of the defense witness's actual involvement in the criminal activity, or other insight about the witness's motives or background, that could be helpful to the prosecutor in formulating questions to ask or for the purpose of impeaching the credibility of the defense witness. Thus, during a trial, prosecutors should consider consulting with a cooperator about these matters, regardless of whether the cooperator has or will testify.[1]

PRESENTING COOPERATORS AS BELIEVABLE WITNESSES

As repeatedly noted here, cooperators do not have reputations for or the appearance of truthful witnesses. Prosecutors can and should take steps in advance of trial, however, to enhance the credibility of cooperators. Some of these steps we have already discussed. Properly drafted proffer and plea agreements help enhance a cooperator's credibility, particularly if they are adequately described during direct examination and explained by the prosecutor during closing argument. Similarly, working to develop corroborating evidence that can be introduced at trial will go a long way toward enhancing the cooperator's credibility as well.

There are still other things that prosecutors can do before trial[2] to enhance a cooperator's believability. First, prosecutors and law enforcement officers should maintain a proper, professional relationship with cooperators. Cooperators sometimes try to ingratiate themselves to prosecutors and officers and try to become friends. And some cooperators are con artists while others are, frankly, just likable people. Prosecutors must maintain a distance from the cooperator. Jurors are likely to pick up on clues if too chummy of a relationship exists between cooperators and the government, especially if the cooperator speaks using terms suggesting he or she is part of the prosecution team or refers to the officers, or heaven forbid the prosecutor, using first names.

Second, prosecutors should ensure that everything the cooperator said was recorded in some way, either in a law enforcement report or recording or in a transcript from a grand jury session or hearing. This includes every false statement the cooperators made during their cooperation. It is common for cooperators to omit information, exaggerate, or outright lie, especially early on during their cooperation. When prosecutors catch cooperators doing this, the cooperators' falsehoods must be noted, the prosecutors must confront the cooperators, and the truthful information then also recorded. Sometimes law enforcement officers believe they need to only record the final, truthful information and not the cooperators' initial falsehoods. This is improper and a mistake. The government has an obligation to disclose any information to the defense that may be exculpatory or impeachment material, and this includes false statements by a cooperator even if the cooperator later corrects them. It is also a mistake, however, because disclosing the information paradoxically can enhance the credibility of the cooperator. When a jury understands that the government caught a cooperator in a falsehood, confronted the cooperator, and elicited the truth, it can provide the jury with some confidence that the government has vetted the cooperator's story and what that cooperator ultimately says can be trusted because the government tested it and exposed any untruths.

Third, prosecutors should fully prepare the cooperator for testifying. Prosecutors must make sure the cooperator has provided the full story, test it again during preparation, and continue to look for holes. Prosecutors should make sure that the cooperator knows they must own up to any prior falsehoods or misconduct. Prosecutors should ensure the cooperator fully understands the terms of any agreement reached with the government, including the limitations of any government promises and the threats of punishment for lying. Even if factually incorrect, if a cooperator believes he is guaranteed a sentence reduction no matter what happens, it has the same adverse effect on his credibility as a witness as if the government did make such a promise.

Finally, prosecutors should prepare cooperators for cross-examination. Prosecutors should ensure the cooperator knows that his character for truthfulness will be attacked and that the cooperator cannot take it personally or fight back with the defense attorney. Prosecutors must make cooperators understand that they should own up to any criminal history or other subjects that are allowable grounds for impeachment by defense counsel. When cooperators readily admit the past wrongs without equivocation or excuse, it mitigates the impact of their past conduct on the jury's assessment of the cooperators' truthfulness. Prosecutors should also fully explain to cooperators the process a defense attorney may use to impeach a witness with a prior inconsistent statement. To do this, a cooperator should review all prior statements and grand jury testimony.[3] The prosecutor should then explain that if at trial the cooperator makes a statement that the defense attorney believes is inconsistent with one of the cooperator's prior statements, the defense attorney will point it out. A prosecutor may want to go through the questions the way a defense attorney might when impeaching a witness with a prior inconsistent statement. The prosecutor should emphasize that the cooperator should admit it if the cooperator made an inconsistent statement, but not to panic. There is usually a valid explanation for inconsistencies and the prosecutor can assure the cooperator that if the defense attorney does not give the cooperator a chance to explain, the prosecutor will do so if the prosecutor thinks it is important.

Chapter Nine

Developing Evidence

Prosecutors have a role, and indeed a responsibility, to help develop the evidence in a criminal case. Law enforcement officers obviously assume the primary investigation role. Law enforcement officers are trained to investigate criminal cases, question witnesses, and identify, seize, and analyze evidence. Law enforcement officers often approach investigations with a goal of obtaining sufficient evidence to support a criminal charge. They do not always conduct criminal investigations with an eye on persuading jurors of a defendant's guilt. Law enforcement officers do not stand before juries and judges, marshal the evidence, and attempt to persuade the fact finders. Prosecutors do. Prosecutors look at how jurors will view and understand evidence. Prosecutors are also better able to anticipate how defense counsel may attack the case. Thus, prosecutors look at evidence through different lenses, and from different perspectives, than do law enforcement officers. So it is incumbent upon prosecutors to work with law enforcement officers to develop the evidence in a way that aids the prosecutor in winning the case.

There are some keys to successfully developing evidence. First, the investigation should never end until the case is over. Second, prosecutors should work closely with the law enforcement officers throughout the investigation whenever possible. Third, prosecutors should visit the crime scene. Fourth, prosecutors should study and understand the contexts in which the crime occurred. Fifth, prosecutors should view the evidence from the rearview perspective. Finally, prosecutors should think creatively and with persuasion as the goal. I will discuss each of these keys in turn.

NEVER STOP INVESTIGATING

A prosecutor should not stop investigating the case until the case is over. Months, or in some cases years, may pass between charging a defendant and the trial or sentencing. It is a mistake for a prosecutor to stop investigating a case after bringing charges. While charges are pending there are several ways in which a case may become stronger if only the prosecutor maintains the investigation.

First, the bringing of charges against a defendant may create opportunities to significantly advance the investigation and uncover additional evidence of the defendant's criminal conduct. The defendant's arrest may embolden recalcitrant or fearful witnesses to cooperate or cause a rift among those remaining in the defendant's criminal organization resulting in conflicts and abandonment. After a defendant's arrest, then, prosecutors should re-evaluate the investigation and consider re-approaching previously reluctant witnesses or co-conspirators. Prosecutors may also want to re-examine and continue to investigate the criminal organization to which the defendant belonged, looking for opportunities to exploit the disruption caused by the defendant's arrest.

Second, defendants often help prosecutors after their arrest by attempting to escape or tamper with witnesses. Law enforcement officers should monitor a defendant's conduct and activities after arrest, whether the defendant is in or out of custody pending trial. Evidence that a defendant made plans to escape custody or flee the jurisdiction after his or her arrest is strong evidence of a defendant's guilt. Law enforcement officers should also stay in close contact with key witnesses after the defendant's arrest to protect the witnesses but also to gather any evidence of a defendant's attempt to influence or tamper with witnesses.

Third, officers should monitor the defendant's communication after his or her arrest. This may involve monitoring his or her public social media communication if the defendant is out of custody, or his or her letters and calls from the jail if the defendant is in custody. It never ceased to amaze me how often defendants would make incriminating statements on social media or on phone calls from the jail even when they knew the calls were monitored and recorded.

Finally, prosecutors should work with law enforcement officers as they prepare for trial to continuously look for clues they missed or avenues of investigation they failed to take before charging the defendant. As prosecutors prepare for trial they organize the evidence and examine the case as a whole in a much more concentrated way than during the investigation before bringing the charges. In trial preparation, prosecutors pull everything together and synthesize the evidence. In doing this, prosecutors often see things they missed before and observe patterns that become apparent only when all of the evidence is laid out. Also, when preparing witnesses for trial, sometimes witnesses provide additional information they had previously failed to mention out of fear or forgetfulness, or because the officer or prosecutor failed to ask the right questions. Prosecutors who remain alert to these insights and developments can seize the opportunities they present to expand the investigation. When prosecutors do this, the government's case only gets stronger as the government prepares for trial.

Nor should prosecutors stop investigating the case after a conviction. The same forces at work after a charge and before conviction continue to be at work after a conviction and before sentencing. The defendant's conviction may embolden recalcitrant witnesses more than the defendant's arrest. The defendant's conviction may spur the defendant to try to escape or tamper with evidence or witnesses more than his or her arrest because the defendant may now conclude he or she has nothing to lose. I once had a case when the defendant, a medical doctor convicted at trial for the illegal diversion of controlled substances, surprised me when, to seek revenge, he tried to hire a hitman to kill two of my trial witnesses. Evidence generated by a continued investigation after conviction may allow the government to seek a more appropriate sentence and may also allow the government to develop a stronger case against the defendant's criminal associates who have not yet been convicted.

It is worth noting that some law enforcement officers are reluctant to expend time and energy continuing to investigate a case after a defendant has been charged and especially after a defendant has been convicted. This is not always the case; some officers fully appreciate the benefits of continuing the investigation. During my career as a prosecutor, I had the privilege to work with some outstanding agents, many of who never stopped investigating the case even if it required listening to hours and hours and hours of recorded jail calls looking for the one time the defendant slipped up and said something incriminating. For those officers who do not fully appreciate the need to continue the investigation, prosecutors should work with the officers to encourage and motivate them to do the work. It will only take a couple instances of success to prove to law enforcement officers the benefit of effort.

WORK WITH OFFICERS IN CONDUCTING THE INVESTIGATION

Prosecutors should work as a team with law enforcement officers in conducting the investigation. Although prosecutors could sit back and let the officers conduct the investigation and present the prosecutor with the results, this would be a mistake. First, prosecutors will have a much better and thorough understanding of the case, its strengths and its weaknesses, when they were deeply involved in the investigation. Second, prosecutors can help direct investigations in a way to develop evidence that will help inform and persuade juries.

This is not to say that prosecutors should become investigators. Prosecutors must stay in their own lane. They should not control witness interviews or direct searches, kick down doors or seize evidence. Nor should prosecutors unnecessarily criticize or second-guess officers' decisions after the fact. Law enforcement officers have training and experience prosecutors often lack. Law enforcement officers' role is to conduct the investigation, and prosecutors' role is to prosecute the case. Thus, although it is important that officers and prosecutors stay in their lanes, they should constantly communicate and work together toward a common goal.

VISIT THE CRIME SCENE

Whenever possible, prosecutors should visit the scene of the crime or criminal conduct. Related to this directive is the broader concept of prosecutors becoming immersed in the context of the criminal conduct. Both are important and are similar, but also different in some ways.

There is no substitute for visiting the scene of a crime. All the photographs and video in the world cannot reveal to prosecutors the details and perspective that can be gained from visiting the scene of a crime. It will be up to the prosecutor to use words to describe to a jury or judge what happened and how it happened. Photographs, videos, diagrams, and the like are all visual aids, but a prosecutor must use words with these aids to persuade the fact finder. That is much harder to accomplish when the prosecutor has never been to the scene and is working off of secondhand knowledge.

Also, by visiting the scene of criminal activity, a prosecutor may be able to identify additional evidence that would aid the prosecutor in persuading the fact finder. For example, in one white-collar fraud case I prosecuted, the government's theory was that the chief executive officer was a hands-on manager with control over the lower-level people in the accounting department whom he had falsifying documents on his behalf. The defense theory was that the CEO was a hands-off, absentee manager with no direct involvement with the accounting department. By visiting the accounting department I was able to observe that the CEO had installed a window in his office that looked directly down upon the desks of the accounting clerks, and that he had a back entrance to his office that led to the accounting department. Although the agent I was working with was one of the best, he did not understand the significance of these facts in relation to the theory of the case, or the jury appeal that photographs of and from that window would have.

Indeed, it is often the case that the prosecutor cannot fully understand how or why the crime occurred in the manner that it did without being at the scene. For example, in a murder case I prosecuted one of the key issues would be whether the defendant was acting in self-defense or whether the victim was trying to flee. The victim was stabbed to death with a machete but had a large cut across the back of his arm that was inexplicable until I visited the scene. Once there we realized that the slice to his arm had to of occurred while he raised his arm in a defensive manner while trying to open the door to escape. We realized this only when we saw how the location of the couch and a wall and the direction the door opened all worked together to explain the wound. Although we had literally hundreds of photographs of the crime scene, none of us was able to discern the layout from the two-dimensional photographs.

LEARN THE CONTEXT OF THE CRIME

For similar reasons, it is also important that prosecutors immerse themselves in the subject matter or context involved in the criminal case. Prosecutors handling drug cases should learn everything they can about the drug trade: where the drugs are coming from, how they are manufactured or grown, importation routes, packaging methods, distribution practices, slang terms, and the like. Prosecutors handling gun cases should learn about firearms, handle them, and shoot them. Prosecutors handling white-collar cases need to learn about the business, profession, or industry that was involved in the fraud. So if the case involves bank fraud, the prosecutor should devote time to learn about the financial transactions involved, the documents generated in the normal course of banking transactions, the flow of funds, and so on. If the case is an environmental criminal case involving the discharge of petroleum from bilge tanks of oceangoing vessels, the prosecutor must learn about the vessels, the process for lawfully handling polluted bilge tank water, and similar information. By delving into the subject matter and understanding the underlying activity or context of the criminal activity, a prosecutor is in a better position to identify evidence that would be important for the fact finder to understand the crime. As important, this knowledge base also puts a prosecutor in a much better position to explain the significance of the evidence to jurors.

REARVIEW PERSPECTIVE

Good prosecutors learn how to view evidence through a rearview perspective. By rearview perspective, what I mean is that prosecutors should look at what evidence needs to be developed from viewing the case from what has to be accomplished in the end. In other words, prosecutors should look at the case backward, from thinking about what evidence will be needed to reference in closing argument to persuade a jury to convict, and by considering the record that will be needed if the government hopes to prevail on appeal. It is too late if the prosecutor is standing before a jury or a panel of appellate judges wishing that the evidence was something different than what it was. It is much better to think about what the prosecutor needs to have in evidence to prove the case to a jury and then set about ensuring that evidence is developed during the investigation.

In assessing what investigation should be conducted and what evidence should be gathered, prosecutors should think about what they would like to show the jury and talk to the jury about during closing argument. Thus, throughout the investigation prosecutors should be thinking about how the evidence will come in at trial and what the prosecutor would say about the evidence in closing argument. Indeed, good prosecutors draft and constantly revise an outline of closing argument well before an indictment is sought. By having the end goal in mind, it helps a prosecutor keep perspective about what evidence needs to be developed to achieve that goal.

Similarly, when working with law enforcement officers to develop evidence in a case, it is important that prosecutors keep in mind what evidence will be necessary to ensure the case survives on appeal if won at the trial court level. The case must withstand not only the scrutiny of a jury or judge as a fact finder; it must also be so strong that on appeal a reviewing court will not second-guess the fact finder's decision. Also, the stronger the case, the more likely it is that an appellate court may find that any mistakes made during the trial constituted harmless error. In prevailing on appeal, it is also important that the record from the trial court is adequate for appellate review. Thus, prosecutors should think about the record from that perspective. It may be necessary, for example, to generate a photograph of a location so that witnesses' testimony about an event is comprehensible to an appellate court reading a cold record.

DEVELOPING PERSUASIVE EVIDENCE

Good law enforcement officers will do a fine job investigating the crime and seizing, analyzing, and producing evidence sufficient to prove a defendant guilty beyond a reasonable doubt. Law enforcement officers may not, however, be focused on identifying and generating evidence that would be optimal for purposes of persuading a jury of the defendant's guilt. There is a difference in the quality and nature of the evidence, and law enforcement officers are not in the best position to recognize it even when they try.

But trial lawyers, including prosecutors, should be focused on how a jury will perceive the evidence. Jurors must be able to understand the evidence in the first place. The evidence must also be persuasive. Prosecutors can and should help the law enforcement officers develop evidence to meet these twin goals. Prosecutors do not have to simply accept and work with the evidence produced by the law enforcement officers. Prosecutors can and should help develop and discover new evidence.

To accomplish this task, prosecutors should view the evidence from a juror's perspective. Prosecutors are immersed in the law and the criminal justice system. It is easy for prosecutors to make connections, understand context, and appreciate the legal significance of evidence. Likewise, prosecutors will be very familiar with the facts of the cases they prosecute and their minds will fill in missing gaps. It is from this perspective that prosecutors generally view their cases.

To understand the jurors' perspective, prosecutors should think about the average juror's background, education, understanding, and influences. The average juror will have little or no background in the law, law enforcement, or the criminal justice system. The average juror is not well educated and will have no legal training. Jurors will have no understanding of the facts of the case or the parties involved. And the criminal justice system is a mystery to the average juror, involving unfamiliar rituals, rules, and procedures. With the jurors' perspective in mind, then, it is incumbent on prosecutors to develop evidence for the purposes of ensuring the jurors' understanding of the case and to persuade the jurors of the defendant's guilt. There are many ways for prosecutors to do this.

First, prosecutors should consider visual aids. People, including jurors, learn best through a combination of audio and visual means. Prosecutors should strive to illustrate with images every significant part of the case. This may mean requesting the agent to go back to locations and take photographs that would aid the jury's understanding of the evidence. For example, after a bank robbery law enforcement officers may have taken photographs of the crime scene in the sense of photographing inside the bank where the robber stood and of the teller's stand and drawer. They likely did not, however, take a photograph of outside the bank, photographs from the teller's perspective looking out from where he or she stood and saw the robber, or from inside the bank and looking out through the windows where the teller will testify he or she saw the robber's car in the parking lot. Nor is it likely that the officer took photographs of the robber's car that the teller would testify he or she saw him or her drive away in. You get the idea. The goal would be to have photographs taken that help the teller tell the story of what he or she saw the day of the robbery so that the jurors can place themselves in his or her shoes in their minds. None of the photographs standing alone may be of any evidentiary value, as such. They may not depict evidence or the suspect or anything else of particular evidentiary value. But when paired with witness testimony, they can greatly aid the jurors' understanding of the testimony and the other evidence.

There are other forms of visual aids that help jurors understand evidence. Flow charts, organizational charts, floor plans, diagrams, and the like may be very helpful. A flow chart may help jurors' understanding of a witness's testimony about a course of action taken or procedure followed. For example, a flow chart showing how loan documents were processed and reviewed by a bank may help the witness explain, and jurors understand, where in the process the defendant was able to introduce fictitious invoices. Organizational charts can help jurors understand the hierarchy and relationships between members of legal and illegal organizations. Floor plans can be invaluable in aiding witnesses in describing where events occurred and further the jurors' understanding of the events. Although photographs can provide a visual picture of the scene, it is often very difficult to get an understanding of a layout of a location from photographs alone. Diagrams and other visual depictions of locations or objects can have the same effect.

Timelines can also be tremendously helpful and compelling visual aids. People tend to think of events in chronological order. Keeping in mind that jurors know nothing about the case when they step into the courtroom, timelines can be very helpful to jurors in understanding the course of events. Timelines also can help jurors make cause-and-effect connections or see relationships between different events. This is especially true in cases involving crimes occurring over a long course of time, or crimes when multiple, interrelated events occurred at or near the same time. Indeed, in some instances it may be necessary to have more than one timeline, for example one timeline for the overall case and others for finite events. Officers can help construct and verify the accuracy of timelines.

Prosecutors should also consider generating summaries, graphs, or charts that synthesize voluminous or complex evidence. The rules of evidence permit the admission of summary evidence in certain circumstances when the underlying data is admissible but too voluminous to be easily understood by the jury. There is no bright line regarding what merits a summary and what does not. Prosecutors should err on the side of creating summaries when there is any doubt. Graphs and charts may also help the jury make connections between various pieces of evidence. Imagine, for example, a complex fraud and money-laundering case where it is important to understand the flow of money for the jury to understand and appreciate the defendant's guilt. A graph or chart showing the flow of money, based on other admissible evidence, may have much more impact than each of the separate pieces of evidence in helping the jury make the connections.

Finally, prosecutors may consider the generation of evidence during the trial itself. In one trial I had that lasted months and had scores of witnesses, we took photographs of each witness on the day they first testified to display to the jury and reference them during closing argument to help the jury recall the face and testimony of witnesses. On other occasions, witnesses may draw diagrams or create other exhibits in the process of testifying. Prosecutors can have these newly created documents marked as exhibits and admitted at trial.

It is the prosecutor's responsibility, of course, to work with law enforcement officers and witnesses to lay the foundation for admission of this evidence under the rules of evidence. In some cases, this will be easy but requires planning and preparation. For example, the teller can lay the foundation for admission of the photographs from the various locations in the bank, but it requires showing the teller the photographs during witness preparation and ensuring that they are accurate and were taken from a point of view that aids in the testimony. If not, the case agent may have to go back out and take more photographs. In other cases, developing the foundation for evidence may take a lot of work with the witness. Drafting flow charts of a complex procedure may require many drafts to both ensure accuracy and make it comprehensible. If the witness is unsure of how some part of the process works, it may require the witness to obtain some firsthand knowledge of that part so that the witness is able to lay a proper foundation for the evidence. In some instances, it may not be possible to lay a sufficient foundation for some visual aid, like an organizational chart, to be entered into evidence, but they may nevertheless be used during the course of the witness's testimony if it would aid the witness in illustrating a point.

Chapter Ten

Working with Grand Juries

Generally speaking, the roles and uses of grand juries differ significantly between federal and state prosecutions. As noted, the Fifth Amendment to the US Constitution requires federal prosecutors to present evidence to grand juries to establish probable cause that crimes occurred, and grand juries must return indictments before the federal government can try or convict defendants for felony offenses. The Fifth Amendment's grand jury requirement is not, however, applicable to the states under the Fourteenth Amendment. *See Hurtado v. California*, 110 US 516, 520 (1884). Although all state constitutions provide for the ability of prosecutors to empanel grand juries, most states do not require grand jury approval for bringing felony charges and others states only use grand juries infrequently.

State and local governments empanel grand juries for different purposes. Sometimes state or local prosecutors will empanel a grand jury only for specific, controversial cases, such as a shooting by a police officer, to display a greater degree of neutrality regarding the decision whether to prosecute. If the county attorney declined prosecution citing a lack of evidence, the victim's family and public may not be as willing to accept that judgment as they would if an independent grand jury declined to return an indictment against the officer. The reverse is also true. If a county attorney charged a law enforcement officer with a crime arising from the shooting, it could impair the county attorney's relationship with law enforcement officers with whom the county attorney must work every day. If a grand jury charges the officer, however, it provides the county attorney a way to avoid bearing all of the responsibility and also demonstrates to other officers that there is a legitimate basis for the charge. Some state and local governments, however, empanel grand juries as a matter of course, having the grand juries deliberate and decide whether to return an indictment on all felony charges. When grand juries are used in this latter manner, the process is largely similar to the way federal prosecutors use grand juries.

This chapter, then, will focus on federal prosecutors' use of grand juries to investigate and charge defendants. A federal prosecutor may use a federal grand jury to investigate any federal criminal offense. This includes felony offenses as well as misdemeanor crimes. There are no rules governing how prosecutors are to conduct grand jury investigations. In other words, a federal prosecutor has wide discretion to determine what documents or things or people to subpoena to appear before the grand jury. A grand jury investigation can be completed in an hour, or it may continue for years so long as the prosecutor is in good faith investigating a possible violation of federal criminal law. The scope of a grand jury's power is limited by the job it is tasked to perform—determining whether there is probable cause to believe a crime has been committed. Thus, a federal prosecutor cannot use a federal grand jury to investigate a defendant after he has been indicted unless the purpose is to pursue additional charges or defendants in a superseding indictment. *See, e.g., Costello v. United States*, 350 US 359, 362 (1956); *In re Grand Jury Subpoena Duces Tecum, Dated January 2, 1985*, 767 F.2d 26, 29-30 (2d Cir. 1985).

A grand jury occupies a "unique role" in the federal criminal justice system. *United States v. R. Enterprises, Inc.*, 498 US 292, 297 (1991). It is an investigatory body that "can investigate merely on suspicion that the law is being violated, or even just because it wants assurance that it is not." *United States v. Morton Salt Co.*, 338 US 632, 642–643 (1950). "The function of the grand jury is to inquire into all information that might possibly bear on its investigation until it has identified an offense or has satisfied itself that none has occurred." *R. Enterprises*, 498 US at 297. "A grand jury investigation 'is not fully carried out until every available clue has been run down and all witnesses examined in every proper way to find if a crime has been committed.'" *Branzburg v. Hayes*, 408 US 665, 701 (1972) (quoting *United States v. Stone*, 429 F.2d 138, 140 (2d Cir. 1970)). The investigative power of the grand jury is necessarily broad, then, if its public responsibility is to be adequately discharged. *Branzburg*, 408 US at 700. Grand juries may not, however, use their investigatory authority "to violate a valid privilege, whether established by the Constitution, statutes, or the common law." *In re Grand Jury Investigation (Detroit Police Dep't Special Cash Fund)*, 922 F.2d 1266, 1269–70 (6th Cir. 1991). Thus, a grand jury may not invade a valid privilege, such as the attorney-client privilege, attorney work product privilege, the psychotherapist privilege, marital and spousal privileges, or the Fifth Amendment privilege against self-incrimination. "The grand jury is, to a degree, an entity independent of the courts, and both the authority and obligation of the courts to control its processes are limited." *In re Grand Jury Investigation of Hugle*, 754 F.2d 863, 864 (9th Cir. 1985).

The use of a grand jury to investigate criminal activity constitutes a critical component in federal criminal cases. Federal prosecutors must develop strategies and practices for working with grand juries. This is particularly true when determining which potential witnesses to subpoena to the grand jury because grand jury time is a limited and valuable resource. Multiple prosecutors vie for time before the grand jury and so prosecutors must use the time they have before the grand jury wisely to take effective advantage of the grand jury. This chapter will discuss strategies for the effective use of grand jury power to subpoena documents, strategies for effectively using grand juries to question witnesses, best practices for determining who and when to question witnesses before grand juries, and the preparation required for effective questioning of witnesses and presentation of cases to grand juries.

STRATEGIES FOR USING THE GRAND JURY TO SUBPOENA DOCUMENTS

One of the most powerful aspects of a grand jury's ability to investigate criminal conduct is its ability to compel the production of documents. A federal grand jury has the authority to issue subpoenas duces tecum to any person or entity, including government agencies, to produce documents or things before the grand jury. Rule 17 of the Federal Rules of Criminal Procedure governs subpoenas issued under the authority of the grand jury. Rule 17 permits the issuance of grand juries subpoenas to secure testimony or to require the production of documents, or both. A grand jury's jurisdiction is limited to investigate offenses that fall within the district where the grand jury has been empaneled. *See Blair v. United States*, 250 US 273, 282–83 (1919). Nevertheless, grand juries "have authority and jurisdiction to investigate the facts to determine the question whether the facts show a case within their jurisdiction," which includes the authority to issue subpoenas to those outside the district to produce evidence relevant to the investigation. *Id.* at 283. A federal prosecutor, then, has the power to subpoena a person or entity located anywhere in the United States or its territories requiring the appearance of the person before or production of documents to a grand jury. Indeed, the grand jury subpoena power extends to US citizens living abroad in foreign countries. So, for example, a prosecutor investigating a fraud scheme in Iowa can issue a subpoena to a company in Puerto Rico to produce documents if there is a good faith belief that doing so could produce evidence that would further the criminal investigation.

The law presumes, absent a strong showing to the contrary, that a grand jury acts within the legitimate scope of its authority. *See United States v. Mechanik*, 475 US 66, 75 (1986) (O'Connor, J., concurring in judgment) ("The grand jury proceeding is accorded a presumption of regularity, which generally may be dispelled only upon particularized proof of irregularities in the grand jury process"). Thus, a grand jury subpoena issued through normal channels is presumed to be reasonable, and the recipient bears the burden of showing unreasonableness.

Generally speaking, the production of documents or objects to a grand jury is not testimonial in nature, and so is not protected by the Fifth Amendment. As a consequence, a prosecutor can serve a grand jury subpoena on a target of the grand jury investigation and compel production of documents to the grand jury. The Fifth Amendment to the United States Constitution states that "[n] o person . . . shall be compelled in any criminal case to be a witness against himself . . . ." The Fifth Amendment applies "when the accused is compelled to make a [t]estimonial [c]ommunication that is incriminating." *Fisher v. United States*, 425 US 391, 408 (1976). Courts have broadly interpreted what constitutes a "testimonial communication." Thus, in *Fisher*, the Supreme Court stated that sometimes "[t]he act of producing evidence in response to a subpoena . . . has communicative aspects of its own, wholly aside from the contents of the papers produced." 425 US at 410. For instance, by complying with a subpoena, the subpoenaed recipient may "tacitly concede [ ] the existence of the papers demanded and their possession or control," as well as his "belief that the papers are those described in the subpoena." *Fisher*, 425 US at 410. Absent a showing like this, proving that the mere production of the documents is equivalent to testimony, however, the Fifth Amendment does not apply.

If a recipient of a subpoena asserts a Fifth Amendment privilege regarding the act of producing documents to the grand jury in response to a grand jury subpoena, a prosecutor may want to consider seeking court authorization to grant act-of-production immunity. Under Title 18, US Code, Section 6002, a court may grant a witness use immunity, regardless of whether the witness agrees. If the court grants the immunity, then the witness must testify, or produce documents. The witness's Fifth Amendment right against self-incrimination is maintained, however, because the statute prohibits the use of "testimony or other information compelled under the order (or information directly or indirectly derived from such testimony or other information). . . ." 18 U.S.C. § 6002.

Like the Fifth Amendment privilege against self-incrimination, the Fourth Amendment's prohibition against unreasonable seizures does not extend to grand jury subpoenas. *United States v. Dionisio*, 410 US 1, 9 (1973). ("It is clear that a subpoena to appear before a grand jury is not a 'seizure' in the Fourth Amendment sense, even though that summons may be inconvenient or burdensome.") That is because, while a search warrant is a judicial authorization authorizing law enforcement officers to search or seize persons or things without prior notice, a subpoena is part of an adversarial process, which includes a right of the person subpoenaed to challenge the subpoena in court before complying with its demands. *Subpoena Duces Tecum v. Bailey*, 228 F.3d 341, 348 (4th Cir. 2000). Nevertheless, the Fourth Amendment does require a grand jury subpoena to be "reasonable." *Id.*, at 11–12. A subpoena is reasonable under the Fourth Amendment if it: (1) commands the production of things relevant to the grand jury's investigation; (2) specifies what must be produced with reasonable particularity; and (3) requests the production of records covering a reasonable time period. *In re Grand Jury Subpoenas*, 906 F.2d 1485, 1496 (10th Cir. 1990).

A grand jury subpoena duces tecum thus provides prosecutors with a valuable tool to investigate criminal activity. Prosecutors should think carefully, however, about when and how to use this tool. In some instances, such as issuing subpoenas to financial institutions in connection with the investigation of certain crimes, the government can prohibit a third party from disclosing the existence of the subpoena to the target. In most other cases, however, the government can only request that third parties not disclose the existence of the subpoena. To the extent that prosecutors want to keep the investigation covert, they should consider the possibility that a recipient of a grand jury subpoena duces tecum may reveal the existence of the investigation to the target of the grand jury investigation. Certainly, when the subpoena is served on the target, the target is at least aware of the investigation, although the target may not be able to always determine the scope or nature of the investigation simply from the subpoena itself.

When drafting a grand jury subpoena duces tecum, prosecutors must take care in identifying the documents sought. This involves specifically describing the documents themselves and the scope of the subpoena in terms of subject and time period. Businesses and industries utilize terms of art to refer to documents and a subpoena that fails to use those terms of art may not result in production of the desired documents. It is important, then, that prosecutors work with the law enforcement officer or others knowledgeable about the subject area to ensure that the proper language is used. This may also involve communicating with the intended recipient of the subpoena so that the prosecutor can explain in general terms what the prosecutor is looking for and have the recipient dictate the language the recipient business would like the prosecutor to use on the subpoena to obtain the desired documents.

Some investigations, like fraud investigations, may involve large amounts of documents. Compliance with subpoenas that ask for too much can be very expensive and time-consuming to review. In some cases, such as those involving financial institutions, the government will pay for the costs of copying and producing the subpoenaed documents, in most cases the recipient is not reimbursed for these costs. Further, in most cases it is counterproductive to obtain too many documents. It may be hard to find the needle if the prosecutor requires the production of a huge stack of hay. Prosecutors should therefore give careful thought to the scope of the subpoena. Prosecutors may, for example, find it more productive to, at least initially, seek production of documents reflecting sample months or weeks, or a limited time period, or for only certain types of transactions or above certain dollar amounts. The initial, limited subpoena may aid the prosecutor in discerning a pattern or identifying the documents that are most important to the investigation. The prosecutor can then issue additional, more tailored, grand jury subpoenas to get at the desired evidence and avoid having to wade through volumes of unhelpful documents.

Finally, the government can use a grand jury subpoena to require a target to provide handwriting exemplars, fingerprints, and voice exemplars. Courts have uniformly held that a defendant's Fifth Amendment right against self-incrimination is not jeopardized by production of these things because it is not the equivalent of testimony. *See, e.g., Gilbert v. California*, 388 US 263, 266–67 (1967) (compelling defendant to provide handwriting exemplars was not a violation of the Fifth Amendment because it was not testimonial); *Kyger v. Carlton*, 146 F.3d 374, 381 n.2 (6th Cir. 1998) (taking fingerprints not a Fifth Amendment violation because it is not testimonial); *United States v. Dionisio*, 410 US 1, 7 (1973) (compelling voice exemplars not a violation of Fifth Amendment because not testimonial).

STRATEGIES FOR USING THE
GRAND JURY TO SUBPOENA WITNESSES

The primary, and required, goal of presenting evidence to a grand jury is to determine whether to seek an indictment charging a subject with a felony offense. Although this is the essential purpose of a grand jury, having witnesses testify under oath before a grand jury can further other objectives. When prosecutors carefully choose and question witnesses, grand jury testimony can generate leads, shore up witnesses, and strengthen the government's case. Prosecutors need to recognize, however, that grand jury time is a finite resource. Grand juries typically meet once a month, for a few days at a time. During that session, there may be a large number of prosecutors wanting time before the grand jury to question witnesses in their cases. There is only so much time during the day, and so many days a week that a grand jury may be in session. So prosecutors must think carefully about who they question before the grand jury, on what topics, and in what detail, keeping in mind the fact that grand jury time is a limited resource.

One of the first decisions a federal prosecutor must make during the investigation stage of a case is who to subpoena as witnesses before a federal grand jury. Prosecutors also need to carefully consider when during an investigation to subpoena which witnesses to the grand jury. To make these decisions, prosecutors should first consider why one would want to subpoena any witness to the grand jury. This requires a basic understanding of the grand jury process, the goals of a grand jury presentation, and consideration of how witnesses can help achieve those goals.

The Grand Jury Process

When a prosecutor causes a grand jury subpoena to be served on a person requiring live testimony, the witness is under a court order to appear and must testify, unless to do so would be incriminating. Witnesses are not always cooperative with law enforcement officers in the field when officers attempt to question them. Some witnesses refuse to talk at all, while others provide only partial or false information. Although some witnesses feel compelled to be honest for fear of being charged with making a false statement to a law enforcement officer, all too many are not intimidated by that danger. Thus, a grand jury subpoena has the power to compel even reluctant witnesses to come forward. If they fail to appear, they are in contempt of the court's order and can be arrested and incarcerated to compel their appearance, if necessary.

On the day the witness appears to testify, a prosecutor may have an opportunity to meet with the witness prior to their testimony, and generally should do so (but always with a law enforcement officer present). The primary purpose of this meeting is to determine if the witness is represented by an attorney or is requesting an attorney, explain the process, and advise the witness of the need to be truthful. Although witnesses may not have their attorneys present in the grand jury room while testifying, they have the right to be represented by an attorney if they wish, and the government can provide counsel to those who are indigent. Prosecutors should not discourage witnesses from obtaining advice of counsel in connection with their appearance before a grand jury. Indeed, attorneys often facilitate cooperative testimony because witnesses are often more receptive and trusting of their attorneys' explanation of the power of the grand jury and the necessity to testify truthfully.

This pre-testimony meeting often has a sobering effect on many witnesses who have never had to testify and many of whom have no idea what a grand jury is or how it operates. Witnesses who previously refused to cooperate with law enforcement officers sometimes suddenly decide to cooperate. Other times, witnesses alert the prosecutor to issues that impair their willingness or ability to cooperate, such as threats made by the target of the investigation. When witnesses raise such issues in this meeting, it provides the prosecutor with an opportunity to address and hopefully mitigate or nullify those impediments.

Grand juries consist of up to twenty-three grand jurors (and a minimum of sixteen to constitute a quorum). The physical layout of rooms used by grand juries varies from courthouse to courthouse, some resembling courtrooms while others look more like conference rooms. However the physical space may appear, it is intimidating for most citizens to enter a room and be faced with that many people. A court reporter is also present, along with the prosecutor. Before the witness takes a seat, the foreperson of the grand jury places the witness under oath. The prosecutor then reads a list of rights and obligations to the witness, including a warning that the witness could be prosecuted for perjury if the witness lies.

It is not uncommon for the atmosphere of the grand jury, the oath, and the warning against committing perjury to cause heretofore reluctant or untruthful witnesses to cooperate and be truthful. Prosecutors should take this truth-compelling influence into account when determining how to use the grand jury. If a witness still refuses to testify in front of the grand jury, a prosecutor has several options to persuade or compel the witness to testify. These include granting the witness testimonial immunity or using contempt proceedings, if necessary.

Who to Subpoena to a Grand Jury

There are several reasons for choosing to question particular witnesses under oath before a grand jury. The power to compel testimony before the grand jury can aid prosecutors in discovering new information or leads, preserving testimony of witnesses for later use, locking down adverse witnesses, persuading a recalcitrant witness to testify, explaining documentary evidence, establishing an essential element of the offense, and assessing the persuasiveness of a potential witness.

First, a prosecutor may decide to subpoena a witness for the obvious purpose of discovering information then unknown to the investigators and the grand jury. These witnesses may include people who have personal knowledge about an offense or the target of the investigation. A prosecutor may have reports of interviews of these witnesses, so may have at least some idea of what the witnesses know relevant to the investigation. Nevertheless, a prosecutor may and usually does have additional or different questions that may lead to the discovery of information that is not contained in the law enforcement officer's report of interview that can be asked during a grand jury appearance. Other witnesses may not have any personal knowledge but may have heard others who have personal knowledge talk about it. Although this may be hearsay and so may not be admissible at trial, it is admissible in a grand jury where the rules of evidence do not apply. Testimony by these witnesses may generate leads or help identify people with personal knowledge.

Second, prosecutors may subpoena witnesses to the grand jury to preserve their testimony. For example, if a witness may be deported, or may be a foreign national who intends to leave the country, or an ill or aged witness who may die, having them testify before the grand jury will at least preserve their testimony. Because only the government is present before the grand jury, and such testimony is necessarily testimonial in nature, issues may arise under the Federal Rules of Evidence and the Confrontation Clause in the Sixth Amendment to the US Constitution regarding the ability of the government to use this testimony in later proceedings. It is beyond the scope of this book to delve into this area, but grand jury testimony can sometimes come into evidence, either as substantive evidence or for purposes of impeachment, even if the witness is not present at trial to testify. The grand jury testimony could also be used in proceedings where the Federal Rules of Evidence do not apply, such as at detention or sentencing hearings. Thus, although there are limits to the use of this grand jury testimony, prosecutors should remember that the grand jury can nevertheless be used to preserve the testimony of one who may not later be available to testify at trial.

Third, prosecutors may subpoena witnesses to the grand jury to lock unreliable witnesses down to some version of a story. Unreliable witnesses may include, for example, cooperators, a target's family, friends, and associates, or other potentially unfriendly witnesses who may have a motive to change their story later, when the case goes to trial. It is important to have an unreliable witness commit to a certain version of events under oath. If the prosecutor suspects a witness may change the version of events later, either volitionally or under pressure by others, a transcript of the witness's grand jury testimony under oath provides the prosecutor with the ability to impeach a witness who later testifies to a different version of events. Although the prosecutor can sometimes rely on a statement the witness previously provided to a law enforcement officer, those statements are not made under oath, usually are not verbatim, and witnesses may not have affirmed or adopted the officer's report. So even when prosecutors have such statements, they are not nearly as effective for the purpose of impeachment as a transcript of the witness's sworn testimony before a grand jury. Indeed, in certain circumstances, the Federal Rules of Evidence allow juries to use statements made before a grand jury as substantive evidence if the witness appears at trial but then refuses to testify or feigns lack of memory.

Fourth, a prosecutor may subpoena a reluctant or recalcitrant witness to the grand jury to obtain information that witness has previously been unwilling to provide to law enforcement officers. As noted, witnesses sometimes do not want to cooperate with a criminal investigation, may be intimidated by the prospect of talking to law enforcement officers, or may be afraid of retaliation from the target if he or she provides information to the police. Officers cannot make witnesses talk to them, but a prosecutor can make the witness testify before a grand jury.

Fifth, prosecutors may have document custodians testify before the grand jury in connection with the production of documents under a subpoena duces tecum. Typically, prosecutors excuse third-party recipients of duces tecum subpoenas from having to actually appear before the grand jury to produce the documents so long as they produce them to the case agent.[1] Sometimes, however, the prosecutor may want to have a document custodian produce documents to the grand jury, particularly if there is some question about whether the witness or entity has fully complied with the subpoena. The prosecutor can question such witnesses about what they did to comply with the subpoena, where they looked for responsive documents, and who may have helped them comply with the subpoena. On other occasions a prosecutor may think it helpful to have a document custodian answer those and other questions not because there is any suspicion that the recipient failed to fully comply with the subpoena but, rather, to help the prosecutor and grand jury better understand the documents. Prosecutors may subpoena other witnesses to the grand jury to explain documents or other pieces of evidence. Sometimes it is helpful for the grand jury to better understand a complex case by having someone with knowledge of the subject introduce a piece of evidence (for example, a forensic analyst to explain a computer forensic report) and explain its meaning and importance to the grand jury.

Sixth, prosecutors may choose to subpoena witnesses to appear before the grand jury simply to present evidence establishing an essential element of the offense so as to allow the grand jury to return an indictment. So, for example, the offense of being a felon in possession of a firearm has three elements: (1) the defendant knowingly possessed a firearm, (2) the defendant had previously been convicted of a crime that was punishable by more than one year in prison, and (3) the firearm was transported in interstate commerce. Thus, to establish probable cause that the target committed the offense and obtain an indictment, a prosecutor must subpoena some witness to the grand jury to testify that the target's criminal history shows a prior conviction and to prove that the firearm was manufactured outside the state. The case agent can perform this role because hearsay is admissible before the grand jury.

Finally, sometimes prosecutors subpoena witnesses to the grand jury just to see how they will perform as a witness. Prosecutors may do this, for example, with child victims of exploitation, elderly witnesses, expert witnesses, witnesses with English as a second language, or mentally disabled witnesses. Prosecutors may subpoena such witnesses not only to testify about information relevant to the investigation, but also so the prosecutor has an opportunity to observe how the witness performs while testifying in front of an audience. This can be valuable in assessing the credibility of witnesses and the strength of the government's case and can serve as a starting point for working with witnesses to improve their performance if they are required as a witness in a later hearing or trial.

Incidentally, case law provides that prosecutors may use the power of the grand jury to subpoena targets of grand jury investigations to appear before grand juries. *See United States v. Wong*, 431 US 174, 179 n.8 (1977). The US Department of Justice has a general policy, however, against issuing subpoenas for targets to appear before the grand jury. UNITED STATES ATTORNEY'S MANUAL 9-11.150. Thus, although a prosecutor may constitutionally subpoena a target before the grand jury, Department of Justice policy requires prior approval of the US Attorney for the district or the responsible Assistant Attorney General. A target may also volunteer to appear before the grand jury. There are advantages and disadvantages of having a target appear before the grand jury investigating him or her. For example, through charisma or by invoking sympathy or by inviting jury nullification, a target may be able to persuade a grand jury not to indict the target. Conversely, a target may make incriminating statements before the grand jury or be caught lying or trying to obstruct the grand jury's investigation, making the target's situation worse. Generally speaking, prosecutors should allow targets to testify before the grand jury because in most instances the target will either make incriminating statements or lie, and seldom will a target be able to persuade a grand jury not to indict if there is indeed sufficient evidence to prove the target committed the crime.

When to Subpoena Witnesses to the Grand Jury

Once a prosecutor determines whom to subpoena as witnesses to the grand jury, the prosecutor must determine when to subpoena those people to testify before the grand jury. In part, it depends on why the prosecutor is calling the witness in the first place. For example, a prosecutor looking to uncover facts might subpoena a witness that serves this purpose before he or she calls a witness simply to determine how the witness performs or to establish an essential element of the offense. Similarly, in trying to unravel a crime or discover who committed it and how it was committed, the nature of the case may dictate questioning certain witnesses before the grand jury before questioning others. Likewise, the natural course of the investigation may dictate the order of grand jury witnesses and their timing; low-level cooperating drug dealer defendants will likely testify before others higher in the drug organization as the investigation works up the chain of supply.

A critical component in determining the timing of subpoenaing witnesses to the grand jury is how the grand jury investigation fits into the overall covert and overt status and nature of the criminal investigation. Unless a prosecutor is subpoenaing a law enforcement officer or someone in a similar position to the grand jury, there is always a risk that the witness may reveal the existence of the investigation to the target. After all, a grand jury witness may lawfully tell anyone about appearing before the grand jury and what the witness said to the grand jury. If there are other covert law enforcement procedures contemplated as part of the investigation, then the prosecutor will probably want to delay subpoenaing witnesses to the grand jury until all other covert operations have been completed.

Ultimately, prosecutors must subpoena all witnesses they wish to question to the grand jury before it returns the indictment. Once an indictment is returned, it is improper to use the grand jury power to gather evidence, conduct pretrial discovery, or otherwise engage in preparation for trial. *See, e.g., United States v. Sasso*, 59 F.3d 341, 351–52 (2d Cir. 1995); *Resolution Trust Corp. v. Thornton*, 41 F.3d 1539, 1546–47 (D.C. Cir. 1994) (collecting cases). Thus, the grand jury process is abused if it is used "for the primary purpose of strengthening the government's case on a pending indictment or as a substitute for discovery." *United States v. Jenkins*, 904 F.2d 549, 559–60 (10th Cir. 1990). Even after an indictment is returned, however, the grand jury may still be used to pursue additional charges or additional defendants in an ongoing investigation, even if the effect is to aid in the prosecution of the original defendant on the original charge. *See, e.g., Sasso*, 59 F.3d at 352; *United States v. Phibbs*, 999 F.2d 1053, 1077 (6th Cir. 1993).

PREPARING FOR QUESTIONING
WITNESSES BEFORE THE GRAND JURY

To be truly effective and efficient utilizing the grand jury as a tool in the investigation, prosecutors must prepare for questioning witnesses. Because no judge is present, there is no defense attorney present to object to questions, the government's burden of proof only a preponderance of the evidence, and often the prosecutor is trying to discover unknown facts as opposed to present known ones, prosecutors may be less motivated to prepare carefully for questioning witnesses before a grand jury than they would be preparing witnesses to testify at a trial. Thus, a busy or lazy prosecutor may be tempted to approach the task of questioning witnesses before the grand jury with little advanced preparation, ready to wing it. This would be a mistake.

It is before the grand jury that a prosecutor can test and probe witnesses for weaknesses, elicit testimony that fully explores the scope and nature of the criminal activity under investigation, and develop a record that enhances the believability of credible witnesses or exposes the lies of others. To accomplish these goals of questioning witnesses successfully takes careful preparation. Just as prosecutors must carefully determine who to call as witnesses, when to call them, and in what order, so too prosecutors must carefully determine the scope of questioning, the questions to ask, and the order in which to ask them. Thus, prosecutors should draft an outline of questions for each grand jury witness, thinking carefully about these factors.

Before drafting such outlines, however, prosecutors should keep in mind how the prosecutor, and the defense attorney, may use the transcript of the witness's testimony. Prosecutors may use the transcripts of grand jury witnesses in several ways. A prosecutor may use the transcript of a grand jury witness to draft an outline of questions for the witness's trial testimony. Trial witnesses should review the transcripts of their testimony before the grand jury to refresh their memories in preparation for their trial testimony. Finally, both prosecutors and defense attorneys can use grand jury transcripts to refresh the recollection of a trial witness, to impeach the witness, and in some instances even use it as substantive evidence. Knowing how the transcript can be used should help prosecutors focus drafting questions to elicit the information they want and need.

In drafting questions for grand jury witnesses, prosecutors should not focus on methods of persuasion. In other words, there are techniques for asking witnesses questions during direct examination at trial that can aid in the persuasiveness of the testimony, such as looping and repetition. Prosecutors should dispense with these techniques before a grand jury because the government need only persuade a grand jury by a preponderance of the evidence standard. That is such a low burden that prosecutors should not be worried about structuring questions in a way to enhance the witness's persuasiveness. It is far better to structure questions in a manner to get at the truth.

Prosecutors should think carefully about how to ask questions of a witness in a way to most likely elicit truth. How to do this will depend on the facts and the witness, but the point is that prosecutors should think hard about this and draft an outline of questions accordingly. With potentially adverse or untruthful witnesses, it is often most effective to draw out the truth if the prosecutor asks questions first that lock the witness into certain facts in a manner that does not clue the witness into the significance before asking questions that would elicit information the witness would recognize as significant. Sometimes this can be accomplished by misdirection. For example, in a case where the target is believed to be an unlawful drug user in possession of a firearm, it would be best to ask questions establishing the witness's long-term knowledge of the target, that the witness has been to the target's house before, and then ask if the witness has ever seen the target selling drugs. The witness is likely to say no to protect the target. Then the prosecutor can ask if the target is "just a drug user." The witness is likely to view testimony that the target just uses drugs as exculpatory and may admit it. Once the witness has admitted seeing the target "just" use drugs, the prosecutor may then ask detailed follow-up questions as to when, where, how, and so on. By the time the prosecutor asks these detailed questions, the witness may realize that mere drug use might get the target into trouble for some reason. But by then the witness has already been locked down on the fact of drug use and would be less able to back out of that testimony.

When questioning cooperators before the grand jury, prosecutors should be sure to pin the cooperator down to the essential facts of the cooperator's version of events. This will allow the prosecutor to test that testimony against other evidence to assess its credibility. It will also ensure that the witness is locked down to the essentials so that the prosecutor can use the transcript to impeach the witness if the cooperator tries to change his story later.

The prosecutor should not try to ask any cooperators or neutral witnesses (such as eyewitnesses or fact witnesses with no biased interest in the case) questions that would elicit needless details. The more detailed the questions, the more likely the witness may make a mistake about a detail. Even though it could be an innocent mistake, at trial a defense attorney could still use that mistake to impeach the witness's credibility. So prosecutors should ask only for details that are important to the case.

Finally, prosecutors should intentionally ask questions of grand jury witnesses designed to draw out and elicit any exculpatory evidence or information that would be damaging to the government's case. This seems counterintuitive, but it is not. Prosecutors should not hesitate to ask questions of grand jury witnesses because they are afraid that the answer may hurt the government's case. It is far, far better to discover adverse evidence in the grand jury than at trial. The government's burden is so low before a grand jury that if adverse testimony in the grand jury could cause the grand jury not to return an indictment, then the prosecutor has no business charging the defendant in the first place. Prosecutors should see the grand jury as the place to discover everything bad there is about their cases.

PRESENTING CASES TO GRAND JURIES FOR INDICTMENT

Presenting a case to a grand jury will consist of questioning witnesses, returning documents subpoenaed through the grand jury's authority, charging the jury, then receiving the grand jury's verdict after deliberations. Although the law permits federal prosecutors to present opening statements and closing arguments to a grand jury, a common practice is not to do so, certainly not in the manner one would do so for a petite jury. Remembering that the burden of proof is only a preponderance of the evidence in the grand jury, prosecutors should not be concerned about persuading a reluctant grand jury to return an indictment. Indeed, if the prosecutor believes the case is so close of a call for indictment that it requires persuasion by the prosecutor, then the prosecutor should think twice before asking the grand jury for an indictment in the first instance. That said, in some complex cases a prosecutor may consider presenting a truncated opening statement focused on providing a roadmap to the grand jurors of the complexities and explaining the course the evidence will take so that the grand jurors are better able to understand the evidence as it is presented.

On the other hand, sometimes it is helpful for the jury to understand the evidence if the prosecutor begins a grand jury session with a simple outline of the business before the grand jury. In other words, at the beginning of a session before a grand jury, a prosecutor may want to identify the target, describe the crimes under investigation, and identify the witnesses that will appear before the grand jury that day. Indeed, identifying the target and witnesses is important to make sure that none of the grand jurors know them and, if they do, to determine if their familiarity with the target or witness would affect their ability to be fair and impartial.

After all of the evidence has been presented to the grand jury, federal prosecutors should then inform the grand jury that the prosecutor is asking the grand jurors to return an indictment. The prosecutor should identify and explain the elements of the offense, unless the grand jury is an experienced one and already familiar with the elements. Depending on the local practice, the prosecutor should either read the indictment to the grand jury or provide the indictment to the foreperson, who will then review it with the other grand jurors during deliberations. After deliberations (during which only grand jurors are present in the room), the foreperson will let the prosecutor know the grand jury has completed its deliberations and voted on the indictment. The prosecutor then re-enters the grand jury room with the court reporter, receives the indictment from the foreperson, and makes a record of the votes (for example, "The record will reflect that the grand jury has deliberated and returned a true bill with twenty-two of twenty-three grand jurors concurring in the finding of probable cause. Ms. Foreperson, is this your signature that appears on the indictment and ballot?"). The prosecutor should then sign the indictment in the presence of the grand jury. The indictment will later be returned to a judge in open court.

Chapter Eleven

Charging Strategies and Tactics

Prosecutors have a tremendous amount of discretion in determining how to charge defendants in criminal cases. They have the discretion to choose who should be charged. If there is more than one target, prosecutors have the discretion to determine whether to charge the targets in a single indictment or multiple indictments. When charging multiple defendants together in the same charging document, prosecutors have discretion in choosing the order of identifying defendants in a multi-defendant indictment and the order of charges in a multi-count indictment. If there are multiple targets and the prosecutor chooses to charge the targets in multiple indictments, the prosecutor has the discretion to determine whether to charge all of the targets at the same time or charge them at separate times, and the order in which to bring the charges if the prosecutor chooses to bring multiple indictments at different times. Prosecutors have discretion in choosing the charges to bring against targets, whether to bring all possible charges or just some. In some cases, prosecutors have discretion in how many charges to bring arising from a criminal course of conduct, depending on the unit of prosecution. Finally, prosecutors have some discretion in the language they use in making the accusations in an indictment.

Prosecutorial discretion is restrained, however, in some ways. Sometimes directives from the Attorney General or other supervisors compel prosecutors to bring certain charges or refrain from bringing certain charges. For example, during some administrations, the US Attorney General required prosecutors to charge the most serious readily provable offense. During other administrations the Attorney General instructed prosecutors not to charge people with distribution of marijuana absent the presence of certain aggravating factors. Also, other things outside a prosecutor's control, such as a looming statute of limitation, may restrict the prosecutor's options. The language of the indictment is dictated in part by the requirement that indictments must contain allegations of facts that meet all of the elements of the offense, jurisdiction, venue, and statute of limitations. Indictments must otherwise have sufficient detail to fully inform the accused so that, under the Double Jeopardy Clause, the accused can ensure they have not previously been charged with the offense.

Prosecutors should give careful thought to the strategic and tactical considerations inherent in making charging decisions. Prosecutors should think strategically in making charging decisions in a manner that will have the greatest impact on the case as a whole, that will effectively shut down the criminal activity or organization, and that will enable proper punishment and, when applicable, vindicate the rights of victims through fines or restitution. Indeed, prosecutors must consider the greater strategic interests involved not only in the case at hand, but must also take into account how the charges in the instant case may affect other unrelated cases currently pending and cases that may be brought in the future. For example, a prosecutor must consider whether charges in the instant case will tax the resources of the office so as to negatively impact the ability of the office to prosecute other pending cases. Similarly, a successful prosecution of the case at hand, or an unsuccessful prosecution, may impact the office's ability to prosecute similar cases in the future or impact the likelihood that defendants in future cases will plead guilty. Prosecutors must also make charging decisions that will have the tactical effect of advancing the overall strategic goals. Each decision to charge each target with particular crimes should focus on the immediate aims, but with an eye toward how it fits with other tactical charging decisions to help achieve the strategic goals. For example, in a drug case the strategic goal may be to shut down a drug organization, and tactical aims may be to charge lower-level dealers with the goal of working up the chain of distribution. In a fraud case, the strategic goal may be to stop the fraudulent activity and make the victims whole, while the tactical aims may be to bring a charge quickly to exert control over the target and his or her assets, and later bring all of the additional charges that may be appropriate after there was time to fully investigate the extent of the criminal activity.

Although I will discuss aspects of each of the charging decisions a prosecutor must make, it is important for prosecutors to think of all of the charging decisions as part of the greater whole. The decision of whom to charge may affect who else could be charged. A decision to charge one crime may preclude charging another, or the ability to prosecute another target. Each charging decision can impact other charging decisions. Thus, like a chess player, prosecutors must think several moves in advance, recognizing that each move affects future moves.

WHO SHOULD BE CHARGED

The most fundamental decision for any prosecutor to make is whom to charge. This seemingly simple question is much more nuanced than at first it might appear. Among the considerations in making this decision is determining the amount of evidence a prosecutor should have before charging someone with a criminal offense. Even when a prosecutor believes there is sufficient evidence to charge a target, the prosecutor must also decide whether to charge a target, find some other way to hold the target accountable, or decline to prosecute the target.

It is axiomatic that the government can charge someone with a criminal offense based on evidence establishing probable cause to believe the person committed the crime. The more difficult but important question is whether a prosecutor should charge every target for whom the evidence establishes probable cause the target committed a criminal offense. Generally speaking, prosecutors should hesitate to charge targets when the evidence currently known to the prosecutor is only sufficient to establish probable cause. Rather, prosecutors should not bring charges against a target until and unless the prosecutor believes the evidence currently known to the prosecutor is sufficient to establish proof beyond a reasonable doubt.

As counterintuitive as this may sound, there are several reasons why prosecutors should only bring charges when there is evidence to prove a defendant's guilt beyond a reasonable doubt, even though the legal burden of proof necessary for indictment is significantly lower. First, at trial the prosecutor will have to persuade a jury of the defendant's guilt beyond a reasonable doubt. It is logical, then, that a prosecutor should desire that quantum of evidence at the charging stage. Second, it is a sound exercise of discretion in a system of justice that prosecutors refrain from charging a person with a crime when a prosecutor only has enough evidence to establish probable cause. Third, if a prosecutor charges a case with only enough evidence to establish probable cause, the prosecutor's case may never get any stronger and the prosecutor may lose at trial. Although it was my experience that the government's case almost invariably got significantly stronger as trial approached, especially when the prosecutor ensured the agents continued to investigate the crime, that is not always the case. And a loss at trial can have significant strategic ramifications. The government wins more than 90 percent of the cases that

proceed to trial, especially the federal government when prosecutors have to-
tal discretion on whether to bring charges. Defendants and defense attorneys
know this, which impacts defendants' decisions whether to enter guilty pleas.
When, however, the government loses at trial it can embolden defendants to
roll the dice at trial. This, in turn, can result in more trials and consequently
a greater strain on the government's resources, which may in turn further
negatively impact the win/loss ratio for the government. Thus, a wise and fair
prosecutor will hesitate to charge a defendant when the evidence then known
to the prosecutor would do no more than establish probable cause.

There are times, however, when other factors may militate toward charging
a target when there is only sufficient evidence to establish probable cause.
Exigent circumstances may dictate the need for immediate charges. If a target is on the verge of fleeing, or people are being victimized by the target,
immediate charges may be required, especially if the prosecutor has good
reason to believe that the government will readily be able to develop more
evidence. Law enforcement officers make these kinds of decisions all of the
time, recognizing that the evidence then known to the officer may not be
overwhelming, but recognizing that the urgency of the circumstances dictates
immediate charges based on probable cause. When prosecutors decide to
charge a defendant based only on probable cause, they should be increasingly
sensitive to the possibility that the defendant is not guilty. Prosecutors should
act as quickly as possible to advance the investigation and determine whether
there is, in fact, additional evidence to prove the defendant's guilty beyond
a reasonable doubt. If a prosecutor concludes there is not such evidence, the
prosecutor should move to dismiss the charge without prejudice. A dismissal
without prejudice permits the government to refile the charges if, at a later
date, more evidence is found. A dismissal with prejudice means that the government is barred under the Double Jeopardy Clause from ever charging the
defendant with the same crime again.

Even when a prosecutor is persuaded that there is evidence beyond a reasonable doubt to establish a target's guilt, the prosecutor must still decide
whether to bring the charge at all. Sometimes justice is best served by not
charging a person with a crime. There may be exceptional circumstances surrounding the crime that call for restraint by the government. For example, it
may not be appropriate to charge a ninety-five-year-old man with murder for
helping his cancer-ridden, ninety-seven-year-old wife die by giving her sleep-
ing pills. Similarly, a prosecutor may decide that justice is best served by having another government charge the defendant because the resulting sentence
would be more just. For example, a federal prosecutor trying to dismantle a
far-flung drug conspiracy may decide that justice is best served by having the
county prosecutor charge a very low-level courier with an offense that carries

a maximum of five years in state prison, rather than charge the courier as part of the federal conspiracy where the person would face a ten-year mandatory minimum sentence. In making these decisions, the prosecutor is considering not what the prosecutor can do, but what the prosecutor should do.

MULTI-DEFENDANT/MULTI-CHARGES CHARGING DECISIONS

Prosecutors frequently work on cases involving multiple targets. At some stage of the investigation, the prosecutor may have developed sufficient evidence to charge more than one of the targets. When this occurs, the prosecutor must decide how to proceed. Prosecutors must decide whether to charge all of the defendants at once in a single indictment or charge the targets separately in a series of indictments. When charging multiple defendants in a single indictment, prosecutors must decide the order the prosecutor identifies the defendants in the caption of the case. When charging a defendant or defendants with multiple offenses, prosecutors must determine the order of the charges in the indictment. When prosecutors choose to charge multiple targets in separate indictments, the prosecutors must determine the order of the indictments: whom to prosecute first, whom second, and so on.

Single Indictment vs. Multiple Indictments

In considering whether to charge all of the targets in a single indictment or in a series of indictments, prosecutors should weigh a number of factors. First, prosecutors must determine whether the defendants could be properly joined together in a single indictment. Rule 8(b) of the Federal Rules of Criminal Procedure provides:

> Two or more defendants may be charged in the same indictment or information if they are alleged to have participated in the same act or transaction or in the same series of acts or transactions constituting an offense or offenses. Such defendants may be charged in one or more counts together or separately and all of the defendants need not be charged in each count.

FED. R. CRIM. P. 8(b). Defendants joined in the same indictment need not be charged in each count together. *United States v. Wadena*, 152 F.3d 831, 847 (8th Cir. 1998). Thus, prosecutors may charge multiple defendants in a single indictment when the defendants have participated in the same act or transaction or when the defendants have participated in the same series of acts or transactions. FED. R. CRIM. P. 8(b). In other words, under this rule the defendants must have acted together in some manner to be charged together in the same indictment. One defendant may be charged in all six counts of an indictment, for example, while another defendant may be charged in only one or two of the counts in the indictment.

A conspiracy charge is an obvious way of charging multiple parties in the same indictment by alleging that they acted together to commit a crime. *United States v. Vasquez-Velasco*, 15 F.3d 833, 838 (9th Cir. 1994). Indeed, members of the same conspiracy generally should be charged together in the same indictment and tried together when possible. *United States v. Mathison*, 157 F.3d 541, 546 (8th Cir. 1998) (noting that courts have repeatedly held that defendants charged in a conspiracy should be tried together). This is the case even when one member of the conspiracy may have occupied a very minor role, while another member of the conspiracy occupied a leadership role.

On the other hand, it is not appropriate to charge multiple defendants in the same indictment if there is no real connection between them and their actions. Thus, it is not appropriate to charge multiple defendants in the same indictment simply because they committed the same offenses at approximately the same time, unless there is some further connection between them. *United States v. Vasquez-Velasco*, 15 F.3d 833 (9th Cir. 1994). In looking to determine whether joinder of defendants in the same indictment is proper, a court will look to the face of the indictment itself. In most cases, it is not appropriate for the court to look at the facts underlying the indictment to determine if joinder was proper. *Costello v. United States*, 350 US 359 (1956).

Prosecutors should also think about practical considerations in determining whether to charge multiple defendants in a single indictment or whether to spread them out in a series of indictments. At a very practical level, prosecutors should consider whether the number of defendants would be manageable if all of them declined to enter guilty pleas and all went to trial. Although more than 95 percent of all defendants plead guilty in the federal system, sometimes they do not. This may particularly be true when prosecutors charge a large number of members of a tightly knit criminal organization in a single indictment. The defendants in such cases may continue to work together, each refusing plea offers, forcing the government to try them all in a single trial. The question for the prosecutor, then, is whether it would be physically and practically manageable to try all of the defendants together in a single trial. The courtroom may only be able to seat a half-dozen defendants at one time. Although courts have, on occasion, used auditoriums or other larger venues for trials of a large number of defendants, that is not an ideal situation and involves a lot of logistical issues.

On the other hand, if a prosecutor is able to charge all of the members of a criminal operation in a single indictment, it may encourage defendants to plead and cooperate with the government more than if they were charged in a series of indictments. An indictment that charges all of the defendants of a criminal operation together can effectively telegraph to the defendants that the government has fully uncovered their criminal operation, it has captured everyone involved, and it has a solid case. As defendants look around the courtroom at their co-defendants, it often results in a rush by defendants to cooperate with the government against the others to get the best deal. In contrast, when an indictment names only a few of the people involved in a criminal operation, those charged may be reluctant to cooperate from fear of retaliation against them or their loved ones by those who have not yet been charged or pressured by those not yet charged to hang tight and go to trial. Even when these defendants do choose to plead and cooperate, they may not fully disclose all of the information they have because they may believe the government does not yet know the full extent of the criminal conduct.

Whenever prosecutors consider charging a group of targets in a single indictment, they should also carefully assess the amount and quality of evidence as to each target. It may be tempting to charge all of the suspected members of a drug conspiracy, believing that the evidence of the conspiracy itself is overwhelming. Although that may be true, the evidence of a particular target's involvement in the conspiracy may not be so strong. Prosecutors must not overlook the weaknesses of the evidence against individual targets because they are focused on the evidence of the larger case. All too often, when prosecutors fail to do this, the one defendant who elects to go to trial and make the government prove its case is the defendant against whom the government has the least amount of evidence. It may be better to charge only those defendants against whom the strongest evidence exists with the hope that some will cooperate and thereby provide additional evidence against remaining targets.

In the end, there is no bright line test for when a prosecutor should charge all targets together in a single indictment and when the prosecutor should charge them in more than one indictment. It is a matter of judgment and weighing of the different factors.

Multiple Charges Considerations

Whether there is a single target or multiple targets, there is sometimes probable cause to support more than one criminal charge. Prosecutors must decide, then, which charges to bring. Assuming there is sufficient evidence to support each possible charge, there are a number of factors prosecutors must consider in deciding which charges to bring.

To begin with, the charges must be properly joined in the same indictment under the criminal procedural rules. Similar to the joinder of multiple parties in a single indictment, prosecutors may charge more than one offense in a single indictment. This is permitted when the offenses are: (1) of the same or similar character; (2) based upon the same act or transaction; or (3) are in some way connected together or part of a common scheme or plan. FED. R. CRIM. P. 8(a). In determining whether multiple charges are properly charged in the same indictment, prosecutors should consider whether the crimes involved the same method of committing the offense (modus operandi) and whether they were committed reasonably close in time. *United States v. Edgar*, 82 F.3d 499 (1st Cir. 1996). There must be some logical connection between the offenses, just as there has to be some logical connection between defendants to charge them in the same indictment.

Prosecutors should also consider the relative strength of the possible charges. Assuming the charges could be properly joined under Rule 8, and assuming there is sufficient evidence to support each charge, still the quality and quantity of evidence supporting each charge will likely vary and sometimes differ significantly. A weak charge may benefit from being coupled with stronger charges, yet stronger charges may also be weakened by being included with charges for which there is relatively little evidence. Prosecutors must carefully weigh the costs and benefits of including charges that seem weak relative to other charges. There may be sentencing considerations or other factors that militate toward including a charge even if it is weak relative to other charges.

There may be strategic reasons to hold off on bringing all possible charges in an indictment, even when the evidence supporting a charge may be strong. Some charges carry mandatory minimum sentences or other harsh sentencing consequences. If a prosecutor brings those charges in an indictment only to dismiss them as part of a plea bargain, it can create an impression among defense counsel that the prosecutor either overcharges cases or is afraid to go to trial and will dismiss charges to avoid the courtroom. If prosecutors hold those charges in a back pocket, however, and let defense counsel know they will be brought if the defendant does not plead guilty, it creates a very different impression among the defense bar. A prosecutor may also delay bringing a charge because the prosecutor would have to disclose information in discovery that could jeopardize other criminal investigations if disclosed. For example, a prosecutor may charge a drug dealer with the distribution of drugs on a particular day but refrain from charging the dealer with money laundering in connection with the larger drug conspiracy because the prosecutor is still investigating the money laundering that involves other targets. Bringing the money-laundering charge at the same time as the drug charge could jeopardize the money-laundering investigation and therefore the prosecutor may want to hold off.

Order of Defendants and Charges in Single Indictments

When a prosecutor indicts a case involving either multiple defendants or multiple charges, or both, a decision must be made as to the order for listing the defendants and charges in the indictment. Although this seems unimportant, and in most cases it is of little importance, still some thought should be put into the decision for a few reasons. First, the order of the defendants listed in a multi-defendant indictment can impact the impression people, including the defendants, have about the case and the defendants. The first name listed will be the shorthand name of the case for all time forward. If John Doe is the first named defendant, it will be known as the Doe case; if Bob Smith is listed first, it will be the Smith case. The first defendant named in the indictment carries the suggestion that that defendant is the leader or the most criminally culpable defendant. This can have a psychological impact on the defendants and others, including jurors. Thus, a prosecutor should put some thought into the order if the prosecutor wants to convey a message through the ordering of the defendants in a multi-defendant indictment. Generally speaking, it makes the most sense to list the defendants in a hierarchical order, all other things being equal, because that is the implied message regardless of whether it was intended. If a prosecutor wants to avoid trying to convey any message by the order of the defendants listed, then listing defendants in alphabetical order is the best way to do this.

When arriving at the order of the charges, other factors should be considered. The verdict form the jury fills out will be in the order of the charges. Thus, prosecutors may want to think about whether a certain order of charges would have an influence in how the jury deliberates. For example, if a defendant is charged with drug distribution and carrying a firearm in furtherance of a drug trafficking offense, it may make the most sense to have the drug charge first and gun charge second. With regard to the gun charge, the jury would be instructed that the first element of the offense is whether the defendant committed the drug trafficking offense. When filling out the verdict form, then, it could help the jury narrow down its decision as to the gun count if the jury had already found the defendant guilty of drug trafficking in Count 1.

Generally speaking, it is also preferable to list group conduct charges before individual crimes. In other words, a prosecutor should list a drug conspiracy charge first, followed by individual counts of distribution of drugs by one or more members of that larger conspiracy. Again, if the jurors find the defendants committed the drug conspiracy offense, their focus on offenses by individual defendants is colored by the decision the jury has already made that the defendant was a member of the conspiracy.

Finally, all other things being equal, charges should be listed in chronological order. Again, when jurors are struggling to reach verdicts in the jury room, they will be trying to go through the evidence in a logical manner. Chronological order is a natural default and likely the way the prosecutor presented the evidence at trial and argued about it in closing argument. Thus, counts chronologically ordered by date of events generally helps the jurors in the deliberation process.

In some cases, however, it may make more logical sense to order the counts by defendant in multi-defendant, multi-count indictments. In some multi-defendant cases, there are a series of offenses committed by individual defendants covering an extended period of time. Rather than list offenses in strictly chronological order, it may make more sense to a jury during deliberations, and to the prosecutor during closing argument, to consider the evidence defendant by defendant. In other multi-defendant, multi-count indictments it may make more sense to group counts by similar crimes, regardless of the chronological order in which the crimes were committed or by the defendants who committed them. One very complex case I had as a prosecutor involved bank fraud, environmental crimes, and immigration violations all committed over the course of a few years by upper management of a company. Some defendants were involved in all of the types of criminal conduct, while others in just one or two of the categories. Thinking about how we wanted to argue the case to the jury and how we wanted the jury to approach the task of reaching a verdict, we decided to order the counts by type of crime and then within each category of criminal conduct by defendant.

The point is that in drafting a charging document, prosecutors should put some careful thought into the message they want to convey (if any) by the order in which they list the defendants and the impact the order of the charges will have on the jury's deliberations.

Multiple Indictments against Multiple Targets

When prosecutors weigh the various factors and decide that it is best to charge a group of targets in more than one indictment, prosecutors must then determine the order in which to charge the targets. This requires some very careful consideration and critical weighing of competing factors. Generally speaking, prosecutors should try to work up the chain of command in a criminal organization. That may suggest that prosecutors would want to indict the least culpable defendants first with the hope and plan that many of them would choose to plead guilty and cooperate against those higher in the organization. Prosecutors certainly do not want to be in the position of using the big fish to go after the little fish and be stuck cutting favorable deals to the big fish. On the other hand, prosecutors must keep in mind the potential that those targets not indicted in the first indictment may flee or attempt to obstruct the investigation by destroying evidence, or by harming or intimidating witnesses or the defendants who were charged in the first indictment. That would suggest that perhaps the prosecutor should indict the most criminally culpable targets first.

There may be case-specific factors that suggest a different order in bringing indictments against multiple targets. As noted, to hobble a criminal organization it may be important to indict key players in the first indictment. A prosecutor may also decide it is important to indict a particular violent or charismatic defendant quickly to embolden recalcitrant targets to cooperate when otherwise they may be too afraid or too under the spell of another to do so. And prosecutors may choose to hold off on charging some defendants until later rounds of indictment when the strength of the evidence is weaker relative to other defendants.

WHAT TO CHARGE

Prosecutors almost always have options regarding what charges they could bring against targets arising from the criminal conduct under investigation. Criminal conduct is often of such a nature, and the scope of some criminal statutes of sufficient breadth, that prosecutors usually could bring multiple and various charges against targets. Prosecutors may use their discretion in determining which offenses to charge, often guided by policy directives from above and influenced by local practices. As noted, during some administrations, at a national level, federal prosecutors were directed to charge the most serious, readily provable offense against defendants, while under other administrations they were directed not to charge defendants with marijuana-related offenses unless the criminal conduct involved certain other aggravating facts. Similarly, due to the long-term culture of a prosecutor's office, local practice in one office may lead to prosecutors bringing certain types of charges while in another local office they do not. For example, some US Attorneys' Offices are much more likely to bring charges under Title 18, US Code, Section 924(c) (using a firearm in furtherance of a drug offense or violent crime) than other offices.

Administrations change, and with them policy directives, and local practices evolve and shift over time. Prosecutors must be responsive to both national directives and influences of local practice. Nevertheless, there are other more stable factors that prosecutors should consider in making strategic and tactical charging decisions. First, prosecutors must decide whether to charge a defendant with every conceivable crime that the evidence might support, and if not, what factors should influence which charges to bring. Second, prosecutors should consider the punishment consequences of their charging decisions, both for the possible sentence in terms of years of incarceration and fines, but also the collateral consequences to defendants and others from the charges.

Before discussing these factors, it is important to note that in making these charging decisions prosecutors should assume that every case will result in a trial. Although the vast majority of criminal cases result in guilty pleas, when cases do go to trial the charging decisions the prosecutors made up front can significantly influence the nature of the trial and the likelihood of success at trial. Trial is the ultimate crucible testing the competency and adequacy of a prosecutor's charging decision. So wise prosecutors make charging decisions assuming that every charge will be tested by trial. Further, thoughtful prosecutors will re-examine their charging decisions as the likelihood of trial increases, keeping in mind that the prosecutor may be able to change the charges before trial. Sometimes prosecutors recognize as trial approaches that the original charging decisions were erroneous or overly aggressive either at the time they were made or in light of changing evidence or circumstances. Discretion is sometimes the better part of valor, and a confident prosecutor will not hesitate to dismiss some or all charges when justice so demands. Conversely, after re-examining the evidence as trial approaches, prosecutors may conclude that additional or other charges are supported by the evidence. If the prosecutor is preparing for trial in a timely manner, there may be enough time to resubmit the case to the grand jury to obtain a superseding indictment changing or adding to the charges.

Choosing Charges

Criminal conduct will often give rise to a variety of possible criminal charges. Setting aside for now the impact certain charges might have on sentencing and collateral consequences, a prosecutor must first decide whether to charge every possible crime that could arise from the criminal conduct. There are a number of factors prosecutors should consider in making this critical decision. These include the strength of the evidence as to each charge, the evidentiary burden on the prosecutor to prove each charge, the impact of plea negotiations, in some cases the unit of prosecution, and the impact on victims and the public.

In considering possible charges, prosecutors should obviously consider the strength of the evidence for each possible charge. Although that may seem obvious, there is often a temptation to charge all possible crimes that the evidence may support, instead of charging just those offenses for which there is proof beyond a reasonable doubt. Prosecutors may be influenced by law enforcement officers, other prosecutors, or just the excitement of the case and lose sight of the need to differentiate between possible charges. Just as jurors must consider each charge separately when deliberating on verdicts, so, too, prosecutors must carefully parse through the evidence for each possible charge. Very often, there is significant evidence the target committed some crimes, strong evidence he or she committed other crimes, and some evidence he or she committed still other crimes. Wise prosecutors charge only the crimes for which there is significant (as in proof beyond a reasonable doubt) evidence.

Some may argue that prosecutors should charge a target with other crimes for which the evidence may not be very strong, so long as there is at least one crime the prosecutor can prove beyond a reasonable doubt. They would argue there is nothing to lose in doing this and that the strong evidence on one charge may bleed over to another charge that lacks evidence in a way that a jury may convict the defendant on the weaker charge. When prosecutors make charging decisions based on this thought process, they abandon their duty to do justice. Prosecutors should hesitate to bring a charge for which they believe there is probable cause but not evidence beyond a reasonable doubt. Although jurors may vote to convict defendants of weaker charges because they are influenced by stronger charges, this is not right and not the basis upon which jurors should rest a verdict.

In any event, charging a defendant with crimes for which there is weak evidence is a poor strategy because it often hurts the government's case as to the stronger charges. Weak charges provide fodder for defense counsel. Defense attorneys should rejoice when prosecutors overcharge their clients because it provides them with grounds for cross-examination and closing argument. The crucible of cross-examination will expose all of the holes in and deficiencies of the government's case on the weak charges. It allows defense counsel to then argue that the entire case against the defendant is as weak as its weakest charge. Although there is a chance the stronger charge will influence a jury to convict a defendant on a weaker charge, more likely the weaker charge may cause a jury to find reasonable doubt about all of the charges.

In deciding which charges to bring, prosecutors must also consider in some cases the unit of prosecution. That is, prosecutors sometimes must decide whether to charge each and every act that may constitute a separate offense when the acts are all part of a criminal scheme or conspiracy. For example, under the Mail Fraud Statute, Title 18 US Code, Section 1341, each separate letter or mailing made in furtherance of a scheme to defraud constitutes a separate offense. In an investment fraud scheme involving the mailing of thousands of letters, then, a prosecutor could literally bring thousands of counts of mail fraud. Similarly, in a drug conspiracy case a prosecutor may have evidence that would support a score of separate drug distribution charges for each occasion when the target distributed drugs in furtherance of the conspiracy. The question for prosecutors to consider is how many of these charges to bring and which ones to choose. Assuming that the evidence is equally strong for all possible counts, the prosecutor could bring every single one of the charges. Again, it comes down to determining what the prosecutor should do, not what the prosecutor can do.

When prosecutors have the ability to charge many counts related to an offense because of the nature of the defined unit of prosecution, prosecutors should, of course, carefully consider all of the other factors that influence charging decisions (strength of the evidence as to each count, the burden of prosecuting each count, the sentencing impact, and the influence it might have on plea negotiations). There are, however, other factors to consider as well in these circumstances. Prosecutors should consider including charges that fully reflect the scope of the criminal conduct. This may include the geographic or temporal scope of the criminal conduct, or the people involved in the criminal conduct. For example, in a wire fraud scheme lasting a number of years, involving numerous victims in various locations, perpetrated by several targets, a prosecutor may want to select as units of prosecution several representative mailings that would encompass all of the time frame, at least one mailing for each victim, and mailings that would have involved in some way each of the targets of the investigation. Prosecutors may also think about choosing units of prosecution in a manner that minimizes the number of witnesses necessary to lay the foundation for the evidence. Finally, prosecutors may want to choose to charge units of prosecution that have some other significance in the case. For example, a particular drug transaction may be important to charge separately as part of a conspiracy case because the transaction involved the largest amount of drugs among the various transactions or involved all of the coconspirators. Similarly, in a mail fraud case a prosecutor may choose as a unit of prosecution a mailing that was directed to a particularly prominent or vulnerable victim, or one that resulted in the largest amount of funds fraudulently obtained among all of the mailings. Prosecutors should not, however, choose the number of charges solely to create the appearance of guilt based on the sheer number of charges. Defense attorneys have a legitimate concern that jurors may presume guilt when they learn that a defendant is charged with scores of counts, when, in fact, the number of counts may have no real connection with the strength of the government's case or the true scope of the defendant's criminal conduct.

Another factor prosecutors should consider in determine which charges to bring against a target is the added burden on the government to prove each additional charge. In making charging decisions, as mentioned, prosecutors should assume the case will proceed to trial. With that in mind, before including a charge in an indictment, prosecutors should consider the additional resources that will be required to prove each charge beyond a reasonable doubt. In some cases, adding charges will have no or only a marginal impact because the same witness or witnesses will testify regarding evidence pertaining to more than one charge and there may be no or only a few additional exhibits to offer into evidence. Consider, for example, a case where officers conducted a controlled buy of narcotics from a target, then arrested him immediately after the buy and found a large quantity of drugs on him. The prosecutor could likely charge the target with distribution of a controlled substance and possession with the intent to distribute the controlled substance without expending any resources beyond that which would be expended in charging the defendant with only the distribution charge. On the other hand, there will be other cases when adding a charge to an indictment would require calling one or more additional witnesses or the introduction of multiple exhibits. In very large cases, adding multiple charges to an indictment may equate to adding multiple days to the anticipated length of a trial. All things being equal, prosecutors should charge the minimal number of charges necessary to accomplish the goals of the prosecution.

Prosecutors may also consider whether there are charges that could counter or defeat an anticipated defense. Some charges may turn on key facts that may be difficult to prove beyond a reasonable doubt while other charges are available that can address the same criminal conduct with the same or similar sentencing ramifications. For example, if a prosecutor believes there may be some difficulty proving the use of the US mail in connection with a fraud scheme, the prosecutor may consider whether the evidence would also support a wire fraud charge as well. In the computer age, the "wires" are almost always in play. I was a prosecutor in a high-profile, complex white-collar bank fraud case. The bank had a very complicated corporate structure and we anticipated that the defense would contest whether the particular entity that loaned the defendant funds was itself insured by the federal government. To counter that possible defense, we simply charged the defendant with wire fraud as well. Although the sentencing consequences were slightly different, it was effective insurance against the anticipated technical defense.

Prosecutors should also understand that charging decisions significantly impact plea negotiations, and thus the likelihood of trial. The plea options are limited when defendants are charged with only a single offense. If that charge also carries a mandatory minimum sentence, the ability to negotiate a plea may be even more constricted. A defendant in his fifties charged with an offense carrying a twenty-year mandatory minimum sentence may have little incentive to plead guilty to what he or she may rightly view to be a life sentence. On the other hand, when defendants are charged with multiple offenses, the ability to negotiate a plea to one or more charges (with an agreement to dismiss the remaining charges) is enhanced, particularly when the charges carry differing sentencing and collateral consequences. So, when prosecutors have the option based on the facts of a case, they may want to make charging decisions that would increase plea negotiation options. This may mean bringing more charges to increase the number of potential charges to which a defendant may choose to plead guilty. It may also mean, at least initially, not bringing charges that would restrict the plea options. For example, a prosecutor may want to initially refrain from charging a defendant with an offense that carries a stiff mandatory minimum sentence, while informing the defendant that if the defendant does not plead guilty to the pending charge, the prosecutor will charge him or her with the more serious offense.

Finally, charging decisions can also have an impact on victims and the public. Although the primary focus in making charging decisions should turn on the factors already discussed, particularly the strength of the evidence, prosecutors cannot lose sight of the impact the charging decision could have on others. All things being equal, prosecutors may choose certain charges to be responsive to the perception the charging decision will have on victims and the public. For example, for the sake of victims of the criminal conduct, prosecutors may want to include or exclude counts related to certain victims depending on whether failure to include a count would offend a victim of that count, or whether the victim of that count would prefer not to be part of the public prosecution. Similarly, in rare cases prosecutors may choose certain charges over other charges based on the public perception, if nothing else would be adversely affected. For example, if charging a defendant with a racketeering charge would have the same sentencing effect and be equally supported by the evidence as charging him or her with mail fraud based on the same conduct, a prosecutor may choose a racketeering charge because the public may perceive the charge as more reflective of nature of the defendant's criminal conduct. Likewise, if a prosecutor could charge a defendant for unlawful possession of a firearm because he or she was a felon and also an unlawful drug user, for general deterrence purposes the prosecutor may want to assert both grounds to increase the public's awareness that it is unlawful to possess firearms as a drug user.

Sentencing and Collateral Consequences

When prosecutors have the choice of bringing multiple charges against a target, prosecutors should also analyze the sentencing impact of each additional charge. In some cases, this analysis may lead to the conclusion that additional charges are appropriate, while in other cases it may lead to the opposite conclusion. When deciding on potential charges, prosecutors should consider the potential punishment they believe is called for or appropriate given the nature of the crime and the characteristics of the target. Once the prosecutor has determined the sentencing goal, charging decisions should be made to accomplish that goal. An especially heinous crime or recidivistic defendant may dictate bringing the types and number of charges necessary to provide the court with the ability to sentence the defendant at the level the prosecutor believes is appropriate.

For example, imagine a federal case involving a felon who stole firearms from a gun dealer and then while burglarizing a home uses one of the stolen firearms to kill the homeowner. Imagine, further, that the federal prosecutor could not charge the defendant with a federal offense in relation to the murder because the murder did not violate any federal offense. The facts, however, support a charge for possession of firearms as a felon and firearm theft charges. It would be appropriate in that case for the prosecutor to bring charges and insist on a plea to both so as to allow the court at the time of sentencing to fashion an appropriate sentence for the underlying murder. The federal sentencing statutes and guidelines direct judges to sentence defendants for the underlying offense, even if that conduct was not directly charged as an offense. A conviction on all counts would allow the sentencing judge to "stack" the maximum sentences for each count and then have the ability to sentence the defendant for the underlying offense conduct of the murder. In contrast, if the prosecutor charged the defendant with only a single count of being a felon in possession of a firearm, it would have capped the potential punishment at the statutory maximum of ten years.

Conversely, imagine a case where a nineteen year old took sexually explicit photographs of his seventeen-year-old girlfriend on his cell phone with her consent. Imagine further that the target has no criminal history. A federal prosecutor could charge the target with simple possession of child pornography, which carries no mandatory minimum sentence and a possible maximum sentence of not more than ten years. 18 U.S.C. § 2252(b)(2). Conversely, the prosecutor could charge the target with production of child pornography, carrying a fifteen-year mandatory minimum sentence and a maximum possible sentence of thirty years' imprisonment. 18 U.S.C. § 2251(d), (e). In making this charging decision, the prosecutor should consider the punishment the prosecutor believes appropriate given the facts of the case and the characteristics of the defendant and may conclude a production of child pornography charge would be unduly harsh.

Similarly, in making charging decisions prosecutors should also think about the collateral consequences of the potential charges. Criminal charges can have significant collateral consequences, such as mandating restitution or repayment of taxes, permitting forfeiture of assets or collection of costs of prosecution, or barring a defendant from conducting business with the US government. Other charges may impact a defendant's immigration status, jeopardize a defendant's professional licensure, or require a defendant to register as a sex offender. Charges may also affect the ability of a court to impose conditions of probation or supervised release. Finally, convictions on some charges may have significant collateral consequences should the defendant commit offenses in the future. For example, a defendant previously convicted of a federal or state felony drug distribution offense may face an enhanced sentence in federal court when charged in the future with a felony drug distribution charge. As with considering the direct sentencing implications of charges, prosecutors should consider the potential collateral consequences of potential charges and fashion charges that are appropriate given the nature of the criminal conduct and the characteristics of the defendant.

HOW TO CHARGE

In making charging decisions, prosecutors must not only decide what charges to bring, but how to bring them. Prosecutors may be able to charge defendants with various types of charging documents, such as a criminal complaint, a criminal information, or an indictment. Prosecutors must also decide what to say in the charging document. In other words, prosecutors must choose the words for the charging document. Some complex charges, such as conspiracy, racketeering, or regulatory type charges, require additional decisions by prosecutors in drafting the wording of the charge. Finally, prosecutors must decide, in certain circumstances, whether to amend charges.

Choosing the Charging Document

Sometimes prosecutors have the option of choosing various methods of charging a defendant using different types of charging documents. In the federal system, a prosecutor may charge a defendant in a criminal complaint, a criminal information, or an indictment. There are benefits and limitations to each type of charging document, and they are designed for different purposes.

Criminal Complaints

A criminal complaint is really a temporary charge. A criminal complaint identifies the defendant, date, location, and crime and is supported by an affidavit sworn by an officer establishing probable cause to believe the defendant committed the crime charged. If approved by a judicial officer, a defendant may be arrested and remain under the charge for up to thirty days until the government either charges the defendant in a criminal information or an indictment.

Prosecutors often choose to charge a defendant through a criminal complaint because of the exigency of the circumstances dictate an immediate charge and there is no time to present evidence to a grand jury to obtain an indictment. Even when a prosecutor may have time to present evidence to a grand jury and seek an indictment, a federal prosecutor may still choose to charge the defendant by way of a criminal complaint anyway. There may be several factors to consider in making this decision. First, although the prosecutor might have enough time to present sufficient evidence to the grand jury to establish probable cause the defendant committed the offense, there may not be enough time to present all of the evidence and question all of the witnesses desired. The additional thirty days generated by charging a defendant by a criminal complaint would allow the prosecutor time to complete the grand jury investigation. In other instances, witnesses may be reluctant or afraid to testify before the grand jury until the defendant is in custody. Charging the defendant in a criminal complaint allows the government to secure the defendant in a way that may give confidence to recalcitrant witnesses.

Second, the return of an indictment triggers certain discovery rights for a criminal defendant that are not triggered by a criminal complaint. A prosecutor may have concerns about the destruction of evidence or the safety of victims or witnesses that could be addressed with some additional time. So, again, charging a defendant by way of a criminal complaint instead of an indictment allows the government to get the defendant under the government's control while still allowing time for the government to take care of security issues before turning discovery over to the defendant.

Third, because a criminal complaint is supported by an affidavit, a significant amount of detail about the criminal offense may be contained in the affidavit that may not be contained in a formal charging document like a criminal information or indictment. Prosecutors are generally barred from discussing details of a case outside what is in the public record. It is sometimes advantageous to the government's investigation, then, to charge a defendant by a criminal complaint so as to be able to unseal the complaint and release that information to the public. For example, if a case involves a large number of potential victims, an affidavit filed in support of a criminal complaint may allow for a fuller description of the criminal scheme than could be included in an information or indictment. This fuller description may then allow the government to provide notice to potential victims of the scheme, permitting those victims to come forth to seek redress or restitution.

Criminal Informations

In the federal system, criminal informations are a form of hybrid charging document. A federal criminal information has the appearance in form of an indictment. Unlike an indictment, however, a criminal information is brought only under the name and authority of the US Attorney. Neither a grand jury, nor a federal judicial officer, reviews or approves the charges in a criminal information.

A defendant cannot be tried or convicted of a felony offense based on a criminal information, absent a waiver of the right to have a grand jury consider evidence against the defendant and return an indictment. The government may, however, try and convict a defendant of a federal misdemeanor crime brought by way of a criminal information. On the other hand, the government may also choose to charge a defendant with a misdemeanor offense by way of an indictment.

When defendants are willing to waive indictment on felony charges, federal prosecutors have the option to charge such defendants by either a criminal information or indictment. Defendants who have worked out a plea agreement with the government are often also willing to waive their right to require the government to present evidence to a grand jury to obtain an indictment. Sometimes the government will work out a plea agreement with a target before any charges have been brought. This happens most often in white-collar cases when the target is aware of the government's long-term investigation, has retained counsel, and has entered into plea negotiations before the government has sought an indictment from the grand jury. On other occasions, the government may have already charged the defendant by way of a criminal complaint, but plea negotiations resulted in an agreed-upon disposition before the government presented the case to the grand jury for indictment. In still other cases, a defendant may already be charged by way of an indictment, but plea negotiations result in an agreement to have the defendant plead guilty to a crime or crimes charged in a criminal information in place of, or in addition to, those charged in an indictment.

When defendants are willing to waive indictment on federal felony charges, prosecutors should almost always accept the waiver and choose to charge the defendant by way of criminal information instead. The practical reason for this is to save limited grand jury resources. If a defendant is willing to waive indictment, it saves the government all of the time it would

take in the grand jury to present the indictment, have the grand jury deliberate, and then return the indictment in open court. There are exceptions,
however, to every rule. If a prosecutor had concerns that the defendant may
later claim his or her waiver was not voluntary because the defendant has a
history in other cases of claiming his or her attorneys gave ineffective assistance of counsel, a more cautious prosecutor may choose to proceed with
obtaining a grand jury indictment. Similarly, if it is a high-profile case and
there is a belief that the public may misinterpret a plea to an information
instead of an indictment as suggesting the government is not holding the
defendant fully accountable, then a cautious prosecutor may again choose
to proceed to the grand jury.

If a prosecutor decides to allow a defendant to waive indictment and plead
guilty to a felony charged in a criminal information, it is imperative that the
waiver is knowing and voluntary. The waiver must be in writing and signed
by the defendant. Further, the judicial officer must address the defendant in
open court and advise the defendant of his or her right to demand that the
government present evidence to a grand jury and obtain an indictment. The
defendant must then orally waive that right on the record.

When prosecutors bring misdemeanor charges against a target, they again
have the ability to choose whether to do so by way of a criminal information
or by way of an indictment. In making this decision, prosecutors should consider several factors. Again, charging a defendant by way of a criminal information avoids the unnecessary expenditure of limited grand jury resources.
On the other hand, it may be helpful to use the grand jury to secure testimony
from witnesses. Prosecutors should be cautious about using the grand jury for
this purpose unless at the time the prosecutor intends to have the grand jury
deliberate on an indictment. Finally, there may be an advantage to have the
benefit of the grand jury's review and evaluation of the evidence, especially
if the case may be perceived as controversial.

Indictments

Indictments are formal charging documents presented to the grand jury
and signed by the grand jury foreperson and the prosecutor. As noted, the
federal government cannot try or convict a defendant of a felony offense
unless a grand jury has returned an indictment against the defendant or the
defendant waives the right to have the matter presented to a grand jury. In
the vast majority of cases, then, federal prosecutors bring felony charges
against defendants by way of indictments. It is the wording of indictments
that will be the primary focus of the following section, even though the
same considerations could apply with equal force to the drafting of a criminal information.

Choosing the Words

In choosing the words to bring charges in an indictment, prosecutors must consider a number of things. First, prosecutors must consider the degree of factual detail to include in the charge. Second, prosecutors must pay attention to the use of conjunctive and disjunctive language. Third, prosecutors must give thought to the date or date range it is alleged the crime occurred. Finally, prosecutors must carefully consider word choices.

The Amount of Factual Detail

Prosecutors may charge an offense with the bare minimum of detail in an indictment. Federal Rule of Criminal Procedure 7(c)(1) states that a criminal indictment "shall be a plain, concise and definite written statement of the essential facts constituting the offense charged." In this type of notice pleading, a prosecutor must include in the charge language that describes the approximate date of the offense, the location that invokes the court's jurisdiction and venue, the name of the defendant, and facts that would satisfy all of the essential elements of an offense. The charge must also contain sufficient information to allow a defendant to make a challenge to double jeopardy under the Sixth Amendment to the US Constitution. There is no requirement that the indictment describe the government's evidence, contain evidentiary detail, or identify all the facts supporting the allegations. *Wong Tai v. United States*, 273 US 77 (1927). Both state and federal governments provide prosecutors with form language for most charges to be used for this purpose.

Prosecutors are not limited, however, to including only the bare minimum factual details in drafting an indictment. In some instances, prosecutors may want to include additional factual detail. Indeed, in some instances, such as in complex fraud or conspiracy cases, prosecutors may want to describe in great detail the entire criminal scheme, including instances of particular acts essential to the scheme and the roles of various individuals in the criminal conduct. These later, detailed indictments are sometimes referred to as speaking indictments or talking indictments. There are, of course, benefits and detriments to including more or less factual detail.

One benefit from including more factual detail is that it can avoid the need for a bill of particulars. "[A] court may direct the government to file a bill of particulars." FED. R. CRIM. P. 7(f). A court may require a bill of particulars may be necessary "[t]o inform the defendant of the nature of the charge against him with sufficient precision to enable him to prepare for trial, to avoid or minimize the danger of surprise at the time of trial, and to enable him to plead his acquittal or conviction in bar of another prosecution for the same offense when the indictment itself is too vague, and indefinite for such purposes." *United States v. Ayers*, 924 F.2d 1468, 1483 (9th Cir. 1991) (internal citation and quotation omitted). In analyzing whether a bill of particulars is necessary, courts look to factors such as the complexity of the charges, the number of charges and defendants, and the clarity of the indictment's language. If an indictment provides sufficient detail, however, it may accomplish the purposes served by a bill of particulars. *United States v. Mitchell*, 744 F.2d 701, 705 (9th Cir. 1984).

Another benefit that can arise from greater factual detail in an indictment is that it may encourage a defendant to plead guilty. When an indictment correctly describes the defendant's conduct in considerable detail, it may have a sobering effect on a defendant, making the defendant and the defendant's attorney appreciate the thoroughness of the government's investigation. This may spur the defendant to seek an early plea agreement, recognizing that the government has, indeed, caught the defendant.

A benefit of a speaking indictment may also arise in districts where the judges either have the indictment read to the jury or when the judges send copies of the indictments back to the jurors during deliberation. When this happens, a properly drafted, detailed speaking indictment may resemble the government's opening statement, marshalling and organizing the facts in a manner that leads to a conclusion of guilt.

Finally, the more factually detailed an indictment, the more facts are known to the public. As mentioned, one of the benefits of charging a defendant initially with a criminal complaint is that it allows great factual detail to be made public by inclusion of the fact in the affidavit filed in support of the complaint. Whether that detail is contained in the indictment or the complaint affidavit, the benefit of public disclosure of greater detail is that it may allow victims of a criminal scheme to become aware of the case and seek redress or restitution.

There are, however, detriments to including too much factual detail in an indictment. The more factual detail included, the more likely it will be that the prosecutor makes a mistake about a fact. That factual error or omission may lock the prosecutor into a specific theory or claim. If the prosecutor was mistaken or omitted facts would permit a different theory of the case, a defense attorney may seize upon this in arguing to a jury that the government has failed to prove its case. Similarly, if the defendant or his or her attorney perceive that the prosecutor is operating on mistaken facts or a mistaken understanding of the events, it may embolden a defendant to proceed to trial, rather than encourage an early guilty plea. Finally, the more factual detail the prosecutor includes in an indictment, the more the indictment may disclose the prosecutor's theory of the case or highlight the critical evidence. This may, in turn, allow a defendant to anticipate the government's argument and counter it by developing other evidence or by tailoring a defense argument to defeat the government's theory.

Conjunctive and Disjunctive Language

Some criminal statutes contain language that would allow proof of the crime by more than one means. The government may charge a defendant using conjunctive language when a statute may be violated in more than one way. *Turner v. United States*, 396 US 398 (1970). Although a statute may be violated in more than one way, the government need only prove at trial that the defendant violated the statute in one of the listed ways. *Id.* So, for example, the government may charge that a defendant conspired to distribute marijuana *and* cocaine, in violation of Title 21, US Code, Section 846. Yet, at trial, it is sufficient if the jury finds that the defendant conspired to distribute one drug, but not the other, as conspiring to distribute either is still a violation of the conspiracy statute. If there is more than one alternative, a jury should be instructed to unanimously agree as to how the defendant violated the statute.

In short, when an offense may be committed in more than one way, prosecutors should use conjunctive charging language. This allows prosecutors flexibility in the presentation of evidence and in arguing the case to the jury. A prosecutor may choose, for example, not to pursue an alternative means by which the defendant could have committed the offense if the evidence at trial is not as strong as the government anticipated. For example, if the prosecutor charged a defendant with possessing a firearm as both a felon and an unlawful drug user, but the evidence of the unlawful drug use turned out to be weaker than anticipated at trial, the government may choose not to pursue that alternative and not have the jury deliberate on it.

Alleging the Date of Offense

Prosecutors do not need to allege the precise date of the offense in an indictment. Rather, it is sufficient for the government to allege an approximate date that the offense took place. *See, e.g., United States v. Severe*, 29 F.3d 444 (8th Cir. 1994); *United States v. Hernandez*, 962 F.2d 1152 (5th Cir. 1992). So, prosecutors should use qualifying language in indictments, such as alleging that the crime occurred "on or about" a certain date, or "between about" certain dates. Too much ambiguity in the date of the alleged offense, however, can violate a defendant's due process rights if it prevents the defendant from being able to determine if the instant prosecution is a violation of the Double Jeopardy Clause or prevents the defendant from being able to mount a meaningful defense. Thus, the date of the offense must be reasonably close to the approximate date alleged in the indictment. *United States v. Summers*, 137 F.3d 597 (8th Cir. 1998).

Word Choice

In choosing the words for a charging document, prosecutors must make sure to omit any pejorative, conclusory, irrelevant, and prejudicial language. The indictment should only include facts, not opinions or judgments, and only those facts relevant and necessary to fully describe the criminal conduct. Rule 7(d) of the Federal Rules of Criminal Procedure provides that "Upon the defendant's motion, the court may strike surplusage from the indictment. . . ." FED. R. CRIM. P. 7(d). The purpose of this rule is to protect a defendant against prejudicial allegations that are neither relevant nor material to the charges made in an indictment, or not essential to the charge. *United States v. Poore*, 594 F.2d 39, 41 (4th Cir. 1979).

Although Rule 7(d) authorizes a court to strike surplusage from an indictment, "[a] motion to strike surplusage from an indictment should not be granted unless it is clear that the allegations are not relevant to the charge and are inflammatory and prejudicial. . . . [T]his is a most exacting standard." *United States v. Awan*, 966 F.2d 1415, 1426 (11th Cir. 1992) (citations and internal quotation marks omitted); *accord United States v. Brye*, 318 F. App'x 878, 880 (11th Cir. 2009) (same). To determine whether the allegations are relevant to the charges and the evidence introduced at trial, "[t]he Court may reserve ruling on a motion to strike surplusage until hearing the evidence and determining its relevance at trial." *United States v. Al–Arian*, 308 F. Supp.2d 1322, 1333 (M.D. Fla. 2004).

A prosecutor's use of descriptive words for the criminal conduct can be relevant to the charged offenses. *See, e .g., United States v. Laurienti*, 611 F.3d 530, 547 (9th Cir. 2010) (finding "characterization of the sales practices as unlawful was relevant, because the government sought to prove that, as conducted by Defendants . . . , the practices were indeed unlawful" and denying motion to strike); *United States v. Anyanwu*, No. 1:12–CR–190–TWT–ECS–1, 2013 WL 1558712, at *4 (N.D. Ga. Mar. 12, 2013) (refusing to strike as surplusage description of marriages as fraudulent because the description was relevant to the alleged visa fraud associated with the marriages at issue); *United States v. Stein*, No. 11–80205–CR, 2012 WL 4089896, at *8 (S.D. Fla. Sept. 13, 2012) (rejecting the defendant's motion to strike use of word "sham" finding term was relevant "because it conveys that the consulting agreements were fraudulent and used to misappropriate assets" as alleged in the indictment). Similarly, "[i]f the language in the indictment is information which the government hopes to properly prove at trial, it cannot be considered surplusage no matter how prejudicial it may be (provided, of course, it is legally relevant). *United States v. Thomas*, 875 F.2d 559, 562 n. 2 (6th Cir. 1989).

Drafting Complex Charges

Some complex charges require more careful drafting decisions than may arise in the mine run case. Complex cases may include conspiracy and racketeering cases, fraudulent schemes brought under mail fraud or wire fraud statutes, or regulatory crimes, such as environmental or tax crimes. For example, in alleging a mail fraud scheme, it can be critical to use precise language regarding the use of the mail that is reflected in the conduct under investigation. Likewise, in charging environmental criminal offense or tax violation, courts have held that certain precise language in an indictment is necessary to support a charge. It is beyond the scope of this book to address the drafting issues that arise in relation to most of these types of complex cases. It will have to suffice for purposes of this book simply to alert the reader that when drafting indictments involving such complex charges a prosecutor will want to research the law in this area and look for guidance in drafting the charging language. I will, however, address here some of the issues involved in drafting more commonly charged conspiracy counts.

There are some rules specific to the drafting of conspiracy indictments. A conspiracy is simply an agreement between two or more people to commit a crime. A conspiracy may have multiple objectives; in other words, two or more people could reach an agreement to commit multiple crimes. *Braverman v. United States*, 317 US 49 (1942). On the other hand, the same two people may reach separate agreements to commit separate crimes. *Kotteakos v. United States*, 328 US 750 (1946).

To illustrate, let me provide some examples. Imagine that two people, John Doe and Jane Doe, reached an agreement to distribute methamphetamine and cocaine. This would properly be charged as a single conspiracy with multiple objectives. On the other hand, imagine that John Doe and Jane Doe reached an agreement to rob a bank. Then three months after robbing the bank, they reached an agreement to sell stolen vehicles through John's car dealership. This would best be charged as two separate conspiracies offenses. Imagine, now, that John and Jane Doe agreed to rob a bank and that three months later, John Doe and Steve Smith decide to rob a different bank. The first bank robbery could be charged as a conspiracy in one count, but the later bank robbery would not be deemed part of that conspiracy with Jane Doe. The second bank robbery could be charged in a separate indictment alleging a different conspiracy between John Doe and Steve Smith.

Common sense guides prosecutors' decisions in charging conspiracy counts. If the parties and time frame of the criminal activity are the same or similar and there is a common goal, it is more likely that there is one conspiracy with multiple objectives. *United States v. McCarthy*, 97 F.3d 1562 (8th Cir. 1996). On the other hand, if there are different people involved in committing the separate crimes, and/or the time periods do not overlap, and/ or there are multiple goals, it is more likely that there are multiple conspiracies. *United States v. Barlin*, 686 F.2d 81, 90-91 (2d Cir. 1982). Prosecutors should take care to ensure that the evidence supports the duration, scope, and nature of the conspiracy alleged in the indictment.

Prosecutors should also be aware that it is inappropriate to name or identify by other means unindicted coconspirators in an indictment. *United States v. Chadwick*, 556 F.2d 450 (9th Cir. 1977); *United States v. Trujillo*, 714 F.2d 102 (11th Cir. 1983). Rather, such individuals should be referred to as unindicted coconspirators or as other persons known and unknown to the grand jury or by some other type of reference. On the other hand, there is nothing improper with identifying unindicted coconspirators in discovery or at trial. *United States v. Smith*, 776 F.2d 1104 (3rd Cir. 1985). Prosecutors need not name or indict all coconspirators in an indictment. *United States v. De Cavalcante*, 440 F.2d 1264 (3rd Cir. 1971). Indeed, prosecutors may allege in an indictment that a named defendant conspired with others, known and unknown to the grand jury, without ever identifying in the indictment the identity of any other coconspirator. *United States v. Howard*, 966 F.2d 1362 (10th Cir. 1992).

Conspiracy counts will often contain three sections: the objects of the conspiracy, the manner and means of the conspiracy, and the overt acts committed in furtherance of the conspiracy. Under the heading "objects of the conspiracy" in a conspiracy count, a prosecutor should describe in a single short paragraph (and usually in a single sentence) the conspirators' objectives. There may be more than one. For example, in a money-laundering conspiracy, the objects of the conspiracy may provide:

> Defendants and other conspirators, known and unknown to the grand jury, engaged in financial transactions using proceeds from the sale of controlled substances for the purposes of (1) paying for past shipments of controlled substances or to pay for future shipments of controlled substances, and (2) to covertly convert the proceeds from the sale of controlled substances into other forms of cash and assets so that the conspirators could personally profit from the unlawful activity.

The "manner and means" of a conspiracy is a short description of how the conspirators accomplished the goals of the conspiracy. This section should also be short and should omit details of when and where and what happened, and instead focus on the how question. Using our money-laundering conspiracy example, under the manner and means heading a prosecutor may describe how the conspirators would collect drug proceeds from lower-level drug dealers, then have runners use the cash to purchase a series of cashier's checks or to wire the funds to drug sources in another state to pay for drugs previously shipped or for future shipments. This section may go on to describe how the conspirators also used some of the cashier's checks and wires to deposit funds into bank accounts in nominees' names so the conspirators could then use the cash to purchase cars and other toys.

The last section of a conspiracy count may be the overt acts section. This section is required when conspiracy charged requires the proving of overt acts in furtherance of the conspiracy. Under federal law, unless the statute specifically requires proof of an overt act, it is not an element of a conspiracy offense. *See Whitfield v. United States*, 543 US 209, 213–14 (2005). The Supreme Court has reasoned that, unless Congress specifically provides otherwise, courts will assume that Congress intended to adopt the common law definition of statutory terms. *See Molzof v. United States*, 502 US 301, 307–308 (1992). At common law, an overt act was not a necessary element of a conspiracy charge. *Whitfield*, 543 US at 214.

When a conspiracy statute requires proof of an overt act, then the government must prove beyond a reasonable doubt that one of the conspirators committed at least one overt act during and in furtherance of the conspiracy. An overt act itself need not be illegal. They must be acts, however, not states of mind. For example, two conspirators meeting on a particular date in a particular location to discuss a step in the conspiracy is an act in furtherance of the conspiracy. A sentence describing the two conspirators' states of mind—they decided to use cashier's checks—does not describe an act.

In the overt acts section of a conspiracy count, the prosecutor should set out in separate one-fact paragraphs the detailed facts about the acts the conspirators took in committing the offense. Generally, prosecutors will want to set out the acts in chronological order. Prosecutors will also generally want to make sure that there is at least one overt act alleged for each charged member of the conspiracy, if factually possible. Finally, prosecutors should try to ensure they allege at least one overt act they know they can prove beyond a reasonable doubt.

CHOOSING WHEN AND HOW TO AMEND CHARGES

Prosecutors may have an opportunity to amend charges. The need to amend charges may be obvious when, for example, the facts change such that it is clear that the charges need to be changed to reflect the facts. On other occasions, prosecutors fail to avail themselves of the opportunity to amend the charges when, although not necessary because of changing facts, it would still be advantageous to do so. As noted in a prior section, prosecutors may want to amend the charges to add more serious charges when the prosecutor charged light to begin with in the hopes of a guilty plea. When, however, it becomes apparent that the defendant intends to go to trial, the prosecutor may want to amend the indictment to seek the more serious charge. On the other hand, a prosecutor may want to amend an indictment to reduce or eliminate charges in light of a re-evaluation of the evidence when it becomes apparent the case will proceed to trial. As noted, weak charges may have a spillover effect with juries, detracting from the strength of other charges. A wise prosecutor will constantly re-evaluate the charges and the evidence and amend as necessary and as possible to ensure only the strongest charges proceed to trial. Finally, a prosecutor may wish to amend an indictment to fix vague or ambiguous language, correct minor errors or typographical mistakes, or add clarifying or explicating language, particularly if the case is likely to proceed to trial.

Federal prosecutors can amend indictments in two ways. The first way is to submit a superseding indictment to the grand jury. The second way is to move to amend the indictment. Although the general rule is that only a grand jury may amend an indictment, federal courts allow amendments when "the change is merely a matter of form." *Russell v. United States*, 369 US 749, 770 (1962). Changes of form include corrections of clerical or typographical errors when they do not alter the charging terms of the indictment. When in doubt, careful prosecutors will use the grand jury to make any changes to an indictment.

Chapter Twelve

Discovery

State v Federal (handwritten)

Most state courts permit fairly broad discovery by both parties in criminal cases. Although written discovery, such as interrogatories or requests for admission, are uncommon in state criminal cases, defendants are often permitted to depose government witnesses to discover what the witnesses know and what they are likely to say should the case proceed to trial. As a result, in state cases, criminal defense attorneys usually have a fairly good idea of exactly what evidence the government has in its possession that implicates the defendant and can reasonably predict what the evidence will look like at trial.

In the federal system, in contrast, the discovery process is very different and generally very limited. There is no constitutional right to discovery in federal criminal cases. *Weatherford v. Bursey*, 429 US 545, 559 (1977); *Wardius v. Oregon*, 412 US 470, 474 (1973). Rather, the scope and nature of discovery permitted the parties in federal criminal cases are governed by statute, the Federal Rules of Criminal Procedure, and case law. *See, e.g.,* 18 U.S.C. § 3500; 18 U.S.C. § 3505(b); Fed. R. Crim. P. §§ 12(I), 12.1, 12.2, 12.3, 16, 26.2 and 46(j); Fed. R. Evid. 404(b), 803(24), and 804(b)(5); *Brady v. Maryland*, 373 US 83 (1963); and *Giglio v. United States*, 405 US 150 (1972). Although in practice most discovery in federal criminal cases is a one-way street with information flowing from the government to the defendant, some of the rules contemplate a degree of reciprocity, often triggered when the government provides discovery to a defendant. Unlike in most state courts, in federal criminal cases depositions of witnesses for discovery purposes are not allowed. Although Rule 15 of the Federal Rules of Criminal Procedure provides a mechanism for preserving testimony of a party's own witnesses by evidence depositions under "exceptional circumstances," the legislative history confirms that Rule 15 does not authorize discovery depositions. Rule 15 depositions are permitted only when, for example, the witness lives overseas and is thus not subject to the court's subpoena power, or when the witness is dying, and a deposition is necessary to preserve the witness's testimony.

The manner in which prosecutors address the government's discovery obligations can have a significant impact on the ability to develop and protect cooperators, conduct ongoing criminal investigations, and provide defendants with due process. To make wise strategic and tactical decisions regarding discovery, it is first necessary that prosecutors understand the law regarding discovery. As with other chapters, this chapter on discovery will focus on federal discovery obligations, recognizing that some of the discussion will be transferrable to state prosecution while other portions will not. I will then discuss the strategic and tactical factors that prosecutors should consider in producing discovery to a criminal defendant.

THE LEGAL PARAMETERS OF DISCOVERY

In federal court, the parties' discovery obligations are governed primarily by the Federal Rules of Criminal Procedure, the Jencks Act, and some of the Federal Rules of Evidence. In addition, the government has an obligation to provide a defendant with exculpatory evidence under Supreme Court precedent and the Due Process Clause. I will discuss the applicable rules, statutes, and case law in turn.

Rule 16, Federal Rules of Criminal Procedure

Fairness dictates that defendants are entitled to some basic information necessary for them to defend themselves against pending criminal charges. Rule 16 of the Federal Rules of Criminal Procedure requires the government to provide defendants with some of this basic information. There are some limitations, however, to discovery under Rule 16. First, a defendant is entitled to discovery under Rule 16 only after indictment. Further, Rule 16 obligations are triggered only by a proper request from the defendant. Third, Rule 16 requires only production of "material" evidence. Evidence is material under Rule 16 if it is "relevant to the development of a possible defense," *United States v. Mandel*, 914 F.2d 1215, 1219 (9th Cir. 1990) (citation and internal quotations omitted), or it "enable[s] the accused to substantially alter the quantum of proof in his favor." *United States v. Marshall*, 532 F.2d 1279, 1285 (9th Cir. 1976). Finally, "[r]eports, memoranda, or other internal government documents made by the attorney for the government or other government agents in connection with the investigation or prosecution of the case" are not discoverable under Rule 16(a). Nondisclosure of Rule 16 material requires reversal only if the nondisclosure prejudiced a defendant's substantial rights. *United States v. Michaels*, 796 F.2d 1112, 1115 (9th Cir. 1986).

Rule 16 requires the government to provide a defendant with several categories of evidence, including a copy of any statements made by the defendant, his or her criminal record, documents and tangible objects, reports of examinations or tests, and expert information.

Defendant's Statements

Under Rule 16, a defendant is entitled to copies of any written or recorded statements the government alleges that he or she made. A defendant's statement, under Rule 16, means any relevant written or recorded statements of the defendant which are in possession or control of the government (including government agencies) regardless of whether the government intends to use those statements at trial. Any statement meeting this definition is included, regardless of the person to whom the defendant made those statements. In other words, the statements are not limited simply to those allegedly made in response to interrogation by a law enforcement officer, but rather, encompasses any statements by a defendant to whomever made.

The term "recorded" does not include statements in officers' reports or in grand jury testimony of third parties. It means actual recorded statements on audio or videotape or recorded by a stenographer in the course of the defendant presenting testimony. In addition to actually recorded statements by the defendant, Rule 16 also requires disclosure of the portion of any written record containing the substance of any oral statements by the defendant if they are: (1) relevant; (2) made in response to interrogation; and (3) made to a person then known to the defendant to be a government agent. Even if not reduced to a written report, a defendant is entitled to the substance of any other relevant oral statement made by the defendant in response to interrogation by any person then known to him to be a government agent, if government intends to use that evidence at trial.

Defendant's Prior Criminal Record

Rule 16 requires the government to provide a defendant with a copy of his or her criminal history. This includes what is known, or could be known with due diligence, about the defendant's past criminal record. Except as required by the notice provisions of Federal Rule of Evidence 404(b), which I will discuss later, the government need not indicate whether or how it intends to use this information.

Documents and Tangible Objects

Rule 16 requires advance disclosure to the defendant of any "books, papers, documents, photographs, tangible objects, buildings or places" that are: (1) in the government's possession and material to the defense, or (2) intended by the government for use as evidence in chief at trial, or (3) obtained from or belonging to the defendant. Disclosure of these items can be conditioned on safeguards necessary to protect the integrity of the government's evidence.

Reports of Examinations and Tests

Rule 16 requires the government to provide the defendant with reports of any examinations or tests. Examples of these would include ballistics tests, urinalysis tests, or similar scientific analysis of evidence or data. To be discoverable, the result of examination must be either material to the preparation of the defense or intended for use by the government in its case.

Expert Information

Rule 16(a)(1)(E) requires that, upon request by the defendant, the government must disclose to the defendant a written summary of expert testimony, describing the witness's opinions, "the bases and the reasons therefore," and the witness's qualifications. The obligation to disclose under this rule is triggered by a request from the defendant. If no such request is made, the rule imposes no disclosure obligation on the government.

Rule 16 places an obligation on a defendant to provide reciprocal discovery to the government. This obligation is narrower than the government's discovery obligations. Rule 16(b)(1)(A) requires criminal defendants to provide reciprocal discovery of documents and tangible objects if the defendant has requested these from the government. Likewise, the defendant is required to provide reports of examinations and tests that are in the control of the defendant, that the defendant intends to use at trial "as evidence in chief," or that were prepared by a witness the defendant intends to call at trial. FED. R. CRIM. P. 16(b)(1)(B). In addition, Rule 16(b)(1)(C) mandates that defendants provide the government with a summary of expert testimony. Although generally speaking, mutual exchange of expert summaries is in the control of the defendant, who must make the first request, there is an exception. If the defendant files a notice of insanity or mental defect under Rule 12.2, the government can request discovery of expert information.

Jencks Act (18 U.S.C. § 3500)

The Jencks Act provides that the government must produce to the defense copies of any prior statements made by government witness if: (1) the statements are in the possession of the government, which means in the possession of either the prosecutor or the investigative agency; (2) the statements relate to the subject matter on which the witness has testified; and (3) the defense has moved for their production. The Jencks Act provides that the court may order the government to produce such statements only after a witness has testified on direct examination. Rule 26.2 of the Federal Rules of Criminal Procedure substantially tracks Section 3500, but also applies it to all suppression hearings, sentencing hearings, probation revocation hearings, and, unless the court orders otherwise, to preliminary and detention hearings. *See also* Rules 5.1, 12(h), 32(e), 32.1(c), and 46(j). The Jencks Act and Rule 26.2 impose reciprocal discovery obligations, meaning that a defendant has the same obligation to produce statements of his witnesses to the government.

The statutory definition of a "statement" in 18 U.S.C. § 3500(e) is: (1) a written statement made by the witness and signed or otherwise adopted or approved by him; (2) a stenographic, mechanical, electrical, or other recording, or a transcription thereof, which is a substantially verbatim recital of an oral statement made by the witness and recorded contemporaneously with the making of such oral statement; or (3) a statement, however taken or recorded, or a transcription thereof, if any, made by the witness to a grand jury. The key to determining whether something is a "statement" within the meaning of the Jencks Act is "whether the statement can fairly be deemed to reflect fully and without distortion the witness's own words." *Palermo v. United States*, 360 US 343, 352-3 (1959); *United States v. Morris*, 957 F.2d 1391, 1401 (7th Cir. 1992). The most common issues in determining whether something is a "statement," under Section 3500, concern whether it is communicative, whether it is reasonably complete, whether it has been "adopted" by the witness, whether it is "substantially verbatim," and for what purpose it has been created. Portions of the statement that do not relate to the "subject matter of the testimony of the witness" can be excised on motion of a party. 18 U.S.C. § 3500(c).

Witness Lists and Exhibit Lists

A defendant charged with treason or a capital offense is entitled to a list of the government's witnesses "at least three entire days" before trial. 18 U.S.C. § 3432. In noncapital cases, the defense is not statutorily entitled to an advance list of the government's witnesses or exhibits. As a practical matter, however, most federal district courts have adopted local rules requiring both the government and the defense to produce exhibits and witness lists at a reasonable time in advance of trial.

Other Acts Evidence

Federal Rule of Evidence 404(b) requires the prosecution to provide reasonable notice of "the general nature" of any uncharged crime, wrong or bad act in advance of trial or during trial, upon request of the accused. The degree of detail required under this notice requirement is not defined by statute. Likewise, there is no strict time frame provided for how far in advance of trial such notice is required. What constitutes reasonable and timely notice depends largely on the nature of the case and the nature of the other bad acts. Rule 404(b) is not limited to use by the government. *See, e.g., United States v. McClure*, 546 F.2d 670 (5th Cir. 1977) (acts of informant offered in entrapment defense). Rule 404(b), however, does not impose any obligation upon a criminal defendant to provide notice to the government of a defendant's intent to present Rule 404(b) evidence.

Brady/Giglio Information

Prosecutors must also disclose to the defense any information tending to exculpate the defendant or mitigate his punishment or tending to impeach government witnesses. *See Brady v. Maryland*, 373 US 83 (1963) (evidence that may tend to exculpate a defendant must be produced to the defendant); *Giglio v. United States*, 405 US 150 (1972) (evidence which tends to impeach government witnesses must be produced to the defense). *Brady* and *Giglio* did not create new rules of discovery, but rather, require disclosure as a matter of due process that may void a conviction when the government does not disclose material evidence favorable to an accused. *Weatherford v. Bursey*, 429 US 545, 559 (1977) (emphasizing that there "is no general constitutional right to discovery in a criminal case, and *Brady* did not create one"). For a defendant to establish a *Brady* or *Giglio* violation, the defendant must show: (1) the prosecution suppressed the evidence; (2) the evidence was favorable to or exculpatory of the defendant; and (3) the evidence was material. *Brady*, 373 US at 87. The government cannot be found to have "suppressed" the evidence if it was equally discoverable by the defendant. *See May v. Collins*, 904 F.2d 228, 231 (5th Cir. 1990) (holding that the government is not compelled to furnish information that is fully available to the defendant or that the defendant could obtain through reasonable diligence). Materiality is judged on whether the evidence could have affected the outcome if disclosed. Under this standard,

> evidence is material only if there is a reasonable probability that, had the evidence been disclosed to the defense, the result of the proceeding would have been different. A "reasonable probability" is a probability sufficient to undermine confidence in the outcome.

United States v. Bagley, 473 US 667, 682 (1985) (Blackmun, J.); *id.* at 685 (White, J., concurring in part). The government's *Brady* and *Giglio* disclosure obligations involve not only a substantive, but also a temporal element. *United States v. De La Cruz-Feliciano*, 786 F.3d 78, 87 (1st Cir. 2015) ("*Brady* also applies in cases where the Government delays disclosure of relevant evidence"). Thus, a prosecutor must disclose exculpatory and impeachment material to the defendant "in time for its effective use at trial." *United States v. Coppa*, 267 F.3d 132, 135 (2d Cir. 2001). Generally, disclosure of *Brady* and *Giglio* material during the trial is deemed sufficiently timely.

Affirmative Defense Discovery Implications

Some discovery obligations arise as a result of affirmative defenses. If a defendant intends to present an alibi defense, he or she may need to provide notice to the government. Under Rule 12.1 the government may serve on the defendant a written demand stating the time, date, and place at which the offense was committed. This requires the defendant to serve on the government a written notice of alibi, stating the place the defendant claims to have been at the time and the names and addresses of supporting witnesses. This creates a reciprocal duty for the government to respond at least ten days before trial with a written notice of the witnesses on whom the government intends to rely to prove the defendant's presence at the scene, or to rebut the alibi witnesses.

On the other hand, Rule 12.2 requires the defendant, without request from the government, to file within the time provided for the filing of pretrial motions written notice of the defendant's intent to rely on a defense of insanity, or a mental disease or defect. If the defense intends to introduce expert testimony concerning the defendant's mental condition, including conditions short of insanity, the defense must give notice to the prosecution of that intention within the time provided for filing pretrial motions or at such later time as the court may direct. FED. R. CRIM. P. 12.2(b). The filing of such a notice entitles the prosecution to request disclosure of the expert testimony. FED. R. CRIM. P. 16(b)(1)(C). Of course, if the government then retains a mental health expert to rebut the defense evidence, it would trigger similar discovery obligations on the government to provide like information to the defense.

Rule 12.3. requires the defendant, without a request, to give notice that the defendant is relying upon a claim that the defendant was acting on behalf of a law enforcement or intelligence agency. This so-called Notice of Defense Based on Public Authority requires the government to file, within the time limits set out by the rule, a written response admitting or denying the defendant's claim. At that time, the government may, but need not, demand the names and addresses of the defense witnesses who will support the claim. After the defendant responds, the government must reply in kind, listing the names and addresses of its contrary witnesses.

STRATEGIC AND TACTICAL CONSIDERATIONS REGARDING DISCOVERY

Prosecutors have a significant amount of discretion and control over the production of discovery to defendants. Although the law requires production of some discovery, it does not require the government to provide defendants everything. Also, prosecutors can adopt practices that can limit some of the information that would become subject to discovery obligations. Prosecutors must also exercise judgment in determining whether a piece of information falls within the parameters of *Brady* or *Giglio* material. Finally, prosecutors have some control over the timing of producing discovery. Prosecutors are, then, in a position to control and limit the information provided to criminal defendants in advance of trial.

A quick perusal of Rule 16 reveals that strict adherence to that rule would result in defendants receiving very little evidence indeed. For example, federal investigations are largely based on agent reports (regarding surveillance, interviews agents conduct of witnesses, collection of evidence, and the like), and grand jury testimony. Rule 16(a)(2) specifically excludes these key documents from being subject to discovery. In other words, there is nothing in Rule 16 that would typically require the government to produce in discovery the very core documents reflecting the government's evidence.

Prosecutors also have some ability to control what information becomes subject to discovery rules. For example, the Jencks Act requires prosecutors to exercise some judgment in determining whether something becomes or is a "statement" under the act. If an agent interviews a witness, that witness interview report does not come within the scope of the Jencks Act unless the witness reviews and adopts the statement or the interview report contains direct quotes. Thus, by giving direction to agents to avoid direct quotes and by not showing the interview report to the witness, a prosecutor can ensure that report does not become discoverable under the Jencks Act.

Determining whether some piece of information is subject to disclosure under *Brady* or *Giglio* can be very difficult. Of course, some information can be clearly exculpatory, but more often information is exculpatory only in context and only in light of a theory of defense. A piece of information may have no apparent evidentiary value to a prosecutor and may not seem to be exculpatory, but it may fit perfectly into a defendant's theory of defense. Prosecutors are often not privy to the defendant's theory of defense, and so they may not be in the best position to determine whether information in the government's possession could be exculpatory. Prosecutors may consequently adopt restrictive interpretations of what evidence may be potentially exculpatory, trusting that on appeal any error may be found harmless. On the other hand, prosecutors may choose to avoid that risk by adopting a broader interpretation, or by making all information available to defense counsel.

Finally, prosecutors have some ability to control the timing of disclosure of discovery. The Jencks Act, for example, does not require production of a witness's statement until after the witness has testified. If a prosecutor delayed producing Jencks Act statements until after a witness testified, it would necessitate a delay in the proceedings so as to allow the defense attorney time to review the prior statements by the witness to conduct an effective cross-examination. Federal district courts often resolve this unrealistic timetable by adopting local rules that require the government to produce Jencks Act statements a few days in advance of trial. Nevertheless, even under such local rules, prosecutors can delay disclosure of Jencks Act material until the last possible moment. Further, as noted, the law requires the government to produce *Brady* and *Giglio* materials to defendants in a timely manner so that it is useful to the defense. Generally, disclosure of *Brady* material during the trial meets this timeliness standard, but not always. Thus, prosecutors can delay production of *Brady* materials until the last possible moment, hoping that a reviewing court will find the delayed disclosure sufficient.

Because prosecutors have some control over the nature of information provided to defendants in discovery, and the timing of disclosure, prosecutors must exercise judgment in making those decisions. If a prosecutor errs in determining what it must disclose to a defendant under Rule 16, under the Jencks Act, or under *Brady* and *Giglio*, the prosecutor risks suppression of evidence, a mistrial, or possibly even dismissal of charges. Likewise, if a prosecutor unduly delays disclosure of discoverable information, the prosecutor risks a continuance, a mistrial, or possibly a reversal of the conviction on appeal. In exercising this judgment, then, prosecutors should consider several factors.

First, keeping in mind that a prosecutor's responsibility is to see that justice is done, discovery decisions should not be a product of gamesmanship. In other words, prosecutors should not decide against disclosure of information, or delay disclosure of information, simply for the purpose of making it harder for defense attorneys to defend their clients. The government should not win convictions because it gained an unfair advantage over defense counsel by playing games with the disclosure of information. Prosecutors must recall that defense counsel are already at a disadvantage compared to prosecutors. Defense counsel often know nothing about a case until their clients have been charged, while prosecutors already know everything about the case. Early and full disclosure of discovery to defense counsel helps ensure defendants are provided effective assistance of counsel.

Second, full and early disclosure of discovery may aid in plea negotiations. The more a defendant knows about the quantity and quality of the government's evidence against him or her, the more likely the defendant is to come to terms with the benefits of pleading guilty. The sooner a defendant makes the decision to plead guilty, the less time and resources the prosecutor has to devote to the case, and the more manageable the prosecutor's trial schedule becomes.

Third, making full and early disclosure of discovery materials will absolve the prosecutor of the responsibility of making the difficult judgment call of whether something is or is not exculpatory. Because a failure to comply with discovery requirements and with *Brady* and *Giglio* has such dire consequences, many US Attorney's Offices have adopted discovery practices of generally providing a copy of the government entire discovery file to the defense for review. Under this practice, the defense attorney has as much access to the material as the government and is equally capable of determining whether there is exonerating or impeaching evidence, thus negating the government's responsibility to make those determinations. *See, e.g., United States v. Newton*, 259 F.3d 964 (8th Cir. 2001) (finding that there was no Jencks Act violation when materials were available to defense in the government's open file discovery); *United States v. Johnson*, 751 F.2d 291, 295 (8th Cir. 1984) (open file discovery makes discovery motions unnecessary because defense has access to as much information as the government). Similarly, by making such full disclosure of discovery, prosecutors may avoid claims of error for failing to provide timely notice of Rule 404(b) evidence. In some districts, US Attorney's Offices reach agreements with the defense bar that full disclosure of discovery will obviate the government's obligation under Rule 404(b) to identify evidence it intends to use under that rule, reasoning that defense counsel is as capable as prosecutors in determining what evidence could fall within the scope of the rule.

Fourth, although full and early disclosure of discovery has many advantages, prosecutors must also consider the security issues. In cases involving national security or risks to witnesses or others, or when disclosure would jeopardize an ongoing criminal investigation, prosecutors may decide in particular cases to alter their usual discovery practices. In such cases, prosecutors may choose to maintain a closed file and provide the defendant only what is required under the Federal Rules of Criminal Procedure, the Jencks Act, or the Constitution. Alternatively, prosecutors could generally provide defense counsel with a copy of the government's discovery file except for holding back on some of the information. Prosecutors may also decide to delay disclosure of certain information for security reasons. Similarly, prosecutors may carefully redact discovery information provided to defense counsel so as to provide as much as possible as early as possible, while still meeting the secu rity needs of the case. When a prosecutor has the practice of usually providing full and open discovery, the prosecutor should alert defense counsel when the prosecutor varies from this practice in a particular case.

Fifth, prosecutors need not disclose purely rebuttal evidence as part of their discovery obligations. *United States v. Delia*, 944 F.2d 1010, 1017-18 (2d Cir. 1991) (holding that Rule 16 does not require the government to disclose rebuttal evidence intended for use against a line of defense); *United States v. Presser*, 844 F.2d 1275, 1285 (6th Cir. 1988) (holding that the government need not turn over impeachment evidence that tends to negate guilt). Prosecutors should determine, then, whether evidence fits within this category. If the prosecutor will not use the evidence in the government's case-in-chief, and the relevance of the evidence only arises if the defendant presents specific evidence, then the prosecutor may determine that the evidence is, indeed, only rebuttal evidence and not disclose it. Nevertheless, prosecutors must be careful to make sure that the evidence is not otherwise exculpatory in some way.

In summary, prosecutors should consider providing full and early discovery to defense counsel. The benefits generally outweigh the detriments. Prosecutors can enhance a defense counsel's ability to provide affective assistance, can increase the likelihood of an early plea, and are much less likely to be found to have violated a defendant's constitutional rights when prosecutors choose to fully disclose the government's discovery file.

RECIPROCAL DISCOVERY AND AFFIRMATIVE DEFENSES

Although the government has an obligation to, and in practice does, provide defendants with a fair amount of discovery, defendants, in turn, have very little obligation to provide the government with reciprocal discovery. Rule

16(b) of the Federal Rules of Criminal Procedure outlines a defendant's reciprocal discovery obligations. Generally speaking, a defendant need only provide the government with expert information and the results of tests or examinations. FED. R. CRIM. P. 16(b)(1)(B) & (C). Although a defendant must provide the government with copies of papers, photographs, and other documents, it need do so only to the extent the defendant intends to introduce those items into evidence in his or her case. FED. R. CRIM. P. 16(b)(1) (A). Defendants sometimes do not know what evidence they will present in the case-in-chief until the government presents its case. When that happens, defense counsel may not be able or required to disclose Rule 16 discovery pretrial and can only disclose the information after the government presents its case. There is no time frame attached to Rule 16 reciprocal discovery. Thus, some defense attorneys wait until the government presents its entire case before deciding what documents, photographs, or other documents to introduce in the defense case. Obviously, discovery of those items at that late date is of minimal value to the government.

Defendants also have an obligation under the Jencks Act to produce statements of witnesses the defendant intends to call as witnesses. This is sometimes referred to as "reverse Jencks Act material." Again, this obligation is triggered only when the defendant decides who he is going to call as a witness at trial. So, a defendant can delay disclosure of this reciprocal discovery to the government by delaying the decision of who to call as witnesses at trial.

Finally, as noted, defendants are obliged to disclose certain affirmative defense evidence to the government. Defendants must provide the government of advance notice and information regarding an insanity defense or a defense based on a claim that the defendant had government authority to engage in the conduct. Defendants must provide this information to the government regardless of whether the government asks for such disclosure. A defendant's failure to do so may result in a court barring admission of the evidence. In contrast, a defendant is obliged to disclose alibi defense information to the government only upon a specific request by the government and upon disclosure by the government of specific date, time, and location information about the offense.

Prosecutors must be vigilant and attentive to defendants' reciprocal discovery obligations. In any case where there is any possibility of an alibi for any act the prosecutor believes the defendant committed in furtherance of the offense, the prosecutor must be sure to make a timely request for notice of an alibi defense. Prosecutors should similarly demand Rule 16 and Jencks Act reciprocal discovery from defense counsel and be alert for possible violations.

Chapter Thirteen

Handling Pretrial Motions

Prosecutors are involved in litigating pretrial motions in almost every criminal case. The number and complexity of the pretrial motions are directly proportionate to the seriousness and complexity of the charges and evidence in the case. In some routine cases, defense counsel may not file any pretrial motions for the very simple reason that there is nothing of merit to litigate pretrial. On the other end of the spectrum, some complex cases can consume months or even years of pretrial litigation, sometimes resulting in interlocutory appeals and multiple subsequent delays in the trial date. As a prosecutor I handled some cases that involved scores of pretrial motions, multiple hearings, and an interlocutory appeal or two.

There are several categories of pretrial motions encountered in federal criminal cases. Generally, they consist of motions to dismiss the indictment, motions to change the indictment, motions to change the trial, motions to suppress evidence, motions regarding discovery, and motions in limine.[1] I will discuss each in turn.

MOTIONS TO DISMISS INDICTMENTS

Defendants may attack indictments on a number of grounds. First, a defendant may challenge an indictment for being insufficient as a matter of law. FED. R. CRIM. P. 12. In some instances a defendant may allege that the indictment fails to allege a federal offense on its face. For instance, a defendant may assert that the indictment failed to include language referencing an essential element of the crime. In a bank robbery case, for example, the indictment would be insufficient on its face if it failed to allege that the financial institution was federally insured. Additionally, a defendant may seek dismissal of an indictment if, on its face, it is clear that the indictment is barred by the statute of limitations.

To avoid having to handle these pretrial motions, prosecutors simply have to be careful and precise when drafting indictments. It is helpful for prosecution offices to have a process that involves a supervisor reviewing and approving indictments drafted by line prosecutors. This review process will often prevent these types of errors. Typically prosecutors can correct these errors easily enough by submitting a superseding indictment to the grand jury to correct the error. In some instances, however, these scrivener's errors can be fatal to a case when, for example, the statute of limitations ran after the return of the initial indictment and before the prosecutor can resubmit the case to the grand jury for a superseding indictment.

Defendants sometimes challenge indictments by alleging that the government has abused the grand jury process in some manner. A defendant may allege a violation of the Fifth Amendment's Due Process Clause by asserting, for example, that the government knowingly presented perjured testimony to the grand jury. Defendants may also bring such motions when a witness testified about irrelevant and highly prejudicial information before a grand jury. In a case involving a felon in possession of a firearm, for example, a defendant may argue a violation of due process if a witness testified that the defendant allegedly sexually abused a child. Similarly, defendants may claim an abuse of the grand jury process based on allegedly improper comments by prosecutors or when a prosecutor erroneously instructed the grand jury regarding the elements of an offense.

To prevail on a Due Process Clause claim, however, a defendant must show that the perjured testimony "substantially influenced the grand jury's decision to indict." *Bank of Nova Scotia v. United States*, 487 US 250, 256 (1988). Courts have, on occasion, relied on their inherent supervisory power over the grand jury to dismiss an indictment upon a showing of knowing or intentional prosecutorial misconduct. *See, e.g., United States v. Hogan*, 712 F.2d 757, 761–62 (2d Cir. 1983) (indictment dismissed when court found prosecutor's conduct was flagrant and extremely prejudicial); *United States v. Broward*, 594 F.2d 345, 351 (2d Cir. 1979) (indictment dismissed when court found misconduct was repetitive and entrenched). The authority of courts to dismiss an indictment on inherent supervisory power is questionable, however, in light of the Supreme Court's holding in *United States v. Williams*, 504 US 36, 46 (1992), in which the Court said that "as a general matter at least" courts do not have supervisory power over grand juries, which are considered entities separate from the court.

To avoid having to deal with these pretrial motions, prosecutors need to exercise careful control over grand jury presentations. Prosecutors should be ever vigilant for possible perjured testimony by grand jury witnesses and when discovered be sure to present evidence to the grand jury correcting the record. Similarly, prosecutors should ensure that grand jury proceedings are not infected by irrelevant and inflammatory testimony. Prosecutors can prevent this in part by preparing grand jury witnesses properly and by asking carefully tailored questions. When, however, a witness testifies about some improper matter, it is incumbent upon the prosecutor to instruct the grand jurors to disregard the testimony. Finally, prosecutors must be cautious about their own performance before a grand jury. They should, of course, ensure that they provide accurate instructions to the grand jury on the elements of the offenses under consideration. Likewise, it is helpful for prosecutors to remind the grand jurors that what prosecutors say is not evidence. Prosecutors should not provide any factual information to the grand jury, even when asked, as sometimes they are, by grand jurors. If grand jurors have questions about the facts of the case, prosecutors should call witnesses to answer those questions. Finally, if prosecutors make opening statements or closing arguments to grand juries, the prosecutor should again remind the grand jury that the prosecutor's comments are not evidence, and the prosecutor should be careful not to make statements that would be improper, such as appealing to the grand jurors' sense of duty, making comments to provoke emotional responses, or providing the prosecutor's personal views about the evidence or the target's guilt.

On rare occasions, defendants assert that the court should dismiss an indictment because of outrageous government conduct. These motions are often based not on how the grand jury reached its decision but based on assertions that the underlying criminal investigation shocked the conscious of the court for some reason. *See, e.g., United States v. Hudson*, 3 F. Supp.3d 772, 778–79 (C.D. Cal. 2014) (dismissing indictment on ground that reverse sting operation was deemed improper), reversed *sub nom United States v. Dunlap*, 593 F. App'x 619, 621 (9th Cir. 2014). These motions seldom meet with success, no matter how egregious the underlying government conduct may have been. *See, e.g., United States v. Nolan-Cooper*, 155 F.3d 221 (3rd Cir. 1998) (denying a motion dismiss for outrageous government conduct even when a federal agent had sexual intercourse with the target, an attorney, during an undercover money-laundering investigation); *United States v. Ornelas-Rodriguez*, 12 F.3d 1339 (5th Cir. 1994) (denying a motion to dismiss for outrageous government conduct even when a federal agent allegedly had sex with a witness and used his influence to persuade the witness to cooperate against the defendant); *United States v. Cuervelo*, 949 F.2d 559 (2d Cir. 1991) (denying a motion to dismiss for outrageous government conduct even when a federal agent conducting a drug conspiracy investigation tried to establish a "love interest" between himself and the defendant, had sexual relations with her on at least fifteen occasions, bought her gifts, and wrote her love letters).

A common thread among the decisions where courts have addressed motions to dismiss for outrageous government conduct is a focus on the knowledge and conduct of prosecutors in relation to the conduct. Courts frequently find dismissal inappropriate when prosecutors were unaware of and did not approve of the misconduct. Similarly, courts comment favorably when prosecutors take corrective action when they do find out about such conduct. Corrective action can include putting an end to the misconduct, removing the offending personnel from the case, fully disclosing the misconduct to a grand jury and defense counsel, and not introducing or relying on evidence obtained as a result of the misconduct when possible.

One important point to remember in federal criminal practice is that a defendant cannot challenge an indictment based on an assertion that it is not supported by the facts, or on the ground that the undisputed facts mandate judgment in favor of the defendant. In civil practice, litigants can bring such motions, called motions for summary judgment, in which the court is called upon to render judgment in one party's favor based upon a finding of certain facts. *See, e.g., United States v. Ferro*, 252 F.3d 964, 968 (8th Cir. 2001) (citing cases). In federal criminal practice, trial is the only time that the judgment is rendered based upon the facts of the case.

MOTIONS TO CHANGE INDICTMENTS

In some instances, defendants do not dispute that the indictment is sufficient as a matter of law, but they may allege that the indictment should be changed for some reason. One of the more common pretrial motions of this nature is a motion alleging improper joinder. Rule 8(a) of the Federal Rules of Criminal Procedure describes properly joined offenses, providing:

> Joinder of Offenses. The indictment or information may charge a defendant in separate counts with 2 or more offenses if the offenses charged—whether felonies or misdemeanors or both—are of the same or similar character, or are based on the same act or transaction, or are connected with or constitute parts of a common scheme or plan.

FED. R. CRIM. P. 8(a). Rule 8(b) of the Federal Rules of Criminal Procedure addresses when criminal defendants are properly joined.

> Joinder of Defendants. The indictment or information may charge 2 or more defendants if they are alleged to have participated in the same act or transaction,

or in the same series of acts or transactions, constituting an offense or offenses. The defendants may be charged in one or more counts together or separately. All defendants need not be charged in each count.

FED. R. CRIM. P. 8(b). Motions alleging improper joinder, either of offenses or defendants, assert that the indictment failed to comply with these rules of Federal Criminal Procedure in some regard. As noted in chapter 11 on Charging Strategies and Tactics, prosecutors must consider the joinder rules when drafting indictments to ensure that they strictly comply with Rule 8.

Another, albeit less common, pretrial motion to change an indictment is a motion to strike language in the indictment. Rule 7(d) of the Federal Rules of Criminal Procedure provides that "Upon the defendant's motion, the court may strike surplusage from the indictment or information." The purpose of Rule 7(d) is to protect a defendant against prejudicial allegations that are neither relevant nor material to the charges made in the indictment. *United States v. Fahey*, 769 F.2d 829, 841–42 (1st Cir. 1985). Thus, defendants may file motions to strike when they believe that the indictment contains allegations, whether true or untrue, which the defendants claim are unnecessary to the pleading and which is somehow prejudicial or damaging to the defendants. Language that is informative (for example, describing a defendant as a member of a gang or organized crime family as part of a RICO indictment) should generally not be stricken simply because it may also be prejudicial. Prosecutors can avoid being subject to Rule 7(d) motions by stripping indictments of pejorative and inflammatory language.

MOTIONS TO CHANGE TRIALS

Rule 14 of the Federal Rules of Criminal Procedure provides for the severance of offenses or defendants, even if properly joined in the first place under Rule 8.

(a) Relief. If the joinder of offenses or defendants in an indictment, an information, or a consolidation for trial appears to prejudice a defendant or the government, the court may order separate trials of counts, sever the defendants' trials, or provide any other relief that justice requires.

(b) Defendant's Statements. Before ruling on a defendant's motion to sever, the court may order an attorney for the government to deliver to the court for in camera inspection any defendant's statement that the government intends to use as evidence.

FED. R. CRIM. P. 14. Thus, if it appears that a defendant or the government is prejudiced by a joinder of offenses or of defendants in an indictment or information or by such joinder for trial together, a court may order an election or separate trials of counts, grant a severance of defendants, or provide whatever other relief justice requires. To be clear, a defendant filing a motion under Rule 8 is alleging that the offenses or defendants were wrongfully joined in that the indictment fails to meet the requirements of Rule 8. On the other hand, a motion under Rule 14 asserts that, even though the joinder of offenses or defendants complied with Rule 8, the offenses or defendants should nevertheless be severed to ensure a fair trial.

One reason either a defendant or the government may move to sever defendants under Rule 14 is because one defendant made a confession in which he incriminated a co-defendant. That confession would be admissible against the confessor as an admission of a party opponent. FED. R. EVID. 801(d)(2). Because each defendant has a Fifth Amendment right to remain silent, however, admitting a confession by one defendant implicating another defendant would prevent that defendant from being able to confront an accuser in violation of that defendant's Sixth Amendment rights. *See Bruton v. United States*, 391 US 123, 137 (1968). Subsection (b) allows a court to order the government to deliver to the court for inspection in camera any statements or confessions made by the defendants which the government intends to introduce in evidence at trial, so that a court can determine whether admission of the statement would violate a defendant's Sixth Amendment rights.

Prosecutors can sometimes avoid having to address motions under Rule 14 by anticipating the issues in advance and choosing to separate charges or defendants even when they could be properly joined under Rule 8. When I had cases that clearly involved *Bruton* issues that could not be solved by redacting one defendant's statements so as not to incriminate a potential co-defendant, I simply indicted defendants separately knowing the court would grant a motion to sever. Sometimes, however, evidence arises after indictment that gives rise to a Rule 14 motion, and in those instances there is little a prosecutor can do except deal with the issue at that time.

Another pretrial motion aimed at the manner in which the trial is to occur, versus an attack on the indictment itself, is a motion for change of venue. Rule 18 of the Federal Rules of Criminal Procedure provides, in pertinent part, that "Unless a statute or these rules permit otherwise, the government must prosecute an offense in a district where the offense was committed." Rule 18 reflects similar dictates in the US Constitution. "The Trial of all Crimes . . . shall be held in the State where the said Crimes shall have been committed. . . ." US CONST. ART. III, § 2, cl. 3. "In all criminal prosecutions, the accused shall enjoy the right to a speedy and public trial, by an impartial jury of the State and district wherein the crime shall have been committed. . . ." *Id.* AMEND. VI. Thus, a defendant may file a motion to move the trial to another district if the defendant believes the offense occurred in another district. Sometimes discerning where a crime was committed can be difficult, depending on the facts and the nature of the offense, and in other cases a crime may occur in multiple districts.

Even when the venue is properly in the district, under Rule 18, a defendant may nevertheless seek to change venue for other reasons. Rule 21(a) of the Federal Rules of Criminal Procedure provide that a "court must transfer the proceeding against that defendant to another district if the court is satisfied that so great a prejudice against the defendant exists in the transferring district that the defendant cannot obtain a fair and impartial trial there." FED. R. CRIM. P. 21(a). Pretrial publicity or notoriety of the offense, such as in the Timothy McVey trial, may be a ground for seeking a change of venue under this rule. A court may also "transfer the proceeding, or one or more counts, against [a] defendant to another district for the convenience of the parties, any victim, and the witnesses, and in the interest of justice." FED. R. CRIM. P. 21(b). Only a defendant may file a motion under Rule 21.

There is often little prosecutors can do to avoid having to respond to Rule 21(a) motions other than avoid generating publicity about a case that would be adverse to the defendant. When responding to Rule 21(b) motions, prosecutors should be careful to ensure that victims' rights are upheld and properly balanced against other factors that may favor a defendant's request to change the venue. The Advisory Committee Notes emphasize that Rule 21(b) "requires the court to consider the convenience of victims—as well as the convenience of the parties and witnesses and the interests of justice—in determining whether to transfer all or part of the proceeding to another district for trial." FED. R. CRIM. P. 21 advisory committee's note to 2010 amendment. Prosecutors should also be wary of defendants using Rule 21(b) motions as a means of forum shopping. Rule 21(b) is not intended to provide a mechanism for forum shopping by defendants and "require[s] that a transfer for convenience satisfy the convenience of both parties." *United States v. Jamal*, 246 F. App'x 351, 369 (6th Cir. 2007).

MOTIONS TO SUPPRESS EVIDENCE

The most common motion filed in federal criminal cases is a motion to suppress evidence. Although the Constitution does not explicitly provide for the suppression of evidence obtained in violation of a defendant's constitutional rights, the courts have fashioned an exclusionary rule. *See Arizona v. Evans*,

514 US 1 (1995) (exclusionary rule is a judicially created remedy). The purpose of the exclusionary rule is to punish law enforcement officers for violating a defendant's constitutional rights and to deter wrongful government conduct in the future by suppressing or excluding evidence obtained in violation of the Constitution. *Evans*, 514 US at 14–15.

Defendants may file motions to suppress statements obtained from a defendant in violation of the Fifth Amendment right to remain silent, or the Fifth or Sixth Amendment rights to counsel. Likewise, a defendant may move to suppress evidence obtained in violation of the Fourth Amendment prohibition against unreasonable searches and seizures. Under the Supreme Court's decision in *Wong Sun v. United States*, 371 US 471, 484 (1963), a defendant may seek to suppress not only the specific evidence obtained directly as a result of a violation of his or her constitutional rights, but also any other evidence derived from that violation, referred to as the "fruit of the poisonous tree."

Suppression motions are some of the most important and difficult pretrial motions that prosecutors handle. In many cases, an order suppressing evidence may require the government to dismiss the case for want of admissible evidence to prove the defendant's guilty beyond a reasonable doubt. Even in those cases when the government may still have enough evidence to move forward with the case, the suppression of evidence may have weakened the persuasiveness of the case. And hearings on motions to suppress evidence inevitably require prosecutors to present evidence, often involving live witnesses. Indeed, some suppression hearings can involve testimony by many witnesses and take hours, if not days.

The way for prosecutors to avoid suppression motions is (1) to work with law enforcement officers to ensure that they do not violate a defendant's constitutional rights and (2) to not bring charges that rely on evidence that was obtained in violation of a defendant's constitutional rights. As noted above, in some cases prosecutors are actively involved with the law enforcement officers throughout the investigation, guiding them in their work. In these cases, it is incumbent upon prosecutors to ensure that the officers fully understand what is and is not allowed under the constitution and that they take actions strictly in compliance with the constitution. In other cases, law enforcement officers bring cases to prosecutors after completion of an investigation in which the prosecutor has little or no oversight or involvement. It is important in those latter cases that prosecutors carefully analyze the evidence, staying alert to any possible constitutional violations. When a prosecutor believes that officers engaged in conduct that may give rise to a motion to suppress, the prosecutor must thoughtfully determine whether the conduct did violate the constitution. If the prosecutor concludes that it did, then the prosecutor must decide whether there is anything the prosecutor can do to remedy the problem (by way of a second search warrant, for example) and, if not, whether the remaining evidence is sufficient to prove the case beyond a reasonable doubt. If the prosecutor concludes that the error cannot be corrected and without the evidence that would be suppressed there is not proof beyond a reasonable doubt, the prosecutor should decline to prosecute the case. It is very important that the prosecutor perform this gatekeeping function well because the integrity of the criminal justice system depends on it. Further, failing to do so often results in case law that can be adverse to the government not only in the instant case but in other cases as well.

As noted, when prosecutors resist motions to suppress it almost inevitably requires an evidentiary hearing. Prosecutors must prepare for these hearings with care and diligence. They must carefully review the asserted constitutional violations and be sure to present all evidence that could be relevant to a court's resolution of that issue. Prosecutors may also need to present evidence on other possible suppression grounds not raised by defense counsel, if the grounds are apparent to the prosecutor. Sometimes defense counsel do not immediately spot all of the possible grounds for suppression or inexpertly articulate the basis for the suppression motion. The prosecutor must conduct an independent review of the evidence, searching for any possible suppression grounds and anticipate it by presenting sufficient evidence to prove the constitutionality of the government's conduct.

In preparing for evidentiary hearings on motions to suppress, it is often helpful to research the case law on the grounds asserted. This research should be focused on identifying any standards or factors courts have identified in these other cases to determine if the law enforcement officers violated the defendant's constitutional rights. But the research should also focus on the underlying facts that the courts found important in each of these cases in deciding the issues. By focusing on these facts, prosecutors can better identify the evidence that the prosecutor should present at the hearing that will be helpful to the court in deciding the issue.

Finally, it is important in handling suppression hearings that prosecutors are vigilant for possible attacks on a law enforcement officer's credibility. If a court finds that a law enforcement officer was not credible at a suppression hearing, it may constitute information that is required to be disclosed under *Giglio*. More important, a judicial finding that a law enforcement officer lied under oath could spell the end of the officer's career. If an officer intentionally lies, it is fitting that the officer's career is irreparably damaged. On the other hand, if the officer merely made a mistake or forgot something, or the testimony is based on the officer's honestly held judgment or perception, then a finding that the officer was not credible may unjustly damage a good officer's career. Thus, when a defense attorney attacks a law enforcement officer's credibility at a suppression hearing (or at any hearing, for that matter), it is very important that the prosecutor address the issue aggressively. Sometimes this involves conducting redirect examination to clarify testimony or evidence, and on other occasions it may involve presenting corroborating evidence. If a judge makes a finding that an officer was not credible when the prosecutor believes the officer was honest, the prosecutor should take measures to protect the officer. A prosecutor may, for example, request that the court clarify that the credibility finding was based on a conclusion that the officer made an honest mistake, had poor memory, or the like, and specifically find that the officer did not intentionally provide false testimony.

MOTIONS REGARDING DISCOVERY

Defendants sometimes file pretrial motions in an effort to obtain greater discovery from the government. For example, Rule 7(f) provides that "[t]he court may direct the government to file a bill of particulars." A bill of particular is intended to inform defendants about the details of the charges against them and to allow them to prepare their defenses. *See, e.g., United States v. Torres,* 901 F.2d 205, 234 (2d Cir. 1990) (quoting 1 C. Wright, Federal Practice and Procedure § 129, at 434–35 [2d ed. 1982]).[2] A defendant may file a motion for a bill of particulars before arraignment, within fourteen days after arraignment, or at such later time as a court may permit. Fed. R. Crim. P. 7(f). A court may permit the government to amend a bill of particulars at any time before the verdict is returned. *Id.*

A bill of particulars is simply a request that the government explain its indictment in more detail. As noted in a prior chapter, Rule 7 requires that an indictment "be a plain, concise, and definite written statement of the essential facts constituting the offense charged." Fed. R. Crim. P. 7(c)(1). Although mere notice pleading is thus all that is required under the Federal Rules of Criminal Procedure, a defendant may be entitled to a bill of particulars if the indictment nevertheless lacks sufficient detail for the defendant to know what crime he or she has been accused of committing, or if necessary for him or her to mount a meaningful defense or determine if he or she is being subjected to double jeopardy. Prosecutors can avoid having to deal with motions for bills of particular by carefully drafting indictments.

Sometimes defendants file pretrial motions seeking to discover the identity of confidential informants or sources of information. As a general matter, the courts are reluctant to require the government to reveal the identity of confidential informants who are not going to be witnesses at trial but will compel disclosure if justice requires. A defendant must make a showing in these cases for why the identity of the informant is necessary. Prosecutors should aggressively protect the identity of informants when justice does not require disclosure of their identities. Even when prosecutors conclude on their own, or a court finds, that an informant's identity should be disclosed, prosecutors can take steps to limit the disclosure only to defense counsel or to ensure that the information is not further disseminated beyond what is necessary for the attorney to defend the case.

Chapter Fourteen

Plea Negotiations and Plea Hearings

More than 90 percent of all criminal cases are resolved by way of guilty pleas. Indeed, the criminal justice system would likely break down if every criminal case went to trial. In most instances if a prosecutor does a good job leading others, overseeing and directing the investigation of the case, developing the case well through the grand jury process, and making wise charging decisions, defendants and defense counsel recognize the inevitability of defeat, the benefits from pleading guilty, and fold their cards. Some cases end up in trials precisely because the prosecutor failed to properly develop, prepare, and charge the case. The efficient and effective operation of the criminal justice system, then, depends upon prosecutors doing their job well before ever entering a courtroom to try a case.

Prosecutors have a responsibility to negotiate appropriate plea deals, that is, deals that result in a just resolution of the case given the strength of the government's case, the nature of the crime, and the characteristics of the defendant. Prosecutors must also negotiate appropriately worded plea agreements that hold defendants to the terms and do not allow a defendant to evade responsibility. Finally, prosecutors must ensure that when a defendant enters a guilty plea, that it fully complies with the law.

NEGOTIATING PLEA AGREEMENTS

It is important that prosecutors successfully negotiate appropriate plea deals. In determining the terms of a plea agreement, prosecutors must consider a large number of factors. These include the strength of the government's case, the potential sentence, the collateral consequences of a guilty plea to the defendant and any victims, and the impact the plea may have on the instant and other criminal cases. It should be noted that individual prosecutors' discretion may be limited by office policies and supervisory approval regarding plea agreements.

The strength of the government's case has a significant impact on a prosecutor's ability to negotiate an appropriate plea agreement. Prosecutors may need to make concessions in plea agreements when the government's case is weak. Perhaps the case was weak to begin with, or it may have become weak due to a court's ruling or a change in the evidence (such as a witness becoming uncooperative or unavailable). Whatever the reason, negotiating from a position of weakness is difficult to do. When appropriate and necessary, prosecutors may have to make significant concessions to extract any degree of justice from the case. On the other hand, sometimes prosecutors must just take a chance at trial if making too great of a concession would result in a miscarriage of justice.

The type of plea negotiated with a defendant should permit the court the ability to exercise its discretion to impose a proper sentence. In other words, prosecutors should be careful to avoid reaching plea agreements that would unduly restrict a judge's discretion. In some instances, prosecutors may insist that a defendant plead to a crime that carries a mandatory minimum sentence, which would naturally restrict the sentencing judge's discretion to impose a lower sentence, when that is deemed the appropriate sentence. Similarly, in the appropriate case a prosecutor may negotiate a plea to charges with a statutory maximum that would naturally restrict the sentencing judge's discretion to impose a greater sentence. On the other hand, although a prosecutor may have a particular sentencing range in mind in a particular case, the prosecutor may want to insist on guilty pleas to a certain charge or charges to permit the court leeway to impose a harsher sentence. In other cases, a prosecutor may want to negotiate a plea in a way that allows the court to impose a lenient sentence and not be bound, for instance, by a mandatory minimum sentence, even if the prosecutor believes the appropriate sentence would be greater than such a mandatory minimum sentence.

In determining an appropriate plea based on the possible sentence in federal cases, prosecutors should consider not only any mandatory minimum and maximum sentence that would apply to a charge, but also how the offense would likely score under the US Sentencing Guidelines. The charge or charges to which a defendant pleas can affect the advisory guideline range for the defendant. Similarly, in negotiating a plea, the parties can reach agreements about how they believe the guidelines should apply to the case. When prosecutors can reach agreements on the application of the guidelines, it reduces contested issues the sentencing judge must decide, simplifies sentencing hearings, and reduces the possibility of errors that can be raised on appeal.

In determining an appropriate plea offer, prosecutors should also consider how the deal may impact the defendant in ways other than time in prison or a fine. Convictions to some charges may affect a defendant's immigration status, result in the loss of the defendant's professional license, determine whether the defendant is barred from engaging in business with the government, require a defendant to register as a sex offender, and affect many other liberty and property interests. In some instances, it may be in the interest of justice to insist on guilty pleas to certain charges to ensure that the defendant is subject to these collateral consequences. For example, to prevent future harm it may be very important to ensure a defendant pleads guilty to a charge that would strip the defendant of a license that permitted the defendant to commit the harm in the first instance. Prosecutors can also negotiate pleas that result in collateral consequences, even when those consequences would not automatically operate as a matter of law. For instance, I prosecuted a police officer once for using his position to sexually abuse female motorists. I insisted as part of the plea agreement that he resign as an officer and not thereafter seek employment as a law enforcement officer for a period of years.

Prosecutors must also consider the impact the plea deal will have on the instant investigation, on other related investigations, and on other unrelated prosecutions. The deal a prosecutor cuts with one defendant may impact, positively or negatively, the government's ability to negotiate plea deals with other defendants in an investigation. A prosecutor who strikes too hard of a deal may end up with more trials. The deal a prosecutor strikes with one defendant may also impact the ability to hold other defendants fully accountable. A prosecutor who strikes too generous of a deal with one defendant may find it difficult to strike deals with other defendants who deserve harsher sentences. Also, the deal a prosecutor strikes with a defendant in one case can impact other related and unrelated investigations. Defense attorneys talk and compare notes. They may perceive, rightly or wrongly, that plea negotiations would be fruitless because a prosecutor seeks plea bargains that are too harsh in a particular case or generally. Conversely, defense counsel may perceive a plea offer made by one prosecutor as too harsh because another prosecutor made a much more lenient offer in a related case or in a different but similar case. For this reason, it is important that a prosecutor's office exercise some oversight and control over the plea offers made by individual prosecutors to ensure an evenhanded and rational basis for negotiated pleas.

DRAFTING PLEA AGREEMENTS

Plea agreements should be reduced to writing to ensure that there is no question regarding the terms of the agreement between the government and a defendant. Of course, a defendant can always plead guilty to charges without entering into a plea agreement with the government. If the prosecutor is giving anything to a defendant—making a concession on charges, sentence, or collateral consequences, or agreeing to forgo taking any future action against the defendant—it should generally be in the form of a written plea agreement. Prosecutors should seldom enter into oral agreements. Again, office policy and supervisory control may dictate much of this.

In drafting a plea agreement, there are a number of factors that prosecutors should consider. First, the plea agreement should be written to specifically and clearly state all terms of the agreement. That includes the offense(s) of conviction, the mandatory minimum and maximum sentence the defendant faces, any collateral consequences the defendant may incur, and any concessions either party is making. These concessions can involve charges dropped, an agreement to forgo charges, sentencing agreements, and agreements as to collateral consequences that could arise from the guilty plea.

Second, a plea agreement should contain an accurate statement of facts that establish the elements of the offense, including venue and jurisdiction. It is incumbent upon prosecutors to make sure that these facts are precisely true and completely sufficient to establish guilt beyond a reasonable doubt. Importantly, the facts need to establish jurisdiction and venue in the court where the defendant is pleading guilty; this is something prosecutors occasionally forget to do. Prosecutors may also want to insist the defendant admit to additional facts regarding relevant criminal conduct or that which would be necessary to trigger sentencing guideline provisions or affect collateral consequences. When a defendant is part of a larger prosecution or criminal enterprise, it is helpful to include facts that would require the defendant to truthfully implicate others in the defendant's criminal conduct, even if the defendant is not a cooperator. Requiring a defendant to identify a cohort by name and admit the cohort's involvement in criminal conduct prevents the defendant from falsely testifying on behalf of the cohort in the future.

Third, prosecutors may consider including a provision in which the defendant waives the right to bar admissions of fact the defendant made during plea negotiations and in the statement of facts. Federal Rule of Evidence 410 generally bars admission of such evidence, unless waived. A waiver provision thus permits the government to use the admissions contained in the fact section against the defendant if the defendant backs out of the plea before entering it, withdraws his or her guilty plea, or breaches the plea agreement. This provision is very helpful when defendants consider trying to withdraw their guilty pleas at a later time. Occasionally a defendant who pleaded guilty will have a change of heart after seeing the draft presentence investigation report and fully comprehending the sentence the defendant is likely to receive.

These defendants will frequently then try to withdraw their guilty pleas by claiming they entered the pleas unknowingly or involuntarily, claiming their attorneys misrepresented the sentence they would receive, or making similar excuses. When, however, the plea agreement contains a waiver of Rule 410, then the defendant realizes that if he or she proceeds to trial the government will have as new evidence the signed plea agreement in which he or she confessed to all of the facts constituting the elements of the crimes. This often discourages defendants from making warrantless motions to withdraw their guilty pleas.

Fourth, the plea agreement should contain a provision for any sentencing agreement that is part of the plea bargain. Sometimes the parties make an agreement to a particular sentence that is binding on the judge if the court accepts the plea agreement. In other instances, the parties may make an agreement as to the sentence or sentencing provisions that is binding on the parties, but not the judge. Parties may be able to reach an agreement as to some sentencing issues and not others. For example, the parties may agree how certain sentencing guidelines apply, but not agree as to others, or may agree as to the appropriate fine, but not be able to agree to the terms of years or months of incarceration. When any agreement is made of any type to any sentencing issue, it needs to be included in the written plea agreement.

Fifth, if the defendant has agreed to cooperate as part of the plea agreement, the full terms of that cooperation should be stated in the plea agreement. Those terms should precisely set out the obligations the defendant has for cooperating, the benefits the defendant may receive and how those benefits are to be determined, and the consequences to the defendant if the defendant fails to comply with the cooperation obligations. In drafting this portion of the plea agreement, prosecutors should consider how the language can be used to hold the defendant to his or her responsibilities under the agreement, how the language can be used to help a jury understand why they can trust the truthfulness of the cooperator's testimony, and how a defense attorney may use the language to undercut the cooperator's credibility.

First and foremost, the cooperation provision of a plea agreement must insist that the defendant be completely truthful in all respects, at all times, and regardless of who asks the defendant a question. It must be clear that a defendant's failure to be completely truthful is a material breach of the plea agreement. Cooperation provisions of plea agreements should not identify the targets against whom the government wants a defendant to cooperate. If a defendant decides to cooperate as part of a plea deal, then the defendant should be expected to cooperate against everyone and anyone. Specifying targets in a cooperation provision implies that the government has pressured the defendant to come up with information against the specific target regardless of whether the defendant has such information. A prosecutor will also usually want a cooperation provision to bar the defendant from revealing to anyone else that the defendant is cooperating. The government should maintain control over that information to prevent the defendant from effectively warning others and protecting them.

In describing the benefits a cooperator receives from the plea deal, the plea agreement should provide some summary of what the benefit may be, how that benefit will be determined, and who will decide what benefit the cooperator receives. Good cooperation plea agreements do not provide any benefit to the defendant before all cooperation is complete and evaluated by the government. A plea agreement that provides a benefit to the defendant at the time the agreement is executed provides no motivation for the defendant to continue to cooperate. Nor should any benefit be conditional on the outcome of the prosecution of any other person or case. Again, this implies that the defendant has been pressured to cooperate against a specific target or else the defendant will not get any benefit. That type of language undercuts the credibility of a cooperator. The benefits should be dependent upon truthful cooperation, regardless of whether that cooperation ultimately results in the successful prosecution of any other person. When I was a prosecutor, I explained to cooperators that so long as the cooperator told the complete truth and did what was asked of the cooperator, then the cooperator should get the benefit of the bargain even if a target is acquitted at trial because juries can acquit defendants for reasons that may have nothing to do with the cooperator's performance. A cooperation provision of a plea agreement should also make it clear that a judge will be the ultimate decision-maker in determining whether the defendant is awarded any benefit from cooperating.

Finally, a cooperation provision of a plea agreement should clearly spell out the adverse consequences that would result if a cooperator fails to comply with the terms of the cooperation provisions. The consequences should include the voidance of the plea agreement, including negating any possible benefit the defendant might otherwise have received as part of the plea bargain. That includes the ability of the government to pursue dismissed charges or new charges and the elimination of any reduction of the defendant's sentence for cooperating. The cooperation provision should also spell out that if the defendant is found to have provided false information, whether favorable or unfavorable to another person, that the defendant is subject to prosecution for perjury or making a false statement.

It is also advisable for plea agreements to contain language that reflects that the defendant entered into the plea agreement knowingly and voluntarily and that the agreement was not the result of pressure, threats, or any promises other than those contained in the plea agreement. This section of a plea agreement should also require the defendant to acknowledge having read the plea agreement (or having had it read to the defendant). To this end, it is best to have a defendant initial every paragraph of a plea agreement so that it reduces the chance in the future that a defendant can successfully claim not to have read some portion of the plea agreement. This section should also have the defendant acknowledge understanding the plea agreement to prevent the defendant from later admitting to having read the plea agreement but claiming not to have understood it.

Finally, the plea agreement should contain a paragraph that states that the written plea agreement constitutes the entirety of any agreement reached by the government with the defendant. It should clearly state that any oral statements made by the parties while negotiating the plea agreement are not part of the plea agreement. This helps prevent a false allegation arising in the future that the prosecutor had made some other promise or guarantee not contained in the written plea agreement.

Prosecutors should not sign any plea agreement to which the defendant or defense counsel has made handwritten changes. If the prosecutor is agreeable to the changes, then the prosecutor should retype the agreement to reflect the changes and have it resigned by the defendant. Handwritten changes or annotations to a plea agreement can sometimes be vague, illegible, ambiguous, or wrong. The process of typing in the proposed changes often helps clarify these matters and prevents mistakes.

CHANGE OF PLEA HEARINGS

A judge will preside over a change of plea hearing. In federal court, the change of plea hearing must comply with the requirement of Rule 11 of the Federal Rules of Criminal Procedure. This mandates that a judge place a defendant under oath and personally address the defendant in open court, informing the defendant of certain things and ensuring the defendant understand them. These include: (a) the government's right to prosecute the defendant for any false statement made during the proceeding; (b) the right to not plead guilty or persist in a guilty plea already made; (c) the right to a jury trial; (d) the right to be represented by counsel; (e) the trial rights including confronting and cross-examining any witnesses, against being compelled to testify against himself, to testify himself and present evidence, and the right to compel the attendance of witnesses; (f) the fact that by pleading guilty the defendant waives all of these trial rights; (g) the nature of each charge to which the defendant is pleading guilty; (h) the maximum sentence for each charge; (i) the minimum sentence for each charge; (j) any applicable

forfeiture; (k) the court's authority to order restitution; (l) the court's obligation to impose a special assessment; (m) the court's obligation to calculate
and consider the US Sentencing Guidelines and the factors set forth in Title
18, US Code, Section 3553(a) in determining the defendant's sentence; (n)
the terms of any plea agreement; and (o) the fact that the defendant may be
removed from the United States if the defendant is not a US citizen. FED. R.
CRIM. P. 11(b)(1). The judge is also required to ensure the plea is voluntary
(FED. R. CRIM. P. 11[b][2]), and that there is a factual basis for the plea (FED.
R. CRIM. P. 11[b][3]). In addition, the case law generally provides that due
process requires that a court advise a defendant of collateral consequences
from entering a guilty plea that could affect a defendant's liberty or property
interests, such as loss of citizenship rights, loss of licensure, disbarment from
government employment or business transactions, sexual offender registration, and the like.

Although it is the judge who presides over the change of plea hearing and
is charged with ensuring the plea complies with the requirements of Rule 11,
it is ultimately a prosecutor's responsibility to ensure that the judge complies
with the rule. The prosecutor will know the case far better than the judge.
The prosecutor must make sure that the judge does not make a mistake,
for instance, in reciting the maximum or minimum punishment. This is not
always as clear as it may seem. Some statutes provide for a maximum fine,
for example, but in the federal code there are sometimes other statutes that
provide alternative fines. Similarly, some statutes provide maximum periods
of incarceration, but those can change, based on other statutory provisions.
Similarly, even a special assessment may not be as straightforward as it may
appear. Under federal law, a defendant generally must pay a special assessment of $100 for each count of conviction. Title 18, US Code, Section 3014,
however, provides an additional special assessment of $5,000 for each count
of conviction of certain child molestation or child pornography charges. Also,
prosecutors are in a far better position to know or be able to learn of all of
the collateral consequences that could arise from a defendant's guilty plea.
A judge would have likely had little basis to know whether a defendant has
a license that could be in jeopardy as a result of a guilty plea, or whether the
defendant's livelihood depended on doing business with the government.
Prosecutors are also in a far better position to know what offenses trigger a
sex offender registration requirement or other adverse consequences. When
the parties have entered into a written plea agreement, the prosecutor should
have thought all these things out in advance and have them included in the
written plea agreement. It is when a defendant is not pleading guilty under
a written plea agreement that prosecutors sometimes fail to put sufficient

thought and preparation into a change of plea hearing to ensure the judge adequately and accurately covers these matters.

Thus, prosecutors must closely monitor change of plea hearings and alert the judge whenever there is a mistake or if the judge omits some portion of the plea colloquy or consequence a defendant could suffer from pleading guilty. Prosecutors must also be prepared to assist the judge and defense counsel when, for instance, a recalcitrant defendant has difficulty admitting to facts that form a basis for a guilty plea. Sometimes it requires the prosecutor to question the defendant in a manner to elicit the necessary facts; the judge will not know the underlying facts so cannot effectively examine the defendant. Finally, prosecutors must be alert to the possibility of a defendant failing to go through with the plea. The judge may then have questions of the prosecutor regarding the status of the case and its readiness for trial.

Chapter Fifteen

Preparing for the Case-in-Chief

Good prosecutors recognize the need to view trials as a whole, from jury selection through closing argument. Presentation of the government's case-in-chief, however, is the most critical part of any trial. The most favorable jury in the world will not return guilty verdicts if the prosecutor does not produce evidence to prove the defendant guilty. The best opening statements and the most persuasive closing arguments are not substitutes for substantive evidence proving a defendant guilty. At the same time, it is not enough to simply disgorge the government's evidence before a jury without thinking about who the jurors are and what they need, and without thinking in advance about how to explain the evidence to the jurors. Too often prosecutors prepare the presentation of their case-in-chief in a vacuum, myopically preparing the presentation of individual witnesses and exhibits as if they stand alone instead of viewing these presentations as a whole and integrating them into the rest of the trial.

To present a persuasive case-in-chief, prosecutors must adopt an integrated approach to determining what evidence to produce and how to produce it within the context of the entire trial. This begins with trying to view the evidence from the perspective of the prospective jurors. Second, prosecutors should structure the presentation of evidence in light of the elements of the offense and how the prosecutor intends to describe and explain the evidence in opening statement and closing argument. Third, prosecutors must organize the evidence, and the presentation of evidence, in a coherent and persuasive manner. Fourth, prosecutors must prepare outlines for the direct examination of individual witnesses in a way that makes individual witnesses persuasive but also integrates the testimony with other witnesses and the manner in which the prosecutor intends to explain the entire case to the jury. Fifth, prosecutors must prepare witness outlines in anticipation of objections and cross-examination. Finally, prosecutors must prepare witnesses for testifying in a courtroom. I will discuss each of these steps in turn.

VIEWING EVIDENCE FROM THE JURY BOX

In contemplating what evidence to present at trial, and how to present it, it is imperative that prosecutors start by trying to view the case from the viewpoint of the prospective jurors. What I mean by this here is not literally viewing it from the jurors' perspective (although as I will discuss later, that is also important), but, rather, I mean it here figuratively. Prosecutors should consider the audience they are playing to in determining the type of play to present. Just as any speaker should consider the audience, so too should prosecutors consider that the audience viewing the evidence is the jury.

In assessing the nature of the evidentiary presentation of the government's case-in-chief, a prosecutor may need to consider the makeup of the prospective jurors in relation to the general nature of the evidence. In some cases this may significantly alter the way the government presents its case-in-chief. For example, I once handled a case involving environmental crimes arising from pollution from oceangoing vessels, and the case was to be tried in Iowa. The prospective jurors would likely have very little general knowledge about the shipping industry, which was going to require me to provide more education to the prospective jurors so that they could understand the nature of the crime.

More generally, prosecutors should consider the background of the likely jurors in relation to the evidence to assess the amount of background information the prosecutor will need to present so that the jurors can understand the evidence. Even in cases where the subject matter is not overly complex, like ocean pollution environmental crimes, jurors are unlikely to be familiar with background information and context that may be second nature to the prosecutor. Drug prosecutors, for example, understand how drug trafficking works. The average juror does not. Fraud prosecutors have a general understanding of bank lending practices, lines of credit, account-receivable pledges, and the like. The average juror does not. Thus, in thinking about what evidence to present and how to present it, prosecutors should think about the jury's likely common knowledge and be prepared to supplement that knowledge with testimony and evidence so that the jury can understand the government's case. It may be necessary, for example, to call a witness solely for the purpose of providing context. When I prosecuted bankruptcy fraud cases, for example, I would often call a bankruptcy trustee just to explain to the jury how the bankruptcy system works, the process involved, and what documents are filed by whom and what they mean. I usually had the witness testify with the aid of diagrams and flowcharts to aid the jury in comprehending the complexity of the system. Without an understanding of the bankruptcy system, jurors would have difficulty fully comprehending the evidence showing that someone defrauded the system. In other cases, this educational or contextual component may be satisfied through general fact witnesses by asking additional questions.

DETERMINING ADMISSIBLE
EVIDENCE BEFORE TRIAL

Throughout the investigation, but especially when preparing for trial, prosecutors must evaluate the evidence to ensure that it is admissible. Prosecutors should analyze each piece of evidence, and each anticipated statement by a witness, to determine whether defense counsel could raise any evidentiary objection to admission of the exhibit or testimony. To do this well, once again prosecutors must step out of their own shoes and into those of the defense counsel. Prosecutors must use mental discipline to reexamine the evidence and anticipated testimony from the eyes of a defense attorney whose desire is to bar admission of the evidence. Prosecutors must use their imagination to think of all of the various objections defense counsel could make to admission of the evidence.

Once a prosecutor has identified the possible evidentiary objections a defense attorney could make, the prosecutor then must evaluate the strength of the potential objections and weigh the relative importance of the evidence. With most evidence, although the prosecutor may determine that an imaginative defense attorney could raise a colorable objection, the basis for the objection would be so weak that it may not cause any realistic concern. There will be other exhibits and testimony, however, for which the prosecutor recognizes the defense attorney may have a stronger argument to keep it out of the trial under the rules of evidence. If this evidence is relatively unimportant, then the prosecutor may consider dispensing with the evidence or finding substitute evidence to avoid error. If, however, the evidence is important to the case, then the prosecutor must develop a strategy for dealing with potential objections to the evidence.

There are several ways for prosecutors to address anticipated evidentiary issues. A prosecutor could discuss it with defense counsel in an effort to work things out, raise it in a pretrial motion with the court, or wait to deal with it at trial. There are many strategic and tactical considerations in deciding when and how and whether to raise evidentiary issues in advance of trial.

A prosecutor could engage in a dialogue with the defense counsel about an evidentiary issue in advance of trial and attempt to negotiate a compromise that would allow some version of the evidence to be admitted while addressing concerns the defense attorney may have about the evidence. Attempting to work out evidentiary disputes in this manner is generally wise. If there is a middle ground that can be reached, then the evidence important to the government can be admitted smoothly at trial without interruption and without risk of error. Even when a compromise cannot be brokered, however, the discussion about the evidence with defense counsel can help enlighten the prosecutor about the defense attorney's concerns and potential evidentiary objections, which in turn will allow the prosecutor to more effectively prepare for and address those concerns with the court.

Another way to address evidentiary issues in advance of trial is through the filing of a motion in limine. *Black's Law Dictionary* defines a motion in limine as "[a] pretrial request that certain inadmissible evidence not be referred to or offered at trial." *Motion in Limine*, BLACK'S LAW DICTIONARY 10th ed. 2014. Or, in other words, a motion in limine is "any motion, whether made before or during trial, to exclude anticipated prejudicial evidence before the evidence is actually offered." *Luce v. United States*, 469 US 38, 40 n.2 (1984). "In limine" is Latin for "at the outset." *In Limine*, BLACK'S LAW DICTIONARY, *supra*. Importantly, "limine" does not mean "to limit." Thus, despite the common definition a party can file a motion in limine to seek a pretrial ruling either to bar or to admit evidence. In this section, then, I am talking about prosecutors filing a motion in limine not to keep out defense evidence, but, rather, to obtain a ruling from the court in advance of trial regarding whether the government's evidence can come in.

Generally, raising evidentiary issues in advance of trial by filing a motion in limine is beneficial. A pretrial ruling on an evidentiary issue helps to avoid prejudice and delay and to ensure an evenhanded and expeditious trial and to focus the issues the jury will consider. *United States v. Brawner*, 173 F.3d 966, 970 (6th Cir. 1999) (holding federal rules of evidence, civil procedure and criminal procedure and interpretive rulings of the Supreme Court all encourage parties to use pretrial procedures, such as motions in limine, to narrow the issues and minimize disruptions at trial); *Jonasson v. Lutheran Child and Family Servs.*, 115 F.3d 436, 440 (7th Cir. 1997); *Bradley v. Pittsburgh Bd. of Educ.*, 913 F.2d 1064, 1069 (3d Cir. 1990) ("motion in limine is designed to narrow the evidentiary issues for trial and to eliminate unnecessary trial interruptions"). A motion in limine is especially helpful to the government in a criminal case when a pretrial ruling on an evidentiary issue would promote the prosecutor's ability to plan for trial.

In making the judgment call of whether to raise an evidentiary issue pretrial in a motion in limine versus waiting to deal with the issue at trial, prosecutors must consider several factors. First, a prosecutor must consider whether there is a difference in the likelihood of success if the prosecutor raises the issue in advance of trial rather than waiting to see if the issue arises during trial and dealing with it then. Trial judges will have more time before trial to research, ponder, and decide evidentiary questions than the judge will have during the trial. This is particularly important for prosecutors because it is understandably and justifiably more likely the judge will rule in favor of a defendant on an evidentiary issue that arises for the first time in the middle of the trial than if the same issue was raised in advance of trial. If a judge does not have a lot of time to fully evaluate an evidentiary issue, the judge is more likely to err on the side of ruling in favor of the defendant whose liberty is at stake. In contrast, when a judge has adequate time to analyze the evidentiary issue, the judge may feel more comfortable ruling in the government's favor. Even if the judge is unable or unwilling to rule on a prosecutor's motion in limine in advance of trial, the filing of a motion in limine may still help the government because the trial judge will be more prepared to deal with the evidentiary issue at trial and therefore more likely to rule in the government's favor. *See Mixed Chicks LLC v. Sally Beauty Supply LLC*, 879 F. Supp.2d 1093, 1094 (C.D. Cal. 2012) (observing that advanced warning of an evidentiary issue allows a judge time to prepare for the issue outside the "pressure and parameters of trial in session"). Pretrial briefing and argument on evidentiary issues may also help the prosecutor flesh out and clarify the basis for the defendant's objection.

Second, the prosecutor must consider the degree to which the issue is ripe. In other words, an attorney will want to consider whether this is a case where the court will lack sufficient facts or context for ruling on an evidentiary issue in advance of trial. A judge might view some evidentiary issues more appropriately raised in a trial brief, rather than a motion in limine. *See* STEPHEN A. SALTZBURG ET AL., FEDERAL RULES OF EVIDENCE MANUAL § 103.02[13] (11th ed. 2017); Jennifer M. Miller, *To Argue Is Human, to Exclude, Divine: The Role of Motions in Limine and the Importance of Preserving the Record on Appeal*, 32 AM. J. TRIAL ADVOC. 541, 553 (2009). Some evidentiary issues in particular are less amenable to a pretrial ruling out of context than others. For example, issues relating to foundation, relevance, and the balancing considerations under Federal Rule of Evidence 403 are much more difficult to decide out of context than, for example, a hearsay objection or the admissibility of a prior conviction under Federal Rule of Evidence 609. Determining whether a statement is a coconspirator statement, and thus not hearsay under Federal Rule of Evidence 801(d)(2)(E), is particularly difficult for a judge to evaluate in advance of trial without context because the government has to show that the statement was made by a coconspirator during and in furtherance of the conspiracy. Without evidence regarding the membership, duration, and scope of the conspiracy, it would be hard for a judge to determine in advance of trial whether a statement fits this definition.

Prosecutors could consider raising unripe evidentiary issues in a trial brief to at least alert the judge of the evidentiary issue. This may help the judge prepare for the issue and thus make a wiser ruling. Nevertheless, it will not help the prosecutor prepare for trial because the judge will not have ruled on the issue. By raising the issue in a trial brief the prosecutor will also have revealed an evidentiary issue the opponent may have otherwise missed.

Third, in some cases it may not be clear whether the defense counsel will object to the admission of a piece of evidence, or upon what basis the defense attorney may object. In these cases, it may be advisable for a prosecutor to raise the issue in advance of trial by filing a motion in limine to flesh out the defense position on this issue. For example, a prosecutor may anticipate eliciting testimony from a witness that could be objectionable on multiple grounds, from hearsay to relevance to unfair prejudice. Rather than waiting until trial to discover the basis for the defense attorney's objection, it would be better for the prosecutor to raise the issue in a motion in limine, identifying the proposed evidence and addressing the potential objections the prosecutor believes the defense attorney may raise. It may be that the defense attorney's basis for objecting to the evidence is something the prosecutor can deal with by adjusting the nature of the evidence proffered or by proposing a limiting instruction to address the defendant's concerns.

Finally, although prosecutors file motions in limine primarily for the purpose of obtaining pretrial rulings for the admissibility of evidence, pretrial rulings on evidentiary issues can also impact the possibility of a guilty plea. A court's ruling on an evidentiary issue can dramatically change the tone of the evidence, the strength of the government's case, or the viability of a defense theory. A pretrial ruling on a particularly key piece of evidence may lead both parties to reassess their plea-negotiating positions and may lead to a guilty plea. Even if the court makes the identical ruling at trial, it may be too late for the parties to negotiate a resolution of the case at that late stage.

A trial judge has wide discretion in ruling on evidentiary issues. That discretion extends to the threshold question of whether a motion in limine presents an evidentiary issue appropriate for review in advance of trial. *See, e.g., United States v. Valencia*, 826 F.2d 169, 172 (2d Cir. 1987). A court considering a motion in limine may reserve judgment until trial to assess admissibility based on the actual factual context. Even when a court rules on a motion in limine, the court's ruling is "subject to change when the case unfolds, particularly if the actual testimony differs from what was contained in the . . . proffer." *Luce*, 469 US at 41. In most cases, trial judges will telegraph the probability that a pretrial ruling is subject to possible reversal at trial. In many cases, the court's pretrial ruling will clearly and firmly state that the evidence is either admissible or inadmissible. In other instances, however, the court's pretrial ruling may reflect reservations by including language that the ruling is based upon the assumption that particular evidence is presented, or on a condition that the opponent opens the door by raising the issue. Sometimes a trial court will even expressly state that its ruling is subject to reversal at trial depending upon the presentation of other evidence at trial. If there is ever any doubt as to whether the court has definitively ruled or left the issue open to some degree, the prosecutor should get the judge to clarify the ruling.

In general, I advise prosecutors to raise as many evidentiary issues in advance of trial as possible. There is little or no downside to raising evidentiary issues with opposing counsel whenever possible. For all important evidence for which the defense has potentially strong evidentiary objections, prosecutors should raise the issue with the judge in advance of trial. Those evidentiary issues capable of pretrial ruling by a judge in advance of trial should be raised in a motion in limine. Prosecutors should address unripe or undeveloped evidentiary issues in trial briefs so that the judge is at least familiar with the evidentiary issue and the law regarding it in advance of trial.

STRUCTURING THE PRESENTATION OF EVIDENCE

In any given case, the investigation will have revealed multiple potential witnesses and quantities of objects, papers, photographs, recordings, and other things that could be presented as evidence. It is the prosecutor's responsibility to identify which people to call as witnesses and what to present as exhibits during the government's case-in-chief. This requires careful thought and planning. The government must present sufficient evidence to prove the defendant's guilty beyond a reasonable doubt, but that does not mean that the government should present every potential witness or introduce every possible exhibit. Jurors have a limited capacity to absorb evidence, and prosecutors who inundate jurors with immaterial detail and evidence run the risk that the jurors will be unable to distinguish and focus on the truly important evidence.

It is often best for prosecutors to begin the process of structuring the case-in-chief by first looking to the elements of the offenses. Prosecutors should create a chart of sorts, listing the elements of the offenses and listing in outline form the possible witnesses who could testify as to each element and the nature of the evidence that could be marked as exhibits to prove each element. By way of illustration, let us assume we are dealing with a bank robbery case. Armed bank robbery under Title 18, US Code, Section 2113(d) has four elements:

1. the defendant took, or attempted to take, money belonging to, or in the custody, care, or possession of, a bank, credit union, or saving and loan association;
2. the money was taken "by force and violence, or by intimidation";
3. the deposits of the institution were federally insured; and
4. in committing or attempting to commit the offense, the defendant assaulted any person, or put in jeopardy the life of any person, by the use of a dangerous weapon or device.

Let us also assume the facts involved a masked man who entered a crowded bank with a gun, demanded cash, left a fingerprint on the counter, and fled in a stolen car driven by the defendant's girlfriend, who is now cooperating with the government. Two tellers and a customer heard the robber demand money, while other tellers and customers saw the robber commit the act to more or lesser degrees. The witnesses in this case may involve numerous customers and bank employees, law enforcement officers and forensic examiners, bystanders, the victims of the stolen car, a bank official to establish that the bank is federally insured, and the girlfriend, to name just a few. The tangible evidence in this case may involve security camera video from the bank and/or surrounding businesses; car registration documents; the FDIC certificate; bank drawer records; latent and known fingerprints; photographs of the inside and outside the bank, the getaway vehicle, and the surrounding area; and any evidence seized from the defendant or his residence, again just to name a few possible exhibits.

The prosecutor should list out next to each element the witnesses and exhibits that *could* be used to prove the case. The chart might start by looking something like this:

Element	Witnesses	Exhibits
Defendant took money from the bank	Teller 1	Cash drawer inventory
	Teller 2	Bank video
	Teller 3	Interior bank photos
	Bank Vice President	Exterior bank photos
	Customer 1	Photos of car
	Customer 2	Photos from car search
	Customer 3	Latent prints
	Customer 4	Cash recovered from car
	Customer 5	
	Girlfriend	
By force/intimidation	Teller 1	Bank video
	Teller 2	
	Customer 1	
Bank insured by FDIC	Bank Vice President	FDIC certificate
Defendant used a weapon	Teller 1	Firearm recovered from car
	Teller 2	Photos from car search
	Teller 3	
	Customer 1	
	Customer 2	
	Girlfriend	
	Officer 1	

In identifying the potential witnesses and exhibits, the prosecutor must ensure that there is sufficient evidence to prove each element of the offense charged beyond a reasonable doubt. But that is not the end of the analysis of how best to structure the presentation of the government's case-in-chief. The prosecutor must also consider how to make the presentation of the evidence persuasive. The best way to do this is for the prosecutor to outline the closing argument. The prosecutor should think about what the prosecutor would like to tell the jury during closing argument and think about what exhibits or things the prosecutor would like to show the jury to persuade the jury that the defendant committed the bank robbery. This analysis may, and most times will, result in the prosecutor identifying additional potential witnesses and exhibits for use at trial.

For example, although motive is not an element of the offense of armed bank robbery, showing that the defendant had a motive to rob the bank may constitute powerful persuasive evidence that the defendant did so. Imagine that the girlfriend told the authorities that the defendant robbed the bank because he needed money to support his methamphetamine habit. The prosecutor then may want to present evidence regarding that methamphetamine habit to establish the defendant's motive for robbing the bank. Certainly the girlfriend could testify to that matter, but so too, perhaps, could some of defendant's friends who used methamphetamine with him. Similarly, a search of the defendant's car or residence may have uncovered methamphetamine-user paraphernalia, such as pipes or syringes.

So the prosecutor should expand the evidence chart to include additional categories beyond the elements alone. Perhaps it would include motive or opportunity categories. Prosecutors may also add witnesses or exhibits to the elements charts for purposes of not just meeting the elements of the offense, but doing so persuasively. For example, to prove the defendant used a firearm during the bank robbery, the prosecutor may add additional potential witnesses in the form of friends who previously saw him with a handgun or records showing the defendant's purchase of the firearm.

Once the prosecutor has identified all of the potential witnesses and exhibits, the prosecutor must then determine which witnesses the prosecutor should actually call and what evidence to actually mark as exhibits. This requires an assessment and weighing of evidentiary issues, the probative value of the evidence, and the quantity and quality of the evidence.

Prosecutors must consider the potential evidentiary problems that may exist with potential witnesses and exhibits and weigh the probative value against the risk of error in presenting the evidence. Some witnesses may, for example, have prior convictions that the defense could use to impeach the witness while others do not. Some witnesses may lack direct evidence and would be testifying based on potential hearsay, whereas other witnesses may have direct knowledge. The prosecutor must also consider how to lay a proper foundation under the rules of evidence as to each exhibit and will need to identify the witnesses necessary to do this. For example, cash recovered from the defendant's vehicle may have been seized by one officer, transported to a lab for fingerprint testing by another officer, and retrieved from the laboratory and returned to the case agent by yet another officer. If the defendant is challenging foundation for admission of the cash, the prosecutor may have to call all of the officers involved in the chain of custody to lay the foundation necessary to get the cash admitted into evidence.

Prosecutors must also assess the persuasiveness of witnesses and exhibits. It is important that prosecutors present persuasive evidence. Although there may be three or four tellers, for example, who could testify about the robbery, the third or fourth teller may add little or nothing to the persuasiveness of the case. Perhaps Teller 3 was too far away, or only saw the robber as he was leaving, and perhaps Teller 4 has only a vague recollection of the robber's appearance or makes a poor witness for some other reason such as excessive nervousness. Similarly, although there may be three or four of the defendant's buddies who could testify as to his use of methamphetamine, perhaps one or two of them have such horrible criminal histories that what probative value they would add to the case would be overcome by the impeachment of their testimony based on their criminal histories. The same analysis applies to some exhibits. For example, officers may have taken scores of photographs of the interior of the bank after the robbery. The prosecutor needs to choose from those photographs the ones that best show what happened, where witnesses were, and what the witnesses could see during the robbery and not mark as evidence photographs that do not add to the persuasiveness of the evidence.

Quantity does not necessarily equate with quality. Presenting too many witnesses or exhibits may have an inverse relationship to the persuasiveness of the evidence for the jury. Although a certain amount of cumulative evidence may be appropriate (for example, multiple tellers or customers to identify the bank robber), too many witnesses or exhibits may overwhelm jurors. The jury may forget the key testimony or evidence because it is surrounded by so much other less important and persuasive evidence. Generally speaking, prosecutors should try to present the government's case-in-chief with the least number of witnesses and amount of evidence possible while still proving the case beyond a reasonable doubt.

At the same time, however, prosecutors should be cognizant of the optics of presenting too little evidence. Criminal cases are important. Much is at stake for the defendant, and the prosecutor is asking much of the jury to convict the defendant. Thus, prosecutors should present a sufficient number of witnesses and exhibits to reflect the seriousness of the case. Imagine a felon-in-possession-of-a-firearm case where a cop seized a handgun from the defendant's pocket during a traffic stop. If the defendant stipulated to his status as a felon and the interstate transportation of the firearm, the only remaining element is the defendant's knowing possession of the firearm. A prosecutor could conceivably present the entire case through a single witness: the officer who seized the firearm from the defendant during the traffic stop. Although that could be sufficient, perhaps, to persuade the jury of the defendant's guilt beyond a reasonable doubt, it may be wiser to present additional evidence, even if the probative value of the additional evidence is not very significant. For example, a prosecutor may call the officer's partner to set the scene of the traffic stop, even though that officer did not seize the gun. Or, perhaps, the prosecutor may choose to present an ATF expert to testify about the interstate nexus of the firearm, even though the defendant was willing to stipulate to the element.

The final step in structuring the case-in-chief is for the prosecutor to create witness/exhibit and exhibit/witness lists. In other words, a prosecutor should create a list of witnesses in one column and a list of the exhibits that could be introduced through that witness in the next column. Then the prosecutor should create the opposite list, with exhibits listed in order and next to them a column of witnesses who could lay the foundation for or who may reference the exhibit during trial. The creation of these lists often reveals gaps in the prosecutor's case. When examining the completed lists a prosecutor may see that some witnesses will have no exhibits to testify about at trial. Sometimes that is fine, but other times it may be preferable to create an exhibit (such as a diagram, map, or some other such item) to enhance the persuasiveness of the witness's testimony. On other occasions, the prosecutor may realize that a particular exhibit requires the identification of one or more witnesses to lay the foundation for admission of the exhibit that the prosecutor had previously overlooked. Ideally, more than one witnesses testifies about each exhibit so that there is redundancy if issues arise with a witness's testimony.

These lists will be works in progress and should be altered multiple times between the first draft and the time of trial. In creating the initial lists, the prosecutor should generally attempt to list the witnesses in the order in which the prosecutor thinks they should appear at trial, but further review of the evidence and preparation for trial will usually result in a reshuffling of the order. Likewise, the prosecutor may want to list exhibits in some order initially, but this order will also likely undergo revision when the prosecutor begins to organize the presentation of the evidence.

ORGANIZING THE PRESENTATION OF EVIDENCE

Organizing the presentation of the evidence involves deciding how to order the presentation of evidence in a manner that will make it the most persuasive. The prosecutor must decide which witness to call first, which to call last, and the order of all of the witnesses in between. The prosecutor must also decide which object should be marked as Exhibit 1, which as Exhibit 2, and so on. Making these decisions requires a lot of thought and consideration of various factors, some of which may be competing or conflicting, if the evidence is to be presented in the most persuasive manner possible.

The organization of the presentation of witnesses can be a very complicated task. The government's case-in-chief is like telling a story to the jury. From the first witness to the last, the government is unfolding a story of the crime for the jury to see. Just as some written stories are more compelling and captivating than others, so too some government cases are more compelling and captivating than others. Part of this has to do with the subject matter itself, of course; a simple gun-possession case is not going to be as fascinating as a murder case. On the other hand, whatever the subject matter that constitutes the government's case, how the prosecutor organizes the presentation of the evidence can make a big difference in its persuasive value.

A prosecutor must first consider how to organize the overall presentation of the case-in-chief. Most often, the most logical and compelling way to organize the presentation is chronological. A chronological presentation generally involves presentation of evidence of the crime in the chronological manner in which it occurred. Jurors tend to mentally place events in chronological order and recall them that way. For that reason, most books and movies are presented in a chronological order. Thus, in presenting a criminal case at trial the government most often presents the evidence largely in chronological order. If the case is a drug conspiracy, for example, the government's first witnesses would typically testify about the events furthest in time, with the last witnesses testifying about the most recent events. This systematic and chronological presentation of evidence permits the jurors to understand, retain, and retrieve the facts of the case most readily. A chronological presentation is often also very persuasive because as the story unfolds in time, the jurors can see the inevitable path it will take leading to the defendant's arrest.

In some cases, however, a strictly chronological presentation of the criminal conduct from start to finish may not be the most persuasive presentation. Prosecutors should consider whether a different organization of the presentation of evidence may be more persuasive. For example, a prosecutor could present the evidence in reverse chronological order. In a murder case, for example, it may be more compelling to start the presentation of evidence with officers arresting the blood-soaked defendant after a high-speed chase, followed by evidence from the scene of the murder, with testimony from witnesses placing him at the scene next, ending with testimony from witnesses showing the defendant had the motive and opportunity to commit the crime.

In another case, a prosecutor may consider presenting the evidence in the order in which the case was investigated. I used this organization in a case where a defendant sent a bomb to a victim through the mail. The case relied completely on circumstantial evidence. When the jurors saw the story unfold in the same way the investigators discovered the evidence that revealed the defendant's involvement, following lead after lead and development after development, it led the jurors to the same conclusion to which it led the investigators. A purely chronological presentation of the same evidence in that case would not have clearly led the jurors to see the connections between the evidence as they did when they saw how each piece of evidence led inevitably to the next and inexorably to the defendant as the perpetrator.

Determining the overall organization of the presentation of the evidence is only the first step in the process. There are a number of other factors a prosecutor must consider in determining the exact order of the presentation of witnesses. First, prosecutors should start the presentation of evidence strong and end it strong. Due to the primacy and recency effects on memory, jurors tend to remember best the first and last things they see and hear. Thus, a prosecutor would not want to start with the weakest witness, even if it would be the first witness chronologically or would otherwise be the first witness to call given the prosecutor's overall presentation strategy. Witnesses with significant baggage, like cooperators, should be presented in the middle of the government's case for this reason.

Second, prosecutors should view each day of trial as a mini-trial in the sense that each day the jurors will recall best the first and last witness who testified. Thus, to the extent possible, each day of the case should start and end strong. This is particularly difficult to accomplish because it is often hard to predict with much precision how long witnesses will be on the stand. Thus, prosecutors must sometimes make minor adjustments to witness order during the trial to start and end each day strong. Generally, judges permit this type of adjustment in witness order, particularly if the prosecutor provides the defense with as much advance notice as possible.

Third, prosecutors must consider how the order of witnesses impacts the persuasiveness of each witness. For example, to make a cooperator as believable as possible prosecutors should try to have witnesses who can provide corroboration of the cooperator's story testify before and after the cooperator. Similarly, it increases the persuasiveness of the evidence whenever a prosecutor can have corroborating evidence directly follow other evidence. In a bank robbery case, for example, it's compelling to have a fingerprint expert testify as to finding the defendant's fingerprints on the demand note immediately after the teller testifies and identifies the defendant in the courtroom as the robber. The same evidence would be much less compelling if the fingerprint expert testified several witnesses before or after the teller.

Fourth, the ability of prosecutors to organize the presentation of the evidence is subject to other practical factors, some of which are outside the prosecutor's control. Witnesses may have scheduling conflicts that prevent the presentation of the witness's testimony in the ideal order. The US Marshals may not be able to transport an incarcerated witness to the courthouse on the date or at the time the prosecutor desires. There may be conflicts between witnesses that requires separation of the witnesses in a manner that prevents one following the other. For example, a witness may have cooperated against another witness in the past, and having them waiting in the same holding cells or waiting room at the same time could lead to problems.

Considering all of these factors, along with many other case-specific and witness-specific issues, a prosecutor must nevertheless arrive at an order of witnesses that is as persuasive as possible under the circumstances. The larger the number of witnesses, obviously, the more difficult this task becomes. Prosecutors must simply make judgment calls when one order of the witnesses enhances one factor (for example, the overall order of the presentation), while another order enhances another factor (for example, starting strong and ending strong). Prosecutors must also remain flexible enough to alter the order, sometimes on a daily basis, in a constant effort to juggle all of the factors in a way that makes the case as persuasive and easy for the jury to follow as possible.

Organizing the presentation of exhibits is relatively easy compared to organizing the presentation of witnesses. Nevertheless, it deserves more thought and consideration than it is often given. Prosecutors can attach exhibit numbers to exhibits in a random manner because the number assigned to an exhibit has no inherent meaning or value. By putting some thought into the order in which exhibits are assigned numbers, however, prosecutors can provide meaning and value to the exhibit numbers. By that I mean that the ordering of exhibits by number categories can help jurors understand the relationship between exhibits and witnesses and between exhibits. Although the manner in which numbers are assigned to exhibits may seem insignificant, it is important for prosecutors to put themselves in the shoes of the jurors. The jurors will know nothing about the case before trial starts, must learn all of the facts of the case, then try to understand the judge's instructions on the law. Then, with no training and often no experience, the jurors must try to work as a group to debate the evidence and deliberate to verdict. Everything a prosecutor can do to organize the evidence in a way that makes it easier for the jury to understand the evidence increases the likelihood that the jurors will understand it in the manner the prosecutor desires.

There are various numbering methods prosecutors can use to organize the presentation of exhibits. First, prosecutors can use numbers to denote events in the chronology of the case. For example, in a drug case exhibits 1 through 10 could be used for exhibits from the first controlled buy (e.g., surveillance photos, copies of the buy money, the drugs purchased, etc.), exhibits 11 through 20 could be used for exhibits from the second controlled buy, and exhibits 21 through 40 could be used for evidence seized from the defendant's house during a search that followed the two controlled buys.

Second, a prosecutor may also assign exhibit numbers based on the elements of the offense. For example, the crime of being a felon in possession of a firearm has three elements: (1) the defendant knowingly possessed a firearm; (2) the defendant was prohibited from possessing the firearm because he was a felon; and (3) the firearm was transported in interstate commerce. A prosecutor could assign exhibit numbers based on each element. For example, the first ten exhibit numbers could be assigned to evidence the defendant possessed the firearm (e.g., the firearm being exhibit 1, photos from defendant's Facebook account holding a similar gun as exhibit 2, fingerprint cards as exhibit 3, etc.). The second five or ten exhibit numbers could be assigned to the defendant's status as a felon (e.g., certified copies of conviction or a stipulation by the parties). The last series of exhibit numbers could be assigned to evidence proving that the firearm was transported in interstate commerce.

Third, in a case where a defendant is charged with multiple offenses, prosecutors could assign exhibits numbers based on the offense category. For example, imagine a case that arose from a single search of a defendant's house, resulting in a defendant charged with one count of possession with the intent to distribute controlled substances, one count of possessing a firearm in relation to a drug trafficking offense, and one count of money laundering. The prosecutor could assign number series for each type of offense, with exhibits 1 through 10 being assigned to the drug evidence, exhibits 11 through 20 being assigned to the gun evidence, and the remaining exhibit numbers assigned to the money-laundering evidence.

Fourth, when a case involves multiple defendants, a prosecutor may choose to assign exhibit numbers for each defendant. For example, a prosecutor could assign the first fifty exhibit numbers to the first defendant, the next fifty to the second defendant, and so on.

Finally, prosecutors may need to combine one or more of these methods depending on whether the case involves multiple offenses or multiple defendants.

In the end, organizing the exhibit numbers in a manner to help the jury only works if the jury can either inherently understand the numbering system or if the prosecutor explains it to the jurors. I found it helpful during direct examination and/or closing argument to point the organization out to the jurors. For example, as part of direct examination a prosecutor could hand a law enforcement witness a notebook with a series of exhibits and ask whether the witness recognizes that the exhibits in the notebook all pertain to a certain defendant, or crime, or element, etc. Similarly, during closing argument a prosecutor could use a demonstrative chart that sets out the elements of the offense in one column, the list of witnesses testifying about each element in the second column, and the exhibits pertaining to each element in the third column.

ORGANIZING THE EVIDENCE

Once the prosecutor has identified the witnesses to call and the exhibits to present and has organized the presentation of that evidence, the prosecutor must then physically organize the evidence. This involves building witness and exhibit folders or binders. The larger the case, the more witnesses and exhibits involved, the more important this step becomes. At trial, a prosecutor must act quickly and efficiently. Jurors may find a disorganized prosecutor less persuasive and may resent the waste of time caused by a disorganized prosecutor. The more organized the prosecutor's folders are, the easier it is for the prosecutor to perform well before a jury.

Witness folders[1] should contain the essential materials that will be needed to prepare and question the witness, refresh the witness's recollection if necessary, impeach the witness if required, and respond to objections during the witness's testimony. These essential materials include an outline of the questions the prosecutor intends to ask the witness, a copy of the witness's prior statements or testimony in the case, the witness's criminal history (if any), and any documents that relate to the witness or the witness's testimony that are not otherwise marked as an exhibit for use at trial. Witness folders may contain other materials as well, including copies of the pertinent rules of evidence or case law regarding evidentiary issues that may arise relating to the witness. A prosecutor may also supplement a witness folder not only with copies of every statement the witness made, but copies of statements that others made about the witness. Prosecutors must find a balance between having too many documents and too few in a witness folder.

Prosecutors also need to mark and make copies of exhibits and organize them in folders or binders. Again, this may require more thought and consideration than at first seems obvious. Prosecutors should think about how the exhibits will be used with witnesses at trial. For example, if there is a series of exhibits that one or more witnesses will testify about as a group (say, for example, a series of photographs from a crime scene), then it may be best to put those exhibits together in a subfile or binder so that the exhibits can be provided to the witness as a group. The witness can more easily handle the exhibits on the stand if they were provided together in an organized fashion rather than handing the witness a bunch of individual exhibits. It can also make the presentation of the testimony more efficient and effective if the prosecutor approaches the witness with a single folder or binder of exhibits as opposed to repeatedly walking up to the witness to hand the witness individual exhibits.

PREPARING OUTLINES FOR DIRECT EXAMINATION

In preparing to present the case-in-chief, prosecutors should draft outlines of questions for each witness. In drafting outlines, prosecutors should consider a number of factors and include a number of references. First, prosecutors should draft the outline in a manner that will allow for the witness to testify in a logical and persuasive manner. Organizing the order of questions requires prosecutors to consider many of the same factors considered in organizing the case itself. Typically, it is best to have the witness testify about events in a chronological order, but prosecutors may consider other sequences of questions if they may be more compelling. Prosecutors should also draft the order of questions in a manner that allows the witness's testimony to start and end strong, and bury unfavorable information in the middle of the witness's testimony. When appropriate, and in most cases it is, prosecutors must also fit in questions that elicit information about the background of the witness so that the jury can understand who the witness is, how he or she got involved in the case, and why he or she is trustworthy and believable, so that the jury can empathize with and relate to the witness.

The outline of questions should also include references to exhibits about which the witness will testify or for which the witness will lay a foundation for their admission. The outline should reference the exhibits by the exhibit number assigned to them. The prosecutor may also want to make a marginal note at that point of the outline regarding the evidentiary rule that pertains to the exhibit's foundation or that may be cited if the defense objects to admission of the exhibit during the witness's testimony.

The outline of the witness's direct examination should also include references to the witness's prior statements or testimony, reports, or other documents that the prosecutor may need to use to refresh the witness's recollection or impeach the witness's testimony. The references should be as precise as possible, citing page and/or paragraph numbers whenever possible. When the need arises at trial to refresh recollection or impeach testimony, the prosecutor must be able to quickly and accurately access the relevant document to use for the purpose. During the witness's testimony is not the time for the prosecutor to be thumbing through the witness's grand jury testimony looking for the place where the witness previously referenced the matter in dispute.

The witness's outline should also contain an outline of questions that the defense attorney may ask the witness on cross-examination. The exercise of drafting these cross-examination questions often prompts a prosecutor to see gaps in the direct examination outline or in the evidence as a whole. The prosecutor can then revise the direct examination outline or fill the gap with other evidence. Further, the outline of possible cross-examination questions will be helpful when the prosecutor sits down with the witness in advance of trial to prepare the witness for testifying.

PREPARING WITNESSES TO TESTIFY

Prosecutors should prepare every witness to testify. The extent of the preparation will depend on the nature of the witness, the subject matter of the testimony, and the proceeding in which the witness is testifying. Preparing a civilian witness to testify at a financial fraud trial before a jury when the government must prove its case beyond a reasonable doubt requires more time and effort than preparing a law enforcement officer to testify regarding relevant criminal conduct at a sentencing hearing. Nevertheless, prosecutors owe it to witnesses to prepare them for testifying. This includes the need to prepare law enforcement officers to testify, even when they have done so many times in the past. Testifying is a difficult, stressful, and trying experience. Cross-examination is considered the "greatest legal engine ever invented for the discovery of truth"[2] because lawyers are skilled at dissecting testimony and impeaching witness. This is especially true of criminal defense attorneys, who have ample opportunity to hone their cross-examination skills.

Preparing a witness to testify is not the same thing as telling a witness what to say or even how to say it. Prosecutors should not improperly try to influence what a witness is going to say. It is also important that prosecutors refrain from trying to influence how a witness is going to testify. In other words, prosecutors should not use witness preparation to provide acting lessons to the witness. Prosecutors should not tell witnesses, for example, that they should be more remorseful or passionate, or act more scared or excited, during the witness's testimony. That is not to say that prosecutors cannot instruct witnesses about inappropriate courtroom behavior, such as swearing unnecessarily. Witnesses should tell only the truth as they know it, and they should testify in a manner that is natural to them. Likewise, it is appropriate to instruct witnesses to be respectful to defense counsel, to answer questions with a "yes" or "no" when appropriate, and to not argue with defense counsel, and the prosecutor should provide similar instructions that will help the witness effectively testify.

It is critically important that when preparing witnesses to testify that prosecutors are clear with witnesses about the absolute necessity to testify truthfully. Witnesses may, however, interpret what a prosecutor says during witness preparation as suggesting that the witness testify in a particular manner. Thus, prosecutors must be ever vigilant and self-conscious about the words they use during witness preparation to ensure that the witness understands that the prosecutor only wants the witness to tell the truth.

When, in relation to the proceeding, prosecutors prepare witnesses may depend on the nature of the testimony, the number of witnesses that need to be prepared, and other logistical considerations. Generally speaking, prosecutors should try to prepare witnesses as close to the proceeding as possible, yet far enough in advance of the proceeding to allow the prosecutor to adjust the presentation of the case in light of information learned or developments that arise during the preparation. Prosecutors will almost always have to revise the outline of questions for witnesses in light of the preparation. Through the preparation session, a prosecutor may come to learn that a witness knows of some fact of which the prosecutor was previously unaware or did not know the witness knew. A prosecutor may also determine there is a need to adjust the form or order of questions as a result of going over the witness's testimony during a preparation session. Also, sometimes witness preparation results in the prosecutor realizing the need to add a witness or exhibit or edit an opening statement. Thus, witness preparation needs to take place sufficiently in advance of the proceeding to allow for these potential changes to the government's case-in-chief. On the other hand, the farther in advance of the proceeding the preparation takes place, the more likely it is that the witness will forget what the prosecutor told the witness during the preparation session. Further, the larger the time gap, more likely it is that something may change with the witness before the proceeding. A witness may be arrested, suffer medical issues, or be approached by a defendant's associate, for example. Although it is possible the witness would bring the matter to the prosecutor's attention, the witness may not, and the prosecutor could be surprised by the information at trial or fail to exploit or act on the information. In the end, the timing of the witness preparation sessions requires prosecutors to exercise judgment and engage in careful planning.

Prosecutors should not prepare civilian witnesses without a law enforcement officer, typically the case agent, present. There are several reasons for this. First, the case agent may have helpful insight during the preparation session or be of assistance in dealing with a recalcitrant witness. Second, the law enforcement officer can serve as a prosecutor's potential witness against false claims that the prosecutor tried to improperly influence the witness's testimony. Indeed, the very presence of the law enforcement officer can deter such false claims. Third, the law enforcement officer can create a report, when necessary, to reflect new and previously undisclosed information revealed by the witness during the preparation session. The government has an ongoing duty to supplement the discovery file. If a witness reveals a new fact, that should be reflected in a new report and provided to defense counsel. Finally, a law enforcement officer may need to generate reports when witnesses change their testimony. If a witness says something different (not new) during witness preparation than the witness previously said, whether favorable or unfavorable to the government, it likely constitutes *Giglio* information that must be disclosed to the defense.

Prosecutors should explain to the law enforcement officer why the officer needs to be present during witness preparation sessions. Officers are busy and may view their presence as unnecessary and wasteful of their time. It helps dispel this notion when prosecutors explain the reasons why an officer's presence is necessary. It is also important that the officer know that the officer is there to serve as a potential witness about what occurred, or did not occur, during the witness preparation sessions. If the officer is unaware of that aspect of his or her role, he or she may not pay sufficient attention to the process to serve as a good witness if necessary down the road. Similarly, officers may not be prepared to generate reports about new information if they do not realize that they may be called upon to do so.

Prosecutors should assume that anything they say to the witness during witness preparation will come out at trial. Thus, the prosecutor should ensure that nothing is said to the witness that the prosecutor would not want the jury or judge to hear. Prosecutors should never criticize or denigrate the judge, defense counsel, the defendant, or anyone else. This includes not suggesting to the witness that the defense counsel will try to "pull wool over the witness's eyes" or use tricky or deceptive questioning. Nor should the prosecutor label the defendant (such as calling him or her an "animal"), attack the defendant's character, call the defendant any names, or even describe the defendant's conduct in pejorative terms. Not only would it be embarrassing and potentially harmful to the government's case for this to come out at trial, making such statements to a witness may also improperly influence the witness's testimony.

When preparing witnesses to testify at trial, it is critical that the prosecutor and officer do not provide information to the witness that the witness did not previously know. Witnesses have finite information about certain facts relevant to a case. The prosecutor and case agent, however, have access to all of the facts of a case. Were the prosecutor to disclose facts to a witness of which the witness was otherwise unaware, it may inadvertently and unintentionally influence the witness's testimony. Even advising a witness that other evidence exists that corroborates the witness's testimony may alter the manner of the witness's testimony. For example, a bank teller may believe that the robber drove away in a blue car with a license plate that had the letter Z in it, but the teller is not sure about the accuracy of that perception or recollection. Were the prosecutor to confirm for the witness during witness preparation that officers seized a blue car registered to the defendant that had a license plate containing the letter Z, the manner of the witness's testimony may change dramatically at trial from being unsure to being confident. It is also often important to prevent witness or evidence tampering or interference with an ongoing criminal investigation that witnesses not learn anything about the government's case. Witnesses should remain ignorant of everything to do with the case outside their own personal knowledge, at least until they are done testifying.

The prohibition against giving information to a witness even goes so far as not describing where the defendant will be sitting in the courtroom whenever the witness may be called upon to identify the witness in the courtroom. I learned this lesson only through experience and luck. I had a case when, during direct examination, I asked the witness if the witness saw the person he or she bought drugs from in the courtroom. The ability of the witness to identify the defendant was critical to the case. The witness said yes and at my request pointed out the defendant and described what the defendant was wearing. On cross-examination, the defense attorney asked if I had prepared the witness for trial and if, during that preparation, I had described where the witness and defendant would be sitting in the courtroom. I normally had done this as a matter of course, just to help witnesses feel acclimated to the courtroom. In this instance, however, I had forgotten to do so, which, by chance, allowed the witness to honestly testify that I had not described where the defendant would be sitting in the courtroom. I never forgot the lesson I learned with this close brush with disaster.

Prosecutors should start and end every witness preparation session by explaining the process and emphasizing that the only thing the government wants from the witness is that the witness tells the truth. Prosecutors should explain that everything else they will discuss during the preparation session is designed to help the prosecutor ask better questions to elicit the truth and prepare the witness for the process so that he or she is better able to convey the truth. It helps to get the witness to verbally acknowledge that he or she understands this and will commit to telling only the truth.

Importantly, prosecutors should emphasize the absolute necessity to testify truthfully even when preparing law enforcement officers. Officers are people, too, and they are subject to the same influences as lay witnesses. Officers may want to please the prosecutor or be concerned lest they testify to something that could negatively affect the government's case. I would tell officers during witness preparation sessions that they should internalize the mindset that when they take an oath to tell the truth, they are no longer law enforcement officers. They are witnesses just like any other witness. From the moment they take the oath, they belong to the court and their only duty is to tell the truth, whatever it is. While on the stand testifying, I told officers that they cannot care about the outcome of the case and must set aside their opinion about the defendant and their feelings about any victims. After they testify they can become advocates again, but while they are on the stand, they cannot consider themselves to be advocates.

It is also important to explain to law enforcement officer witnesses the perception that jurors have of them and how that perception may affect their credibility. The general public still hold law enforcement officers in high esteem. We expect officers to tell the truth. We hold them to a higher standard than others in the community. When jurors perceive that a law enforcement officer is shading the truth, even in the slightest degree, they will likely feel as if the officer has betrayed their trust. They will resent the breach of trust and will be more likely to reject the entirety of the officer's testimony whereas they may only reject a portion of a lay witness's testimony who testified in the same manner. Further, the feeling of betrayal jurors experience when they believe a law enforcement officer has lied will carry over to the government's case as a whole, making the jury doubt the trustworthiness of anything the prosecutor says. When officers fully comprehend this juror perception, they more fully appreciate the absolute necessity of adhering strictly to the truth without any shading or gloss.

Before a witness preparation session, the prosecutor should provide the witness with copies of any prior statements the witness has made on the subject matter about which the witness is anticipated to testify. It is important that when providing the statements to the witness, the witness is told that the purpose of doing so is to remind the witness about what he or she previously said. It should be emphasized that by providing the materials to the witness, the prosecutor is not telling the witness that he or she is compelled to say the same thing at trial. The prosecutor should explain that is it possible that the witness may have previously made a misstatement, or that law enforcement officers accidentally recorded what the witness said, or that the witness may have a different recollection of events. The prosecutor should provide the witness with a pen to use in making notations if the witness finds any errors in the prior statements.

Prosecutors should keep in mind that they are creating Jencks Act material when they provide witnesses with copies of their prior statements under these circumstances. Recall that the definition of a "statement" under the Jencks Act includes not only direct quotes by a witness or sworn testimony, but also any statement the witness has made that the witness adopts. By providing a witness with a prior statement with the opportunity to make changes, the witness necessarily adopts any of the statements the witness does not change. Also, any changes the witness makes becomes new Jencks Act statements. Some prosecutors or prosecutors' offices refrain from showing witnesses their prior statements precisely to avoid creating Jencks Act material. I believe the benefits of showing witnesses the statements to make sure the witness is fully informed and the witness's testimony is accurate and truthful far outweighs the detriment of creating Jencks Act material. Again, the government should not be afraid of the truth, nor should it be afraid of disclosing information to the defense even if the defense can use it to impeach the credibility of the government's witnesses. Frankly, if government witnesses can be impeached, they should be.

Before discussing the subject matter of the witness's testimony with the witness during a trial preparation session, a prosecutor should first inquire of the witness whether there is any change in the testimony or recollection. This inquiry will be aided, of course, when the witness has been provided an opportunity in advance to review prior statements and testimony. The prosecutor should also inquire more generally of the witness whether there have been any other changes in circumstances that could affect the witness's testimony, such as drug use, medications, health issues, memory issues, or contact with people about the witness's status as a witness or the witness's testimony.

During a witness preparation session, the prosecutor should go through the outline of questions the prosecutor prepared for the witness. As a result of going through the draft questions with the witness, the witness will be better prepared for and less anxious about the witness's testimony. A prosecutor can go through the questions informally, in the sense of asking the questions casually, or can have the witness pretend the witness is on the stand and proceed to ask questions as if the witness is in court. Of course, a prosecutor can do both. Sometimes it is helpful for nervous witnesses to go through the process as if they are on the stand to help them adjust to the process as it will actually occur in the courtroom. Either way, when going through the outline of questions, the prosecutor should remember not to influence the witness's testimony. Witnesses will even ask sometimes "Is that what I should say?" or "Is that how you want me to answer?" Again, the prosecutor should emphasize that the witness should simply tell the truth. The prosecutor may, however, want to rephrase the draft question to better elicit the desired testimony. For example, if a prosecutor asks a bank teller "What did you see when the robber approached your teller window?" it may not elicit the detail about the robber's limp as a more precisely tailored question like, "Did you notice anything about the robber's gait as he approached your teller's window?" Inevitably, the process of going through the questions with the witness will result in the prosecutor revising the draft outline of questions at least once.

During the process of witness preparation, the prosecutor should show the witness each exhibit about which the witness may testify. The exhibit should be marked as an exhibit and be in the same condition that it will be when offered into evidence. The witness should review the exhibit carefully, and the prosecutor should ensure that the witness has personal knowledge of the exhibit and, when appropriate, can lay a foundation for admission of the exhibit. To alleviate witness nerves, the prosecutor should explain to a witness the process of presenting an exhibit and moving it into evidence. What is routine for prosecutors can be a strange and quirky process to lay witnesses. It helps put a witness at ease, then, when a prosecutor explains the process: the prosecutor will approach the witness and hand the witness the exhibit, then ask the witness a series of questions about the exhibit to lay a foundation for its admission, then the prosecutor will address the court and move for admission of the exhibit, at which time the defense counsel may or may not object, and the court will then issue a ruling regarding admission of the exhibit. The prosecutor should explain to the witness that only after the court rules that the exhibit is admitted can the witness talk about what the exhibit is or what it says or contains. Again, although this is second nature to lawyers, this is an unfamiliar and perhaps strange process to a layperson.

When the witness being prepared is a government cooperator, it is imperative that the prosecutor cover the nature of the witness's cooperation at great length during the witness preparation session. The prosecutor should have the witness review any cooperation or informant agreements and any plea agreements. It is helpful for the prosecutor to inquire of the witness what they understand these agreements mean for the witness, particularly as to any potential benefit the witness has received or may receive as a result of cooperating. If a witness is incorrect, it is important that the prosecutor work with counsel to correct the cooperator and make sure he or she fully understands the agreement. For example, if a plea agreement provides that the cooperator *may* receive a reduction in the cooperator's sentence, it would be incorrect for the cooperator to testify that the cooperator *will* receive a sentencing reduction. The agreement itself may not, and probably will not, itself be an exhibit at trial. Thus, if the cooperator gets it wrong, there may not be a way to correct it at trial. Also, cooperators need to fully understand, for their own benefit, what they may or may not get as a result of cooperating. Similarly, cooperators must understand the adverse consequences that could arise if they were to lie during their testimony. Because the benefits a cooperator may receive are part of a legal framework, it can sometimes be difficult for cooperators to fully understand the process and what they are and are not getting from their cooperation. Prosecutors need to be prepared to go over this part of the cooperator's testimony as many times as necessary to ensure that the cooperator fully understands it and is capable of articulating that understanding when the cooperator testifies. Whenever cooperators are represented by counsel, which is almost always, the government should insist that the cooperator's attorney is present during the witness preparation session. Although most defense attorneys will insist on being present anyway, some find it a waste of their time. It is important to have the cooperator's attorney present to help work with the cooperator to correct any misunderstandings and also to ensure that the witness understands the necessity of testifying truthfully.

Witness preparation involves more than the prosecutor reviewing direct examination with the witness. It also involves reviewing possible cross-examination questions with the witness. Prosecutors should be careful when addressing this topic with witnesses. First, prosecutors should fully explain that they are reviewing possible cross-examination questions that defense attorneys may or may not ask to prepare the witnesses for testifying. Second, prosecutors should again emphasize that they are not telling the witnesses what to say or not say in response to the questions by defense counsel; the witnesses must only and always just tell the truth. Third, prosecutors should be cautious never to describe defense counsel, or the nature of cross-examination questions, in a negative or derogatory manner. For example, a prosecutor should not describe cross-examination as a process by which the defense attorney will try to "trick" the witness or describe a defense attorney as "sneaky." To the contrary, prosecutors should explain that cross-examination is the opportunity for defense attorneys to ask the witnesses questions and that defense attorneys are duty bound to zealously represent defendants. Prosecutors should instruct witnesses never to take questions personally or get defensive or argue with defense counsel. Rather, witnesses should answer the defense attorneys' questions directly and truthfully.

It is helpful to witnesses when prosecutors explain how the nature of cross-examination questions is different than direct examination questions. Prosecutors should explain the difference between leading and nonleading questions and emphasize that there is nothing at all improper or underhanded for a defense attorney to ask leading questions. Prosecutors can explain that when a witness has already told the whole story during direct examination, it would be a waste of time to make the defense attorney ask nonleading questions to get to the point the defense attorney wants to focus on. So, leading questions allow a defense attorney to get straight to the point. Prosecutors should encourage witnesses to try to answer defense attorneys' questions with "yes" or "no" answers when witnesses can answer the questions with a "yes" or "no," and discourage witnesses from arguing with defense counsel. On the other hand, prosecutors should instruct witnesses to say so if they truly believe that they cannot truthfully answer questions with "yes" or "no."

In preparing witnesses for cross-examination, prosecutors should carefully explain the ways in which defense counsel may attempt to impeach a witness's testimony. These include questions about the witness's potential bias, the witness's memory, any criminal history or other bad acts the witness has committed in the past, and prior inconsistent statements. With bias,

I found it helpful to encourage witnesses to simply be frank about any bias they may have. For example, a witness may actually hate the defendant for some reason, or may have a bias against the defendant's race, gender, or other characteristic. A witness may even stand to benefit in some way if the defendant is convicted. Whatever the potential bias issue may be, that does not mean the witness is necessarily testifying falsely. A witness can have a bias and still testify truthfully as to a fact. What will adversely affect a witness's credibility is to falsely disclaim a bias. If a witness is cross-examined as to a potential bias, it is likely the defense counsel has some evidence to back up the question. If the witness falsely denies the bias, the defense counsel may reveal that evidence either during the cross-examination or later through other evidence. With that explanation provided to the witness, I would then encourage the witness to be frank with me in revealing to me any potential bias the witness may have so that together we would have an opportunity either to dispel it, to prevent the defense counsel from inquiring about it if the rules of evidence should bar the evidence, or to disclose the potential bias up front during direct examination so that it did not appear that the witness was attempting to conceal it.

It is similarly helpful to discuss with witnesses the questions defense attorneys may ask on cross-examination regarding the witness's memory. It is important that witnesses understand that their memory is faulty, as is everyone's memory. Our minds trap some facts and retain them, while others are hardly noticed in the first instance and not long retained. Also, our memory of some facts may be inaccurate because in the process of perceiving the facts they were filtered through preconceptions or biases or underwent alteration through a similar process during recall. The bottom line is that witnesses need to understand that their memories are not infallible. On the other hand, there are some facts that were so clear at the time of perception, are of a nature unlikely to be affected by inherent biases or the like, and so firmly placed in memories that witnesses can have confidence in testifying about them.

With these thoughts in mind, prosecutors should advise witnesses to be firm in their testimony when they have confidence in their memories about events, but refrain from asserting absolute certainty about matters when they are not so confident. Some witnesses may feel pressure to claim certainty when in truth they lack confidence in the accuracy of their own recollections. Prosecutors should assure witnesses that it is acceptable to qualify answers based on their memory. Witness may say, for example, that they are "fairly certain" or "almost absolutely sure," or use similar phrases regarding their memory of a fact. It is also helpful to advise witnesses to dispense with unnecessary detail when testifying. If, for example, the important part of a witness's testimony is that the witness saw the defendant enter the bank with a gun, the exact time the defendant entered the bank may be an unnecessary detail. The more detail included in testimony, the more likely the witness will make an error in recollection. This is particularly true the less important the detail was in the first instance.

When witnesses have prior criminal convictions that are open for use to impeach the witness under Rule 609 of the Federal Rules of Evidence, prosecutors should cover this issue with the witnesses. Prosecutors should explain the rule in laymen's terms. A prosecutor should identify the benefits of having the prosecutor elicit testimony about the prior convictions during direct examination instead of waiting until cross-examination by defense counsel. These benefits include allowing more freedom for the witness to testify in his or her own words, rather than having to respond to leading questions, and avoiding the appearance that the witness is attempting to hide his or her criminal past from the jury. The prosecutors should describe the process by which the prosecutor will elicit the criminal history during direct examination, but also explain that defense counsel may nevertheless cover the same ground a second time on cross-examination. Finally, the prosecutor should tell the witness that it is best to be frank and open about criminal history when asked about it by a defense attorney and not to be defensive or evasive. A witness should simply admit the prior convictions and not try to explain them away or minimize the witness's culpability. It is helpful if the witness understands that the more defensive and evasive the witness is about criminal history, the more the defense attorney will focus on the criminal history and the longer the witness will be asked about it.

Aside from criminal history, defense attorneys can also sometimes impeach a witness's credibility by cross-examining the witness about other bad acts, whether those acts resulted in a conviction under Rule 609. Sometimes, albeit rarely, this type of other act evidence takes the form of reverse Rule 404(b) evidence. That is, a defense attorney will offer evidence the witness committed some other act not for the purpose of showing propensity but for some other reason, such as motive, intent, knowledge, and so on. If a prosecutor called a former store manager as a witness in a case where the government had charged the store owner with arson for burning down the store to collect insurance proceeds, for example, a defense attorney could offer evidence that the witness previously committed arson to show that the witness had a motive or intent to burn the store. More often, however, the other act evidence is offered to attack the witness's credibility. A defense attorney could, for example, offer evidence the witness had lied on a job application or failed to disclose past drug use. In order to prepare witnesses for this type of cross-examination, I found it useful to have witnesses imagine that the defendant will be whispering in the defense attorney's ear about everything bad the defendant knows about the witness. Some of that past bad stuff a defense attorney can use to attack the witness, while some may not be admissible. I would emphasize to the witness that if I did not know of the past bad acts, I cannot prevent a defense attorney from raising them even if they are not admissible. I would also explain that if the witness told me about them, then even if they were fair game for the defense attorney to raise during cross-examination that it would be better for us to bring it out during direct examination for all the same reasons that applied to criminal history. With that explanation, I would then encourage the witness to tell me about any bad thing he or she had ever done in the past that could possibly come out during the trial.

Finally, good prosecutors explain the technique lawyers use to impeach witnesses with prior inconsistent statements. Unless someone has been confronted by a lawyer with a prior inconsistent statement, the process can be startling and disturbing. Jurors may misinterpret a witness's confusion and dismay at the confrontation as an indication that the witness has intentionally lied to the jury. Thus, prosecutors should explain the concept first, then provide advice about responding to a defense attorney's attempt to impeach a witness's testimony in this manner. First, witnesses need to understand that it is very likely that they will say something in court that could be perceived to be inconsistent with prior statements. An inconsistent statement may be a result of a faulty memory, access to new information since making the prior statement, or recent refreshment of recollection, or the apparent inconsistency may have resulted from a poorly worded question in court or when the witness last spoke about the matter or a poorly worded or misworded answer either in court or before. Whatever the case, in all likelihood there is an innocent explanation for what appears to be an inconsistent statement that has nothing to do with the witness's honesty. It is important to emphasize to witnesses that some of the time the inconsistencies tend to be minor or not real inconsistencies at all. The point for prosecutors to get across is that witnesses should not panic when it becomes apparent to them that defense attorneys are attempting to impeach their credibility with prior inconsistent statements.

Second, a prosecutor should explain how the questions will sound during the defense attorney's impeachment attempt. The prosecutor should explain that the defense attorney will likely first reference the in-court testimony that the attorney believes is inconsistent with a prior statement. For example, the defense attorney may ask something like: "Now on direct examination, you said that the robber ran from the bank, didn't you?" Next, the defense attorney will usually refer to the circumstances surrounding the witness's prior statement, noting where and when it was made and often referencing facts that would show that the witness understood the importance of being accurate (such as whether the witness was under oath at the time or speaking to someone the witness knew to be a law enforcement officer). The final step of the impeachment process is the confrontation of the witness with the prior inconsistent statement. A prosecutor should explain to the witness that the defense attorney will usually phrase the confrontation question in a manner that demands only a "yes" or "no" answer: "Isn't it true that in the grand jury you said the robber walked away from the bank quickly?" The prosecutor should encourage the witness to answer such a question with a "yes" or "no" answer, if possible, and not to equivocate or try to explain the apparent inconsistency. The prosecutor should also explain to the witness that the point of impeachment with a prior inconsistent statement is to show inconsistency, and not necessarily to show that one statement is more accurate than the other. Thus, the defense attorney is not looking for an explanation and will not likely give the witness an opportunity to explain an apparent inconsistent statement. Finally, a prosecutor should assure witnesses that if the prosecutor believes the defense attorney pointed out an important inconsistency that needed an explanation, on redirect examination the prosecutor will give the witness the opportunity to explain the apparent inconsistency.

Prosecutors should provide witnesses with some orientation about the physical setting of their testimony. At the very least, prosecutors should show witnesses a floorplan or diagram of the courtroom, pointing out where they will enter the courtroom and the location of the witness chair, the jury, and the judge. Again, prosecutors should be cautious never to tell a witness where the defendant will be sitting if there is any chance the prosecutor will ask the witness to identify the defendant in the courtroom.

In some situations a more extensive courtroom preparation session may be appropriate. Some witnesses, such as children or crime victims, may be especially nervous about testifying. A courtroom can be a very intimidating setting and a jury may misinterpret a witness's nervousness as an indication that the witness is not telling the truth. Thus, in some cases it may be advisable to show the courtroom to the witness and, if possible, even let the witness take a seat in the witness chair. It may even be helpful to go through some questions with the witness while they are sitting in the witness chair to get them accustomed to answering question in that setting.

By the end of the witness preparation session, it will inevitably be necessary for the prosecutor to revise the outline of direct examination questions. Sometimes the changes are minor, reflecting a change in the words used to ask questions in a way that allows the witness to more readily understand the question. In other cases, the witness preparation session may require major revisions to the outline of questions, the addition or removal of exhibits to be shown to the witness, or other significant alterations. Prosecutors should resist the urge to make the testimony fit the outline, or to make do with an outline that does not fully elicit the testimony the witness has to offer. This urge to make do can be hard for prosecutors to resist because witness preparation occurs shortly before trial at a time when there are a lot of other demands on the prosecutor's time, along with all of the other work prosecutors have pending in other cases. Nevertheless, it is important that a prosecutor revise the witness outline as soon after the preparation session as possible to ensure that the prosecutor has captured all of the changes that are needed to make the witness's testimony as persuasive as possible.

PREPARING THE EVIDENCE FOR PRESENTATION

Effectively presenting evidence to a jury requires careful thought and preparation. Too often, lawyers fail to carefully consider the steps necessary to ensure the evidence can be adequately viewed and understood by the jury. Rather, lawyers focus on their own perception of the evidence, which is skewed by their intimate familiarity with the evidence. To prepare evidence for persuasive presentation to jurors, prosecutors should place themselves in the shoes, or more literally the seats, of the jurors.

Prosecutors should first take advantage of the technology available for displaying evidence to jurors. Most paper or visual evidence can be digitized and displayed using trial presentation programs. These programs allow lawyers to manipulate the images in various ways to enhance jurors' ability to view and understand the exhibits. Using the technology, a prosecutor can, for example, enlarge a document; underline, highlight, and annotate portions of an image; superimpose two images against or on top of each other; and so forth, all while displaying the documents to a witness and jury. Almost all courtrooms are also now equipped with document cameras. These devices display a visual image of an object on a screen. Thus, a prosecutor can place a document on the screen so that the witness and jury can see it at the same time. These document cameras can also work to display some objects to the jury as well, depending on the size and nature of the object. As previously noted, prosecutors should also consider creating charts, diagrams, summaries, and other demonstrative exhibits for use with witnesses to help the witness convey and explain information to the jury.

Some cases also involve audio or video recordings. Prosecutors should strongly consider creating transcripts of these recordings when the words stated in them are important to the case to help the jury understand the evidence. Although the transcripts themselves are not evidence and do not go back to the jury during deliberations, they can be extremely helpful for jurors to catch what is said while listening to a recording. The harder it is to hear and understand what people say on a recording, the more important it is to generate a transcript of it. Depending on the number and length of the recordings, this process can sometimes be very time-consuming, especially if the recording is in a foreign language. Prosecutors should work far in advance of trial to determine whether and what transcripts are needed to be prepared in time for presenting the recordings at trial.

Once a prosecutor has prepared all of the exhibits for display to the jury, it is incredibly important that the prosecutor then go and test them out in the courtroom. The prosecutor should pull up every digitized exhibit on the computer and project it on the screen. What may appear clear on the computer screen may be blurry or too dark on the courtroom screen. The prosecutor should practice and practice and practice any intended manipulations of the images, such as enlarging or highlighting, to make sure the prosecutor can smoothly and flawlessly do so when in front of the jury. The prosecutor should likewise practice with the document camera, determining where to place a document or object, how far to zoom in or out, and how to focus the image.

When trying out the exhibits in the courtroom, it is further very important that the prosecutor view the images from the jurors' seats. Prosecutors should make sure that the exhibits are clearly visible from every juror's seat. This includes digitized exhibits as well as demonstrative exhibits, such as charts. It has been my observation that lawyers create demonstrative exhibits in a manner that is easily visible to the lawyer standing two feet from the exhibit, but fail to realize that the exhibit is unreadable to a juror three or more feet away from it while sitting in the jury box. The same efforts must be made for any recordings. Prosecutors should practice playing any audio exhibits in the courtroom to ensure they can smoothly and flawlessly play the recording. Prosecutors should also test the volume and the clarity of any audio recording from the jurors' seats.

In short, in preparing evidence for trial, prosecutors must remember that the jurors are the ultimate fact finders in the case. What matters is what jurors can see and understand.

Chapter Sixteen

Preparing for the Defense Case

While a prosecutor is preparing to present the government's case, the prosecutor must simultaneously be preparing to confront the defense case. Somewhat like a chess player, a prosecutor must anticipate the opponent's potential moves, the opponent's potential reactions to the government's actions. A prosecutor must recognize that a defense attorney may respond to the government's case-in-chief not simply through cross-examination of the government's witnesses and by argument at the close of the case, but also through the affirmative presentation of evidence during a defense case. That defense case may also involve the assertion of affirmative defenses. A good prosecutor, then, prepares in advance of trial for the defense case and does not wait until trial to react to it.

That said, it must be acknowledged that in most criminal cases the defense does not present evidence. Sometimes there simply is not a viable case for the defense attorney to present. The vast majority of criminal trials involve the presentation of government witnesses and evidence only. It is a rare case when the defense calls witnesses or offers its own exhibits into evidence. This is particularly true of the typical street crime, such as drug distribution, firearms possession, and violent offenses. Even when defendants do call witnesses in those cases, those witnesses usually testify as to narrow issues of fact or as to the defendant's character and seldom present much of a challenge for the government. Mainly in white-collar cases is it common for the defense to have a robust case and call many substantive witnesses.

Nevertheless, a prosecutor must be prepared for the possibility of a defense case. Prosecutors need to think ahead of how they can tailor the presentation of the government's case to anticipate defense evidence. Preparing for a defense case requires prosecutors to take advantage of discovery rules to learn of the defense case, investigate defense witnesses, and anticipate the possible cross-examination of the defendant. Prosecutors need to also consider investigating possible defenses and defense witnesses. Prosecutors should prepare outlines for cross-examination of possible defense witnesses. Finally, prosecutors should consider whether a rebuttal case is necessary or advisable and, if so, of what it will consist.

DISCOVERING INFORMATION
ABOUT A DEFENSE CASE

In preparing for a defense case, prosecutors should avail themselves of any procedural or local rules that would require the defense to divulge the existence of a defense case, the nature of any defense, and the identity of defense witnesses or description of defense exhibits. As discussed in chapter 12, there are few reciprocal discovery tools available to prosecutors that will, as a practical matter, realistically provide prosecutors with any real knowledge of potential defense cases. As a result, prosecutors often go into trial rather blind as to what, if any, case defense attorneys may present. Knowing this, it is important then that prosecutors use every tool that is available to elicit information from the defense about defense cases.

As mentioned, defendants are bound by reciprocal discovery obligations regarding experts and Jencks Act material. Similarly, certain affirmative defenses require defendants to provide notice and information to the prosecution in advance of trial. Prosecutors should affirmatively demand from defense counsel the evidence and information required by the rules. Local rules, adopted by courts, sometimes also impose obligations upon defendants to provide the government with advance notice of the identity of potential witnesses and copies of potential exhibits. Again, prosecutors should become familiar with these rules and require defense counsel comply with them. Finally, prosecutors may wish to consider working out an informal agreement with defense counsel to exchange information in a manner different from and greater than that contemplated by the rules. Prosecutors may explore whether an agreement can be reached with defense counsel, for example, to exchange witness lists or copies of exhibits earlier than required, or perhaps offer earlier disclosure of Jencks Act material to the defense attorney in exchange for an early description of anticipated testimony by defense witnesses.

INVESTIGATING DEFENSE WITNESSES

Through local rules, through local practice, or by cooperating with defense counsel, a prosecutor will often get a few days' advance notice of any witnesses a defendant may call. Sometimes defense counsel will provide Jencks Act statements for the witnesses or a general description of the subject matter of their testimony, but most often all the prosecutor will get is the names of potential witnesses. Time will be of essence in researching and investigating the potential defense witnesses because the prosecutor will likely only have a few days before trial starts to complete the work. Although the investigation of defense witnesses can continue while the government is putting on its case-in-chief, that is practically possible only if there are trial team members available to do it while others are trying the case or if it can be accomplished at night after trial.

Prosecutors should research the defense witnesses to the extent possible. Prosecutors should recruit the law enforcement officers working on the case, paralegals, legal assistants, or other members of the trial team to help conduct this investigation. To the extent possible, efforts should be made to learn about the witnesses' criminal history, their employment status and history (when it might be relevant), their relationship with the defendant or other members of the defense team, and any history the witnesses have of having testified in the past. Full use should be made of the internet and access to public records to learn as much as possible about the prospective witnesses. This includes searching publicly accessible social media as much as possible.

Prosecutors should also attempt to interview defense witnesses. As a prosecutor, I was often surprised that defense attorneys seldom tried to interview government witnesses. In contrast, I tried to have agents interview defense witnesses. A witness has no obligation to talk to anyone from either side, of course, but it never hurts to at least attempt to conduct such an interview.

When sending agents out to conduct these interviews, prosecutors should ensure that the agents are instructed carefully about how to handle the interviews. Generally, agents should fully identify themselves to the potential witness, ensuring that the witness understands that the agent is aligned with the government and not the defendant. Further, it is often advisable that the agents make sure the witness understands that the witness is under no legal obligation to talk with the agents and that there will be no negative consequences that would arise from refusing to talk with the agents. Finally, if the witness agrees to be interviewed, the agents may want to tell the witness they must tell the truth and that the witness may be prosecuted for lying to the agent. This warning is necessary for the government to prosecute a witness for making a false statement. In the end, agents must take care not to intimidate or discourage the witness from testifying for the defendant in any way, explicitly or even implicitly.

Agents should be instructed to interview defense witnesses about a wide variety of matters and not just the witness's anticipated testimony. First, agents should ask the witness why he or she believes he or she is being called to testify, what he or she anticipates saying, and the basis for these beliefs. Often the witness knows from talking to the defense attorney generally why he or she is being called as a witness and what the defense attorney anticipates asking the witness. On other occasions, however, the witness may have no idea why they are being called as a witness. Second, agents should question the witness about the subject matter of his or her anticipated testimony in some detail. Agents should explore the basis for the witness's knowledge, looking for weaknesses in the anticipated testimony. Third, agents should ask witnesses about their knowledge of other witnesses, including both government and other defense witnesses. Sometimes one witness will have surprising and helpful information about other defense witnesses, or reveal something unknown but damaging about a government witness. Finally, and at the end of the interview, agents should ask witnesses about their knowledge of the defendant. This is best done last because defense witnesses tend to become recalcitrant when directly questioned about the defendant with whom the witness may be friends or to whom the witness may be related. The witness should be asked not only about the defendant's conduct in the case at hand, but also the defendant's other criminal conduct on other occasions.

When defense witnesses agree to be interviewed, it often results in new leads, such as previously unknown potential witnesses or disclosure of other acts the defendant committed. On other occasions, defense witness interviews will raise potential defenses or explanations that must be probed and tested. Prosecutors should urge agents to follow up on the new leads. It is the prosecutor's responsibility to then determine whether any new information falls within the category of true rebuttal evidence, or whether it constitutes *Brady* or *Giglio* information that may need to be disclosed to defense counsel in advance of trial.

ANTICIPATING TESTIMONY BY THE DEFENDANT

Criminal defendants rarely testify at trials. This is particularly true in federal criminal cases because, among other reasons, the US Sentencing Guidelines provide for a potential increase in a defendant's sentence if the sentencing judge finds that the defendant falsely testified and thus obstructed justice. *See* USSG §3C1.1. Nevertheless, a careful prosecutor prepares for cross-examination of the defendant in every case, even when it seems highly unlikely the defendant will testify.

It has been my observation and experience that cross-examining a criminal defendant is one of the most difficult tasks facing a prosecutor. This is so for many reasons. First, if the defendant committed the offense, then the defendant knows better than anyone else exactly how he or she committed the crime. Thus, the defendant is in the best position to see weaknesses in the government's case or to evade pitfalls in his testimony. Second, the defendant has been thinking long and hard about testifying. A clever defendant, with knowledge of the government's evidence, can sometimes offer a tailored explanation that gives him or her plausible deniability or most often defeat the mens rea element. Finally, defendants have nothing to lose and so may lie with abandon; the oath may well mean nothing to them. Having decided to roll the dice by testifying, defendant witnesses have every motive to lie. Prosecutors cannot, then, count on a witness's obligation to tell the truth serving as a limit on the defendant's testimony.

In preparing for cross-examining a criminal defendant, prosecutors should endeavor to try to put themselves in the shoes of the defendant and try to imagine what the defendant could say that would provide a defense. Having thought of what the defendant may say, the prosecutor should, in the prosecutor's mind, marshal the evidence that would counter each thing the defendant may say. It will not do to confront a defendant witness with this contrary evidence; again, a criminal defendant is unlikely to admit anything on the stand no matter how obvious it may be. Rather, the trick is to formulate questions that box the defendant in and set the defendant up for defeat by rebuttal evidence. For example, in a drug courier case the focus of the defendant's testimony would likely be a denial of any knowledge that drugs were hidden in the vehicle. The defendant might proffer an explanation that some friend just asked him or her to drive the car to another location as a favor and that he or she had no idea there were drugs in the car. The prosecutor may know from the evidence, however, that the defendant drove nonstop from a source state to the destination city, there were fast-food wrappers in the car, the defendant had little cash, the defendant made no phone calls to anyone in the destination city, and the defendant had no discernable way to return to the source state after delivering the car. The goal of a cross-examination in such a case may be to lead the defendant down the path of his or her fake story, trying to get him or her to give more detail, claim he or she took his time driving, had a firm plan for meeting someone in the destination state and a way to get back home, and so forth. It will be important that the prosecutor develop leading questions in advance of trial that would try to persuade the defendant witness to embellish his or her own story to the point that other evidence will show its falseness. The prosecutor must remember to lead and never to ask the defendant for the explanation when the testimony reveals facts that are inconsistent with the defendant's story.

With a general idea of what the prosecutor believes the defendant may say, it is helpful for the prosecutor to draft an outline of the questions the defense counsel may ask to elicit the anticipated story. Once drafted, the prosecutor should go back over the outline looking for questions that may be subject to objections based on the rules of evidence. The prosecutor should make careful notes for the applicable rules of evidence that may come into play and possibly even outline an argument regarding the rules.

The next step in preparing to cross-examine a criminal defendant is for the prosecutor to identify every discrete fact related to the crime that the defendant must absolutely admit. Although defendants will never admit facts that are clearly incriminating, they will often admit facts that are obviously true and are not directly incriminating. Those facts, when admitted, still have the effect of hemming in the defendant and limiting the scope of his or her explanation.

Third, the prosecutor should think carefully about ways to impeach the defendant's credibility. The facts of the crime aside, the defendant's credibility is at issue when the defendant testifies. Thus, anything about the defendant or his or her testimony that is impeaching of his or her credibility is fair game. This includes the defendant's criminal history, to the extent that it qualifies as convictions subject to impeachment under Rule 609. It may also involve other past acts or omissions bearing on the defendant witness's credibility. It is often fruitful when a defendant offers an explanation for the first time at trial to get the defendant to admit he or she did not previously offer this explanation to a spouse or friends or others. Of course, prosecutors should be very cautious here not to ask questions that would comment on the defendant's right to remain silent by not giving the explanation to law enforcement officers after advised of the right to remain silent. Finally, the defendant's testimony may lend itself to impeachment based on prior inconsistent statements.

In outlining a cross-examination of a defendant, prosecutors should generally keep it simple and keep it short. The cross-examination should be focused on making a few key points. The prosecutor should also outline a cross-examination that allows the cross-examination to end on the most powerful note possible. This is often a series of questions regarding obvious facts the defendant must admit.

ASSESSING AND ADDRESSING THE ADMISSIBILITY OF DEFENSE EVIDENCE

Just as a prosecutor should assess the government's evidence to identify possible evidentiary issues and decide whether and how to address the issues in advance of trial, so too should a prosecutor do the same thing for defense evidence. Prosecutors should thoughtfully consider every possible evidentiary objection to anticipated defense exhibits and testimony. Prosecutors should then determine the strength of the possible objection and the importance of the anticipated evidence. For important evidence to which there is a strong evidentiary basis to object, the prosecutor must decide how and when to address the issue.

Just as with the government's evidence, there are several ways for prosecutors to address potential evidentiary issues with anticipated defense exhibits or testimony. First, a prosecutor can informally address the issue with defense counsel in an effort to reach a negotiated compromise. Second, a prosecutor can consider filing a motion in limine to bar the evidence. Third, the prosecutor can raise the evidentiary issue in a trial brief. Finally, the prosecutor can wait to object until the defense attorney offers the evidence at trial. There are factors for prosecutors to consider in deciding the proper course of action.

Raising issues with defense counsel in advance of trial, either informally, through a motion in limine, or in a trial brief, reveals the prosecutor's position. A prosecutor who raises an evidentiary issue in advance of trial will inevitably highlight evidence the prosecutor believes is important and identify the basis for objecting to the evidence. The defense counsel may not have recognized the importance of the evidence or a weakness in its admissibility. Indeed, it is possible that the defense attorney had not even considered the evidence the prosecutor anticipated the defense attorney may offer. Raising the evidentiary issue in advance of trial provides the defense counsel time to research and respond to the issue, which the defense counsel would not have been able to do had the prosecutor raised the evidentiary issue for the first time at trial. Even when a prosecutor is successful in obtaining a pretrial order barring the defendant's proposed evidence, it provides the defense attorney time to react to the ruling and either address it and correct the issue that makes the evidence inadmissible or develop an end-run around the issue by presenting other admissible evidence to prove the same element.

Sometimes evidence may be so potentially prejudicial that it could harm the government's case even if the trial court sustains the prosecutor's objection at trial. Although the trial judge may instruct the jurors to disregard the evidence, the bell has already been rung, so the saying goes, and cannot be un-rung. It is particularly important, then, that prosecutors raise in advance of trial objections to evidence they believe is highly prejudicial. Even if the motion is unsuccessful, the prosecutor is in a better position to address the issue. The prosecutor may, for example, want to address that issue in jury selection, or mention the evidence in opening statement, or elicit the evidence during direct examination so that it does not appear the prosecutor is attempting to hide the adverse evidence from the jury.

In assessing the advisability of raising an evidentiary issue in advance of trial in a motion in limine, prosecutors should also consider the effect making an objection to evidence in front of the jury may have on the jury. Jurors may perceive that a prosecutor objecting to evidence at trial is attempting to conceal evidence from them. There is a popular perception that attorneys and courts hide information from jurors, and there is some truth to this. The purpose of the evidentiary rules, after all, is to bar jurors from exposure to certain evidence. This perception that the court system is hiding evidence from jurors is exacerbated when a prosecutor objects during trial to defense evidence. Even if the prosecutor prevails on the objection, it may harm the government's case. Jurors may first hold an animus against the prosecutor if they believe the prosecutor is hiding information from them. Jurors may also hypothesize the existence of evidence that is far more adverse to the government than the evidence really was. For example, if a prosecutor successfully objects to a question calling for hearsay, jurors may fill in the blank of what they think the witness might have said. The jurors' imaginations may be worse for the government than the answer would have been.

So for a prosecutor who anticipates that the defense will offer evidence that may be objectionable, it may be beneficial for the prosecutor to raise the issue in advance of trial in a motion in limine. The effect of restricting the evidence the jurors will see may be the same, but the impact on the jury will be different because the jurors will be unaware of the ruling and will not have reason to feel animus against a prosecutor for keeping something from them. Also, the jurors will not have the opportunity to speculate as to what might have been kept from them. Even if the prosecutor is unsuccessful with the motion in limine, the prosecutor can adjust the trial presentation in light of the court's ruling.

Sometimes letting the defense present evidence and using cross-examination to undercut that evidence does more damage to the defense than the advantage that could be gained by excluding the evidence in advance of trial. Even though the defendant's evidence may be inadmissible under the Federal Rules of Evidence, there may be times when a prosecutor is better off letting the evidence in and using the inherent unreliability of the evidence to infect the jury's view of the rest of the evidence. Also, greater dividends may be gained by allowing defense counsel to promise the jury in opening statement that the jury will see certain evidence, and then successfully keeping that evidence out by objecting at trial, than would be gained by obtaining a pretrial order barring the evidence.

PREPARING A REBUTTAL CASE

When a criminal defendant presents evidence, the prosecutor must consider whether to present a rebuttal case. That decision will be fact-intensive, of course, dependent upon the evidence the defendant presented and the possible rebuttal evidence the government has at its disposal. Nevertheless, there are some general observations to be made about rebuttal cases.

Generally, rebuttal cases are either spectacularly successful or they fail miserably. A government rebuttal case fails miserably when it fails to definitively rebut the defense case. There is no such thing as a mediocre rebuttal case for the government. Like redirect examinations, most often rebuttal cases add nothing to the government's evidence. Presumably, the prosecutor presented the best evidence available in the case-in-chief and held nothing back. The government has the burden of proof and if the defendant presents evidence and the government attempts to rebut it, but succeeds in making only minor points, it is a failure. If the government announces that it is presenting rebuttal evidence, the jury fully expects the government to destroy the defense case. If the rebuttal evidence fails to destroy the defense case, it does far more injury to the government's case than if the prosecutor presented no rebuttal evidence at all. It has been my observation that a prosecutor knows when the rebuttal case will be completely successful. If a prosecutor has any doubt, the prosecutor should probably refrain from attempting it. During my twenty-plus-year prosecuting career, I successfully presented a rebuttal case in less than a handful of trials.

When a prosecutor believes there is strong evidence that will clearly rebut the defense evidence, the prosecutor should present it quickly and precisely. In other words, truly good rebuttal evidence typically consists of a definitive piece of evidence or testimony that rebuts a key fact presented by the defense. The prosecutor should present the rebuttal evidence in the most concise way possible. A focused presentation of rebuttal evidence draws the jury's attention on the contrasting evidence, highlighting the rebuttal nature of the evidence. Further, a concise and precise presentation of rebuttal evidence narrows the scope of surrebuttal evidence available to the defense. The government's rebuttal case, in other words, is not a place to expand the scope of the evidence or rehash points already established in the government's case-in-chief.

Prosecutors should be careful not to try to sandbag the defendant and be left holding the sandbag. In other words, prosecutors sometimes anticipate the possibility of the defense putting on a case and, trying to be clever, hold back on presenting evidence in the case-in-chief because the prosecutor believes the impact of the evidence will be much greater in rebuttal. That may well be the case, but if the defense ends up not putting on a case after all, the prosecutor is left holding onto the piece of evidence with no opportunity to present it to the jury. I learned this lesson the hard way, to the expense of a colleague who sought my advice. I suggested the prosecutor hold back on a piece of evidence, sure that the defendant would testify. The defendant did not testify, though, and the jury never learned of the evidence we had held back. The defendant was acquitted. Perhaps the jury would have acquitted the defendant even if the jury had learned of the evidence it never saw, but we will never know.

Rebuttal evidence can also be fraught with potential error. A good prosecutor has carefully thought out and orchestrated every aspect of the government's case-in-chief, has weighed out evidentiary issues, and has ensured that the presentation of the evidence does not encroach on the defendant's constitutional rights in any way. Rebuttal cases, however, are by definition a reaction to what the other side has presented. The prosecutor often must make quick decisions about whether to present a rebuttal case, what evidence to present, and how to present it. The potential for error increases with the decrease in time for the prosecutor to carefully consider all of the implications of the potential rebuttal evidence. Also, if the prosecutor held back on disclosing some evidence believing it was only relevant as rebuttal evidence, but was wrong, it could result in a mistrial.

So to counter the potential for error that arises from haste, prosecutors should carefully plan a rebuttal case in advance to the extent possible. This requires the prosecutor to think very carefully and creatively in advance of trial about all of the potential evidence the defense could present, if the defendant puts on a case. Prosecutors need to use mental discipline to imagine themselves in the place of defense attorneys and consider all of the possible defenses that could arise from the evidence. Once the prosecutor has identified various possible defenses and the nature of the evidence that would be presented with each defense, the prosecutor can plan possible rebuttal cases. I would often write outlines on separate pieces of paper, identifying the possible defense and listing the possible ways for the government to respond. Most often, I would conclude that the best response to the defense case was not a rebuttal case but, rather, was to address the defense evidence in closing argument. On occasion, however, it would occur to me that if a defendant presented evidence in support of a particular defense, there may be an opportunity for me to present rebuttal evidence. With that in mind, I would prepare as much as I could in advance an outline of the rebuttal evidence, even drafting questions for potential witnesses and preparing the witnesses for the possible rebuttal testimony.

Finally, there are some cases when the prosecutor knows there will be a rebuttal case because the defendant has asserted an affirmative defense. Alibi, insanity, and entrapment defenses are examples of theories of defense that will almost certainly involve the potential for a rebuttal case. There are two important things for prosecutors to consider in these situations. First, the prosecutor should tailor the presentation of the government's case-in-chief with the affirmative defense in mind. Often the government can present evidence in such a way as to undercut the affirmative defense before the defendant even has a chance to put on the case, negating the need to present a rebuttal case at all. Second, if it is clear that the government will present a rebuttal case, the prosecutor should fully prepare it with the same careful attention and effort as the prosecutor devoted to the case-in-chief.

Chapter Seventeen

Expert Witnesses

It is more and more common that experts of one kind or another are employed in criminal cases. Experts may address everything from forensic evidence (such as fingerprints, ballistics, handwriting analysis, chemical composition of substances, and the like), to computer evidence, to psychology. Sometimes one side or the other uses subject matter experts to educate juries on complex topics, such as bankruptcy, banking, or a particular industry. In still other cases the parties may present experts at sentencing to address financial loss or to present mitigating social science information relevant to a proper sentence for the defendant.

It is increasingly important, then, that prosecutors are fully prepared to work with experts and expert testimony. The focus of this chapter will be on dealing with both government and defense witnesses before and in preparation for their trial testimony. In this chapter I cover discovery obligations pertaining to experts. I will also summarize the rules of evidence as they pertain to experts but will not delve deeply into the evidence rules as this is not a book on evidence.[1] This chapter will also discuss how to identify good government expert witnesses, how to work with them to develop the evidence, and how to prepare them for testifying. This chapter will also address how to handle defense expert witnesses, including how to research their background, analyze their work, and effectively prepare for cross-examination.

DISCOVERY RULES AND EXPERTS

Rule 16 of the Federal Rules of Criminal Procedure imposes on both the government and the defendant certain discovery obligations involving experts. As a general matter, each side must provide to the other side reports and other underlying documents, examinations, and tests forming the basis for an expert's testimony when the other party requests such discovery. The government's obligation is broader in scope, however. The government must provide such documentation if "the attorney for the government knows—or with due diligence could know—that the item exists" and "the item is material to preparing the defense or the government intends to use the item in its case-in-chief at trial." FED. R. CRIM. P. 16(a)(1)(F)(ii) & (iii). In contrast, a federal criminal defendant needs to provide such items to the government only if "the defendant intends to use the item in the defendant's case-in-chief at trial or intends to call the witness who prepared the report and the report relates to the witness's testimony." FED. R. CRIM. P. 16(b)(1)(B)(ii). The difference between the discovery obligation reflects the government's responsibility to provide all relevant documents to the defense, whether they exculpate or incriminate the defendant, while relieving a criminal defense attorney from disclosing to the government evidence that may incriminate the defendant. Prosecutors should be aware, however, that the language of Rule 16(b)(1)(B)(ii) is sufficiently broad that defense attorneys may seek to withhold disclosure until the last minute, even when they offer the evidence in their case-in-chief and call the expert at trial, by claiming that they did not "intend" to do so until the last minute.

Rule 16 also requires both sides to provide summaries of their expert's opinions to the opposing parties. Again, however, the government's obligation is greater than the defendant's in this respect as well. If the defendant requests such disclosure, the government must provide the information to the defendant, which in turn kicks in a reciprocal obligation for the defendant to do the same. If the defense does not make such a request, however, the defendant has no obligation to make such a disclosure to the government, even if asked, unless the defendant is offering a mental defense under Rule 12.2(b) of the Federal Rules of Criminal Procedure.

Prosecutors may want to make Rule 16 disclosure of expert testimony in relation to an agent testifying about criminal methods (e.g., that certain items seized during a search are tools of the drug trade). As I will discuss next, the Federal Rules of Evidence permit lay witnesses can render opinions, but only so long as those opinions are not based on specialized knowledge. If agents only know whether an object is a tool of the drug trade, or a certain slang term has a meaning in the criminal underworld, through the agent's experience as a narcotics officer, for example, then any opinion the agent expresses about the matter may be subject to the rules for expert testimony. If so, then the government would have been obligated to comply with the Rule 16 discovery obligations regarding the expert testimony. In practice, however, prosecutors seldom treat this type of agent testimony as expert testimony under the rules and defense attorneys seldom object. The safer course of conduct may be for prosecutors to make expert disclosures regarding this type of testimony.

EXPERTS AND THE FEDERAL RULES OF EVIDENCE

To understand how to work with and prepare for expert testimony in advance of trial, it is necessary to have some familiarity with the rules of evidence that govern the admissibility of expert testimony. In federal courts, the 700 series of rules in the Federal Rules of Evidence cover expert testimony. Federal case law has also, however, clarified the court's role in acting as a gatekeeper regarding expert testimony to ensure that jurors are exposed only to reliable expert testimony. I will briefly discuss the evidentiary rules and the law pertaining to experts here.

Federal Rule of Evidence 701 addresses the admissibility of opinion testimony by lay witnesses. Rule 701 provides:

Rule 701. Opinion Testimony by Lay Witnesses

If a witness is not testifying as an expert, testimony in the form of an opinion is limited to one that is:

(a) rationally based on the witness's perception;
(b) helpful to clearly understanding the witness's testimony or to determining a fact in issue; and
(c) not based on scientific, technical, or other specialized knowledge within the scope of Rule 702.

FED. R. EVID. 701. The purpose of Rule 701 is to allow opinion testimony when it would be of some value, and exclude it when it would prove unhelpful or a waste of time. *See* 29 CHARLES ALAN WRIGHT & VICTOR JAMES GOLD, FEDERAL PRACTICE AND PROCEDURE § 6252 (2017).

In contrast, Rule 702 of the Federal Rules of Evidence addresses the admissibility of expert testimony. It provides:

Rule 702. Testimony by Expert Witnesses

A witness who is qualified as an expert by knowledge, skill, experience, training, or education may testify in the form of an opinion or otherwise if:

(a) the expert's scientific, technical, or other specialized knowledge will help the trier of fact to understand the evidence or to determine a fact in issue;

    (b) the testimony is based on sufficient facts or data;

    (c) the testimony is the product of reliable principles and methods; and

    (d) the expert has reliably applied the principles and methods to the facts of the case.

FED. R. EVID. 702. Rule 702 codifies the Supreme Court's decisions in *Daubert v. Merrell Dow Pharmaceuticals, Inc.*, 509 US 579 (1993), and *Kumho Tire Co. v. Carmichael*, 526 US 137 (1999). In those two decisions, the Supreme Court held that trial judges have the duty to serve as so-called "gatekeepers," to ensure that only reliable expert testimony is permitted into evidence in federal courts. *Daubert* was limited to scientific evidence, but in *Kumho Tire*, the Supreme Court reinforced the gatekeeping obligations of the trial judge to ensure the reliability of all expert testimony, whether scientific or otherwise. When one party challenges the reliability and, hence, the admissibility of the other side's expert testimony in a federal criminal case, the trial judge must hold what is referred to as a "Daubert" hearing to test the reliability of the expert testimony and decide whether to admit the testimony at trial.

    The Federal Rules of Evidence also place some limitation on the type of facts or data upon which an expert may rely in reaching his or her opinion. Rule 703 provides:

Rule 703. Bases of an Expert's Opinion Testimony

> An expert may base an opinion on facts or data in the case that the expert has been made aware of or personally observed. If experts in the particular field would reasonably rely on those kinds of facts or data in forming an opinion on the subject, they need not be admissible for the opinion to be admitted. But if the facts or data would otherwise be inadmissible, the proponent of the opinion may disclose them to the jury only if their probative value in helping the jury evaluate the opinion substantially outweighs their prejudicial effect.

FED. R. EVID. 703. The facts or data in the particular case upon which an expert bases an opinion or inference may be those perceived by or made known to the expert at or before the hearing. If of a type reasonably relied upon by experts in the particular field in forming opinions or inferences upon the subject, the facts or data need not be admissible in evidence in order for the opinion or inference to be admitted.

    In addition to limiting experts to reliance on facts and data reasonably relied on by others in their field, Rule 703 also raises a couple of important points to remember in conducting direct examination and cross-examination of experts. First, the party who called the expert to testify cannot slip in through the expert evidence which is otherwise inadmissible simply because the expert relied on it in reaching his or her opinion, absent a finding by the court that its probative value substantially outweighs the prejudicial effect. Thus, federal prosecutors must abide by this rule and be alert for defense counsel who do not. Second, a party does not need leave of the court to cross-examine the other side's expert for relying on inadmissible facts and data to reach their opinion. This sometimes is a ready source of ammunition for cross-examination.

In federal court, experts can generally testify to the ultimate issue at trial, unless it has to do with a criminal defendant's mental state. Rule 704 provides:

Rule 704. Opinion on an Ultimate Issue

(a) In General—Not Automatically Objectionable. An opinion is not objectionable just because it embraces an ultimate issue.

(b) Exception. In a criminal case, an expert witness must not state an opinion about whether the defendant did or did not have a mental state or condition that constitutes an element of the crime charged or of a defense. Those matters are for the trier of fact alone.

FED. R. EVID. 704. Also, in federal court, it is usually not necessary to have an expert lay out in detail the basis for his or her opinion; rather, the expert is free simply to state the opinion. Rule 705 provides:

Rule 705. Disclosing the Facts or Data Underlying an Expert's Opinion

Unless the court orders otherwise, an expert may state an opinion—and give the reasons for it—without first testifying to the underlying facts or data. But the expert may be required to disclose those facts or data on cross-examination.

FED. R. EVID. 705. Thus, an expert may testify in terms of opinion or inference and give reasons for the expert's opinion without first testifying to the underlying facts or data that gave rise to that opinion. On cross-examination, however, the attorney can require the expert to disclose the underlying facts or data.

In some cases, a federal prosecutor may choose to first establish the basis for the opinion, then have the expert state the opinion, while in other cases prosecutors may choose to reverse the order. In any event, I do not suggest that prosecutors ever present an expert by simply having the expert state the opinion without at some point providing the jury with some explanation of the basis for that opinion.

GOVERNMENT EXPERT WITNESSES

Prosecutors often call experts to testify at trial or sentencing hearings. In many cases, the expert testimony is critical. Indeed, in some cases, such as a drug trafficking case when the government must prove the substance was a controlled substance, expert testimony is necessary to establish an essential element of the offense. Prosecutors should view experts as a tool, sometimes a necessary one, often an optional tool, to aid the government in the presentation of a persuasive case. Fundamentally, experts help prosecutors present evidence, or challenge evidence, which is outside jurors' common understanding. Experts can provide this assistance both in a consultive role, through testimony, or both.

Whether to present expert testimony on behalf of the United States is one of the initial questions prosecutors may have to decide. When prosecutors decide to present expert testimony, sometimes the expert is a government employee who worked on the investigation and has already, in a sense, been chosen for the prosecutor. In other cases, prosecutors have the option of selecting an expert, and must decide whom to retain. Whether an expert is a government employee who performed work on the case or a privately retained expert selected by the prosecutor, the prosecutor must prepare the expert for testifying. Finally, prosecutors should prepare their experts for cross-examination. I will address each of these steps in turn.

Deciding Whether to Present Expert Testimony

Some government cases cannot be presented without expert testimony. For example, if the United States charges a doctor with prescribing controlled substances outside the usual course of medical practice and without a legitimate medical purpose, the government will necessarily have to present expert medical testimony to support that charge. On the other hand, in many cases expert testimony can be helpful, but not necessary in the government's presentation of its case. For example, in many routine drug trafficking cases, defendants will stipulate to admission of the laboratory report establishing that the substance seized from the defendant was a controlled substance because the defense theory is that the defendant never possessed the controlled substance. In those instances the government can establish the element of the offense without having to call the expert chemist who performed the analysis of the suspected controlled substance.

A prosecutor's first task, then, is to determine whether to retain an expert and present expert testimony. The answer to this question is usually obvious. When a case involves the testing of the chemical content of drugs, fingerprints comparisons, or the analysis of ballistics, the case involves an area of knowledge outside the realm of the average juror and requires expert testimony absent a stipulation. In other cases, the answer may not be so obvious. Prosecutors should carefully examine the nature of the case for evidence that requires explanation because the evidence is outside a juror's common knowledge. This may include topics like drug trafficking terms and patterns, cultural traditions, and business practices. Whenever there is something that only a person with special knowledge can explain and the prosecutor believes that the jury must understand the issue to find the defendant guilty, expert evidence is needed.

The next question to answer, once a prosecutor determines that the case requires expert evidence, is whether the prosecutor should call an expert witness to testify. As suggested above, in some cases prosecutors can dispense with expert testimony because they can get the evidence, such as a laboratory analysis report, admitted into evidence through a stipulation without calling a witness. Prosecutors should think critically, however, about whether to call an expert witness even in those cases when they could get by without one. Prosecutors may want to call experts to testify if presentation of expert testimony will provide proper emphasis to the evidence or provide an opportunity to explain some detail that would be lost if the written report or test result is admitted by stipulation alone, unaided by live testimony.

In some cases prosecutors may want to retain an expert, even though the prosecutor may not ever call the expert to testify at trial. Experts can provide prosecutors with knowledge and insight needed to effectively investigate or prosecute a case. These consulting experts can be utilized at all stages of a federal criminal case. A prosecutor may hire an expert during an investigation to provide the prosecutor with education or guidance in a particular area, to conduct experiments, or to evaluate other evidence to help determine whether a crime has been committed, who committed the crime, and whether the evidence is sufficient to support the filing of charges. Likewise, a prosecutor may choose to hire a consulting expert to provide similar guidance during the trial preparation and trial, or to give the prosecutor the knowledge and understanding needed to effectively cross-examine the defense expert. Finally, prosecutors may even choose to retain an expert solely to assist during the sentencing phase of a federal criminal trial.

Working with Government Experts

In the vast majority of cases, the government's expert is a government employee chosen by default for the prosecutor as part of the investigation process. Law enforcement officers processing a crime scene will send evidence to government laboratories for forensic examination and analysts are assigned to work on the case, often by random assignment. In those cases, the prosecutor is not involved in selecting the expert. Nevertheless, prosecutors should take steps to work with these government experts to ensure that the analysis was valid, the expert's opinions are sufficiently supported, and that the expert's work addresses all of the issues present in the case.

Selecting an Outside Expert

Although in most cases prosecutors work with government experts, in some cases, prosecutors must select outside experts. Sometimes during an investigation the need for an expert becomes apparent and no government employee with expertise in the field is readily available. In one very complex financial fraud case I prosecuted, I hired an outside forensic accountant to analyze the financial transactions to determine how the target committed the fraud and where the money went. In other cases, defendants may raise affirmative defenses after being charged that require retention of an expert. For example, in one murder case I handled the defendant asserted an insanity defense, requiring me to find and retain a mental health expert to address the defendant's affirmative defense.

In choosing an expert, a prosecutor should seek the most qualified expert in the field that the prosecutor can employ within the available budget. A prosecutor should seek to employ objective experts and be cautious to detect experts who may just tell the prosecutor what the expert believes the prosecutor wants to hear. To ensure objective and reliable expert testimony, prosecutors should thoroughly research potential experts. A prosecutor should obtain a copy of the expert's curriculum vitae and then check the references listed and critically analyze the expert's curriculum vitae looking for gaps, inconsistencies, and weaknesses. A prosecutor should determine whether the expert may be biased, or accused of bias, because the expert has always testified for the government, for example, or because of some other association in the expert's background. Experts gain reputations among lawyers, including prosecutors. So, prosecutors should ask around about an expert to find out what the expert's reputation is for honesty in the industry and community. Prosecutors should also research potential experts online and in reported cases, looking for articles or judges critical of the expert's objectivity or methodology. Prosecutors should not be so anxious to hire an expert that they ignore problems; if those problems exist, they will very likely arise later when it will be far more damaging to the case.

A prosecutor should give careful consideration to the initial contact with a potential expert and the information that is provided to the expert. The prosecutor's communication with an outside expert is not confidential, should be disclosed as part of discovery, and is a proper topic for cross-examination by defense counsel. A prosecutor should ensure that what the prosecutor tells the expert about the case, and the materials the prosecutor provides to the expert, do not improperly influence or appear to improperly influence the expert's independence or opinion.

When employing an expert, prosecutors should have a candid discussion with the expert regarding the prosecutor's expectations. The prosecutor should discuss in factual terms the nature of the case and the subject matter of the opinion the prosecutor is looking for, termed in a neutral manner. For example, a prosecutor may explain that the case involves a murder and the prosecutor needs an opinion of whether the defendant was insane at the time of the offense. The prosecutor must make it clear to the expert that the prosecutor wants only the expert's honest assessment, regardless of whether it is favorable or unfavorable to the government. These instructions should also be reduced to writing and provided to the expert as part of the engagement letter. Further, the prosecutor should be careful not to reveal to the expert the government's theory of the case or what outcome of the expert's analysis would be favorable to the government. To give an extreme example, a federal prosecutor should never tell an expert that he or she is looking for someone to testify that the defendant is sane, and then provide the expert with only evidence supporting that conclusion, while excluding evidence suggesting insanity.

Finally, in providing the expert with information from which the expert is to derive an expert opinion, prosecutors should make sure that the expert is given all relevant information, whether favorable or unfavorable to the government. In this regard, it often helps to have the expert identify the information the expert believes is necessary for the expert to render an opinion. Otherwise, there is a danger that the prosecutor may unintentionally influence the result of the expert's analysis by the selection of the information provided to the expert.

Understanding the Expert's Subject Matter and Opinion

A prosecutor cannot effectively work with an expert or elicit compelling expert testimony if the prosecutor lacks at least a fundamental understanding of the expert's subject matter. A prosecutor will have difficulty making an expert's testimony understandable to the jury if the prosecutor does not understand it in the first place. This fundamental understanding is also necessary for the prosecutor to help the expert convey the basis for the expert's opinion and persuade the jury of its correctness.

Whether the area of expertise is chemistry or psychiatry, accounting or physics, prosecutors should become familiar with the methodology and terminology of the subject matter. Some of this comes with experience, while in other cases prosecutors may have to check out books and read articles on the subject matter to understand it enough to work effectively with the expert. This does not mean that the prosecutor must become an expert in the area. It does mean, however, that the prosecutor must know enough about the subject matter to fully comprehend the expert's work and opinion in order to recognize weaknesses or defects in the data, methodology, terminology, and opinion. In some instances, it may be necessary for the prosecutor to visit the expert's laboratory, or have the expert provide a demonstration of the testing or analysis.

The government's own expert can be of great value as a teacher. The government's expert can help educate the prosecutor and can assist in structuring an outline of the direct examination so that the expert can effectively communicate with the jury. The government's expert can first recommend articles or books to read on the subject matter. A prosecutor should also read anything the government's expert has written on the topic about which he or she is testifying; one can be sure that the defense attorney will have done so. A prosecutor should read this material not just to become informed, but to look for inconsistencies or fodder for cross-examination of the government's expert. The government's expert can also provide tutorials to the prosecutor to educate the prosecutor on the subject. This can be of assistance not only in helping to present the government's expert's testimony, but, as will be discussed further, the government's expert can help prepare the prosecutor for cross-examining the defense expert.

Preparing a Government Expert for Testifying

Once the expert has reviewed the necessary evidence and rendered an opinion, and the prosecutor has decided to call the expert to testify, the next step is preparing the expert for testifying. The first task in this process is to work with the expert in the production of the written report or opinion. Prosecutors should not simply accept the expert's written opinion uncritically. Rather, prosecutors should review the written report like the defense attorney will review it. Prosecutors should look for unwarranted assumptions, unsupported conclusions, and erroneous facts. A prosecutor should work with the expert to suggest areas for improvement. Again, prosecutors should keep in mind that all of the communication prosecutors have with experts may be the subject of cross-examination, so they should not say or suggest anything to improperly influence or change the experts' opinions or conclusions.

In preparing experts to testify, a prosecutor should consider what evidence is necessary and what graphs, charts, or other demonstrative exhibits would be effective in helping the expert explain the opinions and persuade the jury that the expert is correct. Expert testimony is often hard to understand for the average juror. Charts, summary exhibits, and demonstrative exhibits help communicate complicated concepts in an understandable way. Prosecutors should work with the expert to determine the appropriate exhibits necessary to persuasively express the expert's opinion and the basis for that opinion. It is important for a prosecutor to rehearse using the demonstrative exhibits to ensure that the demonstrative exhibits are adequate and complete and that the prosecutor and expert both know how to work with the exhibits.

Another part of preparing an expert for trial testimony often involves deflating the expert's ego. All too many experts are egotistical. After all, they have become an expert in their field. If the prosecutor has done well in selecting the expert, the expert is one of the most qualified and accomplished persons in the field. Despite all of the expert's accomplishments, however, they are not experts at testifying or the law. Jurors need to be able to connect with and trust an expert. An arrogant, egotistical expert will likely offend jurors, and the jurors' animosity toward an arrogant expert will interfere with receiving and being persuaded by the expert's message. A defense attorney can exploit an expert's inflated ego, poking at it, hoping to make it burst in the form of angry outbursts. A good prosecutor, then, will have a frank discussion with the government expert about ego, about the need to be humble and relate to the jury. A good prosecutor will warn the expert about possible cross-examination calling into question the expert's education, qualifications, and experience and caution the expert against taking the bait by being offended or responding defensively.

Finally, and somewhat related to deflating an expert's ego, it is important to work with the expert to strip the expert's testimony of any unnecessary jargon and technical terms. Inevitably, there will be some uncommon and complex terms as part of the expert's field of expertise, and the expert may have to use some of those terms to state an opinion or explain how the expert arrived at the opinion. Whenever an expert uses such terms, however, the prosecutor must have the expert explain the term's meaning in plain English, then avoid using the term again. This can become very difficult because some fields of expertise are steeped in complex terminology that to the expert is like a second language. Think about it as a lawyer; we unconsciously use terms in everyday conversations with other lawyers and in the courtroom that are completely foreign to the general public. It is critical, however, that jurors fully understand the expert's opinion. Thus, in preparing an expert for testifying, the prosecutor should go through the expert's testimony in detail and diligently identify, define, and avoid jargon and technical terms and help the expert become disciplined in doing so.

DEFENSE EXPERT WITNESSES

Cross-examining a defense expert witness can be one of the most challenging, yet one of the most rewarding, experiences prosecutors will ever have in the practice of law. It can also be a daunting and intimidating task. Experts, by definition, should know far more than the prosecutor on the topic about which they will testify. Remember, however, that prosecutors should know far more about the law and cross-examination than the expert. The prosecutor's job in cross-examining an expert is not to become an expert on the subject matter and match wits with the defense expert; rather, it is to become an expert in cross-examination of experts.

As mentioned, this is not a book on trial advocacy. I will not, then, talk about the art of cross-examination or, in particular, how to cross-examine an expert. Rather, I will focus on all of the work that a prosecutor must complete in preparing for cross-examination. In truth, it is this preparation that makes the cross-examination possible. The actual cross-examination is just the facade of the structure that stands behind the prosecutor's ability to destroy an adverse expert's testimony.

The absolute key to effective cross-examination of an expert witness is preparation, preparation, and more preparation. A prosecutor must read everything the expert has written on the topic that is the basis of the expert's opinion. The more prestigious the expert, the more the expert has written. And the more the expert has written, the greater the likelihood that the expert has written something that is inconsistent with the expert's opinion or calls into question the basis for the expert's opinion or methodology. In several cases I prosecuted I was able to impeach a defense expert witness's testimony by quoting back to the expert something the expert previously wrote and published in a peer-reviewed journal.

Prosecutors should also search out transcripts from other cases where the expert has testified on the subject. Again, the more prestigious the expert, the more the expert has testified. The more the expert has testified, the more likely the expert is to have previously stated something under oath that conflicts with or calls into question the expert's current opinion. Again, as a prosecutor I repeatedly impeached defense expert witnesses using their prior testimony in other cases.

It is true that reading all of the expert's written work and prior testimony on the subject will take a lot of time. I often spent hours each night after the kids went to bed reading articles and transcripts for this purpose, hours I will never get back. It is also true that a prosecutor will likely find only a single useful sentence or line of testimony for every thousand pages read. Nevertheless, it is a worthwhile investment of time. Not only will it likely produce useful cross-examination ammunition, it will also help the prosecutor become better versed in the subject matter. This will in turn help the prosecutor in working with the government's own expert and in explaining the complex area to the jury in understandable terms.

Prosecutors should also carefully investigate the expert's qualifications and the range of topics in which the witness claims to have developed an expertise. An expert's curriculum vitae (CV) often contains hidden gems or omissions that can be very helpful in cross-examining an expert. Prosecutors may even want to verify the expert's claimed education. There are commercial services that, for a small fee, will verify whether the expert has the degree from the institution claimed on the expert's CV. Although in my career I only found false or inflated credentials twice in this way, in those cases the discovery was devastating to the defense expert. It is also important to pay attention to small details on a CV. For example, in one case when we researched the address the expert listed on his CV, we discovered that he occupied an office adjoining the defense attorney's office. This was, of course, very useful information with which to impeach the expert's claimed neutrality.

In this age, it is also important for prosecutors to get online and research the expert's social medial and internet footprint. Some experts may have backgrounds or engage in other activities that reveal biases that could have influenced the way they interpreted the evidence or colored their opinion. In one case, for instance, I found that an expert who held himself out as a neutral, uninterested professional had railed vociferously against American law enforcement officers in general and prosecutors in particular during an interview with a German magazine. In another case, I discovered on an expert's public social media profile that he was married to the lead defense attorney in the state where he lived. Although normally that would be of little or no import, in this particular case the expert regularly touted his past as a former law enforcement officer to persuade juries that he was only reluctantly rendering an opinion adverse to the government.

It is also important for the prosecutor to read, re-read, and have the government's expert read and critically evaluate any written report or examination produced by the defense expert. If the expert used scientific tests, the prosecutor should learn how those tests work and what limitations they may have. The prosecutor should also examine any device used in the process to look for opportunities the expert could have to manipulate the outcome. In analyzing the expert's opinion, the prosecutor should try to determine whether the expert made assumptions or worked from faulty, biased, or incomplete information. It is not uncommon that experts are provided incomplete or slanted evidence or data from which they formed their opinions. The government's expert may be the best asset in finding weaknesses in the defense expert's opinion and in structuring questions for cross-examination.

I personally believe that experts generally fall into one of two categories: honest and dishonest (or biased). Honest experts may render opinions that are faulty for any variety of reasons: improper assumptions, insufficient or erroneous information provided by the defense, flaws in reasoning, or the like, or because the expert was unqualified, insufficiently educated or experienced, or simply made an honest mistake. Honest experts I found were easier to cross-examine. Most honest experts can be led to recognize the weaknesses in their own opinions and care enough about their reputation that they will acknowledge the weakness and may even agree that their opinion may be in error.

Dishonest experts are more difficult to cross-examine. They will not be swayed from their opinions regardless of what errors or faults in their opinion cross-examination reveals. With these experts, prosecutors should spend less time preparing to attack the expert's opinion and the basis for the opinion. The government's expert can expose those weaknesses during direct examination. Rather, in preparing to cross-examine a dishonest expert witness, the focus should be on attacking the expert, not the expert's opinion. The focus of cross-examination should be on the dishonest expert's bias and lack of credibility, largely leaving the opinion itself alone. Prosecutors will never succeed in persuading a dishonest expert witness to admit an error. If a prosecutor can succeed in discrediting the person, then the opinion will fall as well.

Prosecutors should carefully draft an outline of questions to ask the expert on cross-examination. If the defense expert is an honest one, then the questions should be structured not to discredit the expert but to call into question the expert's conclusion. The prosecutor's outline of questions should be structured in a way to methodically and clearly show the error inherent in the expert's opinion. If the defense expert is dishonest, the prosecutor's outline of questions will have to be craftily designed to box the expert into facts or opinions that the prosecutor can later show with the government's own expert or during closing argument are flawed because the expert lacked credibility.

Finally, prosecutors should take careful notes of the adverse expert's testimony. As much as the prosecutor may prepare for cross-examination, an expert may testify to something on direct examination that the prosecutor did not anticipate. This unexpected testimony may eliminate a line of cross-examination questions or it may open up an entirely new line of cross-examination questions.

Chapter Eighteen

Working with Crime Victims

Many crimes leave victims in their wake. Crimes can injure others either financially, physically, or psychologically. During my career as a prosecutor, I worked on fraud cases in which some defendants stole social security checks from little old ladies and others stole millions of dollars from financial institutions. I worked on other cases involving domestic abuse victims, sexual abuse victims, shooting victims, and the surviving family members of serial killers. I worked with victims who were financially harmed, physically injured, and psychologically traumatized and scarred by what they suffered at defendants' hands. These victims' stories were sad, depressing, and scary. When I think back on my career as a prosecutor, it is often the victims that I think of the most. When I have nightmares, it is of memories of what I saw done to crime victims.

In recent decades there has been an increased focus on victims' rights. Prosecutors have a responsibility to work with and on behalf of crime victims. Yet, the relationship between prosecutors and victims can be problematic and cause issues that can adversely impact a case. Unwary prosecutors can jeopardize their cases, and their careers, by making mistakes in their relationship with victims.

This chapter discusses these issues and provides advice for prosecutors to maintain an appropriate and productive relationship with crime victims. I will start by generally noting the interests victims have in cases and discussing how they may diverge from the government's interests. Second, I will review crime victims' legal rights (particularly focusing on their rights under federal law). Third, I will discuss the characteristics of an appropriate relationship for prosecutors to have with crime victims. Fourth, I will examine some steps prosecutors should take to foster a healthy relationship with crime victims in a manner that fully advances the victims' interests and maintains their rights as crime victims while simultaneously benefiting the prosecution of the case. Finally, I will examine the relationship law enforcement officers have with crime victims and prosecutors' role in monitoring that relationship.

CRIME VICTIMS' INTERESTS

The interest a crime victim has in the prosecution of a criminal may be aligned with the government's interest. The crime victim's interest, however, may also be different from and in some cases diverge from the government's interests. To develop the proper working relationship with crime victims, it is important for prosecutors to have an appreciation of crime victims' interests in a criminal case.

Crime victims will almost always share the prosecutor's goal of seeing the defendant convicted. Most crime victims want defendants behind bars. They want defendants publicly held accountable for crime, which usually calls for incarceration, sometimes for a fine, or sometimes both. In many cases, the prosecutor's goal of achieving justice aligns well with the victim's interests in the outcome of the case.

On the other hand, very often a crime victim's interests do not perfectly align with the prosecutor's interest in achieving justice. That may be because their perspectives of a just outcome differ. In some instances, a crime victim may not want the criminal prosecuted or punished at all. The crime victim may be related to or have a relationship with the criminal. Victims of domestic abuse all too often do not want their abusers prosecuted. In other instances, a crime victim may not want the criminal prosecuted because of philosophical or religious reasons. Another crime victim may, on the other hand, believe that a defendant should be charged with a more serious offense for which the prosecutor believes there is insufficient evidence. Or a crime victim may believe that a defendant should face or receive a sentence that is greater or less than that the law or a judge deems appropriate. Sometimes a crime victim's views are wholly unrealistic and unreasonable, and on other occasions they may be fully justified but practically unachievable because of the evidence or the law.

Crime victims' interests may also go beyond conviction and incarceration. The defendant's humiliation, contrition, and confession may be as important, if not more important, to a crime victim than the number of months or years a defendant spends in prison or the size of a fine imposed. Victims have a personal stake in the outcome of criminal cases, and oftentimes they have personal relationships with defendants. Crime victims seek closure, a sense that their wrong has been righted, and a feeling of justice, which the criminal justice system does not and cannot always advance in a way satisfactory to crime victims.

Finally, crime victims may have a financial or other interest in the outcome of a case. Fraud victims may desire restitution from a criminal defendant. In other cases, crime victims may desire that the prosecution result in depriving the defendant of certain property rights in assets shared with the victim, or legal rights the defendant has in relation to family members, licensure, or organizations. Again, the criminal justice system may not be capable of addressing all of these interests or redressing all of crime victims' injuries.

CRIME VICTIMS' RIGHTS

Crime victims have certain legal rights in criminal cases that prosecutors have a duty to enforce. This is particularly true in federal court. Beginning in the 1980s, Congress enacted a number of laws addressing victim rights.

Congress passed the Victim and Witness Protection Act of 1982 (VWPA) for the purposes of striking a balance between the rights of victims and the rights of the accused. The VWPA created criminal offenses for tampering with or retaliating against victims and witnesses (18 U.S.C. §§ 1512, 1513) and also included a provision that authorizes prosecutors to seek restraining orders to protect victims and witnesses (18 U.S.C. § 1515).

Two years later, Congress passed the Victims of Crime Act of 1984 (VCA). The VCA established the Crime Victims Fund to compensate crime victims. Fines and assessments imposed on defendants constitute the source of the funds.

In the Crime Control Act of 1990, Congress mandated that government officials, including prosecutors, make "best efforts" to ensure that victims' rights are enforced. This includes a duty for prosecutors to confer with victims, protect their privacy, notify them of court proceedings, and provide reasonable protection from the accused. Prosecutors are also required to provide victims with a waiting area out of sight and hearing of the defendant and defense witnesses, inform victims of the filing of charges, any plea agreement, the trial verdict, and any order releasing the defendant from custody. 34 U.S.C. § 20141.

The Antiterrorism and Effective Death Penalty Act of 1996 contained provisions for closed-circuit televised court proceedings for victims of crime when there is insufficient room in the courtroom for all of the victims. 34 U.S.C. § 20142. It also provided for mandatory restitution for certain crime victims (including victims of fraud or violent crime) notwithstanding the defendant's financial inability to pay restitution. 18 U.S.C. § 3663A.

In 1997, Congress enacted the Victims' Rights Clarification Act. Among other things, that act mandated that, notwithstanding any other law or rule, crime victims have a right to be present in the courtroom during a trial even if they may become witnesses at the time of sentencing. 18 U.S.C. § 3510. This law was motivated in part by the capital trial of Timothy McVey where his bombing of a federal building killed and injured so many people that it was physically impossible to have all victims and their family members present in the courtroom.

In 2000, Congress amended the Violence Against Women Act (VAWA) (first enacted in 1994 and amended in 1996). As amended, the VAWA created criminal offenses for interstate domestic violence (18 U.S.C. § 2261), interstate stalking (18 U.S.C. § 2261A), and interstate violations of protective orders (18 U.S.C. § 2262), and a series of firearms offenses related to domestic violence (18 U.S.C. § 922[g][3]).

In 2004, the president signed into law the Crimes Victims' Rights Act of 2004. Title I of the act enumerates specific rights of crime victims in federal criminal cases, codified at 18 U.S.C. § 3771(a). These include "[t]he right to reasonable, accurate, and timely notice of any public court proceeding . . . involving the crime or of any release or escape of the accused," and "[t]he right to be reasonably heard at any public proceeding in the district court involving release, plea, sentencing, or any parole proceeding." 18 U.S.C. §§ 3771(a)(2) and (a)(4).

There are other federal statutes addressing victims' rights under other special circumstances as well. States have also enacted similar victims' rights acts. The bottom line is that prosecutors need to become familiar with these statutes to become fully aware of victims' rights to enforce those rights. As noted above, many of these rights have to do with notice of and an opportunity to be present during judicial proceedings. It is ultimately the prosecutor's responsibility to make sure that victims are notified of proceedings and enforce their right to be present and observe proceedings.

Federal prosecutors also have the responsibility to enforce victims' rights as part of the sentencing proceedings. Federal Rules of Criminal Procedure 32 governs sentencing in federal court. Among other things, it provides that the presentence investigation report must identify any victims of the crime and describe the financial, physical, and psychological impact the offense had on the victim and the victim's family. At the time of sentencing, prosecutors have an opportunity to speak. When there is a crime victim, the prosecutor should address the court regarding the impact the crime had on the victim and the victim's family members. Prosecutors should also ensure that the crime victim or the victim's family members have an opportunity to address the court before imposition of sentence and to submit crime victim impact statements if the victims wish.

MAINTAINING AN APPROPRIATE
RELATIONSHIP WITH VICTIMS

Prosecutors should respect and empathize with crime victims but still maintain a professional relationship with crime victims. Victims come from all walks of life. Some crime victims may have criminal backgrounds themselves, while others may come from backgrounds with which the prosecutor has no familiarity. Many crime victims come from backgrounds and have life experiences very different from those of prosecutors. Some people are victims because the defendant targeted them due to the victim's vulnerability, such as poverty or mental or emotional challenges. And it is also common for crime victims to want to become the prosecutor's friend, to view prosecutors as their lawyers, and for prosecutors to treat crime victims as part of the prosecution team. Thus, proper respect, empathy, and professional relationship are not always easy to achieve.

Crime victims deserve prosecutors' respect. As noted, crime victims have a compelling interest in the outcome of a criminal prosecution. Although prosecutors are properly focused on convicting a defendant, they must at the same time respect the interests that crime victims have in the case. And prosecutors should treat crime victims with respect and dignity, even if those victims do not earn the prosecutors' respect and are themselves undignified. This is true regardless of who the victim is and regardless of how the victim treats the prosecutor. Some crime victims can be mean, vulgar, and unpleasant, or demanding, demeaning, or unreasonable. However a crime victim acts, prosecutors should unfailingly treat him or her with respect.

Prosecutors should also try to empathize with crime victims. Prosecutors should try to understand and appreciate what the victim went through, how the crime impacted the victim, and how the crime might be affecting the victim's current behavior and conduct. To advance the victims' legitimate interests, enforce their rights, and maximize the benefit to the prosecution of the case, however, it is critical that prosecutors try to put themselves in the victims' shoes and see the case from the victims' perspective.

Prosecutors should consider what they do and what they say in light of how it might be viewed by or affect crime victims. It is not always as easy to do this as it may seem. Criminals sometimes intentionally seek out these victims because of their vulnerability. Victims may be unpleasant, uncouth, and uncooperative. Nevertheless, prosecutors should be sensitive to the impact decisions or statements may have on crime victims. Prosecutors should carefully choose the words they use to describe the crime, the victim, and the harm, thinking about how those words might impact the victim.

One of most difficult aspects of working with crime victims, however, is maintaining a proper professional relationship with them. Prosecutors may have a lot of contact with crime victims, sometimes over long periods of time. In many crime victims' eyes, law enforcement officers and prosecutors are special and sometimes viewed as their saviors or heroes. This sometimes leads to victims wanting to be friends with prosecutors. Prosecutors may find the victims to be very likable and sympathetic. Prosecutors should strive, however, to maintain a professional relationship with victims. Prosecutors should be friendly toward crime victims but not become friends with crime victims, at least until the case is over.

Other crime victims view prosecutors as their personal lawyers. Some victims believe that prosecutors should act on the victim's behalf, make decisions with the victim's best interest in mind, and do the victim's bidding. Some crime victims will also seek legal advice from prosecutors, such as asking what civil action the victim can or should take against the defendant or his or her associates. Prosecutors need to make it clear that they do not represent victims and should refrain from giving any legal advice to crime victims. Prosecutors should, if necessary, carefully explain to crime victims the nature of an attorney-client relationship and the absence of such a relationship between the prosecutor and the victim and emphasize that the prosecutor only represents the people and must make decisions based on the peoples' interest.

In some cases, prosecutors may fall into the habit of viewing crime victims as part of the prosecution team. This is especially so when prosecutors work with sympathetic victims over long periods of time. It can be tempting to let the crime victims in on developments in the case, especially if the prosecutor believes it may ease the victims' suffering. For example, in a murder case it may be very difficult not to disclose to the victim's family new information that may lead to the discovery of the victim's body or the killer. It is critical, however, that prosecutors maintain a proper distance from crime victims. Prosecutors should never divulge to victims information that is not publicly available. Nor should prosecutors make derogatory comments about the defendant, defense counsel, judges, or anyone else for that matter to crime victims. Crime victims may divulge what a prosecutor says to them to others, including the press. To some degree, crime victims should not be trusted. Their interests may not completely align with the government's interest, and their emotional and psychological state may impair their judgment and discretion. Thus, before making any statement to crime victims, prosecutors should think about whether they would be concerned if that statement ended up on the front page of the local paper. If so, the prosecutor should not make the statement to the crime victim.

STEPS PROSECUTORS CAN TAKE
TO WORK WELL WITH VICTIMS

There are some crucial things prosecutors can do to develop and maintain a proper relationship with crime victims. First, prosecutors should work closely with victim coordinators. Almost all prosecutors' offices now have staff members trained for and devoted to working with crime victims. Prosecutors should develop a good working relationship with this professional, letting the victim coordinator take the lead in working with crime victims. This requires the prosecutor to keep the victim coordinator informed about developments in the case and to ensure the victim coordinator is maintaining regular and appropriate contact with the crime victims. Prosecutors should make sure, of course, that the victim coordinator understands the same need to maintain a professional relationship with the crime victim as the prosecutor.

Prosecutors should communicate regularly with crime victims. The communication can come directly from the prosecutor, but more often the prosecutor will communicate with victims through the law enforcement officers or the victim coordinator. Prosecutors should keep the crime victims timely informed of public developments in the case. Prosecutors may do this personally, or through the victim coordinators. Sometimes victims deserve to learn of public information before the public disclosure, when this is appropriate and possible. For example, if law enforcement officers have discovered a victim's remains, it is appropriate to let the victim's family know of the discovery before going public with the information so that the family does not learn of it for the first time on the news or from a neighbor. Prosecutors should certainly make sure that victims are aware of any court hearings sufficiently in advance of the hearing to allow their attendance if they desire. It may also be just as important to keep the crime victims aware of the lack of developments in the case so that they know that the case is still under investigation.

When crime victims are uncooperative, prosecutors should work with law enforcement officers and the victim coordinator to try to determine why the victim is uncooperative. In some cases, the root causes of the lack of cooperation can be successfully addressed. Past bad experiences with law enforcement may be overcome by working hard on developing the victim's trust in this case. Fear of retaliation by the defendant or his or her associates may be addressed by speaking with the victim about steps the government can take to ensure the victim's safety. If the victim is uncooperative because of the victim's relationship with the defendant, perhaps the victim's other family members or friends can help persuade the victim of the benefits of cooperating. Opening and maintaining a channel of communication with the crime victim is the key toward trying to turn an uncooperative victim into a cooperative one. Sometimes it simply takes time for the victim to trust and have confidence in the government.

Prosecutors should also manage expectations. Prosecutors should be careful not to over-promise results. However much a prosecutor may hope and perhaps believe the perpetrator will be caught, prosecuted, and punished, the prosecutor should be careful never to promise results. Rather, prosecutors can promise efforts. Part of managing expectations also involves taking the time to provide crime victims with explanations. For victims to understand and appreciate charging decisions, it may be necessary for prosecutors to explain elements of offenses and burdens of proof. For victims to accept the punishment a defendant may receive, prosecutors may need to provide some basic explanation of sentencing statutes, sentencing guidelines, and judicial discretion in fashioning sentences. Finally, for victims to comprehend and accept the likelihood of being made whole, prosecutors may have to explain the practical limitations on collecting restitution from defendants.

Finally, prosecutors should be vigilant in advocating for victims' rights. Prosecutors should ensure that victims have an opportunity to be heard when they have a right to be heard under the law. Prosecutors should also seek proper restitution for victims when the law allows for restitution to be awarded.

LAW ENFORCEMENT
OFFICERS AND CRIME VICTIMS

Law enforcement officers are usually the first to have contact with crime victims and sometimes develop close working relationships with those victims. There is nothing inappropriate with this. Nevertheless, prosecutors should endeavor to make sure that the law enforcement officer's relationship is appropriate in all of the ways outlined above. A prosecutor should explain to the law enforcement officer the proper parameters and limits to a proper relationship with the crime victim and explain why it is necessary. The prosecutor should then monitor the relationship to make sure it stays within the proper bounds and take corrective action if necessary.

Prosecutors should recognize, however, that a law enforcement officer's relationship with a crime victim may be very helpful. That relationship may aid in maintaining good communication with the victim and maximizing the victim's cooperation with the prosecution of the case. Prosecutors should ensure that the law enforcement officer understands the victim coordinator's role, however, and that the law enforcement officer cooperates with the victim coordinator in working with the crime victims.

Chapter Nineteen

Preparing for Jury Selection

Jury selection is a critical part of any trial. The jurors will ultimately decide the fate of the government's case. The evaluation and selection of the citizens who will sit in judgment of the prosecutor's case, then, must occupy a central place in the prosecutor's preparation for trial. Unfortunately, prosecutors often give preparing for jury selection short shrift, devoting little time or effort to it.

Admittedly, jury selection in federal court may be less important than it is in state court. Some federal judges will not permit lawyers to directly question prospective jurors. The remaining federal judges who permit lawyers to directly question prospective jurors will almost always restrict the length and scope of voir dire. In contrast, state and county prosecutors are almost always permitted to question prospective jurors directly, often with few limitations on time or scope of the examination. Nevertheless, there is much more to jury selection than the actual voir dire of the prospective jurors. Thus, even in courts where prosecutors are not permitted to directly question prospective jurors, there remains much a prosecutor can and should do to prepare for jury selection.

In covering the topic of preparing for jury selection, I will start by reviewing the constitutional and statutory provisions relating to jury selection in federal court. I will not be discussing state laws for jury selection; a state-by-state review of the law pertaining to jury selection is beyond the scope of this text. Nevertheless, federal constitutional law provides the underpinnings upon which all of those state procedures are based.

After discussing the laws pertaining to jury selection, I will turn to a discussion of preparing for the jury selection process. There are two steps in the selection process. The first is learning about prospective jurors to identify the basis for challenging them for cause or to formulate a basis upon which to exercise peremptory strikes. Voir dire is one part of the learning process, but not the only one. The second step in the jury selection process involves the removal of prospective jurors either through for-cause challenges or by the exercise of peremptory strikes. There are legal issues that may arise, such as defense requests for additional peremptory strikes or Batson challenges, as well as practical issues for prosecutors to consider in preparing for the selection process.

Finally, I will briefly discuss other legal issues that may arise in the jury selection process for which prosecutors should be prepared. These include motions to change venue because of pretrial publicity, the empanelment of anonymous juries, and addressing juror misconduct issues. Prosecutors need to anticipate these potential problems in advance of trial to successfully address them when they arise at trial.

CONSTITUTIONAL AND STATUTORY
LAWS REGARDING JURY SELECTION

The US Constitution establishes the right to trial by jury in criminal cases. US CONST. ART. III, § 2, cl. 3 ("The trial of all Crimes, except in Cases of Impeachment, shall be by Jury"). Whether a defendant is constitutionally entitled to a jury trial depends on the charges and the degree of punishment to which the defendant could be subjected. The Supreme Court has concluded that the right to trial by jury does not extend to petty offenses, that is to crimes punishable by less than six months in prison. That is so even if the defendant is charged with multiple petty offenses for which, if punishment was aggregated, the sentence could result in the equivalent of punishment for more serious offenses.

Litigants may waive trial by jury and agree to have a judge decide the matter. Rule 23(a) of the Federal Rules of Criminal Procedure provides that, if a defendant is entitled to a jury trial because of the nature of the charges, the case must be decided by a jury unless the defendant and the government both waive a jury trial and the court approves. The Supreme Court upheld the constitutionality of Rule 23(a) and rejected the argument that a defendant should be able to waive a jury regardless of whether the government consents. *See Singer v. United States*, 380 US 24, 35–36 (1965). Further, "Rule 23(a) does not require that the Government articulate it reasons for demanding a jury trial at the time it refuses to consent to a defendant's proffered waiver." *Singer*, 380 US at 36.

The Bill of Rights amended the US Constitution to incorporate two common-law rights regarding jury trials. The Sixth Amendment incorporated the common-law requirement that juries be impartial. The Sixth Amendment provides, in pertinent part, that "[i]n all criminal prosecutions, the accused shall enjoy the right to a speedy and public trial, by an impartial jury of the State and district wherein the crime shall have been committed." US CONST., AMEND. VI. Courts have also found that the Fifth Amendment's Due Process Clause requires an impartial jury. *See Casias v. United States*, 315 F.2d 614, 615 (10th Cir. 1963) (en banc) ("[The] denial of trial by an impartial jury is also the denial of due process").

The Sixth Amendment does not define the words "impartial jury." Courts have interpreted those words as incorporating two concepts. The first is that the pool from which the petit jury is selected represent a "fair cross section of the community." As the Supreme Court explained in *Holland v. Illinois*, the fair cross-section requirement is "not explicit in the text" of the Sixth Amendment, "but is derived from the traditional understanding of how an 'impartial jury' is assembled. That traditional understanding includes a representative venire, so that the jury will be . . . 'drawn from a fair cross section of the community.'" 493 US 474, 480 (1990) (quoting *Taylor v. Louisiana*, 419 US 522, 527 [1975]). As we will discuss in more detail later in the section on jury composition, Congress codified the "fair cross section" requirement in proscribing procedures for district court to form jury venires. *See* 28 U.S.C. § 1861.

The second concept is that the jurors who serve on the jury must not be biased in favor or against either of the parties. A juror is not impartial if the juror's experiences, opinions, predispositions, biases, prejudices, interests, or relationships "would 'prevent or substantially impair the performance of his duties as a juror in accordance with his instructions and his oath.'" *See Wainwright v. Witt*, 469 US 412, 424 (1985) (quoting *Adams v. Texas*, 448 US 38, 45 [1980]).

To select an impartial jury from a venire gathered from a fair cross section of the community, two processes are required. First, there must be a process by which to question prospective jurors to determine who can be impartial. This has resulted in a procedure now referred to as voir dire. Second, there must be a process for removing from the panel of prospective jurors those whom the court or the parties believe are not impartial. This has resulted in two additional procedures. The first is the process of allowing parties to ask the court to remove jurors "for cause," meaning that a party can prove to the satisfaction of the trial judge that a prospective juror cannot be impartial. The second process is to allow parties to exercise peremptory strikes, meaning the parties may remove prospective jurors for any reason, even if the party could not persuade the court that cause existed to remove the prospective juror.

Voir dire is deemed critical to achieve the goal of an impartial jury. *See Rosales-Lopez v. United States*, 451 US 182, 188 (1981) ("Voir dire plays a critical function in assuring the criminal defendant that his Sixth Amendment right to an impartial jury will be honored. Without an adequate voir dire the trial judge's responsibility to remove prospective jurors who will not be able impartially to follow the court's instructions and evaluate the evidence cannot be fulfilled"). Yet, the Constitution is silent as to voir dire. Rule 24 of the Federal Rules of Criminal Procedure addresses voir dire, but it does not require that either the judge or the parties engage in voir dire. Indeed, Rule 24(a) of the Federal Rules of Criminal Procedure leaves it totally within the judge's discretion whether to permit the parties to conduct voir dire at all. The rule does not even require the judge to conduct voir dire. *See* FED. R. CRIM. P. 24(a) (the court "*may* examine prospective jurors or *may* permit the attorneys for the parties to do so") (emphasis added).

Despite the lack of any legal requirement they do so, in practice judges invariably engage in some voir dire, however limited it may be. Rule 24 does not prescribe any procedure for how a judge is to conduct voir dire or have the parties conduct voir dire. It is completely within the court's discretion to control the scope and nature of voir dire, and a trial judge can limit questions by counsel to those it deems proper. *See Rosales-Lopez*, 451 US at 189. Thus, in practice, the degree to which federal judges restrict jury selection varies by judge and by district to a greater degree than probably any other aspect of a federal criminal trial. Although some judges permit wide latitude in conducting voir dire, other judges permit none at all.

The Constitution is also silent as to the exercise of for-cause challenges and the exercise of peremptory strikes by the parties. No federal rule addresses the parties' excise of for-cause challenges. And although Rule 24 of the Federal Rules of Criminal Procedure addresses the exercise of peremptory strikes, it does so only to the extent of establishing the number of peremptory strikes afforded to each side. Nothing in Rule 24 or any other rule prescribes a procedure for parties to use in exercising peremptory strikes.

Finally, the Constitution is silent as to the size and composition of a criminal jury. At common law, juries typically consisted of twelve people. That common-law practice has been codified in federal practice in Rule 23 of the Federal Rules of Criminal Procedure. There are provisions in the rule for a jury of less than twelve to decide a case either by stipulation of the parties or if a juror is excused for good cause after trial begins. A federal statute, Title 28, US Code, Section 1865, establishes the required qualifications necessary for a person to serve as a juror.

Because an understanding of the law of jury selection is necessary for a prosecutor to understand how to prepare for jury selection, I will delve into some of these issues in more detail.

Sources for Jury Pools

People must be chosen from some source to form the pool of potential jurors. The source of prospective jurors in the federal system is dictated by the Jury Selection and Service Act, 28 U.S.C. § 1861 ("the Act"). Section 1861 states in broad terms the government's policy for the composition of juries. It provides:

> It is the policy of the United States that all litigants in Federal courts entitled to trial by jury shall have the right to grand and petit juries selected at random from a fair cross section of the community in the district or division wherein the court convenes. It is further the policy of the United States that all citizens shall have the opportunity to be considered for service on grand and petit juries in the district courts of the United States, and shall have an obligation to serve as jurors when summoned for that purpose.

28 U.S.C. § 1861. The Act goes on in the following section to prohibit the exclusion of people from jury service based on "race, color, religion, sex, national origin, or economic status." 28 U.S.C. § 1862. In Section 1863, the Act refers to Section 1862 as a "right." In other words, Section 1862 must be seen not simply as a restriction upon the jury selection methods, but as a right held by the people to serve on a jury regardless of their race, color, religion, sex, national origin, or economic status. This is important for the exercise of peremptory strikes in relation to some of these factors, which I will discuss later. Further sections of the Act set out procedures for courts to follow designed to achieve Section 1861's policy and Section 1862's rights.

The Act requires district courts to develop plans for the random selection of people to serve on grand and petit juries and to design procedures for the drawing of names of those people to serve on jury venires from which the grand and petit jurors will ultimately be selected. The term "venire" is defined as "[t]he group of citizens from whom a jury is chosen in a given case." BLACK'S LAW DICTIONARY 1556 (6th ed. 1990).[1] Title 28, US Code, Section 1863 sets out in considerable detail how district courts are to go about establishing plans for the random selection of people to serve as prospective jurors and the requirements for such plans. I will not delve into the procedures at length but will discuss the basic nature of the requirements and statutory exceptions to jury service. I will also briefly discuss the procedure for selecting people from among this pool of prospective jurors to serve on venires from which juries are ultimately to be selected.

Section 1863 generally delegates to the districts the responsibility for developing plans for randomly selecting people to serve on juries. This responsibility may further be delegated by the district court to the clerk of court or to commissioners. 28 U.S.C. § 1863(b)(1). The primary sources to identify people to serve on juries are voter registration lists or lists of actual voters. 28 U.S.C. § 1863(b)(2). Courts are required to develop plans, however, that "prescribe some other source or sources of names in addition to voter lists where necessary to foster the policy and protect the rights secured by sections 1861 and 1862 of this title." 28 U.S.C. § 1863(b)(2). In other words, if voter registration lists alone will not result in a jury pool that represents a fair cross section of the community, or results in a jury pool that improperly excludes people based on their race, color, religion, sex, national origin, or economic status, then the court's plan needs to find another way to supplement the list of potential jurors. This may include using city directories, drivers' licenses, or other government-issued identification documents.

The Act mandates that district courts design their plans to include a method of random selection from all of the available people on the lists. Section 1864 prescribes the procedures for randomly drawing names of people from the randomly generated list of people in the jury pool to serve on a particular jury. That section sets out the procedure for notifying the prospective jurors and requires those prospective jurors to fill out and return within ten days a juror qualification form. This qualification form requires the prospective juror to provide some basic information to enable the clerk of court to determine if the person qualifies for jury service. These forms are not the same thing as juror questionnaires, which I will describe and discuss later. Lawyers are not routinely provided with copies of these forms, unlike juror questionnaires.

To form a venire for jury selection for a given trial, prospective jurors are selected at random from the district. If there are multiple divisions within a district, prospective jurors are generally selected from the division where the trial will be held, although prospective jurors can be pulled from anywhere within the district. Typically, once the clerk of court has identified a pool of potential jurors, the clerk will draw from that pool a smaller group of prospective jurors to serve on the venire. The size of the venire depends on the number of trials set on a given day, the length of the trial, or the complexity of the case. Before jury selection begins, the potential jurors are administered an oath that requires them to answer truthfully all questions posed to them regarding their qualifications to serve as jurors.

Qualifications for Jury Service

The juror qualification form mentioned in the prior section requires prospective jurors to answer questions to determine if they have the minimum attributes necessary to serve as a juror. The qualifications for a person to serve on a jury are established by statute. Section 1865(a) provides that any person may serve as a juror unless the person:

1. is not a citizen of the United States eighteen years old who has resided for a period of one year within the judicial district;
2. is unable to read, write, and understand the English language with a degree of proficiency sufficient to fill out satisfactorily the juror qualification form;
3. is unable to speak the English language;
4. is incapable, by reason of mental or physical infirmity, to render satisfactory jury service; or
5. has a charge pending against him for the commission of, or has been convicted in a State or Federal court of record of, a crime punishable by imprisonment for more than one year and his civil rights have not been restored.

28 U.S.C. § 1865(b). Each of these qualifications merits some discussion.

The first qualification is citizenship and age. Although parties have challenged the citizenship requirement on the ground that excluding legal resident aliens and other non-citizens deprives the party of a true cross section of the community, courts have consistently rejected these constitutional challenges. *See, e.g., United States v. Cecil*, 836 F.2d 1431, 1451–52 (4th Cir. 1988); *United States v. Afflerbach*, 754 F.2d 866, 870 (10th Cir. 1985); *United States v. Toner*, 728 F.2d 115, 130 (2d Cir. 1984).

The second and third qualifications pertain to English proficiency. America does not have an official language, but legal proceedings in federal courts are conducted in English (even in districts such as Puerto Rico where another language predominates). The English proficiency requirement is not stringent, however. A juror must be able to complete a juror qualification form and be able to speak English. That does not mean, however, that English needs to be the citizen's primary language or even that the person speak English well. A citizen is not disqualified from service even if the person does not understand everything that is said. *See United States v. Gray*, 47 F.3d 1359, 1637–38 (4th Cir. 1995) (finding no error when jurors spoke English as a second language, did not understand everything said, and needed assistance from other jurors in understanding certain things).

Section 1865(b)(4) bars those with mental or physical infirmities from serving as jurors if the infirmity renders them incapable of "satisfactory service." Though there are few reported cases addressing this provision, presumably this would include people with memory issues or learning disabilities or the like and people who are blind or cannot hear. There has been only one reported case where a defendant has challenged this provision under the Americans with Disabilities Act (42 U.S.C.A. § 12101 et seq.). The challenge was unsuccessful, the court reasoning that the statute only bars service when the infirmity would render it "unsatisfactory," a reasonable basis for excluding any person from jury service whatever the cause. *United States v. Johnson*, No. CR 01–3046–MWB, 2013 WL 1149763, at *1 (N.D. Iowa Mar. 19, 2013).

Finally, anyone facing or having been convicted of a felony offense is disqualified from serving as a juror. The basis for excluding felons is the same as under the Federal Rules of Evidence for allowing a witness to be impeached by a prior felony offense. *See* Fed. R. Evid. 609(a)(1) (permitting a party to impeach a witness's credibility with evidence the witness was previously convicted of a felony offense). The reasoning is that if someone is willing to break the law and commit a serious offense (defined as a felony), then that person is not to be trusted to take an oath seriously, whether it be as a witness or as a juror. If a state has deemed it appropriate to restore a convicted felon's citizenship rights, however, then that person may serve as a juror. Criminal defendants have occasionally, but unsuccessfully, argued that the exclusion of felons as potential jurors results in the exclusion of minorities at a disproportional rate because they are incarcerated at a disproportional rate, and on the ground that excluding felons deprives the defendant of a true cross section of the community. *See, e.g.*, *United States v. Barry*, 71 F.3d 1269, 1273–74 (7th Cir. 1995); *United States v. Greene*, 995 F.2d 793, 797–98 (8th Cir. 1993).

LEARNING ABOUT PROSPECTIVE JURORS

The goal of the jury selection process is selection of fair and impartial jurors to decide the case, which requires learning something about the prospective jurors and eliminating those who cannot be fair. The primary procedure for learning about prospective jurors is voir dire, that is the questioning of prospective jurors in the courtroom. Although I will discuss how prosecutors should prepare for voir dire, there are other ways for prosecutors to learn about prospective jurors. This includes juror questionnaires, investigation of prospective jurors, and the use of juror consultants.

Juror Questionnaires

Most courts, state and federal, use some type of questionnaire to elicit basic information from prospective jurors to assist in the jury selection process. Statutes in England, and then in the United States, mandated that the court provide criminal defendants with basic information about prospective jurors, such as name, profession, and place of residence, in advance of trial.[2] Written juror questionnaires are most often submitted to prospective jurors when they are selected to serve as potential jurors for a given term. In the federal court system, these questionnaires are mailed to prospective jurors well in advance of their service and then collected and kept by the clerk of court. Increasingly, jurors may also now fill out such questionnaires online on the courts' websites. When cases are then called for trial, the clerk's office may distribute to the court and the trial attorneys copies of the questionnaires for the panel of prospective jurors that will constitute the venire for that case. Questionnaires obviously contain personal information about prospective jurors, so they are provided to the trial attorneys in confidence with the requirement that they be used only for court purposes and destroyed or returned to the clerk's office upon completion of the trial.

Federal courts have not adopted a uniform or standard juror questionnaire for use in all federal cases across the country. As a result, the number, nature, breadth, and depth of the questions asked in juror questionnaires vary from district to district. There is a tension between asking enough questions with sufficient detail to elicit helpful demographic and belief information from prospective jurors and generating questionnaires that are too long and too burdensome for prospective jurors to complete. The best questionnaires are ones that obtain basic factual information about the prospective juror's residence, education, and employment history, criminal history, prior jury experience, and prior involvement in the court system as a litigant. Good questionnaires should also elicit information about prospective jurors' beliefs that are relevant to service as a prospective juror. These questions should be open-ended ones, asking jurors things like their opinion of the justice system or if they hold values that would make it difficult for them to sit in judgment of others or of particular people.

Juror questionnaires provide some significant benefits. First, juror questionnaires save time in the courtroom. The questionnaires provide the trial attorneys with a lot of information that they might otherwise have to elicit during voir dire. Second, questionnaires provide prospective jurors the opportunity to disclose sensitive information that they may be hesitant to disclose in open court. Some prospective jurors may feel less inhibited, and more open to sharing information, in writing rather than orally in front of strangers. Third, written questionnaires foster more honest and candid answers by prospective jurors. This is particularly so for controversial topics, such as a prospective juror's views about race or capital punishment. Fourth, written questionnaires may further result in more thoughtful, contemplative answers because prospective jurors have time to think about their answers. Fifth, assuming that prospective jurors complete the questionnaires in private without input from friends and family, the answers in the questionnaires are more likely to reflect the prospective jurors' true beliefs and values because they have not been influenced by the answers of other prospective jurors in the courtroom or attempts by the prospective juror to gauge from others' reactions the most socially acceptable or "correct" answer. Sixth, written juror questionnaires minimize the risk of contamination of the jury pool by answers that are inflammatory or prejudicial to a fair trial, such as an answer that asserts that any criminal defendant who fails to testify is hiding something. When, during voir dire, a prospective juror provides such an answer, it poses the danger of influencing other prospective jurors' views on the issue. Finally, written juror questionnaires provide trial attorneys with some feedback from every prospective juror. Often prospective jurors are reluctant to speak in open court and some pass through the entire voir dire process without speaking once.

There are also some limitations and disadvantages to written juror questionnaires. First, as noted, written juror questionnaires are not standard or uniform across federal district courts. The information sought in the standard juror questionnaires vary considerably in breadth and depth from court to court with some being much more helpful than others. Second, prospective jurors may not provide full and complete information in written juror questionnaires. Prospective jurors may provide only limited information in response to questions for various reasons, including finding the task burdensome or because the prospective juror is hesitant to share information that could be further disseminated. Of course, trial attorneys may gain insight from the very fact that a prospective juror is circumspect in answering a particular question. Third, prospective jurors may not understand a question in a written juror questionnaire because it is vague or ambiguous. There is no opportunity for follow-up or to ask clarifying questions in a written juror questionnaire while the juror is completing the questionnaire, so the answer may be inaccurate if the prospective juror's understanding of the question is inaccurate. Fourth, the prospective jurors' answers to juror questionnaires may be vague, ambiguous, imprecise, or unintelligible. Again, there is no opportunity for the answer to be clarified while the prospective juror is answering the juror questionnaire, and thus any clarification must await voir dire. Fifth, the setting and circumstances surrounding the completion of juror questionnaires do not necessarily ensure complete, accurate, or thoughtful answers. Prospective jurors may rush through the juror questionnaire, viewing the task as a hassle, and so not give careful thought to answers. Further, when prospective jurors complete juror questionnaires at home, there is none of the aura of importance and seriousness present in a federal courtroom that serves to create a sense of responsibility to provide candid, contemplative answers. Finally, answers to written juror questionnaires may not reflect the prospective jurors' own views. When prospective jurors fill out the questionnaires at home, they may seek input from family members and others or receive unsolicited input when completing the juror questionnaire. There is, of course, no way to know the extent to which a prospective juror's answers on a juror questionnaire were influenced by others.

Prosecutors may conclude that certain prospective jurors should be challenged for cause based solely on answers to juror questionnaires. Some appellate courts have affirmed trial judges' removal of jurors for cause based solely on their answers to juror questionnaires, even without the benefit of voir dire to explore answers to written juror questionnaires. When this occurs, however, a trial judge's decision is afforded no deference on appeal because the trial judge did not make the decision based on a credibility assessment of the prospective juror. A better approach is for prosecutors not to seek to strike a prospective juror for cause until voir dire when they can more fully develop a record that would support removing the prospective juror for cause.

There are some jurisdictions where courts do not utilize standard written juror questionnaires. In those jurisdictions, parties may ask the court to submit basic questionnaires to prospective jurors. In such a motion, a prosecutor should educate the judge regarding the effectiveness of juror questionnaires, emphasizing the benefits, including shortening the voir dire process. The prosecutor should also outline a proposed procedure for the distribution, collection, and dissemination of the written questionnaires. Finally, the prosecutor should submit a proposed juror questionnaire to the court as part of such a motion. In asking a court to submit a written juror questionnaire to prospective jurors, prosecutors need to recognize that judges will be protective of courtroom staff time and the costs of submitting written juror questionnaires. In making such proposals, then, prosecutors should structure the protocol in a manner that minimizes the utilization of court resources.

In addition to the standard juror questionnaires routinely issued by courts, parties may also request that the court submit case-specific juror questionnaires to prospective jurors. This type of juror questionnaire seeks much more information from prospective jurors on specific matters at issue in the case at bar. Courts most often utilize supplemental juror questionnaires in complex cases, such as capital cases when juror views on the death penalty are critical in jury selection or in cases when there has been substantial pretrial publicity about the case. Prosecutors should exercise good judgment in deciding when to request courts to submit special juror questionnaires. The submission of the case-specific juror questionnaires poses an additional burden on prospective jurors to complete them and imposes additional costs on the court to submit and retrieve the juror questionnaires. Courts have broad discretion to issue, or refuse to issue, such case-specific juror questionnaires.

In drafting juror questionnaires, there are a number of factors to consider. While prosecutors consider these factors, they should strive to view the questions from the perspective of prospective jurors. Prosecutors should also keep in mind the goal of the juror questionnaire, that is, to elicit specific information helpful in determining whether prospective jurors' views or biases may prevent them from being fair and impartial.

First, questions should be limited to the bare minimum in number, recognizing that prospective jurors will view answering juror questionnaires as a burden. Often, juror questionnaires are too long and too complex, with too many questions and subparts. Unduly long questionnaires will result in prospective jurors providing limited, short, or flippant responses. Prosecutors should also remember that they will have to read the answers to all of the juror questionnaires and attempt to glean conclusions from them, which becomes increasingly difficult the longer and more complex the juror questionnaire becomes.

Second, the questions should be clear and concise. Attorneys tend to overwrite and underanalyze their questions, making them confusing to laypersons. Here, it is helpful to have non-attorney friends or family members answer draft juror questionnaires to ensure the questions are understandable to laypersons.

Third, prosecutors should not view juror questionnaires as a substitute for voir dire, meaning juror questionnaires should not ask every question the prosecutor may like to ask prospective jurors. Indeed, some questions are better left to voir dire. Questions that will necessarily require follow-up or probing may be better left to voir dire rather than a juror questionnaire. Rather, the juror questionnaire should ask a question to flag that topic as a possible issue for a prospective juror and leave to voir dire close questioning of the prospective juror on the topic.

Fourth, careful consideration should be given to whether to formulate open-ended questions or close-ended questions. Open-ended questions will likely elicit more detail and information. On the other hand, open-ended questions may not require a prospective juror to commit to a position in a way that fully informs the trial attorney. For example, an open-ended question asking prospective jurors to state their views about drug legalization may not fully elicit a firm response as well as a close-ended question that asks jurors to state whether they believe marijuana should be legalized. In contrast, close-ended questions are easier for prosecutors to evaluate and categorize. A question that asks prospective jurors whether they are for or against gun control is far easier for prosecutors to use in placing prospective jurors into categories than an open-ended question that asks jurors what they think about gun control. On the other hand, close-ended questions prevent prospective jurors from expressing nuanced or conditional answers that may be important to prosecutors in assessing the prospective jurors' suitability as trial jurors.

In drafting juror questionnaires, it is important that prosecutors view the effort as an information-gathering tool and not as a form of advocacy. Some attorneys and jury consultants attempt to word questions in a manner that is intended to sway or influence the prospective jurors, or to inculcate in them a certain point of view. For example, instead of a neutral question asking if jurors believe marijuana should be legalized, an advocate may propose a question that asks if jurors believe marijuana should be legalized so long as all dangerous drugs remain illegal. This second question clearly implies that marijuana is not a dangerous drug. This is improper. Questions should be worded neutrally and devoid of judgmental or value-laden verbiage intended to influence prospective jurors.

When moving a court for submission of juror questionnaires, prosecutors should try to persuade the court to provide the juror questionnaires at a reasonable time in advance of trial so as to give the trial attorneys as much time as possible to process the answers. Deciphering and synthesizing answers to juror questionnaires can be very time-consuming. Juror questionnaires filled out the morning of trial will also result in much less complete and contemplative answers from prospective jurors than when prospective jurors are provided the juror questionnaires well in advance of trial with ample time to fill them out. In short, prosecutors should attempt to have the court adopt deadlines for the submission, collection, and dissemination of the juror questionnaires in a time frame that results in the trial attorneys receiving the answers at least a week or two in advance of trial.

It is important that prosecutors develop skills to fully and effectively use the information contained in juror questionnaires for purposes of jury selection. This task requires thought, organization, and critical thinking. The difficulty arises in part from the volume of information provided in responses to such juror questionnaires and the need to synthesize the information in a way that it can aid in voir dire and in determining how to exercise peremptory strikes. In approaching this task, prosecutors should also consider how the information may aid in the manner in which to try the case. In other words, the answers to the juror questionnaires will provide insight into the jury pool as a whole, such as the general education level of the pool and the prospective jurors' exposure to or experience with the case or the issues involved in the case. Understanding this macro information should aid prosecutors in determining the most effective way to communicate with the jury during opening statement and closing argument and inform the prosecutor's decisions regarding the nature and manner of presenting the evidence in the case in the most persuasive manner, given the general makeup of the jurors hearing the case.

With these goals in mind, prosecutors need to figure out how to maximize the usefulness of the data provided by the answers to the juror questionnaires. It is best to approach the juror questionnaires in stages. First, prosecutors should read through a dozen or so juror questionnaires to get a sense for which questions generated the most helpful information, which questions appear to have been misunderstood, and which questions provided little helpful information. Despite the prosecutor's best efforts in drafting the perfect juror questionnaire, the reality is that the juror questionnaires will not have resulted in the outcome the prosecutor anticipated. Obviously, the prosecutor's focus in mining the juror questionnaires for helpful information will be on the first category of questions. Prosecutors should nevertheless devote time in analyzing the other two categories of questions for purposes of developing voir dire questions. If it appears that prospective jurors generally misunderstood or misinterpreted questions in the juror questionnaire, then the prosecutor will need to rework the wording of these questions during voir dire to get the useful information the written juror questionnaire was intended but failed to elicit. Likewise, if there were questions in the questionnaire that produced little useful information, the prosecutor should look carefully at those questions with an eye on voir dire at trial. Perhaps the questions were simply unnecessary questions in the first place or, again, perhaps they were poorly worded to elicit helpful information and can be reworked for voir dire to elicit truly helpful information.

Second, prosecutors may want to simply tabulate the answers to the questions that called for "yes" or "no" type answers. This tabulation should be conducted in a manner that both identifies answers by prospective juror, but also in a manner that provides an overall view of the tone of the prospective jurors' answers. In other words, prosecutors will want to know how individual prospective jurors answered each of the "yes" or "no" questions to discern each individual prospective juror's point of view, but they will also want to get a sense of how the jury pool as a whole viewed the issues.

Third, it is important that prosecutors evaluate the juror questionnaires to identify prospective jurors against whom the prosecutor may want to make "for-cause" challenges. A prosecutor should identify each such prospective juror and generate a list of answers to questions that would give support to a for-cause challenge. At the same time, the prosecutor may want to formulate follow-up questions for these prospective jurors designed to confirm and solicit more answers that would support a for-cause challenge.

The majority of the prosecutor's effort should be focused on analyzing the answers to the key questions previously identified that generated the most helpful information. This requires a deep-level study of the answers to the key questions to identify the prospective jurors' attitudes on the key issues and identify jurors who may be biased for or against the government. It is important not only to identify jurors with bias, but to also gauge the depth or strength of that bias. In conducting the analysis of these key questions, it is most effective to adopt some type of scoring system. This can consist of a scale of 1 to 10, or a grade distribution of A to F, or something similar. An effort should be made to grade the prospective jurors' scores on each of the key individual questions, considering the nature of the answer along with the degree of strength to which it appears the prospective juror holds that value or perspective. The prospective juror's overall grade, then, can consist of the average of all of these grades. Prosecutors may, however, want to assign different weights to the questions. For example, a prospective juror's answer to a question pertaining to the presumption of innocence may be deemed much more important to the prosecutor than an answer to a question asking about whether the prospective juror has relatives involved in law enforcement. Careful thought should be given to developing a scoring scheme that reveals the most informative score possible.

A final step in evaluating the results of juror questionnaires is to analyze the answers to identify leaders. Jury selection is really a process of jury de-selection. At most, a prosecutor has a limited ability to use for-cause challenges and peremptory strikes to remove the worst prospective jurors for the government. Thus, it is far more important to remove leaders than to remove followers. Answers to certain questions may help identify leaders. Certainly any answers that show that the prospective juror holds or has held a leadership position in employment or in outside organizations may identify that prospective juror as a potential leader on any jury. But other answers, or the manner in which the prospective juror answers other questions, may reveal a strong personality. These prospective jurors should be flagged for special attention during voir dire.

In the end, prosecutors should maintain a proper perspective regarding juror questionnaires and recognize that they are only a tool in the jury selection process. It is important that prosecutors not form fixed opinions of prospective jurors based on answers to juror questionnaires. They should be open to the idea that the prospective jurors' answers did not truly reflect their beliefs or values, and that the prosecutor's interpretation of the answers may be mistaken or flawed. During jury selection, prosecutors should be prepared to change their score or rating of the prospective jurors in light of answers during voir dire and the prosecutor's observation of the prospective jurors during jury selection.

Investigating Prospective Jurors

Prosecutors may investigate prospective jurors in an effort to discover whether they are qualified to serve and to make more informed and better use of peremptory strikes. It has long been a practice for litigants to investigate those called for potential jury service. With the development of the internet and social media, however, the ability to conduct thorough investigations of prospective jurors has expanded dramatically. This new capability to investigate prospective jurors carries with it some issues, both practical and ethical, that we will address below.

Trial attorneys have been investigating prospective jurors since the early 1700s. When towns were small, it was likely that the trial attorneys or their clients would know some or all of the prospective jurors. As the population expanded and cities grew, the likelihood that litigants and lawyers would know the prospective jurors decreased and the practice of and need for more expanded investigation of prospective jurors increased. Trial attorneys soon began conducting their own research into prospective jurors or hired private detectives to do so. Famous trial attorney Clarence Darrow hired a former deputy US Marshal to investigate prospective jurors in a high-profile case, a step that ultimately led to Darrow's indictment, but ultimate acquittal, for bribing jurors.[3]

Historically, the nature of investigating prospective jurors differed, depending on the size of the community from which the pool was drawn, the nature and notoriety of the case, and the funds available. When the jury was drawn from a fairly small community, an investigation of prospective jurors may have been limited to making a lot of phone calls to find people who knew people who knew prospective jurors and quizzing them about the potential juror. In some cases, however, trial attorneys hired private detectives to investigate prospective jurors.[4]

The emergence of the internet and social media in the investigation of prospective jurors has taken off in a new and expansive direction. The internet has expanded the ability to access information about prospective jurors and has expanded the scope of information available about prospective jurors. It has also increased the speed and reduced the cost of conducting investigations of prospective jurors. Using internet search engines, a paralegal or attorney can obtain a large volume of information about prospective jurors, from the value of the prospective jurors' homes and the cars they drive, to news articles that mention them. Thus, the nature of such investigations is significantly different from, and less expensive than, former methods. In a matter of minutes, and at little cost, a person sitting in front of a computer terminal can learn more about a prospective juror than a gumshoe private detective could learn in a month. No longer do litigants need private investigators or jury consultants to perform juror investigations.

More important, the nature of the information now available has dramatically changed. The advent of social media has opened windows into the private lives of many prospective jurors. The vast majority of Americans have Facebook, Twitter, LinkedIn, or MySpace accounts on which they publicly share a tremendous amount of information about themselves, their families, and their friends.[5] Much of the information on the internet and social media is of little or no use to trial attorneys in trying to identify good or bad prospective jurors. Nevertheless, a significant amount of that information can shed an illuminating light on the personal beliefs and attitudes of prospective jurors that may be very important for trial attorneys to know in conducting jury selection.

There has long been significant criticism of the investigation of prospective jurors, including from the Supreme Court.

> The jury is an essential instrumentality—an appendage—of the court, the body ordained to pass upon guilt or innocence. Exercise of calm and informed judgment by its members is essential to proper enforcement of law. The most exemplary resent having their footsteps dogged by private detectives. All know that men who accept such employment commonly lack fine scruples, often willfully misrepresent innocent conduct and manufacture charges. The mere suspicion that he, his family, and friends are being subjected to surveillance by such persons is enough to destroy the equilibrium of the average juror and render impossible the exercise of calm judgment upon patient consideration. If those fit for juries understand that they may be freely subjected to treatment like that here disclosed, they will either shun the burdens of the service or perform it with disquiet and disgust. Trial by capable juries, in important cases, probably would become an impossibility.

Sinclair v. United States, 279 US 749, 765 (1929).

Despite criticism of the practice by the Supreme Court and others, the investigation of prospective jurors is not illegal or unethical. There is no federal statute or case law prohibiting the investigation of prospective jurors, although districts may impose restrictions on the practice in local rules and judges may issue orders barring the practice in particular cases. Similarly, state bar ethical rules do not prohibit the practice, although, again, they sometimes impose restrictions on the investigation of prospective jurors. Section 5.3(b) of The Prosecution Function, of the American Bar Association Standards, provides:

> In those cases where it appears necessary to conduct a pretrial investigation of the background of jurors the lawyer should restrict himself to investigatory methods which will not harass or unnecessarily embarrass potential jurors or invade their privacy and, whenever possible, he should restrict his investigation to records and sources of information already in existence. (Emphasis supplied)

ABA Model Rules of Professional Conduct, Rule 5.3(b). In the commentary accompanying the approved draft of the standards relating to the prosecution function and the defense function, it is said:

> Pretrial investigation of jurors may permit a more informed exercise of challenges than the voir dire affords and can be justified on that score. The practice of conducting out-of-court investigations of jurors presents serious problems however. It may have a tendency to make jury service, already unpopular with many persons, even more onerous because of the fear of invasion of privacy. It may also have the appearance, even if unintended, of an effort to intimidate jurors. To minimize these risks, counsel should be careful to conduct investigations of jurors in a manner which avoids invasions of privacy.

In a 2014 formal opinion, the American Bar Association's Standing Committee on Ethics and Professional Responsibility explicitly approved the investigation of jurors. *ABA Comm. on Ethics & Prof'l Responsibility*, Formal Op. 466 (2014). The committee stated, "Unless limited by law or court order, a lawyer may review a juror's or potential juror's Internet presence, which may include postings by the juror or potential juror in advance of and during a trial, but a lawyer may not communicate directly or through another with a juror or potential juror." *Id.*

As is reflected in the American Bar Association opinion, it is improper for a party conducting an investigation of prospective jurors (directly, or through a jury consultant or private investigator or any other agent) to have ex parte contact with a prospective juror, and it may constitute grounds for reversal of a verdict or a new trial. Ethical rules prohibit attorneys from engaging in conduct through agents that would be prohibited if conducted by the attorney. Both ethical rules, and most local rules, prohibit attorneys from having ex parte contact with prospective jurors. *See* ABA Model Rules of Professional Conduct, Rule 3.5(b) (prohibiting ex parte unauthorized communication with a prospective juror).

Another issue regarding juror investigation arises when the parties' ability to conduct such an investigation is significantly unbalanced. Defendants may argue that the government has greater resources and access to information for purposes of investigating prospective jurors. A defendant may seek to address this imbalance either by asking the court to prohibit the government from investigating jurors, by asking the court to require the government to share the results of any such investigation with the moving party, or by asking the court to provide funds to allow the defendant to conduct its own juror investigation.

Using Juror Consultants

There are a large number of professional jury consultants, sometimes referred to as trial consultants, who market themselves as experts in the area
of evaluating and selecting juries. Jury consultants can provide a wealth of
information to a prosecutor. Jury consultants can provide a variety of services, including polling the potential community from which the jury will be
drawn, conducting demographic studies of the jury pool, calculating statistical juror profiles based on demographics or answers to juror questionnaires,
organizing mock or shadow juries, and other activities designed to provide
trial attorneys with the greatest amount of information and data points avail
able to utilize in challenging venue due to pretrial publicity, conducting voir
dire, making challenges for cause, and in exercising peremptory strikes. As
with every resource, however, there are real and potential drawbacks to using
jury consultants.

Most jury consultants have degrees in psychology, sociology, or the law,
or a combination of these disciplines. There is no specific education, training,
or professional license required to be a jury consultant. Jury consulting firms
often employ a variety of consultants with various backgrounds; some have
more academic backgrounds based in the social sciences, such as psycholo-
gists or sociologists, while others offer more real-life experiences, such as
former trial attorneys. There is no requirement for jury consultants to follow
any guidelines or ethical rules in their practice. Similarly, the Model Rules of
Professional Conduct do not bar or place any restrictions on attorneys using
jury consultants.

Jury consultants use a variety of tools to assist trial attorneys both in
conducting jury selection and in presenting the case to jurors selected. The
services provided by jury consultants is a result of an agreement reached
between the trial attorneys and the jury consultants. Jury consultants usually
have a menu of service options to choose from, and it is the trial attorney's
responsibility to determine which of those services would be valuable, and
worth the cost, for a given case. These services include jury models, jury pool
studies, focus groups or mock juries, the investigation of prospective jurors,
and observation of prospective jurors.

Jury consultants may construct a model of the ideal juror for the case pending trial, based on the consultant's understanding of the parties and issues
involved in the litigation. This model is to serve as a template for the trial attorney to use in jury selection to identify prospective jurors that fit the model,
and to identify those who do not so as to allow the trial attorney to make a
more informed exercise of peremptory strikes. To a limited degree, a jury
consultant's explanation for how he or she arrived at the ideal juror may also

inform the trial attorney about how best to present evidence at trial to appeal to the characteristics of the ideal juror. Aware of the description of the ideal juror, and the consultants' reasoning, the trial attorney may conduct voir dire and exercise peremptory strikes in a manner designed to identify prospective jurors that come closest to the ideal juror.

Jury consultants may also conduct studies or surveys of the geographic area from which the jury pool will be drawn to develop a sense of what the pool as a whole may know about the case and the parties, the demographics of the pool (such as age, education, and socioeconomic status), and/or the prospective jury pool's general beliefs or values. Consultants commonly conduct these community surveys through telephone polls or in-person interviews. Consultants then analyze the data and generate reports that summarize the findings. These reports may then aid trial attorneys in developing profiles of favorable and unfavorable prospective jurors, in drafting voir dire questions designed to identify prospective jurors' attitudes, and to tailor the trial presentation to the pool's general demographics. This information may also be helpful in determining if there has been so much adverse pretrial publicity about the case that it would be appropriate for the trial attorney to file a motion for a change of the trial venue due to pretrial publicity.

Consultants may also establish focus groups and assemble mock juries to aid the trial attorney in advance of trial. Both focus groups and mock jurors are typically recruited from the same source of citizens who will form the pool of potential trial jurors. Focus groups and mock juries serve different functions, operate in different manners, and serve different purposes. A focus group is formed to provide feedback to trial attorneys on specific or limited issues. For example, a consultant might form a focus group to hear mock closing arguments to assess the strength and persuasiveness of the argument. Or, a consultant might form a focus group to hear mock testimony from a key witness and then provide feedback in an attempt to improve the witness's testimony. Consultants may also form focus groups to gauge the general perception of or reaction to issues particular to the case going to trial. Often, presentations to focus groups will attempt to provide both sides of the issue, or both direct examination and cross-examination of a witness, to assess not only the party's case, but also the anticipated opposing case.

A mock jury, on the other hand, is assembled to hear a mock trial. Typically, the mock trial is a drastically reduced version of the real trial, with very limited presentations (five-minute opening statements or ten-minute closing arguments, for example) to minimize the expenditure of time and resources. Attorneys or staff may pose as the opposition and provide mock witnesses to testify for the opposing party, while its own attorneys and witnesses present the case for the firm. The goal is to present the essence of the case for both sides during a condensed time period. Often these mock trials are followed by having the mock jury deliberate in a closed room, but with an ability of the lawyers to observe the deliberations through a two-way mirror or closed-circuit television. The mock jurors are given a limited time to deliberate and reach a verdict. Afterward, the jury consultant and lawyers debrief the mock jurors to learn what issues they identified with the evidence and to elicit feedback on the performance of the witnesses and lawyers.

Trial attorneys may also employ jury consultants to investigate potential jurors, as described in the prior section. As mentioned, with the advent of the internet and the prevalence of social media, lawyers are now able to perform a significant amount of research on prospective jurors that previously required the resources of jury consultants and private investigators. So routine juror investigations are often performed by lawyers or paralegals and not by jury consultants.

Finally, many jury consultants offer jury selection observation services as well. Here, the jury consultants will sit in the courtroom during jury selection and observe the prospective jurors during jury selection. As noted, jury consultants are often trained and educated in psychology and sociology, and so arguably more qualified to interpret verbal and nonverbal actions and responses. Jury consultants observe the prospective jurors, judging their behavior, body language, and facial expressions as much as their actual answers to questions during voir dire. It is common in providing this service that jury consultants will offer to staff the courtroom with multiple observers so that each observer can limit his or her attention to just a few prospective jurors, watching them at all times, even when they are not answering questions. Jury consultants may similarly observe prospective jurors during breaks in the jury selection process to evaluate how they interact with each other and third parties in the hallways. The jury consultant then provides advice to the trial attorney regarding which prospective jurors may be best and worst for the party based upon the jury consultant's interpretation of the observed verbal and nonverbal actions and reactions. The trial attorney can then make a more informed, and in theory better, decision in exercising peremptory strikes.

It will be a rare case when the government's budget can justify, or supervisors approve, a prosecutor's hiring of jury consultants. Prosecutors need to be aware, however, that defense counsel may do so, particularly in high-profile cases or cases involving wealthy defendants in white-collar cases. I never hired a jury consultant as a federal prosecutor. When I was in private practice, I represented a doctor charged with various federal offenses. My firm hired a jury consultant who performed many of the services described above. Having also used jury consultants in a couple civil cases while in private practice, my general assessment is that their value is overstated, at best. Jury consultants often claim and advertise that they are successful in impacting the outcome of jury trials and, with their services, trial attorneys will increase their likelihood of success. There is, however, no independent, empirical data to support these broad marketing claims. On the other hand, as a general matter many of the services provided by jury consultants will increase the amount of information trial attorneys have to work with in trying to effectively conduct jury selection. The more information a trial attorney has about prospective and actual jurors, presumably the better the decisions the trial attorney makes about jury selection and other aspects of the trial.

There are several disadvantages and detrimental effects from using jury consultants. First, their services do not come cheap, and the cost can be justified only in the most important cases. In addition, there is a danger of over-reliance on the advice of jury consultants at the expense of the trial attorney's own experience and judgment. Jury consultants are engaged in a profit-making venture. They are motivated to inflate the impact of their services and exaggerate the importance of their advice. Jury consultants may emphasize their quasiscientific methods and their education and training in social sciences to persuade the trial attorney that their judgment is superior to the trial attorney's judgment, when it may not be any better at all.

Further, sometimes complications arise, depending upon the type of case and nature of work the jury consultant performed, regarding an obligation to disclose information to the opposing party. This is especially the case for the government in a criminal case. Under the Jencks Act, for example, the government must provide to the defendant any statement made by a witness on the subject matter on which the witness will testify. If the government had a witness testify in a focus group or mock trial, then the government may have to divulge that information to the defendant. Similarly, there may be obligations to disclose to the defense the results of surveys or jury investigations if that information could affect the defendant's rights. For example, a survey may reveal pervasive negative opinions about the defendant's guilt due to pretrial publicity, affecting the defendant's ability to have a fair trial in the venue. Thus, before engaging the services of a jury consultant, prosecutors should first research the extent to which they may have to turn over to the opposing side information learned from employment of the jury consultant.

Finally, if the real jury learns of work performed by the jury consultant, it may adversely affect the jurors' views of the party. Jurors are unlikely to look favorably upon the party responsible for investigating them, for example, particularly if that investigation involved techniques like surveillance of prospective jurors. Jurors would likely find it uncomfortable to know that they were being observed closely in the courtroom or hallways by juror consultants. Jurors may also view the use of focus groups or mock juries as a method to game the system or exert improper influence on the testimony of witnesses. Prosecutors cannot always control the extent to which they can keep the use of a jury consultant confidential. As noted, in some instances prosecutors may be obliged to disclose the information to the defense. In other instances, the defense may discover it. In short, prosecutors should view jury consultants as a potentially useful aid in conducting jury selection, but engage them with caution and after fully evaluating the pros and cons of their services. And prosecutors should be alert to a defendant using jury consultants.

PREPARING FOR VOIR DIRE

Voir dire, pronounced vwar dear, derives from the French verbs voir and dire, and means, literally to see, to tell. In Old French, "voir dire" meant to speak the truth. *See* David Mellinkoff, *The Language of the Law*, 101–2, 106 (1963). Voir dire generally refers to the process of conducting a preliminary examination of a person to determine competency, interest, bias, or some other factor that would disqualify the person from appearing in court as a juror or witness. BLACK'S LAW DICTIONARY (7th ed. 1999). Thus, incidentally, the process of voir dire is used not only to examine potential jurors, but also to examine witnesses if one party believes that there exists some fundamental flaw that should prevent the witness from giving testimony.

As noted, in federal court the trial judge will conduct the initial questioning of prospective jurors. Typically, the court provides a brief description of the case and then questions the panel as a whole. These questions typically cover topics that relate to obvious biases or prejudices. The judge's sole interest is in weeding out prospective jurors who cannot be impartial. Some judges will ask follow-up questions, while other judges will simply elicit answers that suggest that a prospective juror may be biased, depending on the attorneys to ask the necessary follow-up questions. So, in courts when judges permit the lawyers to directly question the prospective jurors, prosecutors need to be prepared to ask follow-up questions, if necessary, either to determine if a prospective juror is prejudiced or to rehabilitate a prospective juror who may at first appear prejudiced or biased, but who turns out not to be biased upon further examination.

One of the judge's primary obligations during jury selection is dealing with prospective jurors who claim they are unable to serve as a juror because of some other commitment, such as work or family obligations. Most judges handle these issues with tact and in a manner designed to discourage prospective jurors who simply want to shirk their civic duties. Quite often, however, prospective jurors will remain on the panel who clearly do not want to serve as jurors and have been frustrated in their attempts to fabricate excuses for being excused. Prosecutors may want to use peremptory strikes to eliminate such prospective jurors, as they will not do justice to the case, to the United States, or to the defendant.

After the court conducts its voir dire, many federal judges will permit the government to conduct voir dire, though it is not required by Rule 24. Again, it is fully within the trial court's discretion to permit or deny direct participation by the parties in voir dire as there is no constitutional requirement that it even occur. *Mu'Min v. Virginia*, 500 US 415, 430 (1991) (district courts have broad discretion in deciding whether to allow specific questions by attorneys during voir dire). If the government was permitted to conduct voir dire, then of course defense attorneys will be permitted to question potential jurors. When there are multiple defendants, the courts will usually permit counsel for each defendant to conduct separate voir dire. The Federal Rules of Criminal Procedure provide no time limits on voir dire by the parties. A trial judge's discretion in controlling jury selection extends to the time permitted attorneys to conduct voir dire, if they're allowed to do it at all. Thus, judges will often impose a time limitation on counsel.

REMOVING PROSPECTIVE JURORS

The second part of the two-part process of selecting a fair and impartial jury is the removal of prospective jurors that the lawyers believe, after voir dire, cannot be fair and impartial. There are two ways for lawyers to remove prospective jurors. The first method is through a challenge for cause. These are instances when a prospective juror's prejudice or bias is so clearly obvious that the prospective juror simply cannot be impartial. *See Wainwright v. Witt*, 469 US 412, 424 (1985) (standard for determining whether a venire member may be removed for cause depends on whether the juror's views would prevent or substantially impair the performance of his duties as a juror in accordance with his instructions and his oath) (internal quotations omitted). Either party can challenge a juror for cause, but it remains in the court's discretion whether to grant the motion. *See United States v. Parmley*, 108 F.3d 922 (8th Cir. 1997) (striking for cause is a matter committed to the discretion of the district court). There are no limits on the number of for-cause challenges. The second method for removing prospective jurors is through the exercise of peremptory strikes. Lawyers may remove a limited number of prospective jurors they believe are biased for or against their party, for frankly for any reason at all other than based on the prospective juror's race, national origin, and gender. To be successful, prosecutors need to understand how these two removal methods work, appreciate their limitations, and prepare in advance of trial for using them during jury selection.

Challenges for cause and peremptory strikes relate to each other in important ways. First, if a party succeeds in removing a prospective juror for cause, then the party will not need to use a peremptory strike to remove an undesirable prospective juror. If the challenge is unsuccessful, however, then the trial attorney will likely need to use a peremptory strike to remove the prospective juror. This is especially true if the trial judge requires for-cause challenges to be made in open court, in front of the juror who is the subject of the motion. If a prospective juror is aware that the attorney unsuccessfully sought to remove the prospective juror for cause, that prospective juror will certainly not look favorably upon that attorney. Second, the exercise of a peremptory strike to remove a prospective juror effectively waives any right the party might have to claim error by the trial judge for wrongfully denying a for-cause challenge. *Skilling v. United States*, 561 US 358, 395 n.31 (2010) ("[U]se [of] a peremptory challenge to effect an instantaneous cure of [a trial judge's erroneous for-cause ruling] exemplifies a principal reason for peremptories: to help secure the constitutional guarantee of trial by an impartial jury") (citation and internal quotation marks omitted). So defense attorneys must carefully consider whether it is better to remove the prospective juror and waive any claim for error or leave the prospective juror on the jury and preserve the right to raise the claimed error. Prosecutors frankly need not worry about this because if the government loses at trial, the Double Jeopardy Clause bars it from appealing.

Preparing to Make For-Cause Challenges

As a general matter, trial judges are often reluctant to grant challenges for cause. In part, this may be because judges know that the parties have peremptory strikes available to eliminate prospective jurors. The availability of peremptory strikes allows trial judges to avoid making difficult calls on striking prospective jurors for cause. Judges may also be reluctant to remove prospective jurors for cause because of practical concerns. In any given trial the clerk of court will have called in a limited number of prospective jurors to form the jury venire; thus, a judge may run out of prospective jurors if too many for-cause challenges are granted. Finally, judges may be reluctant to remove prospective jurors for cause because they do not want to cause error. Although a trial judge's decision to grant a for-cause challenge is reviewed for abuse of discretion, an appellate court may find that the trial judge abused that discretion, requiring a new trial. As noted, if a judge denies a for-cause challenge and a party subsequently exercises a peremptory strike to remove that prospective juror, the judge's denial of the for-cause challenge cannot be raised on appeal.

Judges may be particularly reluctant to grant a prosecutor's for-cause challenge. When in doubt, judges may tend to favor the defendant, whose liberty is at stake. Prosecutors cannot appeal an erroneous ruling on a for-cause challenge. Thus, prosecutors need to become skilled at making effective for-cause challenges.

Challenging jurors for cause is an important, but difficult, trial skill. When making challenges for cause, prosecutors must make quick decisions, under pressure, whether to challenge a juror for cause, recognizing that there may be important ramifications regardless of whether the trial judge grants or denies the challenge. When prosecutors decide to challenge prospective jurors for cause, they must then make effective arguments for doing so. With a trial judge's reluctance to grant for-cause challenges in mind, prosecutors should recognize how important it is that they make persuasive arguments when challenging a prospective juror for cause.

If a prosecutor is considering basing a for-cause challenge on an answer the prospective juror provided in a questionnaire, it is usually necessary to conduct some voir dire of the prospective juror regarding the answer at issue. It is a rare case when a judge will sustain a for-cause challenge based solely on the answer a prospective juror gave in response to a questionnaire without the prospective juror having an opportunity to explain it. Indeed, an appellate court may very well find that a trial court has abused its discretion in sustaining a prosecutor's for-cause challenge based on a questionnaire answer alone, without permitting the prospective juror to explain that answer. That is because a prospective juror may offer an explanation for or elaborate upon a questionnaire answer in a way that removes the perception of bias. Even when that does not occur, defense counsel may want to attempt to rehabilitate the prospective juror by asking whether, whatever the opinion or belief, the prospective juror could set it aside and follow the law as given to him or her by the judge.

All good advocacy starts with preparation. With the extensive use of juror questionnaires, and perhaps the investigation of prospective jurors through other means, prosecutors will likely enter the jury selection phase of trial with an idea of which prospective jurors they will likely seek to challenge for cause. Prosecutors should highlight or otherwise flag entries in the prospective jurors' questionnaires that may give rise to a reason to challenge a prospective juror for cause. Prosecutors should then make a list of such prospective jurors and sketch out the grounds for challenging the prospective juror for cause. In doing so, prosecutors should also draft some questions for use in voir dire to draw out more information from the prospective juror that would aid in making the for-cause challenge.

Another attribute of a good prosecutor is to look for places for compromise. In reviewing information about prospective jurors, good prosecutors should be able to identify prospective jurors whom the opposing side may also wish to challenge for cause. In some cases, a compromise may be possible between the prosecutor and defense attorney in some cases to agree to removal of prospective jurors adverse to each side, preserving peremptory strikes for both sides. I did this once in a death penalty case where both sides agreed that certain prospective jurors had such extreme views about the death penalty, for and against, that they could not fairly sit as jurors in the case.

Conducting voir dire of prospective jurors targeted for for-cause challenges can be, well, a challenge. To do it well requires carefully preparing questions in advance of jury selection that are designed to expose the problems with those prospective jurors the prosecutor has identified that are problematic. Of course, answers to questions posed during voir dire may reveal other prospective jurors whom the prosecutor may also wish to challenge for cause. There is no way to prepare questions specifically for those prospective jurors, but the preparation for other prospective jurors can form a guide for questioning those newly identified problematic jurors.

If the basis for the challenge is a lack of qualification, such as lack of proficiency in the English language or some type of mental illness or disability, the very lack of ability to communicate with the prospective juror may constitute the best evidence for the challenge. If the basis is bias, on the other hand, prosecutors need to carefully craft questions to reveal that bias. Unless the prospective juror is trying to get out of jury service, it is unlikely that direct questions will get direct answers. People generally do not like to admit biases. Imagine a juror questionnaire that reveals that a prospective juror has resisted arrest multiple times and has sued the police for false arrest. Asking that juror if he or she has a "problem with police officers" is unlikely to elicit an honest answer. Generally, open-ended questions are more likely to be successful; it is a matter of giving the juror enough rope to hang him- or herself. It may be better to ask the juror what the juror thinks about police officers. The goal would be to provide an opportunity for the prospective juror to talk enough about police officers to reveal a bias that would subject him or her to removal for cause.

It should be apparent, then, that it takes careful thought and intentional design to ask questions likely to elicit answers that truly draw out bias from recalcitrant prospective jurors. To be successful, prosecutors must strategize about how to approach the difficult issue and carefully draft questions designed to expose the problem sufficiently that the trial judge will see the problem and remove the prospective juror for cause. At the same time, prosecutors need to craft questions that will not offend the prospective juror or the other prospective jurors. Likewise, in carefully drafting questions designed to expose a prospective juror's bias, prosecutors must simultaneously be careful not to elicit answers that would poison the beliefs or views of the rest of the panel members.

Prosecutors also need to anticipate possible for-cause challenges defendants may assert and be prepared to address the issues during voir dire. This is because prosecutors will not have another chance to rehabilitate a prospective juror after the defendant's voir dire. Imagine a prospective juror indicated in a questionnaire that the prospective juror thinks that anyone charged with a crime is likely guilty. If given an opportunity during voir dire, the prospective juror might indicate an ability to set that belief aside and follow the court's instructions. If the prosecutor does not provide the prospective juror an opportunity to address the issue, the defense attorney may attempt to elicit answers from the prospective juror that makes it seem the belief is firmly held. Without a further record, the defense attorney may then successfully argue that grounds exist to strike the prospective juror for cause.

Finally, it is very important that prosecutors take good and careful notes during voir dire, particularly for prospective jurors prosecutors believe should be struck for cause. It will be important in arguing the motion to strike the prospective juror for cause that the prosecutor be able to point to the prospective juror's answers to the written questionnaire or cite what the prospective juror said during voir dire that supports the for-cause challenge. The more the prosecutor can recite the prospective jurors' exact words and phrasing, the more likely it is that the prosecutor will be successful not only with the trial judge, but also on appeal if it becomes an issue there.

It is important that prosecutors exercise judgment and discretion in choosing when to challenge prospective jurors for cause. It is seldom advisable for prosecutors to challenge a large number of prospective jurors for cause. Trial judges are likely to view such a shotgun approach to exercising for-cause challenges as indicative that the prosecutor lacks good grounds for any of the challenges. The judge may very well discount the prosecutor's good arguments along with the bad ones. Rather, a good prosecutor will make a challenge for cause only when there is a solid basis for doing so, and only for those prospective jurors that are truly unqualified or unfairly biased. Thus, in preparing for jury selection, prosecutors should think very carefully about who, among the potential problem prospective jurors, is the most problematic and plan on focusing the efforts during voir dire on those few.

Prosecutors should also be cognizant of the relationship between for-cause challenges and peremptory strikes. In deciding whether to make a for-cause challenge, prosecutors should have a sense of how many prospective jurors they want to remove from the jury and how many peremptory strikes the prosecutor has to work with. If the number of objectionable prospective jurors is less than the number of available peremptory strikes, or close to that number, then the prosecutor may not need to challenge a prospective juror for cause and risk a possible appellate issue. Prosecutors should take actions with an appeal in mind, so if a prosecutor can avoid challenging a prospective juror for cause, the prosecutor will never have to defend on appeal the judge's granting of that challenge.

Preparing to Exercise Peremptory Strikes

The Federal Rules of Criminal Procedure afford each party a number of peremptory strikes through which the parties may remove prospective jurors for any reason, or no reason at all. As noted, however, no federal rule prescribes the process by which parties are to exercise those peremptory strikes. In other words, there is no established procedure in federal court to establish the body of prospective jurors against whom the peremptory strikes are to be exercised, directing which party is to exercise peremptory strikes first and second, in what order parties are to exercise peremptory strikes, how many strikes each party is able or required to exercise at a time, or whether the parties are required to exercise all of their peremptory strikes or only some of them. Rather, the process is left entirely to the discretion of trial judges. Courts must, however, provide the parties with adequate notice of the method to be used. *United States v. Turner*, 558 F.2d 535, 538 (9th Cir. 1977). The only apparent restriction on this judicial discretion is that the method chosen by the trial judge "must not unduly restrict" (*id.*) or "embarrass"[6] a criminal defendant's use of peremptory strikes.

There are four general methods for exercising peremptory strikes that courts have been developed over time: (1) the jury box method; (2) the struck juror method; (3) the serial strike method; and (4) the sequential strike method. Courts sometimes use other methods that are variations of these four methods. I will discuss each briefly.

In the jury box method, lawyers are limited to exercising strikes against only the twelve prospective jurors seated in the jury box. The process starts with the court seating twelve prospective jurors in the jury box and limiting voir dire to those twelve. If a prospective juror is successfully challenged for cause, a new prospective juror replaces the challenged juror in the box, retaining the original number. After voir dire is complete and the parties have passed the prospective jurors for cause, the court calls upon the parties to exercise peremptory strikes. For each prospective juror struck, another prospective juror must take that prospective juror's place. When prospective jurors are replaced with new prospective jurors, then, some voir dire examination of the new prospective jurors is necessary. Once the parties complete any additional voir dire, and any of the new prospective jurors are removed for cause, the parties are then called upon to exercise any remaining peremptory strikes, if they have preserved any. Any prospective jurors remaining not struck by either party would then automatically be on the jury.

In the struck juror method, the court seats the number of prospective jurors in or in front of the jury box equal to the number of jurors needed for the trial plus the number of peremptory strikes each side has. In a federal felony trial, this number would be 28 (12 jurors + 10 defense peremptory strikes + 6 government peremptory strikes). Once all challenges for cause have been made and any struck jurors replaced, and after all voir dire has been completed, the parties then exercise their peremptory strikes against this panel of prospective jurors. Typically, the parties exercise their peremptory strikes by taking turns, marking jurors off the list of prospective jurors. When each side has exercised all their peremptory strikes, the petit jury will consist of those prospective jurors not struck.

The sequential method is similar in the number and formation of the panel. It is different, however, in the exercise of strikes. Rather than having the parties exercise their peremptory strikes against the entire panel, the judge has the parties exercise their peremptory strikes on prospective jurors one at a time. Starting with the first juror randomly seated, the judge will call upon one party at a time to determine if the party wishes to exercise a peremptory strike. If either party exercises a peremptory strike, the prospective juror is struck and the judge moves on to the next prospective juror in line. If neither party exercises a peremptory strike, then that juror is on the petit jury and the judge moves on to the next prospective juror.

The sequential method of exercising peremptory strikes involves voir dire of individual jurors, followed by a requirement that each side decide whether to challenge an individual prospective juror immediately after that juror has been passed for cause. In other words, the court and, when permitted, the lawyers, would start by questioning the first prospective juror. The judge would then inquire of the parties whether either was challenging the prospective juror for cause. If neither party challenged the prospective juror for cause, the parties would then be given a chance to exercise a peremptory strike to remove the juror. Then the process would be repeated for the next prospective juror in line. A variation of this method involves attorneys conducting voir dire on "blocks" or "groups" of jurors by one side, followed by that party's exercise of peremptory strikes, before the opposing side takes its turn conducting voir dire and exercising peremptory strikes on the remaining prospective jurors.

Each of these different methods for exercising peremptory strikes has its advantages and disadvantages. Discussing each method in detail is beyond the scope of this book. It is imperative, however, that a prosecutor determines which method the judge in his or her case utilizes and then prepare in advance for how to exercise peremptory strikes most effectively given the method used.

With each of the methods of jury selection summarized above, discretion is left with the trial judge to determine the sequence and, depending on the method, sometimes the number of peremptory strikes a party may exercise when it is that party's turn to do so. In other words, there are no rules establishing whether the government exercises its peremptory strikes first, whether the defendant goes first, whether they trade off strikes, or whether they exercise the strikes simultaneously. Further, when the method allows for parties to exercise more than one peremptory strike at a time, as in the struck juror method, there are no rules on how many peremptory strikes a party must exercise at a time. All of these procedures are left to the sole discretion of the trial judge, and many options are available.

There is nothing in the Federal Rules of Civil Procedure or the Federal Rules of Criminal Procedure requiring an equitable, alternating exercise of peremptory strikes. A court may, for example, require the government in a criminal case to exercise three strikes, the defendant five, the government its remaining three, leaving the defendant the final choice of strikes. Indeed, in theory a court has the authority to require the government to exercise all six of its peremptory strikes first before requiring the defendant to exercise any of his or her peremptory strikes. Or, the judge could come up with some other variation of the parties taking turns exercising peremptory strikes. Similarly, regarding the sequential strike method discussed above, there is nothing that would prevent a court from requiring the government to go first in choosing whether to exercise a peremptory strike on each prospective juror as the court moved down the rows from one prospective juror to the next. This is because trial judges have broad discretion to control jury selection in federal court.

How judges choose to exercise this discretion can be important to the parties in jury selection. The order of striking and the number of strikes the parties are required to exercise when it is their turn can provide a tactical advantage to one side or the other. A party who goes second in order of exercising strikes has the advantage of seeing what the other party has done, which may inform the second party's decision. Further, the first party to exercise peremptory strikes may strike a prospective juror the second party was considering striking. It is not uncommon for both parties to want to strike the same prospective juror for the same or different reasons. So, the party who goes second may not have to waste a peremptory strike if the first party has already struck that prospective juror. Likewise, the more peremptory strikes a party is required to exercise on its turn, the greater the advantage to the following party because the second party has the advantage of knowing more people the first party struck and having a smaller pool against which the second party has to exercise the limited peremptory strikes.

Some judges have adopted a method by which each side exercises strikes simultaneously. This method is available with the jury box or struck juror methods, but not the serial or sequential strike methods. In the simultaneous strike method, each party is given a list of all the prospective jurors in the venire. Each party then strikes the prospective jurors they choose, and the lists are then compared. Sometimes parties strike the same prospective jurors; oftentimes not. When parties do happen to strike the same prospective jurors, courts may have the parties alternate on choosing a substitute prospective juror, with the plaintiff going first.

Given the method used by the judge in a particular case, a prosecutor must develop a strategy in advance of jury selection on how the prosecutor will exercise peremptory strikes. In arriving at a strategy for exercising peremptory strikes, it is important for prosecutors to remember that the voir dire process is more accurately described as juror de-selection. Peremptory strikes provide prosecutors with a limited opportunity to eliminate some prospective jurors they believe are biased or, for whatever reason, may not be the best juror for the case. The reality is that prosecutors are stuck with the panel of prospective jurors pulled by the court and have only a limited ability to remove certain prospective jurors from that group. Thus, the appropriate perspective for a prosecutor to adopt is not determining which prospective jurors the prosecutor wants on the jury, but rather, which prospective jurors the prosecutor would least like on the jury. Given that perspective, prosecutors should exercise peremptory strikes only after significant preparation and careful thought. Also, a trial attorney's strategy in exercising peremptory strikes may vary dramatically depending on the method used by the court for exercising peremptory strikes.

In making the decision of how to exercise peremptory strikes, prosecutors must not only think about who they want to strike, but also must try to figure out which prospective jurors the defense is likely to strike. There are often prospective jurors that harbor views that are adverse to both sides or are generally undesirable for other reasons. The goal, of course, is for trial attorneys to preserve as many peremptory strikes as possible so that each one counts most effectively. If the defense attorney uses a peremptory strike to remove a prospective juror that was also someone the prosecutor wanted removed, it saves the prosecutor an extra peremptory strike. So prosecutors should attempt to avoid exercising peremptory strikes on such prospective jurors until toward the end of the process to wait to see if the defense might strike them first. The ability of a prosecutor to use this strategy of preserving peremptory strikes, however, will depend not only on the method for exercising peremptory strikes the judge uses, but also on the order in which the judge requires the parties to exercise peremptory strikes.

Obviously, prosecutors should first strive to strike those jurors who are most clearly biased against the government or in favor of the defendant. Other prospective jurors may just appear to pose potential problems because of other factors, like a lack of formal education or inattention or general hostile views of the justice system, making them undesirable for either party. Generally speaking, prosecutors will want to exercise peremptory strikes to remove the following categories of prospective jurors, usually in the following order: (1) adverse leaders; (2) unsuccessful for-cause challenged; (3) adverse non-leaders; (4) other problem prospective jurors.

As mentioned, in reviewing juror questionnaires and in conducting voir dire, one of the primary goals is to identify leaders. Prospective jurors who will be leaders in the jury room, and who appear to hold views adverse to a party, should be the first recipients of the attorney's peremptory strikes. All things being equal, an adverse leader in the jury room is more dangerous to a party than a person who holds hostile views but otherwise appears to be a passive person. Passive jurors are more likely to be swayed by other jurors, despite their views, while leaders are more likely to sway others to their points of view. The primary consideration for prosecutors, then, is to identify those prospective leaders that show leadership qualities who are biased against the government or in favor of the defendant and use peremptory strikes to remove those leaders.

If a prosecutor has unsuccessfully challenged a prospective juror for cause, then the prosecutor must feel strongly that that prospective juror is very biased. If the court denies the for-cause challenge, it follows that the prosecutor should use a peremptory strike to remove that prospective juror, even if the person is not considered a leader. It may be important to remove this prospective juror because, regardless of whether the person would attempt or be able to sway others in the jury room, the person's view may be so adverse to the government that it would nevertheless influence other jurors. Further, during voir dire the prosecutor may have asked questions designed to reveal the prospective juror's bias to support a for-cause challenge, and the answers may have revealed biased views. Removing that prospective juror may, then, convey a message to the other jurors that that view is unacceptable and discourage them from holding those views.

Prosecutors should next consider using the remaining peremptory strikes to remove any other prospective jurors who hold views adverse to the government, even if those prospective jurors did not appear to be leaders. Prosecutors should rate the prospective jurors on some scale, as previously discussed, and exercise peremptory strikes in a manner, of course, to remove the worse prospective jurors first.

Should the prosecutor have any remaining peremptory strikes, the prosecutor should exercise them against other problem prospective jurors. These are individuals who may not be biased against the government or in favor of the defendant necessarily, but who may hold views detrimental to the system of justice generally or would likely perform poorly as a juror, introducing an element of risk to the jury deliberation process. Jurors who were unsuccessful in attempting to be excused for hardship might be one such category of prospective jurors who would best be left off a jury if possible. One of the judge's primary obligations during jury selection is dealing with prospective jurors who claim they are unable to serve as a juror because of some other commitment, such as work or family obligations. Most judges handle these issues with tact and in a manner designed to discourage prospective jurors who simply want to shirk their civic duties. Quite often, however, prospective jurors who unsuccessfully tried to get excused from jury service will be left on the panel. These prospective jurors clearly do not want to serve as jurors and have been frustrated in their attempts to fabricate excuses for being excused. Prosecutors may want to use their peremptory strikes to eliminate such prospective jurors, as they may not do justice to the case or to either party.

In answers to juror questionnaires or to questions posed in voir dire, it may also have become apparent that some prospective jurors hold negative attitudes about the lawyers or criminal justice system generally. As jurors, these people may not take their role seriously. Or, they may seize the opportunity as a juror to do what they think is right, as opposed to what the law requires. These may be untrustworthy people who are better off not serving on a jury.

It may also have become apparent that other prospective jurors would simply have difficulty making a decision, or sitting in judgment on a case. This could be because they have the personalities of wallflowers, or perhaps they have deeply held religious or moral beliefs that would make it difficult for them to make a decision that could adversely affect another person's life. Generally speaking, these prospective jurors are most adverse to the party with the burden of proof: the government. So prosecutors should consider exercising peremptory strikes to remove them.

During voir dire, a prosecutor may also have observed that some prospective jurors were inattentive and unresponsive, seldom if ever raising their hands or, when answering questions, gave monosyllabic replies. These same prospective jurors may have been equally uncommunicative in written answers to juror questionnaires. The danger with these prospective jurors is that they are major question marks. So little is known about them that it is hard for anyone to truly know what they think. Prosecutors may want to remove the danger of the unknown by using peremptory strikes to remove such enigmatic prospective jurors.

Finally, prosecutors should develop a strategy considering the alternate jurors for those occasions when the trial judge does not provide additional peremptory strikes for alternates. The Federal Rules of Criminal Procedure provide that the court should give additional peremptory strikes to attorneys for alternate jurors. Some courts, by the fiat of local rules or trial management orders, do away with this provision absent an objection by a party. In these courts, the last unstruck prospective juror(s) seated becomes the alternate juror(s). For example, if three prospective jurors were struck for cause during voir dire and replaced by three new prospective jurors, and the court intends to seat one alternate juror, then the alternate juror would be the last juror not struck by a peremptory strike. This may be the last prospective juror of the original panel seated, if all three of the replacements are struck, or it may be one of the three replacements: whichever unstruck prospective juror was the last to take a seat. The strategy point here is that when exercising peremptory strikes, it is important for the prosecutor to keep in mind which prospective jurors will be alternates. Since alternate jurors rarely deliberate, exercising a peremptory strike on a prospective juror who will be the alternative if not struck would be a waste of a peremptory strike. Thus, all things being equal, prosecutors should not focus on the likely alternate jurors when exercising peremptory strikes.

Much of a prosecutor's efforts in preparing for and conducting jury selection comes down to the moment in the trial when the court calls upon the parties to exercise their peremptory strikes. It is at this point in jury selection when the prosecutor uses all the information obtained through any jury investigation conducted, in reviewing juror questionnaires, and by way of engaging prospective jurors in voir dire, to decide which prospective jurors to strike, and thus which jurors will decide the case.

As a practical matter, regardless of the jury selection method the trial judge employs, when it comes time for the parties to exercise peremptory strikes the judge will expect the attorneys to do so quickly. The jury, too, will be waiting and impatient and, in many cases, still sitting in the courtroom watching the attorneys as they exercise their strikes. So prosecutors need to be prepared to move quickly when exercising peremptory strikes. This means that prosecutors should be assessing throughout the jury selection process which prospective jurors they may want to strike and why. As noted previously when discussing juror questionnaires, it is most helpful for prosecutors to come up with some type of scoring system for assessing prospective jurors. Any system may work, so long as everyone on the trial team providing input to the prosecutor uses the same system. That system may consist of grades, as in school (an A for the best prospective jurors and an F for the worst), or a point system (10 points for the best prospective jurors and 0 points for the worst), or even a color-coded system (green for the best, amber for the middle, and red for the worst). Generally speaking, however, a scoring system that provides multiple gradations (such as grades or numbers) is preferable to one (such as colors) that permit only a few categories. There may be fine lines between which prospective jurors are better or worse than others, and a scoring system that permits reflection of these fine lines is better than a system that does not. Finally, the larger the trial team involved in evaluating and scoring prospective jurors, the more important it is that the team share the same grading system and philosophy. In other words, the lead prosecutor needs to indicate whether, for example, an A grade should be reserved for the truly outstanding prospective juror or whether an A grade should be awarded for any prospective juror for whom there are no obviously negative factors present.

Prosecutors should enter the courtroom having already assigned tentative scores to each of the prospective jurors based on whatever they have learned before voir dire through reviewing answers to juror questionnaires and through whatever investigation they may have conducted. To keep track of the scores and make notes relating to the prospective jurors during voir dire, prosecutors should create a chart reflecting the seating arrangement of the prospective jurors in the courtroom. Each member of the trial team participating in the evaluation and scoring of the prospective jurors should have a copy of the chart. This chart is especially helpful if the trial judge has the attorneys exercise peremptory strikes while the prospective jurors are outside the courtroom. A chart prepared by a prosecutor in advance of voir dire may look something like this:

Juror 1	Juror 2	Juror 3	Juror 4	Juror 5	Juror 6	Juror 7	Juror 8
Juror 9	Juror 10	Juror 11	Juror 12	Juror 13	Juror 14	Juror 15	Juror 16
Juror 17	Juror 18	Juror 19	Juror 20	Juror 21	Juror 22	Juror 23	Juror 24
Juror 25	Juror 26	Juror 27	Juror 28				

During voir dire, prosecutors should make notes on the chart regarding the most important information relevant to the decision of whom to strike. Prosecutors should adjust the scores assigned to the prospective jurors in advance of voir dire in light of the prospective jurors' answers during voir dire and the trial team members' observations of the prospective jurors. When the time then comes in jury selection when the judge instructs the parties to exercise their peremptory strikes, the prepared prosecutor can use these charts, and the scores assigned to the prospective jurors, to intelligently, but quickly, exercise peremptory strikes. The larger the trial team and the greater the number of charts, of course, the more difficult the task of comparing and reconciling scores becomes. To the extent possible, given the time restraints and the timing of any breaks, the trial team should attempt to calculate average scores for each prospective juror based on input from each person scoring the prospective jurors.

It also aids the speed and wisdom of the peremptory strikes if the members of the trial team discuss the prospective jurors whenever possible in advance of trial and during the jury selection process. Before entering the courtroom, the trial team should have met to discuss the prospective jurors and the scores assigned to the prospective jurors based on answers to juror questionnaires and any juror investigation. Then, during any break the judge provides during jury selection, the trial team should huddle and compare scores and discuss their views of the prospective jurors. The focus, as always, should be on identifying the leaders among the prospective jurors who are deemed to hold views most adverse to the client.

Finally, when the time comes to actually exercise the peremptory strikes, the lead prosecutor may wish to confer with co-counsel or other trial team members before exercising peremptory strikes. If the jury is still in the courtroom at this time, the trial team should be circumspect about these discussions. Obviously, they should be conducted quietly so that prospective jurors do not hear what the team is discussing, but team members should also be cautious about looking at the prospective jurors during this process. Prospective jurors may reach adverse inferences from stares or glances by members of the trial team looking at the prospective jurors. The prospective jurors are aware that they are being evaluated at this point and know that the attorneys are deciding which of them to strike. None of us like being evaluated and judged by others, and prosecutors should be conscious of the prospective jurors' position because those not struck will ultimately be judging the prosecutor and the facts of the case in the end.

FACTORS FOR EXERCISING PEREMPTORY STRIKES

Trial attorneys have typically relied on instinct, intuition, and stereotypes when deciding which prospective jurors to remove using peremptory strikes.

As discussed, it is unconstitutional for trial attorneys to strike prospective jurors based on race, national origin, and gender, but nothing bars them from basing strikes on grounds such as a prospective juror's religion, appearance, occupation, age, political or other personal beliefs, characteristics, or demographics. I will discuss first permissible factors prosecutors may use in exercising peremptory strikes, and then I will discuss impermissible factors and the process for challenging a party for using impermissible factors.

Permissible Factors

Many trial manuals and articles embrace the use of stereotypes and generalizations as a basis for exercising peremptory strikes, each author expressing his or her opinions about what conclusions trial attorneys should make from prospective jurors' occupations, ages, and other demographic information.[7] Other theories abound regarding conclusions trial attorneys should make about prospective jurors based on everything from facial features to clothing to posture.[8] There may be some basis for drawing conclusions about people based on these factors, and perhaps some have sufficient training to "read" things into a prospective juror's posture or manner of speech. It is beyond this author's expertise to provide any advice regarding such non-substantive matters. Studies have also shown that attorneys often draw inaccurate conclusions about prospective jurors relying on such stereotypes.[9] Some trial attorneys still cling to stereotypes, or follow the pseudoscientific advice of jury consultants, in exercising peremptory strikes. Other attorneys form their own stereotypes based on their personal experiences trying cases. A trial attorney who experienced a jury trial hung by a juror who worked as a hairdresser may thereafter conclude that all hairdressers make poor jurors.

Most good, experienced prosecutors place little credence on such generalized or personalized stereotypes. Rather, these prosecutors understand that people do not necessarily act consistently with stereotypes. They recognize that many stereotypes are based on erroneous assumptions in the first place. So, although it is permissible for prosecutors to exercise peremptory strikes based on a prospective juror's facial expressions, or occupation, club memberships, or other generalities, doing so may be unwise.

Rather than base peremptory strikes on stereotypes, good prosecutors will exercise their strikes on more solid ground. Recognizing that every case is different, that the parties vary, and that issues in one case may not be present in another, good prosecutors will focus on the case at hand, consider the particular group of prospective jurors at issue, and base peremptory strike decisions on factors important to the intersection of the two. For example, if the case involves insurance fraud, the prosecutor would likely conclude that a prospective juror who works as an accountant in the insurance industry would make a good juror for the government. In a different case involving purely circumstantial evidence of a murder, the prosecutor may believe that same prospective juror would not be a great juror for the government.

Good prosecutors also attempt to look behind generalities and consider the prospective jurors individually. By appearance or occupation, a prosecutor may consciously or subconsciously place a prospective juror in a generalized category. But when the prosecutor then considers the rest of the information known about the prospective juror through the juror questionnaire and voir dire, those generalities may be confirmed or denied. For example, a prosecutor may assume that a prospective juror whose son is in prison would be adverse to the government. But that prospective juror, if asked, may state that prison saved his or her son's life because he was on a downward trajectory that otherwise would have led to his death. The prospective juror may indicate that the government treated his or her son fairly and that the son deserved the punishment he received and is a better person because of the experience. This is one reason it is important for prosecutors to attempt to engage every prospective juror in some conversation during voir dire; generalities tend to disappear when the person is viewed as an individual.

In short, in exercising peremptory strikes good prosecutors not only dispense with exercising peremptory strikes unlawfully based on attributes such as race, gender, and national origin but also dispense with exercising peremptory strikes based on broad generalities. Rather, prosecutors should exercise peremptory strikes by evaluating each prospective juror as a unique person, and in light of the facts and legal issues in dispute in the case at bar.

Impermissible Factors

During the process of exercising peremptory strikes, lawyers for both the government and the defendant must ensure that their exercise of peremptory strikes is not motivated by an improper or unconstitutional reason. Attorneys may not strike a prospective juror because of the prospective juror's race, sex, or national origin. *See Batson v. Kentucky*, 476 US 79 (1986) (government's use of peremptory strikes to remove African Americans from jury panel unconstitutional). This prohibition is based on a defendant's right under the Equal Protection Clause and jurors' rights in the judicial system. Thus, a white defendant can object to the government using strikes to remove minorities from the jury (*Powers v. Ohio*, 499 US 400 [1991]), an African-American defendant can challenge the government's use of strikes to remove white prospective jurors (*Roman v. Abrams*, 822 F.2d 214, 227–28 [2d Cir. 1987]), and the government can object to a defendant's similarly improper use of strikes (*Georgia v. McCollum*, 505 US 42 [1992]). Just as race is irrelevant to whether a person can serve as an impartial juror, so too other characteristics, such as gender, are irrelevant. Thus, it is improper to strike a juror simply because of the juror's gender. *See J.E.B. v. Alabama ex rel TB*, 511 US 127 (1994). The Supreme Court has not expanded scope of this prohibition beyond race, gender, and national origin. So, for example, there is no prohibition for a lawyer to strike a potential juror based on sexual orientation or religious beliefs.

If one side believes that the other exercised a peremptory strike for an unconstitutional reason, that is, one side believes the opposing counsel based the peremptory strike on the prospective juror's gender, ethnicity, or nationality, then the party may make a so-called *Batson* challenge, which requires the trial court to hold a *Batson* hearing. This three-part procedure, borrowed from a similar process used in employment discrimination cases, begins with the objecting party making an initial prima facie showing that the peremptory strike was unconstitutionally motivated. If the moving party is able to make such a showing, the burden shifts to the party who exercised the peremptory strike to articulate a neutral explanation for the challenges. The standard here is not high. "Although the prosecutor must present a comprehensible reason, '[t]he second step of this process does not demand an explanation that is persuasive, or even plausible'; so long as the reason is not inherently discriminatory, it suffices." *Rice v. Collins*, 546 US 333, 338 (2006) (quoting *Purkett v. Elem*, 514 US 765, 767–68 [1995]).

If the non-moving party articulates a non-discriminatory reason, the court must then decide whether it was the real and legitimate reason, or rather was merely a pretext for striking the prospective juror for an unconstitutional reason. "This final step involves evaluating the 'persuasiveness of the justification' proffered by the prosecutor, but 'the ultimate burden of persuasion regarding [the alleged discriminatory] motivation rests with, and never shifts from, the opponent of the strike.'" *Rice*, 546 US at 338 (quoting *Purkett*, 514 US at 768). If the trial court finds the peremptory strike was motivated by a constitutionally improper reason, the court may remedy the improper use of peremptory strikes by discharging the entire venire and selecting a new panel, or by disallowing the improper challenge and seating the struck juror. If the *Batson* objection is incorrectly dismissed but found on appeal, the remedy is a new trial.

OTHER ISSUES DURING JURY SELECTION

Prosecutors need to prepare for other legal issues to arise during jury selection. These include motions by the defense to change venue due to pretrial publicity, the use of anonymous juries, and juror misconduct during jury selection. Although these issues rarely arise, when they do arise prosecutors must be familiar with the law and the process by which these issues arise and are addressed to handle them successfully. I will discuss each of these issues in turn.

Motions to Change Venue

The US Constitution provides that criminal trials should occur in the "district wherein the crime shall have been committed." US CONST. AMEND. VI. The Federal Rules of Criminal Procedure authorize courts to make an exception, however, when pretrial publicity warrants a change of venue to ensure that a defendant can receive a fair trial. Rule 21(a) provides:

> Upon the defendant's motion, the court must transfer the proceeding against the defendant to another district if the court is satisfied that so great a prejudice against the defendant exists in the transferring district that the defendant cannot obtain a fair and impartial trial there.

FED. R. CRIM. P. 21(a). It is important to note that in a criminal case the right to change venue due to pretrial publicity belongs only to the criminal defendant. The government does not have a right to seek a change in venue, even if the publicity in the venue is pervasive and adverse to the United States.

Impartiality is presumed "so long as the jurors can conscientiously and properly carry out their sworn duty to apply the law to the facts of the particular case." *Lockhart v. McCree*, 476 US 162, 184 (1986). A change of venue is warranted if "extraordinary local prejudice will prevent a fair trial— a 'basic requirement of due process.'" *Skilling v. United States*, 561 US 358, 378 (2010) (quoting *In re Murchison*, 349 US 133, 136 [1955]). The burden is on the defendant to establish such prejudicial pretrial publicity. Transfers for a change of venue based upon pretrial publicity are generally disfavored because careful voir dire and the exercise of challenges for cause and peremptory strikes are thought to be sufficient in most cases to mitigate the prejudicial effects of pretrial publicity.

A trial court retains broad discretion to grant or deny a change of venue motion. When pretrial publicity is the basis for a motion for change of venue, courts typically engage in a two-step analysis. The first step is to determine whether the pretrial publicity was so extensive and corrupting that a reviewing court is required to "presume unfairness of constitutional magnitude." *Dobbert v. Florida*, 432 US 282, 303 (1977). If a court finds this to be the case, then the court must order a change of venue and will not move on to the second step. If the court does not find prejudice to be presumed, then in the second step the court will then determine whether the evidence regarding the knowledge and views of the prospective jurors shows actual prejudice. *Id.* The second step occurs at the time of jury selection. Actual prejudice may be discovered either in answers to juror questionnaires, during voir dire, or both.

For a presumption to apply under the first step, there must be a showing not only of extensive pretrial publicity, but a showing that the publicity was corrupting, meaning that it was adverse to the defendant. An impartial jury does not mean that the jurors must be totally ignorant of the case. *See Skilling,* 561 US at 380 ("Prominence does not necessarily produce prejudice, and juror impartiality . . . does not require ignorance"); *see also Irvin v. Dowd,* 366 US 717, 722 (1961) (jurors are not required to be "totally ignorant of the facts and issues involved"; "scarcely any of those best qualified to serve as jurors will not have formed some impression or opinion as to the merits of the case"). In other words, for the presumption to apply, the pretrial publicity must be so pervasive and inflammatory that juror bias will be all but inevitable.

In seeking a change of venue due to adverse pretrial publicity, defendants must present the court with some evidence of the publicity. Toward this end, it is common for defendants to support these motions by submitting collections of the publicity to the court. This may include copies of newspaper and magazine articles, audio clips of radio broadcasts, video clips of television coverage, and, increasingly, copies of social media communication, such as blogs, YouTube postings, tweets, and the like. Defendants may also supplement this evidence by producing results of surveys conducted in the venue from which the jury would be selected. The polls may attempt to assess the degree to which the community is aware of and has formed opinions about the case based on pretrial publicity.

There are a number of factors that courts may consider during step one in determining whether the pretrial publicity is so pervasive and so corrosive as to require a change of venue. These factors include the size of the district from which the jury pool will be drawn, the inflammatory nature of the publicity, the temporal proximity of the publicity, as well as the source of the publicity. "[T]he size and characteristics of the community in which the crime occurred" is important in determining whether the pretrial publicity can be presumed to have created an inevitably biased jury pool. *See Skilling,* 561 US at 382. In districts with a large population, there is a greater chance of finding people who have not heard of the case, whereas in districts with small populations, that is less likely. *See Mu'Min v. Virginia,* 500 US 415, 429 (1991) (potential for prejudice mitigated by the size of the "metropolitan Washington [D.C.] statistical area, which has a population of over 3 million, and in which, unfortunately, hundreds of murders are committed each year"). A court may conclude that the publicity was not inflammatory, even if it was not entirely dispassionate, neutral, or factual. On the other hand, a court is more likely to find inflammatory publicity charged with emotion and factual inaccuracies, or publicity that is so clearly one-sided. The recency of the publicity in relation to the trial is important because if a significant amount of time has passed since the adverse publicity before the trial is to occur, the less likely jurors will have remembered it and the less likely it would be for that publicity to have an impact on the prospective jurors' current views. Finally, if the defendant is a source of the pretrial publicity, it is less likely the court will grant a change of venue. In other words, if there is significant publicity because the defendant, his or her family, or his or her lawyers have instigated the publicity or sought it out, then the defendant has little right to complain about the impact of that publicity on the ability to find unexposed prospective jurors.

If, under step one, the court does not find that the pretrial publicity was so pervasive or corrosive as to create a presumption of prejudice, the court will move on to the second step. As a general rule, "the effect of pretrial publicity can be better determined after the voir dire examination of the jurors." *Narten v. Eyman*, 460 F.2d 184, 187 (9th Cir. 1969) (internal quotation marks and citation omitted). At step two, the court looks at the evidence regarding the prospective jurors' actual views to determine if there is a showing of actual prejudice. The court may consider here information from juror questionnaires and answers during the voir dire itself. The trial court must probe whether prospective jurors have been exposed to pretrial publicity, the extent of their knowledge from the pretrial publicity, whether they have formed opinions as a result of the exposure to the publicity, and whether the jurors can set that knowledge and those opinions aside and render a verdict based only on the evidence admitted at trial. *Irvin*, 366 US at 722–23. If a trial judge is convinced that an impartial jury can be impaneled, a change of venue is not justified. On the other hand, if the trial judge determines through the course of the step two analysis and voir dire that too many jurors have been too prejudiced by the pretrial publicity that an impartial jury cannot be empaneled, then the judge should grant a change of venue.

As can be imagined, it is a time-consuming and expensive process for the court and parties to go through a failed jury selection process only to change venue and start it again in another jurisdiction. So, in cases when there has been significant pretrial publicity, courts may engage in other efforts to counter the publicity and increase the possibility of seating an impartial jury. Courts may, for example, increase the number of prospective jurors called into court to constitute the venire for a particular trial. In a typical federal criminal case, a clerk of court might call in fifty prospective jurors to constitute a venire from which the trial jury would be selected. In a case of significant pretrial publicity, on the other hand, the court may have the clerk of court double, triple, or quadruple that number of prospective jurors. The court may also expand the geographic range of the pool of citizens from which the venire may be constituted. Most federal districts consist of several geographic divisions, and juries are typically pulled from the divisions closest to the court site. In a case involving pretrial publicity in the area near the court site, a trial judge may instruct the clerk of court to pull prospective jurors from more distant parts of the district. This would, of course, increase the inconvenience to the prospective jurors and the costs of transportation and housing jurors that the court would have to cover, but it may be less than the costs involved if the court had to change venue. Finally, a court may impose a gag order on the parties in the case when it becomes apparent early on that the case will generate a large amount of publicity. There is a right of free speech under the First Amendment, of course, but courts have the discretion to bar the parties from communicating with the press when doing so may jeopardize the defendant's right to a fair trial.

In addressing a defense motion for change of venue due to adverse pretrial publicity, there are several things prosecutors should do. First, a prosecutor should thoroughly review the pretrial publicity and, if necessary, collect more samples to present to the court. The prosecutor should then carefully analyze the publicity to determine whether it truly is adverse, its volume and geographic range, whether it reports only facts that will come out as part of the evidence, whether the defendant or his or her associates are the source of any adverse publicity, and the age of the adverse publicity. As noted above, for a change of venue to be warranted, the publicity must be not only pervasive, but also adverse. If the publicity reports only facts that will come out in the evidence, it may not really be adverse. If the publicity is dated in relation to when the trial will occur, or was distributed in only a limited geographic location, it may not be adverse.

Second, the prosecutor should assess whether there truly is pervasive adverse publicity such that the defendant cannot get a fair trial in the district, or whether there are steps the court can take to counteract the publicity. The prosecutor should be prepared, in the appropriate case, to concede the need to change venue to ensure the defendant receives a fair trial. On the other hand, the prosecutor should help the court identify means by which some adverse publicity could be counteracted by a larger pool of prospective jurors, or one drawn from a different geographic part of the district, for example.

Once a trial judge decides to change the venue of a trial due to pretrial publicity, whether in a criminal or civil case, it is generally within the trial judge's discretion to choose a new venue for the trial. In choosing a new venue, the trial court's first focus, of course, is finding a venue where there has been little or no pretrial publicity about the case. Courts may consider other factors as well, such as (1) the convenience of the court, parties, witnesses, and attorneys; (2) security, transportation, and other logistical considerations; (3) the costs associated with trying the case in the new venue; and (4) the impact on the court system in the new location. Generally speaking, trial judges tend to try to move the trial to another location within the district first, and, failing that, to an adjoining district.

Anonymous Juries

Generally speaking, the identity of prospective jurors is public knowledge once they appear in the courtroom for jury selection. Court personnel, the trial attorneys, and the parties generally know the names and other identifying information about prospective jurors. "In the usual case, the parties know the names, addresses, and occupations of potential jurors, as well as those of any spouses, and use this information during voir dire to formulate questions probing for potential biases, prejudices, or any other considerations that might prevent a juror from rendering a fair and impartial decision." *United States v. Ross*, 33 F.3d 1507, 1519 n.22 (11th Cir. 1994). During voir dire, trial attorneys commonly refer to the prospective jurors by name, and the names of those struck during jury selection and the names of those selected to serve as jurors become part of the public record for all to see, including the public and the press. After all, the practice of holding public trials is one of the core principles of an open and democratic justice system in America. Jurors are also generally permitted to leave the courthouse and return home each day after trial, returning the following day to resume jury service.

On occasion in criminal cases, however, for reasons of security or publicity, courts will withhold some or all of this information about prospective jurors from some or all of the participants or public. These juries are generally referred to as "anonymous." This term can be misleading, however, as there are degrees of anonymity. For prosecutors to decide when to seek anonymous juries, it is important to understand the rights implicated by anonymous juries, the legal standards courts apply in determining whether to empanel anonymous juries, and the various degrees of anonymity that courts may adopt.

Empaneling an anonymous jury may interfere with a defendant's Sixth Amendment right to trial by an impartial jury. *See United States v. Darden*, 70 F.3d 1507, 1532 (8th Cir. 1995). That is because "the use of an anonymous jury may interfere with defendants' ability to conduct voir dire and to exercise meaningful peremptory challenges." *United States v. Shryock*, 342 F.3d 948, 971 (9th Cir. 2003); *cf. United States v. Mansoori*, 304 F.3d 635, 650 (7th

Cir. 2002) (holding that juror anonymity deprives defendants of information that might help them make appropriate challenges during jury selection"). The empaneling of "anonymous juries may also infer that the dangerousness of those on trial required their anonymity, thereby implicating defendants' Fifth Amendment right to a presumption of innocence." *Mansoori*, 304 F.3d at 650 ("'An anonymous jury raises the specter that the defendant is a dangerous person from whom the jurors must be protected, thereby implicating the defendant's constitutional right to a presumption of innocence'") (quoting *Ross*, 33 F.3d at 1519). Anonymous juries arguably may also impact the group dynamic of a jury during deliberations. Because of this potential adverse impact on defendants' rights, empaneling anonymous juries has been variously described as "extreme," *Mansoori*, 304 F.3d at 650, "a last resort," *United States v. Edwards*, 303 F.3d 606, 613 (5th Cir. 2002), and "drastic" *United States v. Sanchez*, 74 F.3d 562, 564 (5th Cir. 1996) (quoting *United States v. Krout*, 66 F.3d 1420, 1427 (5th Cir. 1995).

On the other hand, courts have recognized that "'neither the right to a presumption of innocence nor the right to exercise peremptory challenges is a constitutional absolute; each, at times, must yield to the legitimate demands of trial administration and court-room security'" *Mansoori*, 304 F.3d at 650 (quoting *United States v. DiDomenico*, 78 F.3d 294, 301 [7th Cir. 1996]). The interest in protecting jurors from dangers posed to their safety by a criminal defendant or his or her associates, or from harassment and intimidation by the parties, the news media, or the public, may outweigh the defendant's rights. *See Darden*, 70 F.3d at 1532; *accord Shryock*, 342 F.3d at 971. "[E]very court that has considered the issue has concluded that *in appropriate circumstances* the empanelment of an anonymous jury does not infringe on the right to an impartial jury." *Darden*, 70 F.3d at 1532 (citing cases so holding) (emphasis added). So courts "weighing the need for an anonymous jury must balance the defendant's interest in preserving the presumption of innocence and in conducting a useful voir dire against the jurors' interest in their own security and the public's interest in having a jury assess the defendant's guilt or innocence impartially." *Mansoori*, 304 F.3d at 650. *See also Edwards*, 303 F.3d at 613 ("This interest in juror protection must be balanced against the defendant's interest in effective voir dire and the presumption of innocence").

In light of the concerns that anonymous juries may adversely impact a defendant's rights, courts have fashioned standards for empaneling anonymous juries designed to balance the defendant's interests against the interest in protecting the jurors. In federal courts, a court may empanel an anonymous jury when "the interests of justice so require." 28 U.S.C. § 1863(b)(7) (noting that "[i]f the plan [for the random selection of jurors] permits these names to be made public, it may nevertheless permit the chief judge of the district court, or such other district court judge as the plan may provide, to keep these names confidential in any case when the interests of justice so require"). In assessing whether justice so requires, the general standard applied is that courts should not empanel an anonymous jury without "a) concluding that there is strong reason to believe the jury needs protection, and b) taking reasonable precautions to minimize any prejudicial effects on the defendant and to ensure that his fundamental rights are protected." *United States v. Paccione*, 949 F.2d 1183, 1192 (2d Cir. 1991). *See also Darden*, 70 F.3d at 1532. A district court's decision to empanel an anonymous jury is entitled to deference and is subject to abuse of discretion review. *Shryock*, 342 F.3d at 970 (citing cases).

Courts have identified various factors to guide the discretion in deciding whether to empanel an anonymous jury. In assessing the need to protect the jury, courts have looked at: (1) the defendant's involvement in organized crime or an extensive criminal network, (2) the defendant's participation in a group with the capacity to harm jurors, (3) the defendant's past attempts to interfere with the judicial process, (4) the potential that, if convicted, the defendant will suffer a lengthy incarceration, death, or substantial monetary penalties, and (5) whether there is extensive publicity about the case that could enhance the possibility that jurors' names would become public and expose them to possible intimidation or harassment. *Darden*, 70 F.3d at 1532. These five factors, however, "are neither exclusive nor dispositive, and the district court should make its decision based on the totality of the circumstances." *Shryock*, 342 F.3d at 971. Indeed, courts have considered other factors, such as whether the defendant has associates who were not incarcerated and a record of previous attempts to interfere with the judicial process, for example, by intimidating or bribing or harming witnesses, jurors, law enforcement officers, or others involved in the judicial system.

In determining whether the government has satisfied these factors, courts may conduct evidentiary hearings and hear testimony or examine exhibits. Courts may also consider the indictment and affidavits submitted by the parties. Courts should also consider the totality of the circumstances, including "the climate surrounding a trial and a prediction as to the potential security or publicity problems that may arise during the proceeding." *United States v. Branch*, 91 F.3d 699, 723–24 (5th Cir. 1996) (quoting *United States v. Childress*, 58 F.3d 693, 702 [D.C. Cir. 1995]).

Courts have also identified measures that will satisfy the second requirement for empaneling an anonymous jury, that is, whether reasonable precautions can be taken "'to minimize any prejudicial effects on the defendant and to ensure that his fundamental rights are protected.'" *Darden*, 70 F.3d at 1532 (quoting *Paccione*, 949 F.2d at 1192). To avoid jurors concluding they are being referenced by numbers instead of names because the defendant is dangerous, courts may tell prospective jurors that it is empaneling an anonymous jury to avoid having members of the media or others ask them questions or to ensure that no extrajudicial information could be communicated to them during trial, either by the public or by media representatives. Some courts have told jurors that "the use of anonymous juries was commonplace in federal court, and that the reasons for the use of such a jury here had nothing to do with the [defendants'] guilt or innocence," even though this may not be entirely accurate. *Ross*, 33 F.3d at 1521–22). Although anonymous juries are not unprecedented in federal courts, the practice of empaneling anonymous juries is hardly routine or commonplace.

Courts have also found that a thorough voir dire of prospective jurors by the judge and/or by the trial attorneys sufficient to protect defendants' right to an unbiased jury, even though the parties may be deprived of certain identifying information about the prospective jurors. To this end, courts have endeavored to provide as much information as possible about the prospective jurors while still protecting them. For example, although a court may not let the parties know a prospective juror's address, it may allow the parties to know the town or area where the prospective juror resides. Or a court may not reveal the name of the prospective juror's employer, but may reveal to the parties the nature of the prospective juror's job or profession. Some courts have also submitted more detailed questionnaires to prospective jurors in an effort to increase the amount of other information the parties know about the prospective jurors.

Finally, courts may use instructions to emphasize the jurors' duty to remain neutral, despite the circumstances. A court may instruct jurors on the presumption of innocence, perhaps repeatedly, for example, in an effort to mitigate the effect of an anonymous jury.

There are various degrees to which a jury may be "anonymous." These degrees may be referred to as innominate juries, limited anonymous juries, and significantly anonymous juries. An innominate jury is one for which the court provides the parties with a list of the names, employers, and places of residence of each prospective juror but requires that during jury selection the parties refer to prospective jurors by only number and not name. In other words, the parties and lawyers are still provided all of the information about the prospective jurors, but that information is not revealed publicly so as to protect prospective jurors from outside influences. This is, perhaps, the lowest degree of juror anonymity, and hence, the lowest degree of juror protection and the least infringement on a defendant's Sixth Amendment right to an impartial jury. A jury may also be innominate as to the parties, as well as the public. In such a case, the parties would have access to all biographical information concerning prospective jurors except their names. This limitation on information would only provide limited protection to the prospective jurors and mildly infringe upon a defendant's ability to select a fair and impartial jury.

A limited anonymous jury involves the court concealing from the parties and the public the prospective jurors' names, places of employment, and their addresses, with courts sometimes releasing the town or zip code of prospective jurors' residences. In limited anonymous juries, however, courts will release to the parties significant other information about the prospective jurors from questionnaires. Courts also tend to allow voir dire of the prospective jurors in limited anonymous juries, either by submission of questions for the judge to ask or by allowing the trial attorneys to ask questions, so long as they do not solicit the concealed identifying information.

Some courts have empaneled significantly anonymous juries in which the court conceals from the parties and the public the names, places of employment, addresses, or other identifying information about the prospective jurors and their immediate families. In these cases, courts may not even disclose general information about the prospective jurors, such as the town or zip code of residence or even the nature of the prospective jurors' employment. The judge may also preclude or severely limit voir dire of the prospective jurors, particularly regarding anything that would reveal their identities. This form of anonymous jury provides the greatest degree of juror safety but the greatest infringement on a defendant's Sixth Amendment right to an impartial jury.

In determining whether to seek an anonymous jury of any degree, a prosecutor should carefully consider all of the factors the court will consider, as outlined above, in determining whether an anonymous jury is warranted under the circumstances. The prosecutor should also carefully weigh the practical implications for the government if the court empanels an anonymous jury. If that happens, it may seriously limit the information the prosecutor knows about the prospective jurors and thereby impair the prosecutor's ability to effectively challenge prospective jurors for cause or intelligently exercise peremptory strikes. Prosecutors should also recognize that the court's decision to empanel an anonymous jury will likely be an appellate issue and, if erroneous, may require a new trial. Finally, if a prosecutor requests an anonymous jury, the prosecutor should seek the least anonymity possible given the security concerns.

Sequestered Juries

As noted, generally jurors are allowed to return home each day after jury service and return the following day to resume such service. Courts may, however, sequester juries, that is, bar jurors from returning home after the trial day. Courts may also sequester juries during jury deliberation, even if the court did not sequester the jury during trial. Sequestered juries are essential held in the care and custody of the US Marshal Service or a sheriff's office throughout the trial and until the jury returns with a verdict. The motivation for sequestering jurors is similar to the motivations for empaneling anonymous juries. Typically, courts sequester juries either because of a concern over juror safety or tampering or to avoid having the jurors influenced by outside contact or publicity in high-profile cases.

Sequestration may at times be the only means available to the judge to protect the integrity of the trial process. A defendant does not have a constitutional right to a sequestered jury. *See Young v. Alabama*, 443 F.2d 854, 856 (5th Cir. 1971) (holding jury sequestration is not a fundamental right). Failure to sequester the jury is rarely a successful ground for reversal and is proper only upon a showing of actual prejudice. *United States v. Salerno*, 868 F.2d 524, 540 (2d Cir. 1989). On the other hand, a court may order a sequestrated jury notwithstanding a defendant's objection. *United States v. Shiomos*, 864 F.2d 16, 18 (3rd Cir. 1988). In *Wheat v. United States*, 486 US 153, 161 (1988), the Supreme Court noted that "trial courts confronted with [sequestration decisions] face the prospect of being 'whipsawed' by assertions of error no matter which way they rule."

Prosecutors should hesitate before asking a court to sequester a jury. Sequestration is considered one of the most burdensome and problematic methods of assuring a fair trial. Sequestration of citizens serving as jurors constitutes a significant infringement of the jurors' liberty. Sequestration could also reduce the number of potential jurors who could serve and narrows the cross section from which a jury is drawn because it eliminates prospective jurors for whom sequestration would constitute an extreme hardship (such as a single parent of minor children). Judges will also be reluctant to sequester jurors since it can be exorbitantly expensive, depending on the length of sequestration, because the court must pay for housing, meals, and enforcement. Finally, just as with empaneling anonymous juries, there is a real danger that the very act of sequestering the jurors could influence the jury's verdict if the jurors believe the sequestration is the result of a danger posed by the defendant. Jurors may also develop animosity toward the defendant because of the sequestration order. At the same time, sequestered jurors' significant contact with the law enforcement officials responsible for overseeing the sequestration may make jurors feel more favorable toward the government. For all these reasons, trial judges consider sequestration of a jury only as a last resort.

Sequestration of a jury is committed to the sound discretion of the trial judge. In deciding whether to order sequestration of a jury, courts will consider the totality of the outside influence that could influence the jury.

Courts may consider a number of factors in deciding whether to sequester a jury: (1) inconvenience to jurors; (2) the possibility of hastened verdicts to avoid prolonged sequestration; (3) lack of adequate lodging; (4) and the extent of the publicity given to the case. Sequestration may be proper in high-profile cases in which jurors would be exposed to significant publicity and attempts by third parties to contact them. The First Amendment bars courts from placing restrictions on the press and others from expressing their opinions. So if the sources cannot be silenced because of their right to free speech, sometimes the only option available to the court is to keep jurors from hearing the speech. On the other hand, sequestration may be ineffective if the jurors have already been influenced by significant pretrial publicity. Should a judge decide to sequester a jury, the judge should provide the jurors with a neutral instruction to prevent any negative inference being drawn from the sequestration order. *See, e.g.*, *United States v. Tutino*, 883 F.2d 1125, 1133 (2d Cir. 1989); *United States v. Barnes*, 604 F.2d 121, 137 (2d Cir. 1979).

As with anonymous juries, there are degrees of sequestration, and trial courts have a lot of discretion in determining the extent of sequestration. Courts may sequester jurors for the entire trial or only part of a trial (if, for example, during trial it becomes apparent that sequestration is required). Sometimes juries are sequestered only during deliberations, the time period perhaps when the jurors are most susceptible to outside influence or contact. Courts may also vary the degree to which sequestered jurors are allowed contact with family or employers. Sometimes sequestered jurors have virtually unlimited access to family and employers, so long as they remain in the physical care of the law enforcement agency supervising the sequestration. In other cases, courts may strictly limit such access to certain days or hours of the week. In extreme cases, courts may bar all contact with family and others during the sequestration.

Juror Misconduct

During jury selection, prospective jurors sometimes engage in misconduct. That misconduct can include making material omissions of information in response to written or oral questions, or making materially false statements. Misconduct may also occur during the jury selection process when, for instance, prospective jurors conduct their own investigation or research into the case, or have contact with outside parties about the case. Of course, the latter type of misconduct can also occur during the course of a trial and deliberations. It is important that prosecutors become familiar with the law regarding jury misconduct. The law relating to juror misconduct during the jury selection phase of a trial is somewhat different from the law that applies during trial and deliberations.

As noted, the foundation of the American jury system is to have fair and impartial jurors decide legal disputes. Voir dire is a critical component of the tools employed to empanel a fair and impartial jury. Underlying the reliance on voir dire to identify fair and impartial jurors is the presumption that prospective jurors will be accurate and honest in answering questions. Human nature, however, dictates that prospective jurors will not always be accurate and honest. Prospective jurors may make mistakes in answering questions, perhaps because they misunderstood the question or because of faulty memory. It is also in the nature of humans to lie or shade the truth for various reasons. Prospective jurors may lie in answering questions because they feel embarrassed or believe a truthful answer would subject them to harassment by the court or lawyers. Jurors may falsely conceal or omit information because they want to keep the information private, or because they want to get on or off the jury.

Generally speaking, courts recognize that people make honest mistakes. Courts will not invalidate a trial when prospective jurors provide incorrect answers as a result of a mistake absent a showing that a correct answer would have subjected the prospective juror to removal for cause. *McDonough Power Equip., Inc. v. Greenwood*, 464 US 548, 556 (1984). As the court explained:

> To invalidate the result of a three-week trial because of a juror's mistaken, though honest response to a question, is to insist on something closer to perfection than our judicial system can be expected to give. A trial represents an important investment of private and social resources, and it ill serves the important end of finality to wipe the slate clean simply to recreate the peremptory challenge process because counsel lacked an item of information which objectively he should have obtained from a juror on voir dire examination.

Id. at 555. So for a defendant to prevail in a motion for a new trial on the ground of juror misconduct based on inaccurate or false statements during jury selection, the defendant must first show that a juror failed to answer correctly a material question on voir dire, and then show that a correct answer to the question would have "provided a valid basis for a challenge for cause." *McDonough*, 464 US at 556.

Under the so-called *McDonough* test, then, a defendant seeking relief based on a claim of juror misconduct during voir dire must show by a preponderance of the evidence five things: (1) A juror gave an inaccurate answer to a question that was asked on voir dire; (2) the question was material; (3) the inaccurate response was dishonest, meaning knowingly and intentionally false, rather than the result of a good faith misunderstanding or mistake; (4)

the reasons for the knowingly and intentionally false response relate to the juror's ability to decide the particular case based solely on the evidence and, thus, call into question the juror's ability to be impartial; and (5) a correct response would have provided a valid basis for a challenge for cause and would have required or resulted in the excusal of the juror for cause based on actual bias, implied bias, or inferable bias. *Id.* The Supreme Court has held the *McDonough* test to be an exception to the rule that "once the jury has heard the evidence and the case has been submitted, the litigants must accept the jury's collective judgment." *United States v. Powell*, 469 US 57, 67 (1984).

An incorrect answer does not satisfy *McDonough*'s first prong if it was honestly given. *McDonough*, 464 US at 555–56. When a prospective juror truly just makes a mistake, there is no assumption that the prospective juror was biased. A juror "who is trying as an honest man to live up to the sanctity of his oath is well qualified to say whether he has an unbiased mind in a certain matter." *Dennis v. United States*, 339 US 162, 171 (1950). So, in determining whether error occurred, the only question is whether the truthful answer may constitute cause for removal. Imagine, for example, a juror previously convicted of a felony offense who mistakenly believed that the state had restored his civil rights and thus honestly, though mistakenly, believed that he was not a felon. The fact that the state had not restored his civil rights would not necessarily constitute grounds for removal of the prospective juror for cause if the juror was simply, honestly mistaken.

When there is evidence that a prospective juror lied, as opposed to having just making a mistake, however, the effect may be different. When there is evidence of intentional falsehood by the prospective juror, it raises the specter of bias. In that case, then, the grounds for removing the prospective juror expands to include grounds for removal for either actual, implied, or inferred bias. So, using our example again, if the prospective juror intentionally lied about having a prior conviction, it may constitute grounds for a new trial if the prospective juror's lie shows actual or implied bias. This is so even if the jurors' constitutional rights had been restored such that the conviction did not make the prospective juror unqualified to serve on a jury.

Occasionally, prospective jurors engage in other misconduct during the jury selection phase of a trial. To label it as juror misconduct is a bit of a misnomer because although sometimes the "misconduct" is the result of prospective jurors' intentional acts, other times problems arise because of the conduct of third parties. Jurors may engage in intentional misconduct when, for instance, they initiate contact with one of the parties, witnesses, lawyers, or others involved in the litigation. Sometimes jurors also take it upon themselves to conduct their own investigation of the case, researching the facts or the parties online, going to the scene of an event at issue in the case, or the like.

On other occasions, third parties initiate potentially improper contact with prospective jurors during the jury selection process. Sometimes this involves intentional misconduct, such as a party or associate trying to threaten or bribe prospective jurors. On other occasions, it involves accidental or unintentional contact. For example, in one case a defendant made a claim of juror misconduct when a federal agent helped change a flat tire on a prospective juror's car. Sometimes prospective jurors speak with lawyers or parties during or immediately before jury selection. In other cases, prospective jurors may talk or have contact with lawyers, parties, or witnesses during the trial or during jury deliberations.

Prosecutors cannot keep prospective jurors from giving mistaken or false answers during voir dire or prevent other types of juror misconduct, but they can take steps to prevent misconduct that arises from contact with third parties within the orbit of the prosecutors' control. Prosecutors should take affirmative steps to educate every member of the trial team and every potential witness of the absolute necessity to have no contact whatsoever with jurors and to immediately report any accidental contact that may occur. Careful prosecutors will repeatedly remind trial team members and witnesses of this admonition and the importance of complying with it.

When, during the course of a trial, parties discover alleged juror misconduct makes a difference on the nature and extent of an investigation into that misconduct. Trial attorneys sometimes discover inaccurate or false statements in juror questionnaires before jury selection even begins. On other occasions, attorneys uncover inaccurate or false statements in the process of conducting voir dire. Attorneys may also learn, during the jury selection phase, that a prospective juror had contact with a witness or another party, or conducted an independent investigation, or was subject to influence by an outside party. More often, however, trial attorneys do not discover potential juror misconduct during the jury selection process. Rather, trial attorneys typically do not discover juror misconduct, of whatever shade, until after the trial is over.

There is a significant difference in a trial attorney's ability to investigate juror misconduct before trial and after the verdict. The difficulty of investigating juror misconduct during jury selection is one of practical impediments, such as incomplete information and lack of adequate time. In contrast, the difficulty with investigating juror misconduct after a trial is posed primarily by a rule of evidence that bars jurors from testifying in a way that would jeopardize the jury's verdict.

When the potential juror misconduct involves outside influences on the prospective jurors, courts generally should investigate the incident. This often involves questioning the prospective jurors individually regarding their exposure to the outside information. The first question is whether the prospective jurors were exposed to the outside information. The second question is whether, if exposed to the outside information, it would influence the prospective jurors' ability to be fair and impartial. Mere exposure to outside information does not automatically disqualify prospective jurors. So long as the prospective jurors can disregard that information, they may still serve. "Qualified jurors need not . . . be totally ignorant of the facts and issues involved. . . . 'It is sufficient if the juror can lay aside his impression or opinion and render a verdict based on the evidence presented in court.'" *Murphy v. Florida*, 421 US 794, 799–800 (1975) (quoting *Irvin v. Dowd*, 366 US 717, 723 [1961]).

On the other hand, trial judges have broad discretion under the federal rules to control jury selection. This includes the discretion to simply replace a prospective juror when there has been outside contact with the prospective juror without inquiring further into whether that contact would influence the prospective juror's ability to be fair and impartial. Appellate courts will find this solution within a trial judge's broad discretion unless an objecting party can show actual bias or prejudice.

If the alleged misconduct involves an inaccurate or false statement by a prospective juror in response to a juror questionnaire, or in response to a question posed during voir dire, it is again within a trial judge's discretion whether to conduct a hearing to investigate the matter. In determining whether to conduct an evidentiary hearing to investigate the alleged juror misconduct, courts have to balance practical concerns, such as invading the prospective juror's privacy and the disruption such a hearing would have on the progress of the trial, against the extent and seriousness of the alleged erroneous or false statements. The very nature of the alleged misconduct—that is, an erroneous or false statement during jury selection—implies that the movant must provide some evidence to prove that the prospective juror's answers during jury selection were incorrect or false. This evidence may consist of documents that could be admitted without testimony, or it may require testimony. Of course, the easiest and quickest way to address the issue would be with the prospective juror during voir dire. To avoid embarrassment of the prospective juror, such an inquiry would best be conducted at side bar or outside the presence of the rest of the jury. When, however, the alleged misconduct is discovered after the close of voir dire, then the court may have to convene a separate hearing to inquire into the merits of the allegation. The hearing may even take place while the trial is still underway, if the alleged misconduct is discovered in time.

Most often, however, parties do not discover potential juror misconduct until after a trial has been completed. At that stage, investigating the alleged misconduct becomes more difficult. Under *McDonough*, a party must show prejudice. Presumably, the best way to determine prejudice is to inquire into the jury deliberations, to ask the jurors if the misconduct influenced the jury's verdict. Generally speaking, however, judges do not favor post-verdict interrogation of jurors. Questioning jurors as part of a post-verdict investigation of juror misconduct is also permitted only in the most limited circumstances, and only to the degree permitted by the Federal Rules of Evidence. Federal Rule of Evidence 606(b) provides:

> During an Inquiry into the Validity of a Verdict or Indictment.
>
> (1) Prohibited Testimony or Other Evidence. During an inquiry into the validity of a verdict or indictment, a juror may not testify about any statement made or incident that occurred during the jury's deliberations; the effect of anything on that juror's or another juror's vote; or any juror's mental processes concerning the verdict or indictment. The court may not receive a juror's affidavit or evidence of a juror's statement on these matters.
>
> (2) Exceptions. A juror may testify about whether:
>   (a) extraneous prejudicial information was improperly brought to the jury's attention; or
>   (b) an outside influence was improperly brought to bear on any juror.

Fed. R. Evid. 606(b). Courts often refer to Rule 606(b) as the "no-impeachment rule," meaning that the rule bars parties from impeaching a verdict based on testimony by the jurors who rendered it.

The policy considerations underlying Rule 606(b) include verdict finality, maintaining the integrity of the jury system, encouraging frank and honest deliberations, and the protection of jurors from subsequent harassment by a losing party. *Tanner v. United States*, 483 US 107, 120 (1987) (noting that without this rule, "[j]urors would be harassed and beset by the defeated party in an effort to secure from them evidence of facts which might establish misconduct sufficient to set aside a verdict"). In short, courts rely on the adversarial voir dire process to ferret out most misconduct and look to other evidence to prove juror misconduct post-verdict, to avoid invading the sanctity of the jury deliberation process. *Warger v. Shauers*, 574 US 40, 51 (2014) ("Even if jurors lie when answering questions during voir dire in a way that conceals bias, juror impartiality is adequately assured by the parties' ability to bring to the court's attention any evidence of bias before the verdict is rendered, and to employ nonjuror evidence even after the verdict is rendered").

Rule 606(b) thus makes it difficult for a party to meet the second prong of the *McDonough* test, that is, showing that the juror would have been subjected to removal for cause. A further difficulty, however, is that the inaccurate answer by a prospective juror may not be, and often is not, on a matter that would clearly make the prospective juror unqualified from serving on the jury. Sometimes parties may learn after the trial that a juror's truthful answer to a voir dire question would have disqualified the juror from serving, or that an accurate and truthful answer would have reflected actual bias. More typically, however, the movant must prove implied bias, meaning that the juror's truthful answers, and the circumstances that led the juror to provide incorrect answers, leads to the conclusion that the juror could not be fair and impartial. As we previously discussed, it is inherently more difficult to prove the juror would have been subject to removal based on implied bias.

In 2017, the Supreme Court significantly shifted the legal framework of Rule 606(b), at least as it relates to the issue of race. In *Pena-Rodriguez v. Colorado*, ——US ——, 137 S. Ct. 855 (2017), after a jury convicted the defendant of harassment and unlawful sexual contact, two jurors described racist statements made by another juror during deliberations. In determining whether to create an exception to Rule 606(b), the Court observed that "discrimination on the basis of race, 'odious in all aspects, is especially pernicious in the administration of justice.'" 137 S. Ct. at 868 (quoting *Rose v. Mitchell*, 443 US 545, 555 [1979]). The Court distinguished prior cases in which the Court maintained the no-impeachment rule, explaining:

> Racial bias of the kind alleged in this case differs in critical ways from the compromise verdict in *McDonald*, the drug and alcohol abuse in *Tanner*, or the pro-defendant bias in *Warger*. The behavior in those cases is troubling and unacceptable, but each involved anomalous behavior from a single jury—or juror—gone off course.

137 S. Ct. at 868. Thus, the Court held that "where a juror makes a clear statement that indicates he or she relied on racial stereotypes or animus to convict a criminal defendant, the Sixth Amendment requires that the no-impeachment rule give way to permit the trial court to consider the evidence of the juror's statement and any resulting denial of the jury trial guarantee." 137 S. Ct. at 869.

From the language of the Supreme Court's opinion, it appears that the Court does not intend to readily carve out other exceptions. In a dissenting opinion, Justice Alito expressed a concern, though, about the future sanctity of jury deliberations:

> When jurors retire to deliberate, however, they enter a space that is not regulated in the same way. Jurors are ordinary people. They are expected to speak, debate, argue, and make decisions the way ordinary people do in their daily lives. Our Constitution places great value on this way of thinking, speaking, and deciding.

The jury trial right protects parties in court cases from being judged by a special class of trained professionals who do not speak the language of ordinary people and may not understand or appreciate the way ordinary people live their lives. To protect that right, the door to the jury room has been locked, and the confidentiality of jury deliberations has been closely guarded.

Today, with the admirable intention of providing justice for one criminal defendant, the Court not only pries open the door; it rules that respecting the privacy of the jury room, as our legal system has done for centuries, violates the Constitution. This is a startling development, and although the Court tries to limit the degree of intrusion, it is doubtful that there are principled grounds for preventing the expansion of today's holding.

137 S. Ct. 874–75. It is too soon to tell what impact this decision will have on jury selection and the investigation of jury misconduct.

Prosecutors should consistently try their cases with an eye toward appellate review. This applies to potential juror misconduct to the same extent as it applies to other aspects of trial error. As with other errors, the general rule is that parties must raise the issue as soon as it is discovered or risk waiving the right to raise it later. A party waives a claim of juror misconduct if the party had the information underlying the claim before the verdict and failed to raise it with the court. In other words, "[a] defendant cannot learn of juror misconduct during the trial, gamble on a favorable verdict by remaining silent, and then complain in a post-verdict motion that the verdict was prejudicially influenced by that misconduct." *United States v. Jones*, 597 F.2d 485, 489 n.3 (5th Cir. 1979). This requirement to raise the issue of juror misconduct applies equally to alleged misconduct during jury selection and alleged misconduct during trial and deliberations.

Chapter Twenty

Preparing Openings and Closings

As I have repeatedly emphasized, this is not a book on trial advocacy skills. Rather, the focus of this book is on all of the skills and work that are required and take place outside the courtroom. Thus, the reader should not anticipate that this chapter will discuss how to present a compelling opening statement or closing argument. This chapter will not provide guidance on how to draft an opening statement or closing argument, what to say or not say, or how to say it. Rather, this short chapter will only discuss the work that should go into preparing for crafting and presenting an opening statement and closing argument, without delving into the actual art of the presentation.

A key part of preparing for oral advocacy before a jury is knowing when to prepare. The short answer is that a good prosecutor prepares as early as possible and never stops preparing. Even during the course of the investigation itself, before any charges are brought, a prosecutor should be thinking about how to talk about the evidence to a jury. A good prosecutor should even begin to take notes and jot down an outline of things to talk about to the jury. Thinking of those things in advance may affect how the prosecutor oversees the investigation. Anticipating the need to explain a defendant's financial motive for the crime to the jury, for example, a prosecutor may direct the agents to obtain financial records. Those records may not do anything to prove an essential element of the crime, but they may be absolutely necessary to persuade a jury that the defendant had a motive to commit the crime.

Opening statements and closing arguments should remain works in progress, and evolving, living things, until the moment the prosecutor presents them. Prosecutors should constantly reconsider and revise outlines of both opening statements and closing arguments as the investigations continue, after charges are brought, and throughout the pretrial preparation of the evidence and witnesses. A prosecutor may even alter the opening statement after jury selection, in light of the makeup and backgrounds of the jurors. A prosecutor most definitely should revise a closing argument multiple times during the trial in light of the evidence as it developed at trial.

A prosecutor should also consider well in advance of trial what visual aids would assist in persuading the jury of the validity of the government's case during opening statement and closing argument. People learn best when they both see and hear things. So a prosecutor should identify exhibits that could be displayed to emphasize or illustrate a point when the prosecutor is speaking to the jury. A prosecutor should consider creating charts, timelines, or other demonstrative exhibits for use during opening statement and closing argument. It is best for the prosecutor to create these visual aids early because the process of creating them often helps clarify the argument in the prosecutor's mind and may reveal holes or other defects in the prosecutor's presentation.

Lawyers often use PowerPoint or similar presentation software in opening statements and closing arguments. This method of presentation can be effective, but it can also be a terrible distraction and detract from the power of the prosecutor's presentation. When prosecutors choose to use PowerPoint slides, the fewer the words in the presentation, the better. A prosecutor does not want jurors focused on reading the slides at the expense of listening to the prosecutor's words. Worse yet is when lawyers read the slides to the jurors. PowerPoint slides should be few and concise. It is important to prepare these slides as early as possible and to have other members of the trial team or others from the prosecutor's office review the presentation to make sure it is understandable, persuasive, and free of error.

Opening statements preview the evidence the government anticipates the jury will see and hear during trial. To prepare for presenting an opening statement, therefore, a prosecutor must be able to identify the evidence the prosecutor is certain the jury will actually see and hear. This, again, is when motions in limine are important. If it is important to mention a disputable piece of evidence in opening statement, then the prosecutor needs to file a motion in limine in an effort to have the court resolve the evidentiary dispute in advance of trial. If there is any possibility the evidence will not be admitted at trial, the prosecutor would be wise not to mention it during opening statement.

In preparing to present closing arguments, prosecutors should re-evaluate the evidence in light of how it came in at trial. In the early drafts of a closing argument, a prosecutor may have focused more on some evidence and less on other, but at trial the weight of the evidence may have shifted. A prosecutor needs to revise the closing argument accordingly. It is also important the prosecutor identifies the key pieces of evidence to display and highlight during closing argument and ensures they are easily found and retrieved during closing argument, or segregated from other evidence for easy retrieval. Nothing detracts from a closing argument more than when a lawyer spends time during the argument sorting through evidence trying to find the exhibit the lawyer wants to talk about with the jury.

It is critical that prosecutors prepare a rebuttal closing argument in advance, to the extent possible. Prosecutors should know or be able to anticipate much of a what the defense counsel is likely to say during closing argument. Although a prosecutor may not be able to anticipate everything a defense attorney will say during a closing argument, if the prosecutor thinks carefully and endeavors to mentally take the place of a defense attorney, a good prosecutor should be able to anticipate almost everything the defense attorney will say. Defense attorneys are bound to talk about the government's burden of proof and the presumption of innocence. Other defense themes may become obvious from the defense counsel's opening statement or through the nature and tone of the cross-examination questions asked of government witnesses. Knowing this, a prudent prosecutor prepares outlines of rebuttal arguments addressing each of the things the prosecutor anticipates the defense attorney might say in closing. I recommend that prosecutors prepare on separate sheets of paper outlines of rebuttal arguments as to each topic. When the defense presents a closing argument, the prosecutor can then set aside any sheets on topics the defense attorney did not address and gather together the sheets on topics the defense attorney did address. Those sheets then provide the prosecutor with a ready-made outline of a rebuttal closing argument.

Just as haste in presenting rebuttal evidence can lead to error, so too may haste in responding to a defense closing argument lead to error. Indeed, a prosecutor is far more likely to improperly reference a defendant's right to remain silent, or make some other serious error, during a rebuttal closing argument than during an opening closing argument. After hearing a defense closing, a prosecutor may be emotionally worked up, especially if the defense closing involved attacks on the agents or the prosecutor. Emotions have a way of interfering with judgment. Further, when prosecutors fail to prepare for rebuttal closing arguments, they are more apt to make gaffs or use improper phrasing or words that could intrude on a defendant's constitutional rights and a fair trial. That is why it is important for prosecutors to prepare careful rebuttal closing arguments in advance of trial to the extent possible.

Chapter Twenty-One

Handling Sentencing Hearings

Although not every criminal defendant will go to trial, every convicted criminal defendant will be sentenced. A sentencing hearing is the culmination of the criminal case before the trial court. The sentence imposed on a criminal defendant reflects the seriousness of the nature of the offense, considering the history and characteristics of the defendant. Prosecutors have a heavy burden to prepare for and handle sentencing hearings so as to ensure that the public's interests are fully advanced, that victims' rights are ensured, and that the sentence sought is sufficient but not greater than necessary to achieve the goals of sentencing.

A prosecutor's goal should not be to seek the harshest sentence possible in every case against every defendant. Rather, prosecutors should seek just punishment for the crime and the criminal. Sometimes, a just punishment is the harshest sentence permitted by law. Some crimes demand severe sentences; some criminals require harsh punishment. Other crimes and other criminals may deserve leniency and mercy.

Prosecutors have a tremendous amount of discretion to affect a defendant's sentence. Although a judge will ultimately impose the sentence, by choosing the charges the prosecutor has the ability to set the parameters of the judge's sentencing options. Prosecutors may also influence the sentence through plea negotiations or by the positions they take regarding sentencing issues. Prosecutors should be thinking of the sentencing implications their decisions may have, then, at each stage of prosecution.

In the federal system, prosecutors are responsible for ushering the case through a series of steps in the sentencing process. Although the practice may differ from district to district, it is generally advisable for prosecutors to provide the US Probation Office with an offense conduct statement to assist the probation officer in drafting the Presentence Investigation Report (PSR).

Once the probation officer issues a draft PSR, the prosecutor must review it and file any objections deemed appropriate. Prosecutors need to decide whether to seek upward or downward departures or variances from the advisory guidelines sentence. Once the prosecutor has identified the contested sentencing issues, the prosecutor must identify the witnesses and exhibits that will be necessary to present at the sentencing hearing. Prosecutors should file sentencing briefs in contested cases, setting forth the facts and applying the relevant law to those facts. Prosecutors must also be cognizant of any victim issues, including the right of victims to speak at the sentencing hearing and the obligation to seek restitution for victims. Prosecutors should prepare remarks or arguments advocating for the sentence they believe is warranted and just. Finally, during the sentencing hearing prosecutors should ensure that the judge fully complies with the procedural requirements and law regarding sentencings and alert the court of any mistakes or omissions. I will briefly discuss a prosecutor's responsibilities at each of these stages in the sentencing process.

DRAFTING AN OFFENSE CONDUCT STATEMENT

The first step in the sentencing process after a defendant has pleaded guilty or been found guilty is the preparation of a Presentence Investigation Report. A US Probation Officer prepares the PSR. A PSR contains a significant amount of information, including basic identification information about the defendant; a summary of the procedural history of the case; a summary of the defendant's performance while on pretrial release when applicable; a summary of any plea agreement; an offense conduct section in which the probation officer summarizes the pertinent offense conduct and relevant criminal conduct; a calculation of the US Sentencing Guidelines as applied to the offense; a determination of the defendant's criminal history category under the guidelines; a section regarding the defendant's history and characteristics, including his or her family, education, and employment, physical and mental health, and substance abuse history; and sections addressing any victim or restitution issues. Both the government and the defendant may submit position papers to the probation officer for all of these and any other sentencing issues. The government's position paper is often entitled an Offense Conduct Statement, which is a bit of a misnomer. A good position paper should address far more than a summary of the defendant's offense conduct. Nevertheless, for ease of reference I will refer to the government's position paper as an Offense Conduct Statement, or OCS.

Prosecutors should take advantage of this step in the process and provide the probation office with an OCS. This is an opportunity for the prosecutor to summarize the facts of the case in a manner that the prosecutor believes is accurate and pertinent to the sentencing issues in the case. Probation officers will review the government's discovery file and draft an offense conduct section based on the officer's own assessment of the facts. By providing the probation officers with a thorough OCS summarizing the facts of the case, however, the prosecutor has the ability to influence the manner in which the probation officer drafts the fact section and ensure the accuracy and completeness of the facts. The more accurate the prosecutor is, the more likely the probation officer will adopt the facts as summarized by the prosecutor. I found it particularly helpful to reference source materials in the OCS whenever possible, such as referencing specific exhibits or transcripts, to make the probation officer's job easier and to ensure the probation officer would accurately summarize the facts.

In drafting the offense conduct section of an OCS, it is important that the prosecutor focus on the facts relevant to sentencing. The case may have involved a lot of facts, particularly if it went to trial, that were important to persuade a jury of the defendant's guilt or the credibility of witnesses but that have no bearing on the sentence to be imposed. For example, in a bank robbery case the fact the bank was insured by the FDIC is an essential element of the offense. Nevertheless, whether the bank was federally insured has no impact on the sentence the court should impose. There may also be facts contained in the government's discovery file that are relevant to the sentence that were never presented at trial for any number of reasons. For example, the prosecutor may have evidence the defendant engaged in other criminal conduct that the prosecutor chose for strategic reasons not to introduce at trial under Federal Rule of Evidence 404(b). For purposes of sentencing, however, those other crimes may constitute relevant criminal conduct that could impact the defendant's sentence. Thus, prosecutors must critically re-evaluate the evidence with a view of identifying the facts that are relevant and important for purposes of sentencing instead of those facts that were important to establish the defendant's guilt.

In the fact section, it is important that prosecutors include all of the facts that are part of the defendant's relevant criminal conduct. A judge may sentence a defendant not only for the criminal conduct that constituted the offense of conviction, but also for any other relevant criminal conduct. Relevant criminal conduct can even include criminal conduct of which the jury acquitted the defendant. *United States v. Watts*, 519 US 148, 154 (1997) ("In short, we are convinced that a sentencing court may consider conduct of which a defendant has been acquitted"). Section 1B1.3 of the US Sentencing

Guidelines describes in broad terms the conduct that a sentencing court may consider in determining the applicable guideline range. This includes "all acts and omissions . . . that were part of the same course of conduct or common scheme or plan as the offense of conviction." USSG §1B1.3(a)(2). The commentary to that section states: "Conduct that is not formally charged or is not an element of the offense of conviction may enter into the determination of the applicable guideline sentencing range." USSG §1B1.3, comment., backg'd. Section 1B1.4 of the guidelines, in turn, reflects the policy set forth in 18 U.S.C. § 3661:

> In determining the sentence to impose within the guideline range, or whether a departure from the guidelines is warranted, the court may consider, without limitation, any information concerning the background, character and conduct of the defendant, unless otherwise prohibited by law. *See* 18 USC § 3661.

USSG §1B1.4. So prosecutors should include in the fact section any facts that a sentencing judge may consider in determining a defendant's sentence.

There is a legion of reported cases addressing the issue of whether a sentence is appropriate when the defendant's sentence is based more on conduct that was not part of the crime of conviction than on the conduct that resulted in the conviction. For example, a defendant who was convicted of being a felon in possession of a firearm could be sentenced for murdering the person from whom he stole the firearm, even though proof of the murder was not required for his conviction. Some courts and commentators have criticized sentences based on such relevant criminal conduct by analogizing it to a tail wagging the dog. Some courts attempted to address this perceived imbalance by requiring the government to prove this other criminal conduct by clear and convincing evidence, instead of a preponderance of the evidence that is the usual burden of proof at sentencing. The fact that the guidelines are merely advisory now, however, renders that debate academic. *United States v. Reuter*, 463 F.3d 792, 793 (7th Cir. 2006).

A prosecutor's OCS should contain far more than a summary of the relevant criminal conduct. A prosecutor should also include a section regarding any misconduct on pretrial release, when applicable, a calculation of the guidelines score and the defendant's criminal history category, identification of any grounds for a departure or variance from the guidelines and the grounds for that position, and, when applicable, information regarding victims, restitution, and any other collateral sentencing matters. Probation officers are usually not lawyers, yet they will interpret the guidelines and case law and apply them to a case in the manner the officer believes is appropriate. Most probation officers become experts on the guidelines and perform this task as well as most lawyers. Nevertheless, it is incumbent upon the prosecutor to set forth how the prosecutor believes the guidelines should be applied. When appropriate, the OCS should contain case citations and argument regarding why the prosecutor believes the guidelines should be applied in a particular manner. The same need to cite authority and explain the government's position is true for any assertion that a departure or variance from the guidelines is appropriate.

Finally, the prosecutor's OCS should contain information for any other facts that are relevant to a defendant's sentence. Those facts include anything that would be relevant to the factors set forth at Title 18, US Code, Section 3553(a). Prosecutors will seldom have information about the defendant's personal life, physical or mental condition, education, employment, or substance abuse history. When, however, the prosecutor does have access to such information, the prosecutor should include it in the OCS.

REVIEWING AND OBJECTING TO A DRAFT PSR

Once a probation officer completes a draft PSR, the officer distributes copies to the parties. Prosecutors should review the PSR for any errors. Obviously, the prosecutor should review the offense conduct section for factual accuracy and compare the guidelines calculations against the prosecutor's calculations as reflected in the government's OCS. The prosecutor's review of the draft PSR for possible errors must extend beyond these sections, however. The prosecutor should ensure that the probation officer applied the proper version of the guidelines. The prosecutor should also review the scoring of criminal history points and make sure that the probation officer properly scored prior convictions. In short, the prosecutor should not assume that any portion of the draft PSR is correct and double-check all of the probation officer's work. As an officer of the court and a prosecutor whose duty it is to seek justice, the prosecutor should be equally alert to, and point out, errors that favor the defendant as much as those that would favor the government.

When prosecutors find errors in the draft PSR, they should file objections to the draft report. Failure to do so may constitute a waiver of any claim of error. When making objections to the draft report, it is important that prosecutors be precise. A prosecutor should cite the specific paragraph of the draft PSR at issue and state precisely the nature of the government's objection. If the objection is to a fact in the offense conduct section, the prosecutor should provide a reference to evidence that would back up the prosecutor's objection, or explain in some detail the expected testimony or evidence the prosecutor intends to provide at the time of the sentencing hearing to establish the disputed fact.

If the objection is to the calculation of the guidelines, either for the offense level or the scoring of defendant's criminal history, it is again important that the prosecutor cite with precision the disputed paragraph of the PSR and articulate with clarity the basis for the objection. Prosecutors may also want to provide case authority in the objection letter explaining the legal basis upon which the prosecutor is making the objection. A probation officer may change the PSR in light of the prosecutor's authority. Even if a prosecutor is unable to persuade the probation officer to change the PSR, a thoroughly articulated and supported objection still serves to clarify the legal issue that the judge will have to resolve at the time of sentencing.

DETERMINING WHETHER TO
SEEK DEPARTURES OR VARIANCES

Probation officers will often indicate whether the officer has identified any grounds for a departure or variance. A prosecutor may or may not agree with the probation officer's assessment. If the prosecutor disagrees, then the prosecutor should object and state the reasons, and perhaps the case law, just as the prosecutor would object to any guidelines issue. Regardless of the probation officer's view, however, the prosecutor should make an independent assessment of whether a departure or variance from the advisory guidelines range is appropriate.

Prosecutors should carefully consider each and every possible departure provision in Chapter 5 of the US Sentencing Guidelines. Prosecutors should fairly evaluate whether the facts of the case or the characteristics of the defendant merit either an upward or downward variance. Similarly, prosecutors should consider each of the factors set forth at Title 18, US Code, Section 3553(a) to determine if the court should vary either upward or downward from the advisory guidelines range. The credibility of the prosecutor at sentencing, and by extension the US government, may turn on a prosecutor's willingness to concede that there are valid grounds for either a downward departure or downward variance. Even if a prosecutor believes that the sentencing judge should not exercise the discretion to depart or vary downward from the advisory guidelines range, the prosecutor should be willing to concede, when they exist, that there are facts upon which a court could depart or vary downward. The prosecutor may then, with greater credibility, argue that the judge should nevertheless not exercise the discretion to depart or vary downward. Prosecutors need to remember that even, and perhaps especially, at the sentencing stage the prosecutor's goal is to seek justice.

PREPARING THE EVIDENCE

When a prosecutor is faced with a contested sentencing hearing, the prosecutor must determine whether there will be a need to present evidence. Many contested sentencing issues do not require new evidence. The factual basis upon which the contested issue turns may be contained in the unobjected-to portions of the PSR. In other cases, the factual basis may already be in the record as a result of the trial. In still other contested sentencing hearings, the dispute is over the application of the law to undisputed facts.

In some cases, however, there may be a need for prosecutors to present evidence at the sentencing hearing. Prosecutors need to be sensitive to the requirement to prove any facts in the PSR to which the defendant has lodged an objection. Sentencing judges cannot rely on facts in the PSR to which a defendant has lodged an objection without making a factual finding based on an evidentiary showing. A prosecutor may also need to present evidence at the sentencing hearing to support a sentencing enhancement based on relevant criminal conduct that was not part of the facts of conviction, or to support an upward departure or variance motion.

When preparing to present evidence at a contested sentencing hearing, prosecutors should tailor the presentation for the audience and the setting. What I mean by that is that prosecutors need to remember that the judge is the finder of fact at the sentencing hearing, the standard of proof is by a preponderance of the evidence, and the Federal Rules of Evidence do not apply. Prosecutors should not prepare evidence, in other words, as if they are preparing to prove their case to a jury beyond a reasonable doubt within the confines of the evidentiary rules. With this in mind, prosecutors should streamline the evidentiary presentation, using the minimal number of witnesses and exhibits necessary to meet the evidentiary burden. Prosecutors should dispense with the type of background questions often asked of witnesses at trial designed to personalize the witness for the jury. Prosecutors can also safely assume that the sentencing judge has a base of knowledge that obviates the need for witnesses to provide explanations of things that prosecutors would normally need to have explained to a jury (e.g., what it means to front drugs). So prosecutors should excise such surplusage from the outlines of questions for witnesses. Of course, prosecutors must still be aware of the need to make an adequate record for appeal, which may require the prosecutor to ask some questions, the answers to which are obvious to everyone in the courtroom, including the judge. For example, even though judges are aware that firearms are tools of the drug trade, if a prosecutor needs to establish that a sentencing enhancement is appropriate in a felon-in-possession-of-a-firearm case because the felon possessed the firearm in connection with the felony offense of distributing drugs, then the prosecutor will need to establish that fact as part of the record through testimony.

The Sixth Amendment's confrontation clause does not apply to sentencing hearings. Nevertheless, the government may violate a defendant's Fifth Amendment due process rights when presenting hearsay evidence at a sentencing hearing where the defendant was deprived of the opportunity to confront the witness. Generally speaking, in determining whether a defendant's inability to confront the witness violates the defendant's due process rights, courts look at two factors. First, a court will assess the explanation a prosecutor offers as to why confrontation is undesirable or impractical, such as when live testimony would pose a danger to the witness or the burden of producing the witness would be inordinately difficult or expensive. Second, a court will consider the overall reliability of the hearsay testimony that the prosecutor offers in place of live testimony. A cautious prosecutor will strive to produce live testimony whenever possible even though the confrontation clause does not apply at a sentencing hearing. When a prosecutor presents hearsay testimony, however, the prosecutor should present evidence that satisfies the court of good cause for not producing live testimony and establishes that the hearsay testimony was otherwise reliable.

Aside from tailoring the presentation of evidence at a sentencing hearing for the judge as fact finder, prosecutors should otherwise prepare for an evidentiary sentencing hearing much as they would for trial. Some sentencing hearings can resemble mini-trials. Indeed, I had several sentencing hearings that involved calling more than a dozen witnesses and consumed days of testimony. Thus, prosecutors should devote time and attention to preparing for the presentation of evidence in contested sentencing hearings. This means that exhibits should be organized in an understandable and logical manner. Prosecutors should prepare witnesses for direct examination and cross-examination, including reviewing marked exhibits with the witnesses. Prosecutors should also consider the need to generate charts, graphs, summaries, or other demonstrative exhibits that would aid the judge in understanding the disputed facts.

DRAFTING THE SENTENCING BRIEF

The parties may, but generally are not required to, file sentencing briefs in advance of contested sentencing hearings. Whether required or not, prosecutors should take advantage of this opportunity to advocate for the government's position in writing by filing a sentencing brief in any contested sentencing. In a sentencing brief, a prosecutor has the ability to logically address each of the contested sentencing issues, summarize any pertinent facts, and provide legal authority for the government's position. Effective advocacy involves taking every opportunity to argue one's position. This is particularly true for the government when advocating a position to a judge. Judges may be inclined to rule in favor of a criminal defendant whenever they are unsure of the correct answer. Judges are more likely to feel comfortable that they know the right answer when they have adequate time to learn the facts and the law on a disputed issue. So judges are more likely to rule in the government's favor, when the facts and law warrant it, when judges are prepared. Sentencing briefs serve as a means of preparing a judge in advance of the sentencing hearing.

In drafting sentencing briefs, prosecutors should be sure to write to the audience. The audience includes, of course, the sentencing judge. But prosecutors should keep in mind that the audience may also include others. Sentencing briefs are public documents. What the prosecutor says in the sentencing brief may be read by the defendant, the victims, the public, and the press. Thus, although the prosecutor should write the sentencing brief with the goal of persuading the judge—the fact finder and legal arbiter—prosecutors need to keep in mind the effect of what the prosecutor writes may have on the others who may read the sentencing brief. This means that a prosecutor may want to change the tone or verbiage the prosecutor uses so as not to offend a victim or risk the press quoting something in the brief out of context, for example.

With the primary goal in drafting a sentencing memorandum of persuading the judge to rule in the government's favor, prosecutors should endeavor to write the sentencing memorandum in a manner that is designed to help the judge. To do this, prosecutors should think about how judges approach sentencing hearings. In federal court, judges first determine the application of the US Sentencing Guidelines (including any departure issues), then consider whether a variance from the advisory guidelines range is appropriate, followed by the resolution of any collateral matters that may be in dispute (such as restitution). So to be the most helpful to a sentencing judge, prosecutors would be wise to organize their sentencing briefs in the same manner.

Further, judges are properly focused on procedural error. In other words, although a federal judge will ultimately decide a sentence based on the totality of the factors at Title 18, US Code, Section 3553(a), they must make sure before they reach the ultimate decision that they do so in a procedurally correct manner. Significant procedural errors include failing to calculate the guidelines correctly, failing to calculate the guidelines range at all, or treating the guidelines as mandatory. It can also include, for example, a judge should not resolve a variance issue before first determining the applicable advisory guidelines range. Similarly, in determining a defendant's sentence a judge cannot consider something in the PSR to which the defendant objected unless

the judge has properly overruled the objection. A sentencing judge may also commit a procedural error by failing to consider the factors at Title 18, US Code, Section 3553(a), or by relying on clearly erroneous facts. This means for prosecutors that they should ensure that their sentencing briefs call upon the judge to resolve issues in a procedurally correct order and manner, and that they do not invite the sentencing judge to commit a procedural error in any way.

To further aid the sentencing judge, prosecutors should be careful to cite to the portion of the presentence investigation report that is at issue in the dispute. The dispute may relate to the facts in the offense conduct section, or it may relate to something in the calculation of the defendant's criminal history score. It is important that prosecutors cite to every paragraph of the PSR affected by the dispute. For example, a factual dispute about the offense conduct may impact the calculation of the offense level under the guidelines. Prosecutors should identify how the resolution of the dispute will affect the calculation of the guidelines.

It is also important that prosecutors provide citations to the factual record and legal authorities upon which they are basing their arguments. Prosecutors should provide sentencing judges with firm grounds upon which to rule in the government's favor such that an appellate court will affirm the district court's decision. It is incumbent upon prosecutors to provide that basis for the sentencing judge instead of trusting that the sentencing judge will make the record for the prosecutor.

Finally, the prosecutor's sentencing brief should fully address every contested issue. This includes all sentencing guidelines issues, criminal history scoring, departures, and variances. Prosecutors should also fully address any collateral consequences that are at issue, such as restitution, deportation, and the like. In short, in their sentencing briefs prosecutors should strive to provide sentencing judges with a road map for resolving all disputed issues at the sentencing hearing.

Judges have a vast amount of discretion in determining a criminal defendant's sentence. In the federal system, this discretion is reflected in the very broad factors set forth at Title 18, US Code, Section 3553(a). In short, judges can base sentences upon the nature and circumstances of the offense, the history and characteristics of the defendant, and the need to accomplish the goals of sentencing, including such things as deterrence and protection of the community. With this in mind, prosecutors' sentencing briefs should fully address all of the factors a judge should consider in determining sentences. This is an area where I find prosecutors' sentencing briefs often lacking. Prosecutors will usually fully address the application of the guidelines but completely fail to address other factors, particularly the goals of sentencing.

Prosecutors should use sentencing briefs to advocate for the government's position regarding why the requested sentence would advance all of the applicable goals of sentencing.

ASSESSING VICTIM ISSUES

When crimes have resulted in victims, certain issues may arise at sentencing hearings regarding the crime victims. These include the right of victims to be heard, victim restitution, and victim expectations. Prosecutors need to assess the crime victim issues and be prepared to address them at the sentencing hearing.

As noted in chapter 18, crime victims have certain statutory rights, and it is the prosecutor's duty to ensure that those rights are maintained. Those rights include the right of crime victims to address the court at the time of sentencing. Crime victims may do this by providing the sentencing judge with written victim-impact statements, but they also have the right to orally address the court at the time of the sentencing hearing. In advance of the sentencing hearing, prosecutors need to meet with the crime victims, or have a victim coordinator do so, to ensure the victims are fully informed of their rights and to determine if any of them want to provide victim-impact statements in writing or orally. If victims wish to address the court orally, prosecutors should ensure they are fully briefed about the layout of the courtroom, they are aware of the sentencing procedures so that they understand when during the hearing they will have an opportunity to speak, and they understand that their statements should be made to the judge and not at the defendant.

Some crime victims may be due restitution. Sometimes the amount of restitution is not in dispute, but often a criminal defendant will contest whether a particular victim is factually entitled to restitution at all, or contest the amount of restitution the victim has claimed. Prosecutors owe it to crime victims to try to obtain restitution that will make crime victims whole. It is the crime victim's—and thus the prosecutor's—burden to prove the basis for the victim's restitution. This means that prosecutors must work hard to develop the evidence necessary to prove crime victims' claims. Victims may have difficulty understanding the need for them to prove anything and may be defensive about the obligation. Prosecutors have to tread carefully here to make sure that victims understand the need to help the prosecutor help them by gathering whatever evidence is required to establish a basis for the court to award restitution to the victims. This may also involve preparing the crime victims to testify at the sentencing hearing about restitution claims.

Finally, sentencing hearings are also one of, if not the most, emotional and difficult proceedings for crime victims to endure. Crime victims are likely to have certain expectations coming into a sentencing hearing regarding both the procedure and the sentence that the court will impose. These expectations may not be realistic or correct. Victims' expectations may be based on popular culture or a misunderstanding of the facts or the law. Prosecutors need to manage these expectations. Although victim coordinators can help prepare victims for sentencing hearings, I firmly believe that this is one area where prosecutors should not fully delegate this duty. Rather, prosecutors should meet personally with crime victims to prepare them for all aspects of the sentencing hearing. Prosecutors should explain the judge's sentencing discretion, describe any statutory limitations on sentencing, describe the role of sentencing guidelines, and answer questions from the victims about the sentencing hearing.

PREPARING REMARKS

Before a sentencing hearing, a prosecutor should prepare for making an argument to the judge regarding the appropriate sentence to be imposed. During every sentencing hearing, prosecutors have an opportunity to address the judge and articulate the government's position regarding the proper sentence. This opportunity comes after the judge has ruled upon any contested issues. Thus, prosecutors should prepare for argument with variations that may depend upon how the judge rules on the issues.

Prosecutors should not just wing this opportunity to orally advocate for the government's position. Rather, a prosecutor should prepare careful notes regarding the sentence the judge should impose and why. Just as with the sentencing brief, this argument should specifically address the factors judges consider in arriving at the appropriate sentence. In federal courts, those factors are found at Title 18, US Code, Section 3553(a). In particular, prosecutors should address how the sentence the government is seeking furthers the goals of sentencing.

It is important in making argument to the judge that a prosecutor not simply repeat what the prosecutor wrote in the sentencing brief. As with any oral advocacy, the best advocates use the written word as a basis upon which to base oral argument and do not simply orally repeat the written word. It is also important that prosecutors address any evidence that may have been offered, or findings made by the judge, during the sentencing hearing. Further, in cases involving victims, prosecutors should be certain to address how the victims' interests are advanced by the sentence the government is seeking.

In making argument, prosecutors should keep in mind the audience, just as the prosecutor should consider the audience in drafting the sentencing brief. Again, the primary audience is the sentencing judge, the decision-maker who will decide and impose the sentence. At the same time, prosecutors should consider the impact their remarks may have on others, such as victims, and how the remarks may be viewed by the public, the press, and other potential defendants.

MONITORING THE COURT'S COMPLIANCE WITH PROCEDURES

Although the sentencing judge is required to comply with all sentencing procedures and constitutional requirements when imposing a sentence, prosecutors have a duty to monitor this and ensure that the judge fulfills this responsibility. In federal court, as noted, judges may commit procedural error by failing to consider sentencing factors or applying them in the wrong order. Similarly, an appellate court may reverse and remand for resentencing a case when a judge forgets to give a defendant the opportunity to exercise the right of allocution or fails to advise the defendant of the right to appeal. Prosecutors should go to sentencing hearings with a checklist and make sure that the judge covers everything and does so in the correct order.

Chapter Twenty-Two

Appeals

A prosecutor's job is not over until the case has been successfully defended on appeal. Criminal defendants have a right to appeal any conviction or sentence to a higher court unless that right is waived. If a criminal defendant pleads guilty, the defendant waives the right to appeal any prior order (such as an order denying a motion to dismiss an indictment or suppress evidence). By entering into a conditional plea agreement, however, a defendant may negotiate with the government the right to appeal such orders after sentencing. For example, a defendant may plead guilty, but on condition that the defendant have the right to appeal the court's order denying a motion to suppress evidence. In such a case, the matter would proceed to sentencing and after judgment is entered file an appeal. If a criminal defendant goes to trial, the defendant may appeal both the conviction and any order the court previously entered. Criminal defendants generally have the right to appeal the sentence the court imposes, whether the defendant pleaded guilty or was found guilty after trial, unless, again, the defendant waives that right as part of a plea agreement. The government will sometimes require an appeal waiver as part of a plea agreement, barring a defendant from appealing the sentence. Prosecutors may consider whether to require defendants to waive appeal as part of a plea agreement whenever the government provides a significant concession to a defendant as part of a plea bargain, especially if that concession is related to sentencing issues. As a general observation, although some defendants waive appeal and others chose not to appeal, a significant number of criminal cases result in an appeal of some issue. During my twenty years as a prosecutor, about one-third of the cases I prosecuted were appealed.

In some prosecutors' offices, the prosecutor who handled the district court litigation is also responsible for handling the appeal. In other offices, particularly larger offices, there is an appellate attorney or division with multiple attorneys who are responsible for handling all appeals. Other offices may have a hybrid method for handling appeals, with the trial attorney responsible for handling the briefing but not argument, or for handling certain appeals but perhaps not the appeals in more complex cases. Whatever the arrangements for handling appeals, there are a number of things for prosecutors to consider in preparing a criminal case for a possible appeal. There are other things prosecutors should consider doing in preparing for appeal of criminal cases after a defendant has filed a notice of appeal. Once again, this is not a trial advocacy book, so I will not talk about appellate advocacy here. Rather, my focus will be on the work that prosecutors do outside the courtroom.

PREPARING FOR POSSIBLE APPEALS

A prosecutor should think about a possible appeal throughout the life of a criminal case. Some of the decisions that prosecutors make during the course of an investigation and prosecution may affect both the likelihood of an appeal and the likelihood that the government would prevail on appeal. Some searches and interrogations are more constitutionally questionable than others. Some charges are more aggressive than others, based on the evidence in the case. The admissibility of some evidence is riskier under the rules of evidence than other evidence. As I noted in the first chapter of this book, prosecutors have a lot of discretion. Discretion is sometimes the better part of valor. In other words, prosecutors should weigh the costs and benefits when making decisions. Among the primary considerations when prosecutors make decisions are the probability that a decision will result in an appeal and the prosecutor's ability to defend that decision on appeal. Also, when making the decisions, and in making a record below regarding the decisions, prosecutors should take the actions and present the evidence necessary to enhance the government's position on appeal.

Knowing how to enhance the record for appeal requires prosecutors to be familiar with appellate decisions. It is important that prosecutors keep abreast of the law, including paying attention to the facts the appellate judges found important in reaching decisions. In other words, prosecutors should not just focus on the holdings of cases, but rather also carefully consider the factual basis for the decisions. An awareness of the facts that were critical to appellate decisions can inform a prosecutor's decision about what type of record the prosecutor needs to make at the trial level to make sure that the case is in the best position for success on appeal. When prosecutors spot issues in their cases that they recognize may result in an appeal, they may want to perform some research specifically looking for the facts in similar cases that affected the outcome of similar cases. When prosecutors are able to identify the type of facts that are important for the legal analysis, they may be able to take steps to enhance the record so as to increase the chances of success on appeal.

For example, in a case where a defendant has challenged the constitutionality of an officer's conduct in stopping the defendant and performing a pat-down search, the case law indicates that courts look to the totality of the circumstances to determine if the officer had reasonable suspicion to justify the stop. The phrase "totality of the circumstances" is not helpful. What is helpful is knowing what specific circumstances courts have found important in finding that officers had reasonable suspicion. If courts within the circuit have repeatedly noted whether the location of the stop was a high crime area, or whether it was dark out, or whether the stop took place in a public area where others were present, then a prosecutor knows to elicit that information from officers during a hearing.

PREPARING FOR A GOVERNMENT'S APPEAL

The government is the appellant in relatively few criminal cases for very practical reasons. Unless the government seeks an interlocutory appeal, the government waives the right to challenge any pretrial ruling, such as an order suppressing evidence. Similarly, if a jury acquits the defendant, the Double Jeopardy Clause prohibits the government from appealing the decision and retrying the defendant. On the other hand, the government may seek interlocutory appeal of a judge's pretrial orders in certain circumstances and does do so in some instances. The government may also appeal a judge's sentencing order.

When appealing a district court's decision, the government has an especially heavy burden. Trial judges' rulings on constitutional issues are reviewed by appellate courts on a de novo basis regarding the judges' legal conclusions, but almost always the trial judges' factual findings are reviewed under a deferential abuse of discretion standard. Similarly, appellate courts will review a trial judge's evidentiary rulings under the deferential abuse of discretion standard. Finally, judges have a lot of discretion when imposing sentences, so most sentencing decisions are generally reviewed under a deferential standard except for application of the law, such as the sentencing judge's interpretation of the US Sentencing Guidelines.

The government should use caution in deciding whether to appeal a district judge's decision. An adverse trial court decision affects a single case and often a single defendant. And although it provides some precedent, the impact is usually limited and local. On the other hand, if the government unsuccessfully appeals a trial judge, an adverse appellate decision may impact many cases and set adverse precedent that can have a much more wide-ranging and long-lasting impact. For that reason, in the federal system supervisory approval is required before line prosecutors are allowed to file an appeal. In the federal system, there is a fairly formal and involved approval process whereby line prosecutors must first get approval from the US Attorney to appeal, and then obtain approval from the Solicitor General's Office in Washington, D.C., before prosecutors can file an affirmative appeal of a district court judge's ruling.

When prosecutors are given permission to appeal a district judge's decision, the stakes are high. Ensuring success on appeal begins with writing a compelling appellate brief. This is when excellent writing skills are imperative. An appellate brief must be concise, precise, and persuasive. It must identify the narrow issue on appeal and firmly establish the legal basis upon which the government asserts the district court erred. Appellate judges will expect the prosecutor to provide an adequate factual basis, with reliable citations to the record, so that the judges have a firm and clear understanding of the facts. I have heard from many appellate judges how important the facts are to them; one can trust that they generally know the law and what they often need the most help with is understanding the material facts of the case of which they have no knowledge. The importance of facts to appellate judges should reinforce how important it is for prosecutors to know what facts are important in advance of litigating an issue at the district court level, and to develop those facts with an eye toward a possible appeal.

Writing to the audience—appellate judges who know the law and not the facts—is paramount. Prudent prosecutors will subject their appellate briefs to multiple layers of review by other prosecutors to hone the finished product to be the best that it can be. There are many books written on effective and persuasive legal writing, and still others on writing appellate briefs. It is not my goal to replicate or elaborate on these tracts. Rather, the point I endeavor to emphasize here is how important it is that the government's appellant's brief be the best possible example of legal writing. Prosecutors should read and consult these other books on writing in an effort to achieve that goal. Too much is at stake.

Prosecutors should devote a lot of effort when preparing to argue an appellate case when the government is the appellant. First, a prosecutor should ask for as much time to argue the case as possible. Appellate arguments go incredibly fast, and the more time the prosecutor has to explain the case and the government's position, the better the chance of success. Typically, appellate courts will schedule only ten or fifteen minutes per side for argument.

When the government is the appellant, the prosecutor should ask for twenty or thirty minutes. If the case is important enough for the prosecutor to appeal the district court's decision, it is important enough to secure enough time before the appellate court to fully air the issue. Second, a prosecutor should know the record cold; indeed, a prosecutor should memorize key portions of it. In advance of argument it may be helpful to tab portions of the transcript or other portions of the record for easy and quick reference to those portions most likely to be the focus of judicial inquiry during the oral argument. Third, a prosecutor should prepare remarks that are not a mere repetition of the prosecutor's brief, but rather a synthesized version of the essential part of the argument. A prosecutor can fairly safely assume that the appellate judges will be especially prepared for a case when the government is appealing a district judge in a criminal case and will have read the prosecutor's brief.

Again, oral advocacy is a subject of many books and entire law school classes. This is not a book on advocacy and so I will not attempt here to substitute my views for those who are experts in this area. Again, my goal here is to simply emphasize the need for prosecutors to be especially prepared for oral arguments when the government is the appellant. An adverse decision could have significant adverse consequences. A good appellate argument, however, can make a huge difference in the appellate judge's understanding of the issues. In my experience, I can think of only a handful of cases when I believe my appellate arguments made a difference in the outcome of the case; four of them occurred when the government was the appellant.

PREPARING FOR A DEFENDANT'S APPEAL

The government is the appellee in the vast majority of criminal cases considered on appeal. In stark contrast to cases when the government appeals a district judge's decision, appeals by defendants pose a much lower risk to the government. The defendant has the burden on appeal, and the standard of review is generally deferential to the trial judge on most issues. Further, if the prosecutor made wise decisions throughout the case, the possibility of reversible error is usually small. It follows, then, that the government wins the vast majority of appellate decisions in which it appears as appellee.

A prosecutor must, nevertheless, take criminal appeals very seriously and prepare assiduously for them. A poorly executed appellate case can snatch defeat out of the jaws of victory. An adverse ruling on appeal can also, in some cases, have an adverse impact far beyond the instant case. It can establish unfavorable precedent that the prosecutor, and other prosecutors, must live with for years to come.

After a defendant has filed a notice of appeal, the prosecutor has a lot of work to perform in preparing for the appeal. Prosecutors should ensure that the appellate record, that is the record that the appellate judges will have, is complete. Although the district court clerk of court is responsible for getting the record to the court of appeals, prosecutors should endeavor to double-check the record and seek to supplement it when necessary.

Prosecutors should also monitor the defendant's compliance with appellate rules. Defendants must meet a deadline for filing a notice of appeal, and that deadline is jurisdictional. Further, defendants have a responsibility to file timely designations of the records and briefs. Prosecutors should hold defense counsel to the obligation to comply with these rules.

I will not repeat here the need for the government's brief to be well written; as well written when the government is the appellee as when the government is the appellant. Appellate judges will often read the government's appellate brief first, even when the defendant is the appellant, because they expect the government's brief will be better written and more concisely and precisely state the facts and the law. Appellate judges will, again, focus much attention to the facts of the case, which emphasizes how important it is for prosecutors to adequately develop the facts for the record on appeal, and to then make sure the full record reaches the appellate court.

It bears mentioning that prosecutors should be willing to concede error when it becomes clear that error occurred below. If, after the heat of battle is over and upon reflection and review of the record a prosecutor believes the trial judge erred, perhaps because of a position the prosecutor urged, the prosecutor should concede that error. Perhaps the error is harmless, or perhaps there is some other ground upon which, despite the error, the government may prevail on appeal. Nevertheless, if the district court erred, then the prosecutor should be willing to concede it, and if the error was a result of the government's urging, the prosecutor should confess it.

Preparing for oral argument in cases when the defendant has appealed is generally less stressful than when the government is seeking to reverse the trial court. Nevertheless, prosecutors should prepare thoroughly for oral argument. A poor oral argument could cause defeat. That said, in many criminal appeals the case is not a close one, and prosecutors need not feel compelled to use all of the time allotted them in argument if it is clear that the appellate judges are not concerned.

Notes

CHAPTER ONE

1. Nick Drees graduated with honors from Harvard with a bachelor's degree and the University of Chicago with a law degree. After working for years in state and federal courts as an assistant public defender, he became the Federal Public Defender for Iowa in 1994. He remained in that position until he passed away in 2011 after a courageous battle with a rare form of thyroid cancer.

CHAPTER FOUR

1. Before lawyers use phrases, it is helpful to know what they actually mean. A red herring is a cured and salted herring. The phrase originated in late 1700s, but it came into vogue after 1805 when an English journalist claimed he used red herrings to mislead bloodhounds on a trail. The story quickly became a metaphor for misleading someone.

CHAPTER FIVE

1. Roberta Flowers, *An Unholy Alliance: The Ex Parte Relationship between the Judge and the Prosecutor*, 79 NEB. L. REV. 251, 253 (2000) ("This constant contact causes the relationship to take on characteristics that are different from the relationship between the judge and other lawyers. The creation of this interdependent relationship may produce a 'team spirit' between the court and prosecutor, which is counter to the fundamental philosophy of the adversary system") (footnote omitted). *See also* Walter W. Steele Jr., *Unethical Prosecutors and Inadequate Discipline*, 38 SW L. J. 965, 972 (1984) (referring to the development of "team-member" mentality between judges and prosecutors).

2. Stephen Lubet, *Ex Parte Communications: An Issue in Judicial Conduct*, 74 JUDICATURE 96, 97 (1990).

3. *See United States v. Leon*, 468 US 897, 920–21 (1984) (holding that disputed evidence will be admitted if it was objectively reasonable for the officer executing a search warrant to have relied in good faith on the judge's determination that there was probable cause to issue the warrant).

4. *See, e.g., Dennis v. United States*, 339 US 162, 182 (1950) (Frankfurter, J., dissenting) ("The appearance of impartiality is an essential manifestation of its reality"); *Offutt v. United States*, 348 US 11, 14 (1954) (stating that "justice must satisfy the appearance of justice").

CHAPTER SEVEN

1. I was involved tangentially in the prosecution of a couple people tied to a mobster who attempted to set up a drug trafficking organization in our district and dealt with a cooperating witness who was a "made" member of a mafia family. I also served on the Attorney General's Capital Crimes Review Committee, where my duties included reviewing potential capital cases, several of which involved murders committed by mobsters.

CHAPTER EIGHT

1. Of course, prosecutors should keep in mind the sequestration rule and not disclose to the cooperator what another witness said if the cooperator may also be a witness.

2. Although there are ways of presenting the government's case and questioning a cooperator at trial that can also enhance the believability of a cooperator, as noted this book is not about trial advocacy but, rather, all the work involved in prosecution outside the courtroom. The reader should, however, consult trial advocacy and other texts on this subject before questioning a cooperator at trial.

3. The prosecutor will need to disclose any changes or corrections to defense counsel.

CHAPTER TEN

1. At some point, the government must make a return of the documents to the grand jury and make the documents available for the grand jury to review. When subpoena recipients produce the documents to the case agent, then the case agent will appear before the grand jury and fulfill that requirement.

CHAPTER THIRTEEN

1. A motion in limine is a motion filed in advance of trial asking the judge to make an advance ruling regarding the admissibility or inadmissibility of evidence. I discuss motions in limine in more detail in chapter 15. There is an excellent text by James A. Adams and Daniel D. Blinka, *Pretrial Motions in Criminal Prosecutions* (4th ed. 2008), which I commend to the interested reader. This text covers in much more detail the law regarding the pretrial motions I discuss here, along with many other types of pretrial motions. My text is less focused on the law and more focused on the strategy, tactics, and practical issues for prosecutors in handling pretrial motions practice.

2. Abrogated on other grounds by *United States v. Marcus*, 628 F.3d 36 (2nd Cir. 2010).

CHAPTER FIFTEEN

1. I will use the term folders here for ease of reference instead of referring to folders or binders. Some prosecutors prefer to organize materials for each witness in folders or a series of folders, while other prosecutors have witness binders. I found folders easier to use at trial, as binders can become unwieldy. I experimented with keeping the materials in virtual folders on my laptop but found that it was more difficult to toggle between documents and folders on the laptop than it was to do so with physical files. The important thing is for prosecutors to choose a method for organizing the documents pertaining to witnesses in some manner that works best for them.

2. *California v. Green*, 399 US 149, 158 (1970) (quoting 5 J. WIGMORE, EVIDENCE § 1367, p. 29 [3d ed. 1940]).

CHAPTER SEVENTEEN

1. For an evidence book that includes an examination of the Federal Rules of Evidence dealing with expert testimony, see C. J. Williams, *Advanced Evidence: Using the Federal Rules of Evidence in Pretrial and Trial Advocacy* (2018).

CHAPTER NINETEEN

1. The word "venire" means "to come" in Latin. It may be helpful to think of a venire, then, as the group of people asked to come to the courthouse to potentially serve as jurors in a particular case.

2. Katherine Allen, *The Jury: Modern Day Investigation and Consultation*, 34 REV. LITIG. 529, 531 (2015) (citing the English Treason Act of 1708 and the 1790 Public Acts of the First Congress).

3. *See* Geoffrey Cowan, *The People v. Clarence Darrow,* 179–80 (New York: Three Rivers Press, 1993).

4. Thaddeus Hoffmeister, *Investigating Jurors in the Digital Age: One Click at a Time*, 60 U. KAN. L. REV. 611, 616 (2012).

5. *See* Allen, *supra* note 10 at 534 ("About 73% of adults use social media regularly; that number jumps to 90% for adults under the age of 30").

6. *St. Clair v. United States*, 154 US 134, 148 (1894) (holding that "any system for the impaneling of a jury that prevents or embarrasses the full, unrestricted exercise by the accused of his right of peremptory challenges must be condemned"); *see also Pointer v. United States*, 151 US 396, 408 (1894) (holding, in almost identical language, that "[a]ny system for the impaneling of a jury that prevents or embarrasses the full, unrestricted exercise by the accused of that right [to exercise peremptory strikes] must be condemned"). The court used "embarrassed" here to mean "impede," as if referring to a method that decreased the effective exercise of peremptory strikes.

7. *See, e.g.*, Thomas A. Mauet, *Trial Techniques*, 43–48 (6th ed., New York: Aspen Publishers, Inc., 2002) (discussing various theories for assessing prospective jurors); Steven Lubet, *Modern Trial Advocacy*, 48–49 (Notre Dame, IN: The National Institute for Trial Advocacy, Notre Dame University, 1993) (also discussing various theories for assessing prospective jurors).

8. *See generally*, Jamie Bigayer, 21 DUKE J. GENDER L. & POL'Y 369 (2014) (summarizing various theories regarding desirable characteristics of prospective jurors).

9. Caroline C. Otis et al., *Hypothesis Testing in Attorney-Conducted Voir Dire*, 38 LAW & HUM. BEHAV. 392, 401–2 (2013) (summarizing the conclusion from one such study, showing it was consistent with past studies finding that attorney generalizations about prospective jurors are often mistaken).

Bibliography

PRIMARY SOURCES

US Constitution

US CONST. ART. III, § 2, cl. 3
US CONST., AMEND. IV
US CONST., AMEND. V
US CONST., AMEND. VI

Statutes

18 U.S.C. § 922(g)(3)
18 U.S.C. § 924(c)
18 U.S.C. § 1341
18 U.S.C. § 1510(b)
18 U.S.C. § 1512
18 U.S.C. § 1513
18 U.S.C. § 1514
18 U.S.C. § 2113(d)
18 U.S.C. § 2251(d)
18 U.S.C. § 2251(e)
18 U.S.C. § 2252(b)(2)
18 U.S.C. § 2510 *et seq.*
18 U.S.C. § 2261
18 U.S.C. § 2261A
18 U.S.C. § 2262
18 U.S.C. § 2705(a)(A)
18 U.S.C. § 3103a(b)
18 U.S.C. § 3104

18 U.S.C. § 3122
18 U.S.C. § 3142
18 U.S.C. § 3142(f)
18 U.S.C. § 3144
18 U.S.C. § 3432
18 U.S.C. § 3500
18 U.S.C. § 3505(b)
18 U.S.C. § 3510
18 U.S.C. § 3553(a)
18 U.S.C. § 3661
18 U.S.C. § 3663A
18 U.S.C. § 3771(a)
18 U.S.C. § 6002
21 U.S.C. § 846
28 U.S.C. § 1861
28 U.S.C. § 1862
28 U.S.C. § 1863
28 U.S.C. § 1864
28 U.S.C. § 1865
28 U.S.C. § 2255
34 U.S.C. § 20141
34 U.S.C. § 20142
42 U.S.C. § 12101 et seq.

Federal Rules of Criminal Procedure

FED. R. CRIM. P. 3
FED. R. CRIM. P. 5
FED. R. CRIM. P. 5.1
FED. R. CRIM. P. 6(e)
FED. R. CRIM. P. 7(a)
FED. R. CRIM. P. 7(c)(1)
FED. R. CRIM. P. 7(d)
FED. R. CRIM. P. 7(f)
FED. R. CRIM. P. 8(a)
FED. R. CRIM. P. 8(b)
FED. R. CRIM. P. 10
FED. R. CRIM. P. 10(a)(3)
FED. R. CRIM. P. 11
FED. R. CRIM. P. 11(b)(1)
FED. R. CRIM. P. 11(b)(2)
FED. R. CRIM. P. 11(b)(3)
FED. R. CRIM. P. 12(h)
FED. R. CRIM. P. 12(i)
FED. R. CRIM. P. 12.1

FED. R. CRIM. P. 12.2
FED. R. CRIM. P. 12.3
FED. R. CRIM. P. 14
FED. R. CRIM. P. 15
FED. R. CRIM. P. 17
FED. R. CRIM. P. 21(a)
FED. R. CRIM. P. 21(b)
FED. R. CRIM. P. 23(a)
FED. R. CRIM. P. 24
FED. R. CRIM. P. 26.2
FED. R. CRIM. P. 29(c)
FED. R. CRIM. P. 32
FED. R. CRIM. P. 32.1(c),
FED. R. CRIM. P. 33(b)(2)
FED. R. CRIM. P. 41(b)
FED. R. CRIM. P. 41(f)(3)
FED. R. CRIM. P. 46(j)

Federal Rules of Evidence

FED. R. EVID. 404(a)
FED. R. EVID. 404(b)
FED. R. EVID. 606(b)
FED. R. EVID. 609
FED. R. EVID. 701
FED. R. EVID. 702
FED. R. EVID. 703
FED. R. EVID. 704
FED. R. EVID. 705
FED. R. EVID. 801(d)(2)
FED. R. EVID. 803(24)
FED. R. EVID. 804(b)(5)

Cases

Adams v. Texas, 448 US 38 (1980)
Arizona v. Evans, 514 US 1 (1995)
Bank of Nova Scotia v. United States, 487 US 250 (1988)
Batson v. Kentucky, 476 US 79 (1986)
Berger v. United States, 295 US 78 (1935)
Blair v. United States, 250 US 273 (1919)
Bradley v. Pittsburgh Bd. of Educ., 913 F.2d 1064 (3d Cir. 1990)
Brady v. Maryland, 373 US 83 (1963)
Branzburg v. Hayes, 408 US 665 (1972)

Braverman v. United States, 317 US 49 (1942)
Bruno v. Rushen, 721 F.2d 1193 (9th Cir. 1983)
Bruton v. United States, 391 US 123 (1968)
California v. Ciraolo, 476 US 207 (1986)
California v. Green, 399 US 149 (1970)
California v. Greenwood, 486 US 35 (1988)
Casias v. United States, 315 F.2d 614 (10th Cir. 1963)
Costello v. United States, 350 US 359 (1956)
Daubert v. Merrell Dow Pharmaceuticals, Inc., 509 US 579 (1993)
Dennis v. United States, 339 US 162 (1950)
Dobbert v. Florida, 432 US 282 (1977)
Dow Chemical Co. v. United States, 476 US 227 (1986)
Fisher v. United States, 425 US 391 (1976)
Florida v. Riley, 488 US 445 (1989)
Georgia v. McCollum, 505 US 42 (1992)
Giglio v. United States, 405 US 150 (1972)
Gilbert v. California, 388 US 263 (1967)
Holland v. Illinois, 493 US 474 (1990)
Hurtado v. California, 110 US 516 (1884)
In re Grand Jury Investigation (Detroit Police Dep't Special Cash Fund), 922 F.2d 1266 (6th Cir. 1991)
In re Grand Jury Investigation of Hugle, 754 F.2d 863 (9th Cir. 1985)
In re Grand Jury Subpoenas, 906 F.2d 1485 (10th Cir. 1990)
In re Grand Jury Subpoena Duces Tecum, Dated January 2, 1985, 767 F.2d 26 (2d Cir. 1985)
In re Murchison, 349 US 133 (1955)
Irvin v. Dowd, 366 US 717 (1961)
J.E.B. v. Alabama ex rel TB, 511 US 127 (1994)
Jonasson v. Lutheran Child and Family Servs., 115 F.3d 436 (7th Cir. 1997)
Kotteakos v. United States, 328 US 750 (1946)
Kumho Tire Co. v. Carmichael, 526 US 137 (1999)
Kyger v. Carlton, 146 F.3d 374 (6th Cir. 1998)
Kyllo v. United States, 533 US 27 (2001)
Lockhart v. McCree, 476 US 162 (1986)
May v. Collins, 904 F.2d 228 (5th Cir. 1990)
McDonough Power Equip., Inc. v. Greenwood, 464 US 548 (1984)
Mixed Chicks LLC v. Sally Beauty Supply LLC, 879 F. Supp.2d 1093 (C.D. Cal. 2012)
Molzof v. United States, 502 US 301 (1992)
Mu'Min v. Virginia, 500 US 415 (1991)
Murphy v. Florida, 421 US 794 (1975)
Narten v. Eyman, 460 F.2d 184 (9th Cir. 1969)
Offutt v. United States, 348 US 11 (1954)
Palermo v. United States, 360 US 343 (1959)
Pena-Rodriguez v. Colorado, ____ US ____, 137 S. Ct. 855 (2017)
Pointer v. United States, 151 US 396 (1894)

Powers v. Ohio, 499 US 400 (1991)
Purkett v. Elem, 514 US 765 (1995)
Resolution Trust Corp. v. Thornton, 41 F.3d 1539 (D.C. Cir. 1994)
Rice v. Collins, 546 US 333 (2006)
Roman v. Abrams, 822 F.2d 214 (2d Cir. 1987)
Rosales-Lopez v. United States, 451 US 182 (1981)
Rose v. Mitchell, 443 US 545 (1979)
Russell v. United States, 369 US 749 (1962)
Sinclair v. United States, 279 US 749 (1929)
Singer v. United States, 380 US 24 (1965)
Skilling v. United States, 561 US 358 (2010)
Smith v. Maryland, 442 US 735 (1979)
Subpoena Duces Tecum v. Bailey, 228 F.3d 341 (4th Cir. 2000)
St. Clair v. United States, 154 US 134 (1894)
Tanner v. United States, 483 US 107 (1987)
Taylor v. Louisiana, 419 US 522 (1975)
Turner v. United States, 396 US 398 (1970)
United States v. Afflerbach, 754 F.2d 866 (10th Cir. 1985)
United States v. Al-Arian, 308 F. Supp.2d 1322 (M.D. Fla. 2004)
United States v. Anyanwu, 2013 WL 1558712 (N.D. Ga. Mar. 12, 2013)
United States v. Awan, 966 F.2d 1415 (11th Cir. 1992)
United States v. Ayers, 924 F.2d 1468 (9th Cir. 1991)
United States v. Bagley, 473 US 667 (1985)
United States v. Barlin, 686 F.2d 81 (2d Cir. 1982)
United States v. Barnes, 604 F.2d 121 (2d Cir. 1979)
United States v. Barry, 71 F.3d 1269 (7th Cir. 1995)
United States v. Bernal-Obeso, 989 F.2d 331 (9th Cir. 1993)
United States v. Branch, 91 F.3d 699 (5th Cir. 1996)
United States v. Brawner, 173 F.3d 966 (6th Cir. 1999)
United States v. Broward, 594 F.2d 345 (2d Cir. 1979)
United States v. Brye, 318 F. App'x 878 (11th Cir. 2009)
United States v. Calandra, 414 US 338 (1974)
United States v. Cecil, 836 F.2d 1431 (4th Cir. 1988)
United States v. Chadwick, 556 F.2d 450 (9th Cir. 1977)
United States v. Childress, 58 F.3d 693 (D.C. Cir. 1995)
United States v. Collins, 642 F.3d 654 (8th Cir. 2011)
United States v. Coppa, 267 F.3d 132 (2d Cir. 2001)
United States v. Cuervelo, 949 F.2d 559 (2d Cir. 1991)
United States v. Darden, 70 F.3d 1507 (8th Cir. 1995)
United States v. De Cavalcante, 440 F.2d 1264 (3rd Cir. 1971)
United States v. De La Cruz-Feliciano, 786 F.3d 78 (1st Cir. 2015)
United States v. Delia, 944 F.2d 1010 (2d Cir. 1991)
United States v. DiDomenico, 78 F.3d 294 (7th Cir. 1996)
United States v. Dionisio, 410 US 1 (1973)
United States v. Edgar, 82 F.3d 499 (1st Cir. 1996)

United States v. Edwards, 303 F.3d 606 (5th Cir. 2002)

United States v. Fahey, 769 F.2d 829 (1st Cir. 1985)

United States v. Ferro, 252 F.3d 964 (8th Cir. 2001)

United States v. Gray, 47 F.3d 1359 (4th Cir. 1995)

United States v. Greene, 995 F.2d 793 (8th Cir. 1993)

United States v. Hernandez, 962 F.2d 1152 (5th Cir. 1992)

United States v. Hinton, 222 F.3d 664 (9th Cir. 2000)

United States v. Hogan, 712 F.2d 757 (2d Cir. 1983)

United States v. Holmes, 413 F.3d 770 (8th Cir. 2005)

United States v. Howard, 966 F.2d 1362 (10th Cir. 1992)

United States v. Hudson, 3 F. Supp.3d 772 (C.D. Cal. 2014)

United States v. Jamal, 246 F. App'x 351 (6th Cir. 2007)

United States v. Jenkins, 904 F.2d 549 (10th Cir. 1990)

United States v. Johnson, 751 F.2d 291 (8th Cir. 1984)

United States v. Johnson, 2013 WL 1149763 (N.D. Iowa Mar. 19, 2013)

United States v. Jones, 565 US 400 (2012)

United States v. Jones, 597 F.2d 485 (5th Cir. 1979)

United States v. Krauth, 769 F.2d 473 (8th Cir. 1985)

United States v. Krout, 66 F.3d 1420 (5th Cir. 1995)

United States v. Laurienti, 611 F.3d 530 (9th Cir. 2010)

United States v. Leon, 468 US 897 (1984)

United States v. Macklin, 902 F.2d 1320 (8th Cir. 1990)

United States v. Mandel, 914 F.2d 1215 (9th Cir. 1990)

United States v. Marshall, 532 F.2d 1279 (9th Cir. 1976)

United States v. McCarthy, 97 F.3d 1562 (8th Cir. 1996)

United States v. McClure, 546 F.2d 670 (5th Cir. 1977)

United States v. Mechanik, 475 US 66 (1986)

United States v. Milk, 447 F.3d 593 (8th Cir. 2006)

United States v. Mitchell, 744 F.2d 701 (9th Cir. 1984)

United States v. Nolan-Cooper, 155 F.3d 221 (3rd Cir. 1998)

United States v. Phibbs, 999 F.2d 1053 (6th Cir. 1993)

United States v. Powell, 469 US 57 (1984)

United States v. Mansoori, 304 F.3d 635 (7th Cir. 2002)

United States v. Mathison, 157 F.3d 541 (8th Cir. 1998)

United States v. Michaels, 796 F.2d 1112 (9th Cir. 1986)

United States v. Morris, 957 F.2d 1391 (7th Cir. 1992)

United States v. Morton Salt Co., 338 US 632 (1950)

United States v. Newton, 259 F.3d 964 (8th Cir. 2001)

United States v. Ornelas-Rodriguez, 12 F.3d 1339 (5th Cir. 1994)

United States v. Paccione, 949 F.2d 1183 (2d Cir. 1991)

United States v. Parmley, 108 F.3d 922 (8th Cir. 1997)

United States v. Poore, 594 F.2d 39 (4th Cir. 1979)

United States v. Presser, 844 F.2d 1275 (6th Cir. 1988)

United States v. R. Enterprises, Inc., 498 US 292 (1991)

United States v. Reuter, 463 F.3d 792 (7th Cir. 2006)

United States v. Rivera, 971 F.2d 876 (2d Cir. 1992).
United States v. Ross, 33 F.3d 1507 (11th Cir. 1994)
United States v. Salerno, 868 F.2d 524 (2d Cir. 1989)
United States v. Sanchez, 74 F.3d 562 (5th Cir. 1996)
United States v. Santiago, 46 F.3d 885 (9th Cir. 1995)
United States v. Sasso, 59 F.3d 341 (2d Cir. 1995)
United States v. Severe, 29 F.3d 444 (8th Cir. 1994)
United States v. Shryock, 342 F.3d 948 (9th Cir. 2003)
United States v. Smith, 776 F.2d 1104 (3rd Cir. 1985)
United States v. Stein, 2012 WL 4089896 (S.D. Fla. Sept. 13, 2012)
United States v. Stone, 429 F.2d 138 (2d Cir. 1970)
United States v. Summers, 137 F.3d 597 (8th Cir. 1998)
United States v. Thomas, 875 F.2d 559 (6th Cir. 1989)
United States v. Tomsha-Miguel, 766 F.3d 1041 (9th Cir. 2014)
United States v. Toner, 728 F.2d 115 (2d Cir. 1984)
United States v. Torres, 901 F.2d 205 (2d Cir. 1990)
United States v. Turner, 558 F.2d 535 (9th Cir. 1977)
United States v. Tutino, 883 F.2d 1125 (2d Cir. 1989)
United States v. Trujillo, 714 F.2d 102 (11th Cir. 1983)
United States v. Valencia, 826 F.2d 169 (2d Cir. 1987)
United States v. Vasquez-Velasco, 15 F.3d 833 (9th Cir. 1994)
United States v. Wadena, 152 F.3d 831 (8th Cir. 1998)
United States v. Watts, 519 US 148 (1997)
United States v. Williams, 504 US 36 (1992)
United States v. Wong, 431 US 174 (1977)
United States v. Young, 470 US 1 (1985)
Viereck v. United States, 318 US 236 (1943)
Wainwright v. Witt, 469 US 412 (1985)
Wardius v. Oregon, 412 US 470 (1973)
Warger v. Shauers, 574 US 40, 135 S. Ct. 521 (2014)
Weatherford v. Bursey, 429 US 545 (1977)
Wheat v. United States, 486 US 153 (1988)
Whitfield v. United States, 543 US 209 (2005)
Wong Sun v. United States, 371 US 471 (1963)
Wong Tai v. United States, 273 US 77 (1927)
Young v. Alabama, 443 F.2d 854 (5th Cir. 1971)

SECONDARY SOURCES

Books

James A. Adams and Daniel D. Blinka, *Pretrial Motions in Criminal Prosecutions* (4th ed. Dayton, OH: LexisNexis, 2008).
Geoffrey Cowan, *The People v. Clarence Darrow* (New York: Three Rivers Press, 1993).

David Mellinkoff, *The Language of the Law* (Eugene, OR: Wipf & Stock Publishers, 1963).

Stephen A. Saltzburg et al., *Federal Rules of Evidence Manual* § 103.02[13] (11th ed., Dayton, OH: LexisNexis, 2017).

J. Wigmore, *Evidence* § 1367 (3d ed., Netherlands: Wolters Kluwer, 1940).

C. J. Williams, *Advanced Evidence: Using the Federal Rules of Evidence in Pretrial and Trial Advocacy* (Minneapolis, MN: West Academic Publishing, 2018).

C. Wright, *Federal Practice and Procedure* § 129 (2d ed., Ann Arbor, MI: Thomson Reuters, 1982).

Charles Alan Wright and Victor James Gold, *Federal Practice and Procedure* § 6252 (Ann Arbor, MI: Thomson Reuters, 2017).

Articles

Katherine Allen, *The Jury: Modern Day Investigation and Consultation*, 34 REV. LITIG. 529 (2015).

Roberta Flowers, *An Unholy Alliance: The Ex Parte Relationship between the Judge and the Prosecutor*, 79 NEB. L. REV. 251 (2000).

Thaddeus Hoffmeister, *Investigating Jurors in the Digital Age: One Click at a Time*, 60 U. KAN. L. REV. 611 (2012).

Robert H. Jackson, *The Federal Prosecutor*, 24 J. AM. JUD. SOC. 18 (1940).

Jennifer M. Miller, *To Argue Is Human, to Exclude, Divine: The Role of Motions in Limine and the Importance of Preserving the Record on Appeal*, 32 AM. J. TRIAL ADVOC. 541 (2009).

Miscellaneous

UNITED STATES ATTORNEY'S MANUAL 9-11.150

United States Sentencing Guideline §1B1.3

United States Sentencing Guideline §1B1.4

United States Sentencing Guideline §3C1.1

BLACK'S LAW DICTIONARY 10th ed. 2014

ABA MODEL RULES OF PROFESSIONAL CONDUCT, Rule 3.5(b)

ABA MODEL RULES OF PROFESSIONAL CONDUCT, Rule 5.3(b)

ABA Comm. on Ethics & Prof'l Responsibility, Formal Op. 466 (2014)

Index of Cases

Adams v. Texas, 448 US 38 (1980), 263
Arizona v. Evans, 514 US 1 (1995), 180

Bank of Nova Scotia v. United States, 487 US 250 (1988), 174
Batson v. Kentucky, 476 US 79 (1986), 299
Berger v. United States, 295 US 78 (1935), 5, 6
Blair v. United States, 250 US 273 (1919), 117
Bradley v. Pittsburgh Bd. of Educ., 913 F.2d 1064 (3d Cir. 1990), 198
Brady v. Maryland, 373 US 83 (1963), 7, 8, 161, 166
Branzburg v. Hayes, 408 US 665 (1972), 116
Braverman v. United States, 317 US 49 (1942), 156
Bruno v. Rushen, 721 F.2d 1193 (9th Cir. 1983), 43
Bruton v. United States, 391 US 123 (1968), 178

California v. Ciraolo, 476 US 207 (1986), 75–76
California v. Greenwood, 486 US 35 (1988), 76

Casias v. United States, 315 F.2d 614 (10th Cir. 1963), 263
Costello v. United States, 350 US 359 (1956), 116, 136

Daubert v. Merrell Dow Pharmaceuticals, Inc., 509 US 579 (1993), 242
Dennis v. United States, 339 US 162 (1950), 313
Dobbert v. Florida, 432 US 282 (1977), 301
Dow Chemical v. United States, 476 US 227 (1986), 75

Fisher v. United States, 425 US 391 (1976), 118
Florida v. Riley, 488 US 445 (1989), 75

Georgia v. McCollum, 505 US 42 (1992), 300
Giglio v. United States, 405 US 150 (1972), 7, 8, 25, 166
Gilbert v. California, 388 US 263 (1967), 120

Holland v. Illinois, 493 US 474 (1990), 263

Hurtado v. California, 110 US 516 (1884), 115

In re Grand Jury Investigation (Detroit Police Dep't Special Cash Fund), 922 F.2d 1266 (6th Cir. 1991), 116
In re Grand Jury Investigation of Hugle, 754 F.2d 863 (9th Cir. 1985), 117
In re Grand Jury Subpoena Duces Tecum, Dated January 2, 1985, 767 F.2d 26 (2d Cir. 1985), 116
In re Grand Jury Subpoenas, 906 F.2d 1485 (10th Cir. 1990), 119
In re Murchison, 349 US 133 (1955), 301
Irvin v. Dowd, 366 US 717 (1961), 302, 303, 315

J.E.B. v. Alabama ex rel TB, 511 US 127 (1994), 300
Jonasson v. Lutheran Child and Family Servs., 115 F.3d 436 (7th Cir. 1997), 198

Kotteakos v. United States, 328 US 750 (1946), 156
Kumho Tire Co. v. Carmichael, 526 US 137 (1999), 242
Kyger v. Carlton, 146 F.3d 374 (6th Cir. 1998), 120
Kylo v. United States, 533 US 27 (2001), 76

Lockhart v. McCree, 476 US 162 (1986), 301
Luce v. United States, 469 US 38 (1984), 198, 201

May v. Collins, 904 F.2d 228 (5th Cir. 1990), 166
McDonough Power Equip., Inc. v. Greenwood, 464 US 548 (1984), 312–13, 315–17
Mixed Chicks LLC v. Sally Beauty Supply LLC, 879 F. Supp.2d 1093 (C.D. Cal. 2012), 199

Molzof v. United States, 502 US 301 (1992), 158
Mu'Min v. Virginia, 500 US 415 (1991), 284, 302
Murphy v. Florida, 421 US 794 (1975), 315

Narten v. Eyman, 460 F.2d 184 (9th Cir. 1969), 303

Palermo v. United States, 360 US 343 (1959), 165
Pena-Rodriguez v. Colorado, 137 S. Ct. 855 (2017), 317–18
Powers v. Ohio, 499 US 400 (1991), 299
Purkett v.Elem, 514 US 765 (1995), 300

Resolution Trust Corp. v. Thornton, 41 F.3d 1539 (D.C. Cir. 1994), 126
Rice v. Collins, 546 US 333 (2006), 300
Roman v. Abrams, 822 F.2d 214 (2d Cir. 1987), 299
Rosales-Lopez v. United States, 451 US 182 (1981), 264
Rose v. Mitchell, 443 US 545 (1979), 317
Russell v. United States, 369 US 749 (1962), 159

Sinclair v. United States, 279 US 749 (1929), 277
Singer v. United States, 380 US 24 (1965), 262
Skilling v. United States, 561 US 358 (2010), 285, 301, 302
Subpoena Duces Tecum v. Bailey, 228 F.3d 341 (4th Cir. 2000), 119

Tanner v. United States, 483 US 107 (1987), 316–17
Taylor v. Louisiana, 419 US 522 (1975), 263
Turner v. United States, 396 US 398 (1970), 154

United States v. Afflerbach, 754 F.2d 866 (10th Cir. 1985), 267

United States v. Al-Arian, 308 F. Supp.2d 1322 (M.D. Fla. 2004), 155

United States v. Anyanwu, 2013 WL 1558712 (N.D. Ga. Mar. 12, 2013), 155

United States v. Awan, 966 F.2d 1415 (11th Cir. 1992), 155

United States v. Ayers, 924 F.2d 1468 (9th Cir. 1991), 153

United States v. Bagley, 473 US 667 (1985), 167

United States v. Barlin, 686 F.2d 81 (2d Cir. 1982), 157

United States v. Barnes, 604 F.2d 121 (2d Cir. 1979), 311

United States v. Barry, 71 F.3d 1269 (7th Cir. 1995), 268

United States v. Bernal-Obeso, 989 F.2d 331 (9th Cir. 1993), 92

United States v. Branch, 91 F.3d 699 (5th Cir. 1996), 307

United States v. Brawner, 173 F.3d 966 (6th Cir. 1999), 198

United States v. Broward, 594 F.2d 345 (2d Cir. 1979), 174

United States v. Brye, 318 F. App'x 878 (11th Cir. 2009), 155

United States v. Calandra, 414 US 338 (1974), 54

United States v. Cecil, 836 F.2d 1431 (4th Cir. 1988), 267

United States v. Chadwick, 556 F.2d 450 (9th Cir. 1977), 157

United States v. Childress, 58 F.3d 693 (D.C. Cir. 1995), 307

United States v. Collins, 642 F.3d 654 (8th Cir. 2011), 41

United States v. Coppa, 267 F.3d 132 (2d Cir. 2001), 167

United States v. Cuervelo, 949 F.2d 559 (2d Cir. 1991), 175

United States v. Darden, 70 F.3d 1507 (8th Cir. 1995), 305–07

United States v. De Cavalcante, 440 F.2d 1264 (3rd Cir. 1971), 157

United States v. De La Cruz-Feliciano, 786 F.3d 78 (1st Cir. 2015), 167

United States v. Delia, 944 F.2d 1010 (2d Cir. 1991), 171

United States v. DiDomenico, 78 F.3d 294 (7th Cir. 1996), 306

United States v. Dionisio, 410 US 1 (1973), 119, 120

United States v. Dunlap, 593 Fed. App'x 619 (9th Cir. 2014), 175

United States v. Edgar, 82 F.3d 499 (1st Cir. 1996), 138

United States v. Edwards, 303 F3d 606 (5th Cir. 2002), 306

United States v. Fahey, 769 F.2d 829 (1st Cir. 1985), 177

United States v. Ferro, 252 F.3d 964 (8th Cir. 2001), 176

United States v. Gray, 47 F.3d 1359 (4th Cir. 1995), 267

United States v. Greene, 995 F.2d 793 (8th Cir. 1993), 268

United States v. Hernandez, 962 F.2d 1152 (5th Cir. 1992), 154

United States v. Hinton, 222 F.3d 664 (9th Cir. 2000), 75

United States v. Hogan, 712 F.2d 757 (2d Cir. 1983), 174

United States v. Holmes, 413 F.3d 770 (8th Cir. 2005), 43

United States v. Howard, 966 F.2d 1362 (10th Cir. 1992), 157

United States v. Hudson, 3 F. Supp.3d 772 (C.D. Cal. 2014), 175

United States v. Jamal, 246 Fed. App'x 351 (6th Cir. 2007), 179

United States v. Jenkins, 904 F.2d 549 (10th Cir. 1990), 126

United States v. Johnson, 751 F.2d 291 (8th Cir. 1984), 170

United States v. Johnson, 2013 WL 1149763 (N.D. Iowa Mar. 19, 2013), 268

United States v. Jones, 565 US 400 (2012), 76

United States v. Jones, 597 F.2d 485 (5th Cir. 1979), 318

United States v. Krauth, 769 F.2d 473 (8th Cir. 1985), 75

United States v. Krout, 66 F.3d 1420 (5th Cir. 1995), 306

United States v. Laurienti, 611 F.3d 530 (9th Cir. 2010), 155

United States v. Macklin, 902 F.2d 1320 (8th Cir. 1990), 74

United States v. Mandel, 914 F.2d 1215 (9th Cir. 1990), 162

United States v. Mansoori, 304 F.3d 635 (7th Cir. 2002), 305–06

United States v. Marshall, 532 F.2d 1279 (9th Cir. 1976), 162

United States v. Maryland, 442 US 735 (1979), 75

United States v. Mathison, 157 F.3d 541 (8th Cir. 1998), 136

United States v. McCarthy, 97 F.3d 1562 (8th Cir. 1996), 157

United States v. McClure, 546 F.2d 670 (5th Cir. 1977), 166

United States v. Mechanik, 475 US 66 (1986), 118

United States v. Michaels, 796 F.2d 1112 (9th Cir. 1986), 163

United States v. Milk, 447 F.3d 593 (8th Cir. 2006), 43

United States v. Mitchell, 744 F.2d 701 (9th Cir. 1984), 153

United States v. Morris, 957 F.2d 1391 (7th Cir. 1992), 165

United States v. Morton Salt Co., 338 US 632 (1950), 116

United States v. Newton, 259 F.3d 964 (8th Cir. 2001), 170

United States v. Nolan-Cooper, 155 F.3d 221 (3rd Cir. 1998), 175

United States v. Ornelas-Rodriguez, 12 F.3d 1339 (5th Cir. 1994), 175

United States v. Paccione, 949 F.2d 1183 (2d Cir. 1991), 307

United States v. Parmley, 108 F.3d 922 (8th Cir. 1997), 284

United States v. Phibbs, 999 F.2d 1053 (6th Cir. 1993), 126

United States v. Poore, 594 F.2d 39 (4th Cir. 1979), 155

United States v. Powell, 469 US 57 (1984), 313

United States v. Presser, 844 F.2d 1275 (6th Cir. 1988), 171

United States v. R. Enterprises, 498 US 292 (1991), 116

United States v. Rivera, 971 F.2d 876 (2d Cir. 1992), 42

United States v. Reuter, 463 F.3d 792 (7th Cir. 2006), 326

United States v. Ross, 33 F.3d 1507 (11th Cir. 1994), 305–06, 308

United States v. Salerno, 868 F.2d 524 (2d Cir. 1989), 310

United States v. Sanchez, 74 F3d 562 (5th Cir. 1996), 306

United States v. Santiago, 46 F.3d 885 (9th Cir. 1995), 42

United States v. Sasso, 59 F.3d 341 (2d Cir. 1995), 126

United States v. Severe, 29 F.3d 444 (8th Cir. 1994), 154

United States v. Shiomos, 864 F.2d 16 (3rd Cir. 1988), 310

United States v. Shryock, 342 F.3d 948 (9th Cir. 2003), 305–07

United States v. Smith, 776 F.2d 1104 (3rd Cir. 1985), 157

United States v. Stein, 2012 WL 4089896 (S.D. Fla. Sept. 13, 2012), 155

United States v. Stone, 429 F.2d 138 (2d Cir. 1970), 116

United States v. Summers, 137 F.3d 597 (8th Cir. 1998), 155

United States v. Thomas, 875 F.2d 559 (6th Cir. 1989), 156

United States v. Tomsha-Miguel, 766 F.3d 1041 (9th Cir. 2014), 42

United States v. Toner, 728 F.2d 115 (2d Cir. 1984), 267

United States v. Torres, 901 F.2d 205 (2d Cir. 1990), 182

United States v. Trujillo, 714 F.2d 102 (11th Cir. 1983), 157

United States v. Turner, 558 F.2d 535 (9th Cir. 1977), 289

United States v. Tutino, 883 F.2d 1125 (2d Cir. 1989), 311

United States v. Valencia, 826 F.2d 169 (2d Cir. 1987), 201

United States v. Vasquez-Velasco, 15 F.3d 833 (9th Cir. 1994), 136

United States v. Watts, 519 US 148 (1997), 325

United States v. Wedena, 152 F.3d 831 (8th Cir. 1998), 135

United States v. Williams, 504 US 36 (1992), 174

United States v. Wong, 431 US 174 (1977), 125

United States v. Young, 470 US 1 (1985), 41

Viereck v. United States, 318 US 236 (1943), 42

Wainwright v. Witt, 469 US 412 (1985), 263, 284

Wardius v. Oregon, 412 US 470 (1973), 161

Warger v. Shauers, 574 US 40 (2014), 316–17

Weatherford v. Bursey, 429 US 545 (1977), 161, 166

Wheat v. United States, 486 US 153 (1988), 310

Whitfield v. United States, 543 US 209 (2005), 158

Wong Sun v. United States, 371 US 471 (1963), 180

Wong Tai v. United States, 273 US 77 (1927), 152

Young v. Alabama, 443 F.2d 854 (5th Cir. 1971), 310

Index

ABA Model Rules, 278
appeals, 1, 8, 37, 66–68, 109–10, 169, 173, 186, 271, 285–86, 288–89, 300, 329, 335, 337–42
arraignment, 45, 57–59, 182
attorney-client: communication, 17, 25; privilege, 17, 116; relationship, 258

Batson challenges, 262, 299–300
bill of particulars, 60, 152–53, 182
Black's Law Dictionary, 198, 265, 283
Brady information, 7, 8, 161, 166–70, 230
Bruton issues, 178

case agent. *See* Officers
change of venue, 60, 178–79, 301–04
charges: affidavits, 55–57, 149, 153; amending, 148, 158–59; conjunctive language, 152, 154; conspiracy, 135–40, 143–44, 148, 152, 154, 156–58; criminal complaints, 6, 46, 55–58, 148–50, 153, 176–78; criminal informations, 56–57, 59, 135, 148–51; generally, 7, 14–15, 21–22, 29–30, 50, 53–57; indictments, 6, 28–29, 53–59, 116, 125–26, 129, 135–45, 148–57, 159, 173–77, 182; multiple, defendant and charges,

135–41; sentencing consequences, 147–48; speaking indictment, 152–53; strategies, 87, 131–59
closing arguments, 3, 35, 39–43, 62, 96, 101, 110, 113, 129, 140, 143, 175, 195, 203, 210, 236, 252, 273, 319–21
communication: defense counsel, 61; experts, 247–49; judges, 46; jury, 248, 273, 278, 287; monitoring of, 73–76, 86, 106; officers, 13, 16–17, 108; prosecution team, 28, 31, 33; victims, 259–60
compelling testimony, 47, 97, 118, 120–22
confrontation clause. See Constitution, United States
Constitution, United States: Article III, §2, 178, 262; Bill of Rights, 262; confrontation clause, 123, 330; double jeopardy clause, 132, 134, 152, 154, 182, 285, 339; due process clause, 49, 154, 162, 166, 174, 192, 263, 301, 330; equal protection clause, 299; Fourth Amendment, 75, 119, 180; Fifth Amendment, 53, 115–20, 174, 178, 180, 263, 306, 330; Sixth Amendment, 68, 123, 152, 178–80, 262–64, 301, 305, 308–09, 317, 330; voir dire, 264

cooperators: debriefing, 23, 99;
generally, 30, 61, 84, 86–87, 162,
208; grand jury, 123, 128; plea
agreement, 189–90; preparing for
testimony, 219–20; working with,
91–103
confidential source, 20
criminal complaint. *See* charges
criminal informations. *See* charges
cross examination: ; of cooperator, 99,
101–02; of defendant, 227–28, 230,
321–32, 234, 330; of experts, 239,
242–45, 247–52; generally, 41–42,
59, 62, 66, 143, 169, 191, 196, 321;
preparing witnesses for, 62, 212–13,
216, 220–23, 330

defense attorneys: attacking,
constitutional implications with,
42–43; generally, 8–9, 60, 63, 187;
post–conviction relief litigation,
68; referring to, 38–40; responding
to attacks from, 40; working with,
35–47, 95–96
defenses: alibi, 81, 167, 172, 236;
entrapment, 166, 237; insanity,
164, 167,172, 237, 246–47; public
authority, 168
demonstrative exhibits. *See* evidence
Department of Justice, US, 1–2, 18, 57,
61, 125,
depositions, 7, 59, 161–62
detention hearing, 45, 57–59, 123, 165
direct examination: generally, 41, 165,
210, 234–35, in grand jury, 127; of
cooperators, 101; of experts, 242,
248, 252; outlines for, 62, 66, 195,
211–12; preparing witnesses for,
220–24, 330
discovery: experts, 239–40, 247,
generally, 7, 39–40, 59–60, 98, 126,
138, 149, 161–72, 214; motions
regarding, 173, 182–83; reciprocal,
164–65, 167, 171–72, 227–28, 240

ethics, 9, 36, 37, 47, 49, 276–79
evidence: demonstrative, 112, 210,
225–26, 249, 320, 330; developing,
30, 105–113; exclusionary rule,
47, 179–80; exculpatory, 7, 38,
102, 128–29, 162, 166–67, 169–71;
foundation for, 113, 144, 199,
204, 206, 212, 219; rebuttal, 171,
230–31, 235–36, 321; rules. *See*
Federal Rules of Evidence; exhibits:
defense, 233; lists, 165–66, 205–06,
228; numbering, 206–07, 209–10;
preparing, 195, 211, 226; selecting,
201–05, 320; technology, 225
experts: cross-examining, 250, 252;
defense experts, 250–52; discovery,
164; exhibits, 249; generally, 239–
252; government experts, 244–250;
preparing, 248–50; selecting, 246–47

Federal Rules of Criminal Procedure:
Rule 3, 55; Rule 4, 56; Rule 5, 57–58;
Rule 5.1, 58, 165; Rule 6(e), 47,
77–78, 90; Rule 7, 56, 152, 155, 177,
182; Rule 8, 135, 138, 176–78; Rule
10, 59; Rule 11, 62, 191–92; Rule 12,
161, 165, 173; Rule 12.1, 161, 167;
Rule 12.2, 161, 164, 167, 240; Rule
12.3, 161, 168; Rule 14, 177–78; Rule
15, 162; Rule 16, 161–64, 167–69,
171–72, 239–40; Rule 17, 117; Rule
18, 178–79; Rule 21, 179, 301; Rule
23, 262, 264; Rule 24, 264; Rule 26.2,
161, 165; Rule 29, 63; Rule 32, 165;
Rule 32.1, 165; Rule 33, 63; Rule 41,
76; Rule 46, 58, 161, 165
Federal Rules of Evidence:
Applicability, 7, 54, 58, 59, 123,
232, 329; hearsay, 54, 58, 59, 123,
125, 200, 204, 234, 330; Rule 403,
199; Rule 404(b), 161, 163, 166,
170, 222, 325; Rule 410, 188–89;
Rule 606, 316–17; Rule 609, 200,
222, 232, 268; Rule 701, 241; Rule

702, 241–42; Rule 703, 242–43; Rule 704, 243; Rule 705, 243; Rule 801, 178, 200; Rule 803, 161; Rule 804, 161

firearms, 109, 146, 147, 227, 256, 329

fruit of the poisonous tree, 25, 180

Giglio information, 7, 8, 25, 161, 166–71, 181, 215, 230

grand jury: accusatory, 54–55; investigatory, 54–55; presentation to, 53–55, 174–75; subpoenas, 117–120

Guidelines, United States Sentencing. *See* sentencing

hearings: arraignment, 45, 57–59, 182; change of plea, 191–93; detention, 45, 57–59, 123, 165; initial appearances, 46, 57–59; preliminary, 57–59, 165; probable cause, 58

impeachment of witnesses, 759, 100–03, 123–24, 127–28, 166–67, 170–71, 204–05, 211–13, 218, 220, 222–24, 232, 250–51, 268

indictments. *See* charges

informants: disclosure, identity of, 182–83; interviews, 23; use, 73, 91–92, 95, 166, 30

initial appearances. *See* hearings

investigations: controlled buy, 17, 30, 53, 73, 84, 86, 91–93, 145, 209; covert techniques, 73–78, 80, 86, 119, 126; of lone criminals 81–83; mail cover, 75; of organized crime 85–87, 177; overt, 73, 78, 80, 126; pen registers, 75; public records search, 76–77, 229; search warrants. *See* search warrants); surveillance, 19–20, 53, 75–76, 168, 209, 282; trap and trace, 46, 75; trash rip, 76; unorganized crime, investigation of, 8–83; wiretap, 21–22, 46, 74, 86,

Jackson, Robert H., 5

Jencks Act, 7, 162, 165, 168–72, 217–18, 228–29, 282

jurors, 111–12,

juries: anonymous, 305–09; cause challenges, 262, 264, 274–75, 284–88; consultants, 279–83; investigation of, 275–77; misconduct by, 311–18; peremptory strikes, 262–65, 273, 275–76, 279–81, 284–85, 287–300; selection, 261–66; sequestered, 309–311; qualifications for, 266–68; questionnaires, 268–75; venire, 263, 265–67, 269, 284–85, 292, 300, 303–04; voir dire, 62, 261–64, 268–75,278–81, 283–84, 288–90, 292–97, 299, 301–03, 305–06, 308–09, 312, 314–17

Kennedy, John F., 9

Leon good faith, 47

mail cover. *See* investigations

manner and means, 157–58

McVey, Timothy, 179

Miller, Jennifer M., 199

motions: bill of particulars, 60, 66, 152–53, 182; discovery, 182–83; change venue, 60, 178–79, 301–04; dismiss, 60, 134, 142, 146, 168, 173–76, 180, 337; generally, 60; in limine, 63, 173, 198–201, 233–34, 320, 312–13; judgment of acquittal, 63; new trial, 63, 278, 285, 300, 309; sever, 177–79; strike, 60, 155, 177; summary judgment, inapplicability, 176; suppress, 25, 60, 66, 165, 169, 173, 179–82, 337, 339

National Advocacy Center, 1

offense conduct statement ("OCS"), 64, 323–27

officers: case agent, 15, 54–55, 58–59, 90, 113, 124–25, 204, 214–15; conflicts, 1–18, ; leading, 15–19; preparing for testimony, 25; rewarding, 18–19; surveillance, 19–20; state law enforcement, 24–25; working with, 12–15

opening statements, 1, 3, 42, 62, 96, 129, 153, 175, 195, 214, 234, 259, 273, 280, 319–21,

organizational charts, 85–86, 112

outrageous government conduct (motions to dismiss for), 175–76

overt acts, 88, 157–58

paralegals, 9, 15–16, 27, 90, 101, 185, 229, 276, 281

plea agreements, 1, 35, 61, 99, 185–91, 219,

plea hearings, 45, 62, 69, 185, 191–93,

plea negotiations, 60–61, 66, 69, 79, 142, 144–45, 150, 170, 185–188, 323

post–conviction litigation, 8, 37, 67–69

presentence investigation report ("PSR"), 64–65, 188, 256, 323–24, 327–29, 331–32

privileges: against self-incrimination, 116–18; attorney-client, 116–17; attorney work product, 116; grand jury, 116, 118–19; marital, 116; psychotherapist, 116; spousal, 116; wiretaps, 74

proactive cases, 50, 52–55, 71–73, 91

probable cause, 14, 53, 55–58, 72, 74, 115–16, 125, 130, 133–34, 137, 143, 149,

proffer agreement, 91, 95, 99–101

proffer interview, 23, 61, 91

proffer of evidence, 58, 201, 231, 300

prosecution team: conflicts among, 18, 32 ; coordination, 31–32; cooperators, 101; discovery; judges, 47; leading, 15–16; size, 27–29; victims, 257–58; working with, 25, 27–33

reactive cases, 50–56, 69, 71–73, 80

rebuttal argument, 41–43, 321

rebuttal evidence, 171, 228, 230–31, 235–37, 321

restitution, 62, 132, 148, 150, 153, 192, 255, 260, 324, 326, 331–33

Saltzburg, Stephen A., 199

searches: affidavits, 24–25; computer-aided, 89–90, 276; delayed notification warrants, 76, 78; generally, 46–47, 51, 53, 72, 75–76, 78, 89, 108, 119, 180–81, 204, 209–10, 240, 338–39; nighttime warrants, 24; no-knock warrants, 24; piggyback warrants, 24

sentencing: brief, 65, 330–33; collateral consequences, 62, 142, 146–48, 185–88, 192, 326, 331–32; departures, 6, 65, 324, 326–329, 331–32; guidelines, 6, 61, 64–65, 147, 186, 189, 192, 230, 260, 324–28, 334, 339; hearings, 15–16, 45, 64–66, 123, 165, 186, 213, 244, 323; mandatory minimum, 63, 79, 135, 138, 146–47, 186, 188, 191–92; maximum, 7, 135, 147, 186, 188, 191–92; statutory factors. *See* 18 U.S.C. § 3553(a); variances, 6, 65, 324, 326–29, 331–32; victims, 333–34

solicitor general, 340

special assessments, 192

statutes: 18 U.S.C. § 924(c), 141; 18 U.S.C. § 1341, 143; 18 U.S.C. § 1510, 78; 18 U.S.C. § 2113, 202; 18 U.S.C. § 2251, 147; 18 U.S.C. § 2252, 147; 18 U.S.C. § 2510, 74; 18 U.S.C. § 2705, 76; 18 U.S.C. § 3014, 192; 18 U.S.C. § 3103a, 76; 18 U.S.C. § 3122, 75; 18 U.S.C. § 3142, 58; 18 U.S.C. § 3144, 58; 18 U.S.C. § 3432, 165; 18 U.S.C. § 3500, 161, 165; 18 U.S.C. § 3505, 161; 18 U.S.C. § 3553(a), 192, 327–28, 331–

32, 334; 18 U.S.C. § 3661, 326.; 18 U.S.C. § 6002, 118; 21 U.S.C. § 846, 154; 28 U.S.C. § 1861, 263, 265–66; 28 U.S.C. § 1862, 265–66; 28 U.S.C. § 1863, 265–66, 306; 28 U.S.C. § 1864, 266; 28 U.S.C. § 1865, 264, 266–67; 28 U.S.C. § 2255, 67; 34 U.S.C. § 20141, 255; 34 U.S.C. § 20142, 255; 42 U.S.C. § 12101, 267

subpoenas, 51–54, 75, 77–78, 81, 86, 89, 116–26, 129, 162,

superseding indictments, 116, 142, 159, 174,

Sutherland, Justice, 5, 6

taint teams, 25

task force, 18, 84,

timelines, 88, 98, 112, 320

transactional immunity, 91

trash rip. *See* investigations

undercover: agents, 84, 86, 93; buys, 17; operations, 73–74, 86, 91, 175

United States Attorney, 5

United States Attorney's Manual, 125

unit of prosecution, 131, 142–44

use immunity, 91, 118

victim: Advocate (coordinator), 15, 27, 30; charging decisions influenced by, 142, 144, 146, 149, 150, 153; child, 9, 50, 125, 192, 224; communications with, 77, 259–60; generally, 1–2, 9, 19, 31–32, 50, 72, 73, 82, 84–85, 97, 115, 134, 179, 326, 331; impact statements, 333; plea agreement impact for, 181, relationships with, 257–58; rights, 65, 132, 179, 255–56, 323–24; sentencing hearings, 333–35

voir dire, 62, 261–64, 268–75, 278–81, 283–84, 286–90, 292–97, 299, 301–303, 305–06, 308–09, 312, 314–17

wiretap, 21–22, 46, 74, 86

witness: as cooperators, 101–103; coordinators, 27; impeachment of, 223–24; lists, 165–66, 205, 210, 228; officers as, 216–17; outlines, 211–12; preparing, 101–103, 213–25

About the Author

C. J. Williams received his undergraduate degree in 1985 and his law degree in 1988, both with High Honors from the University of Iowa. In 1997, he was awarded a Master's of Law degree with an emphasis in criminal law from the University of Missouri School of Law. He was sworn in as a US Magistrate Judge on February 16, 2016, and served in that capacity until he was elevated to the district court bench on September 12, 2018.

Before taking the bench, Judge Williams served as a federal judicial law clerk, as a trial attorney with the Criminal Division of the US Department of Justice in Washington, D.C., as a trial attorney in a large Kansas City firm, and as an Assistant US Attorney.

As a federal prosecutor, Judge Williams was involved in the prosecution of cases across the country, from Idaho to Puerto Rico, Pennsylvania to Arizona. As an Assistant US Attorney based in the Northern District of Iowa, Judge Williams prosecuted hundreds of felony cases involving almost every type of crime from drug trafficking to multimillion-dollar white-collar fraud cases. Judge Williams was the lead prosecutor in two federal death penalty cases and served a yearlong detail with the Capital Crimes Section in Washington, D.C. Judge Williams won many awards, including three Director's Awards from the Department of Justice, along with awards from many law enforcement agencies and organizations.

Judge Williams has served as an instructor for the Department of Justice at the National Advocacy Center in Columbia, South Carolina, and has taught as an Adjunct Professor of Law at the University of Missouri-Kansas City, University of South Dakota Law School, and the University of Iowa College of Law. He has published more than a dozen law review articles, coauthored a textbook entitled *Federal Criminal Practice* (2016), and authored another textbook entitled *Advanced Evidence: Applying the Federal Rules of Evidence in Pretrial and Trial Advocacy* (2018).